THE
ECCLESIASTICAL HISTORY

OF

EUSEBIUS PAMPHILUS

BISHOP OF CESAREA, IN PALESTINE

TRANSLATED FROM THE ORIGINAL

WITH AN INTRODUCTION

BY

CHRISTIAN FREDERICK CRUSE

AND

AN HISTORICAL VIEW

OF

THE COUNCIL OF NICE

By ISAAC BOYLE

BAKER BOOK HOUSE
Grand Rapids, Michigan

Library of Congress Card Number 55-10437

ISBN: 0-8010-3306-3

First Printing, September 1955
Second Printing, February 1962
Third Printing, October 1964
Fourth Printing, January 1966
Fifth Printing, April 1969
Sixth Printing, August 1973
Seventh Printing, September 1974
Eighth Printing, April 1976
Ninth Printing, August 1977
Tenth Printing, November 1979
Eleventh Printing, September 1981
Twelfth Printing, June 1984

PRINTED IN THE UNITED STATES OF AMERICA

INTRODUCTION

TO THE

ECCLESIASTICAL HISTORY OF EUSEBIUS.

NOTE —In Part I. of the following Introduction, the references show the Book and chapter; in Part II. they show the page. Occasionally there is a double reference.

———◆———

PART I.—GENERAL ABSTRACT OF EVENTS.

This work, the most important that has come down to us from Eusebius of Cesarea, and the most important of any, perhaps, that have came to us from the earlier Fathers of the Church, embraces the events of the first three centuries, down to the time when Constantine became sole master of the Roman world. It is divided into ten books, in chronological order, and opens with a preliminary discourse, the matter of which is strictly theological. It is an apology and exposition of Christian doctrine. The design is chiefly to exhibit the Christian Religion in its true antiquity, dignity and excellence, on grounds derived from the titles, offices, and exalted Nature and Dignity of its Blessed Author, and from a comparative view of facts and passages of the Old Testament, showing that the Person and Doctrine of Christ had been the object of faith and hope from the most remote ages.

Here, then, we have a summary of Christian Doctrine in the Primitive Church. In this connection also, Eusebius accounts for the seeming difficulty that the Gospel was not sooner introduced;

or rather, why this Divine Dispensation was so long delayed. After this summary of Christian Theology, commences what is properly the object of the work—the History of the Church. (B. I. p. 28.) The time when our Lord was born, being an important historical fact, authorities are given corroborating the statement of St. Luke, and settling the question in general, to what particular period this happy event is to be referred. (B. I. ch. 5.) The coincidence with the language of Prophecy is then illustrated by a reference to the state of the Jewish Government at the time, and the seeming discrepancy between the gospels of Matthew and Luke on the genealogy of Christ, is reconciled. (B. I. ch. 7.) Historical sketches are given respecting those who acted a prominent part in our Lord's trial and death, elucidating both the time of His Ministry and the retributive visitations of Providence. (ch. 8.)

The last chapters of this book are chiefly occupied with accounts of John the Baptist, in his relation to the Messiah, and closes with the correspondence attributed to Christ and Agbarus. and which Eusebius translated from the records of Edessa.

The second book, in connection with the martyrdom of Stephen and James the Just, shows the organization of the mother Church at Jerusalem, under the latter of these martyrs as its bishop. The origin of the Syrian Church, at Edessa, is interwoven with the account of Thaddeus, deputed thither by St. Thomas. The persecutions at Jerusalem having scattered the disciples, and, Providence overruling this calamity for greater good, the truths of the Gospel were also scattered abroad with this dispersion. The apostles had, thus far, limited their operations to the Jews ; but henceforth commences the period of extension and catholicity.

Phenice, Cyprus, Antioch, are thus visited by believers, and even Ethiopia receives intelligence of Christ, (ch. 1 ;) but the apostles were not fully prepared to establish the Church among the Gentiles, until the vision of Peter and the conversion of St. Paul dissipate all doubts. A period of peace under Tiberius is favorable to their work. Churches now every where arise, and Greeks at Antioch are the founders of the Christian name, and of the first Church among the Gentiles. The churches of Palestine and Syria are the mothers of all other churches. (ch. 3.)

The celebrated Judao-platonic Philo, flourished under Tiberius and Caligula, and becomes prominent as an expounder of mystical philosophy. He is also noted for an embassy to Rome in behalf of the Jews. The storm that had been gathering, burst upon that people under Caligula, and ended with the destruction of their city and temple, under Vespasian. Returning to the prominent actors at our Lord's death, the historian characterizes Pilate and Herod, noting the manner and circumstances of their death. (ch. 9, 10.) St. Luke's account of the impostor Theudas is confirmed by a passage from Josephus, together with other facts stated by the evangelist, from monuments existing in the days of Eusebius.

The Gospel now spreads in the city of Rome. Simon Magnus is conspicuous as its antagonist, and as a leader in heresy and licentiousness. Eusebius, following Justin, Irenæus, Clement, Papias, and a general tradition, (ch. 13, 14,) speaks of Peter's successful mission against Simon, and the compilation of St. Mark's gospel, under the authority of the apostle. Tradition also refers the foundation of the Church in Egypt, to St. Mark. (ch. 15, 16.) The extracts from Philo, in regard to the Therapeuta, incline the historian to the opinion that they were either a sect of Christians, or else derived their institutions from the latter. (ch. 17.) The works of Philo are now stated and briefly noticed, when the history returns to the condition of the Jews at this time ; their seditions and their sufferings under the emperors Claudius and Nero ; their insurrections under the notorious Egyptian impostor, mentioned in the Acts of the Apostles, when Felix was governor. (ch. 18–21)

The history next traces the different parts visited by St. Paul, as deduced from his own writings, with a view to determine also the time of his death. (ch. 22.) Now follows a more full account of the death of James the Just, (coll. p. 49, 77,) the first bishop of

Jerusalem, of whose Epistles there is a brief notice in connection with what are called the Seven Catholic Epistles. (ch. 23.) The history then relates the martyrdoms of Peter and Paul, referring as authority to Caius, an Ecclesiastical writer who flourished soon after the events; and also to Dionysius of Corinth. This book closes with a review of the great miseries now thickening around the Jews; but does not carry us yet, as far as the destruction of Jerusalem, and may be said to comprise between thirty and forty years after our Lord's ascension.

The third book commences with a succinct statement of the regions evangelized by some of the apostles. The epistles of the apostles are reviewed according to their canonical authority, and in a digression, is subjoined to this the account of those who immediately succeeded the Apostles Peter and Paul in their labors. (ch. 4.) The narrative returns then to the affairs of the Jews; details the destruction of Jerusalem under Titus; compares the predictions of our Lord with the sign of the times, and refers to the contemporary testimony of Josephus. The works of the latter are mentioned and reviewed, together with the Canon of the Old Testament, (ch. 10,) and a notice of those who, under Vespasian, Titus and Domitian, were bishops of Jerusalem, Rome, and Alexandria. ch. 11, 13.)

About this period occurred the dissensions in the Church of Corinth, (ch. 16;) the persecution also under Domitian, which, connected with the origin of the Apocalypse, furnishes occasion to detail some parts of St. John's history, and the relatives of our Lord, (ch. 20,) John's return from the Isle of Patmos, the episcopate of Ignatius at Antioch, the history of the youth recovered to the Church by the efforts of St. John, are spread before us from the writings of the Alexandrian, Clement and Irenæus.

Eusebius now, from the writings of St. John, passes to the order and authors of the gospels, and reconciling apparent discrepancies, lays down that important statement of the Canon of the New Testament, which was received in the primitive Church, together with the distinction between the *acknowledged* (ὁμολογούμενοι,) the *disputed* (ἀντιλεγόμενοι,) and the *spurious* (νόθοι.) (ch. 25.)

A new subject offers next, in the rise of heresies. (ch. 27.) The gross errors taught by Menander, the Ebionites and Cerinthus, the delusions of the Nicolaitans are exhibited on the authorities of Irenæus, Justin, Clement, and the Caius, already quoted above. The reference to the last of these errorists, as if by contrast, introduces the subject of marriage, and an account of those apostles who lived in this state. (ch. 30.) The Epistle of Polycrates of Ephesus, throws light on this subject, whilst the extracts from Hegesippus also shows the purer state of the Church, and the period about which the apostolic chair became extinct. (ch. 23.)

Persecution now reared itself again under Trajan, and this occasions the Epistle of Pliny, and the answer of the Emperor. At Rome, Clement is succeeded by Euarestus, whilst Simeon, who died at 120 years of age, is succeeded by Justus at Jerusalem. The Epistles of Ignatius, and his martyrdom, are noticed from the writings of Irenæus and Polycarp. A general account of some, about this time distinguished for prophetical gifts and miracles, (ch. 37,) the notice of the genuine epistle of Clement, with interesting extracts from the last works of Papias, close the third book. This brings the history down to the beginning of the second century, comprising a range of more than thirty years.

The fourth book exhibits the churches of Rome and Alexandria, becoming more and more prominent in their influence on the rest of the Christian world. With the growth of Christianity we also see the growing misery of the Jews. The eighteenth year of Trajan's reign was a time of great calamity to them, in consequence of insurrectionary movements. In the reign of Adrian, his successor, the enemies of Christianity created persecutions which drew forth apologies from Quadratus and Aristides. The series of bishops at Jerusalem, before the destruction of the city, the delusion of the impostor Barchochebas in the eighteenth year of Adrian's reign, (ch. 6,) and the entire exclusion of the Jews from their ancient Jerusalem, now called Ælia, fix our attention on the re-markable changes of that city.

Turning aside from political events to doctrines, Eusebius reviews the heresies that grew out of those already mentioned, of which Menander Saturninus and Basilides were the leaders. They were successfully opposed by Agrippa Castor. (ch. 7.) A new aspect is given to heretical speculations by Carpoerates, who is pronounced the father of Gnosticism. The effects of these wild speculations, and the successful triumph over them, stand connected with a notice of the writers who shared in the defence of the truth. Hegesippus is marked with much distinction. From Justin Martyr extracts are also given against Cerdon and Marcion. Melito, bishop of Sardis, is also quoted. (ch. 13.) Much space is allotted to the character and martyrdom of Polycarp, as detailed by Irenæus. (ch. 14.) The machinations of Crescens against Justin, the death of the latter, and the martyrdom of many Christians, are followed by extracts from the works of Justin. (ch. 18.) The works of Hegesippus are reviewed, (ch. 22,) on whose authority the names of different sects, both Christian and Jewish, are giv n, with a reflection on the Apocrypha, sufficient to exclude them from the Canon. (ch. 22.)

We are now introduced to an acquaintance with the character and writings of the excellent Dionysius of Corinth, the loss of whose works we are led to deplore, from the value of the fragments here preserved. His Christian lenity in regard to certain rigid measures proposed, the good effects of his epistles, his sound judgment on the writings of others, and the deep interest he every where manifests for the true edification of the Church, entitle him to high consideration. Theophilus of Antioch, and Philip of Gortyna, were distinguished by their writings—the former against Hermogenes and Marcion; the latter, with great perspicuity, against Marcion. The works of Melito, bishop of Sardis, and Apollinaris of Hierapolis, are enumerated, particularly the former, whose epistle to Onesimus, gives us the Canon of

the Old Testament as we have it at the present day. (ch. 26.)
Tatian was a disciple of Justin, but according to Irenæus, fell
into some errors on Christian duty. His Diatessaron, a kind of
Harmony of the Gospels, is noticed by Eusebius. The last author
noticed in the fourth book, is the Syrian Bardesanes, against
Marcion, and it closes about A. D. 170, comprising nearly fifty
years of the second century.

The fifth book opens with the persecutions under Verus. Lyons
and Vienna, the two capitals of Gaul, are distinguished for martyrs. Remarkable instances of Christian faith and fortitude are
exhibited in Vittius Epagathus, Maturus, Attalus, Blandina and
others. The restoration of the lapsed, through the mediation of
the martyrs, a remarkable vision of Attalus, one of them, and the
successful prayer of the Christian legion, are among the incidents
related. (ch. 4–6.)

The succession of Roman bishops is given from Irenæus, from
whom also the account of miracles performed by believers, is taken.
Irenæus is also cited on the Canon, (ch. 8,) particularly on the
Septuagint. The school founded by Pantænus, at Alexandria,
who was succeeded by Clement, together with the eulogium of the
latter on his master, gives a favorable view of the Egyptian Church.
The succession of Gentile bishops in the Church of Jerusalem,
now, seems to have been a consequence of the exclusion of Jews
from Ælia. Rhodo of Asia Minor, wrote about this time, on the
divisions caused by Marcion. (ch. 13.) The Phrygian heresy and
the schism of Blastus at Rome, are among the troubles of the
Church noticed by the same writer. He has also transmitted to
us what we know of Miltiades and his works, especially on the
Montanists. Extracts from Apollonius of Rome, caused much zeal
in refuting the pretended prophets. (ch. 18.) Serapion, bishop of
Antioch, is cited on the same subject; Irenæus writes against
schism, and the learned Apollonius dies a martyr at Rome, under
Commodus. The question on the Passover being started about
this time, occasions great offence. Victor presumes to excom-

municate the eastern churches,—a memorable prelude to the arrogance of other days. (ch 20.) The fifth book ends with an
account of the errors of Artemon, revived by Paul of Samosata.
The close of the book coincides with the reign of Severus, abou:
the beginning of the third century.

The sixth book begins with the persecutions under S. Severus.
It is occupied chiefly with the life and labors of Origen. These
memoirs are introduced with accounts of Clement, Origen's master, Narcissus of Jerusalem, Serapron of Antioch, Heraclas, the
translator Symmachus, Ambrose of Alexandria, and other writers,
consulted by Eusebius in the library of Ælia. Origen's review of
the Scriptures, the deference paid him by the bishops of Alexandria,
Cesarea, and Jerusalem, (ch. 27,) show the estimation in which he
was held. About this time flourished Africanus, author of a
Chronography, who also wrote to Aristides on the geneology o
Christ. (coll. p. 31, 32 and 250.) Beryllus of Bostra, noted for
his errors, is refuted by Origen. An instance of ecclesiastical discipline in the case of the emperor Philip, Origen's controversy
with Celsus, the Arabian errorists and the Helcesaites, the Decian
persecution, which occurred about the middle of the century ;
these events, with the sufferings of Origen, are prominent features
of this book. It closes with some account of the Novatian agita-
tions. For the removal of these, a council is held, and both Cornelius and Cyprian write to heal the threatened breach. Dionysius
of Alexandria, in an epistle to Germanus, gives an account of his
own sufferings, (ch. 40,) and those of the Alexandrian Church, in
an epistle to Fabius of Antioch. (ch. 41.) The latter is also addressed in an epistle from Cornelius. (ch. 43.) An extract from
Dionysius, relates the death of the aged Serapion, and the same
Dionysius addresses Novatus in an epistle, urging peace and reconciliation. His different works are enumerated in the last chapter of the book, which embraces about half of the third century.

The seventh book continues the extracts from Dionysius, and
the persecution under Decius. About this time is agitated the

question on the rebaptism of heretics. (ch. 3.) The easter;
churches act independently of the west, in this matter. (ch. 5.
Stephen of Rome holds no communion with them, and Cypriar
writes to him. About the same time arose the erroneous loctrine
of Sabellius, and the Novatian schism reached its height. (ch. 8.
Besides these points, Dionysius writes on others of interest to the
Church, details the persecutions under Valerian, and his own sufferings (ch. 9) at that time, makes his defence against the insinua-
tions of Germanus on that occasion, (coll. p. 255, 283,) and gives
many names of sufferers for the faith, in Egypt. (ch. 11.)

The persecution was not as violent in Palestine, but yet not
without its victims (ch. 12) at Cesarea. Paneas (Cesarea Philippi)
acquires celebrity for two remarkable traditions. (ch. 17, 18.)
The see of Jerusalem is held in great veneration in these times.

Eusebius now states the labors of Dionysius on the Canon for
Easter, the first attempt of the kind in the Church. The misery
and sufferings of Alexandria during the plague, are graphically de-
scribed by Dionysius, who also relates the schism caused by
Nepos in Egypt, takes part in the controversy on the book of
Revelation, (ch. 20,) in which he displays much critical acumen.
He dies after an episcopate of seventeen years.

Paul of Samosata, notorious about this time, for his errors and
arrogance, is refuted by Malchion, and deposed in a council. (ch.
29, 30.) The heresy of Manes now appears in the Church, (ch.
31,) a sad mixture of oriental philosophy and perverted truth.
The seventh book gives us an account of the prominent characters
contemporary with Eusebius, of the school established by his friend
Pamphilus, at Cesarea, and the martyrdom of Peter, bishop of
Alexandria. (ch. 32.) It embraces more than half a century.
Eusebius gives the number three hundred and five years from the
beginning to the present time.

The eighth book relates the greatest and last of the memorable
persecutions during the first centuries of the Church. Churches
are demolished. Martyrs in Egypt, Syria, Phrygia, attest the faith

Nicomedia is distinguished for violence to the Christians. Maxentius and Maximian are the great enemies. (ch. 14.) Violence reigns the whole time of the persecution, even among the persecutors themselves. (ch. 15.) To the eighth book is appended the celebrated Book of Martyrs. (p. 348–378.)

The ninth book records the revocation of the decrees against the Christians, as also various public acts in their favor. It also relates the calamities now assailing the empire, and the deaths of Maximian, Maxentius and Maximus.

The tenth book winds up the history with a view of the pleasing reverse of events, the oration of Eusebius commemorative of the happy change, and copies of public documents confirming privileges granted to Christians.

C. F CRUSE

March 1, 1850.

ANNOTATIONS

ON THE

LIFE AND WRITINGS OF EUSEBIUS PAMPHILUS

BY VALESIUS.

TRANSLATED* BY THE REV. S. E. PARKER,

AUTHOR OF THE ARTICLES 'PROSODY,' 'QUANTITY,' AND 'VERSIFICATION,' IN
DR. REES'S CYCLOPÆDIA.

According to the testimony of Socrates,† a book relative to the life of Eusebius, was written by Acacius, the scholar of that prelate, and his successor in the see of Cæsarea. This book, however, through that negligence in antiquity to which the loss of many others is to be ascribed, is not now extant; but from the testimonies of the several writers that have mentioned Eusebius, no exertions of ours shall be wanting to supply the defect.

It appears that Eusebius was born in Palestine, about the close of the reign of Gallienus. One proof of which is, that by the ancients, particularly by Basilius and Theodoret, he is frequently termed a Palestinian. It is not *impossible*, indeed, that he might have received that name from his being the bishop of Cæsarea, yet *probability* is in favour of his having derived it from his country. In short, he himself affirms,‡ that he was educated, and when a youth, dwelt in Palestine, and that there he first saw Constantine, when journeying through Palestine in the suit of Diocletian Augustus. Eusebius, too, after repeating§ the contents of a law, written in favour of the Christians, by Constantine to the Palestinians, observes, "This letter of the Emperor's is the first sent to us."

On the authority of Eusebius himself, it may be affirmed, that he

---

* In this version, the sense, more than the expression of Valesius, is regarded.
† Eccles. Hist. lib. 2. c. 4.
‡ In his first book concerning the life of Constantine, chap. 19.
§ Life of Constantine, book ii. chap. 43, where see note *a*. Cambr. edit. 1692

was born in the last part of the reign of Gallienus; for, in his Ecclesiastic History, he informs us, that Dionysius, bishop of Alexandria, lived *in his own age.** Eusebius, therefore, since Dionysius
died in the twelfth year of the reign of Gallienus, must have been
born before, if he lived within the time of that prelate. The same
inference, also, follows, from his stating,† that Paul of Samosata, had
revived the heresy of Artemon, *in his‡ age.* And in his history of
the occurrences during the reign of Gallienus, before he begins the
narrative of the error and condemnation of Paul of Samosata, he observes, " but now, after the history of these things, we will transmit
to posterity an account of *our own age.*"

Whom he had for his parents is uncertain; neither do we know by
what authorities, Nicephorus Callistus is warranted in affirming, that
his mother was the sister of Pamphilus the martyr. Eusebius of
Cæsarea, in Arius's letter,§ is termed brother to Eusebius of Nicomedia. Though he possibly might, on account of his friendship,
have received this appellation, yet it is more probable that he was
nearly related to the Nicomedian bishop; especially since, Eusebius
of Cæsarea only, though many others there are mentioned, is termed
by Arius, brother to that prelate. Besides the Nicomedian Eusebius
was a native of Syria, and bishop first of Berytus: nor was it then
the usage, that foreigners and persons unknown, should be promoted
to the government of churches.

Neither is it known what teachers he had in secular learning; but
in sacred literature, he had for his preceptor Dorotheus, the eunuch,
presbyter of the Antiochian church, of whom he makes honourable
mention, in his Seventh Book.|| Notwithstanding Eusebius there
says only, that he had heard Dorotheus expounding the Holy Scriptures with propriety, in the Antiochian church, we are not inclined
to object to any·one hence inferring, with Trithemius, that Eusebius
was Dorotheus's disciple. Theotecnus being at that time dead, the
bishopric of the church of Cæsarea was administered by Agapius, a
person of eminent piety and great liberality to the poor. By him
Eusebius was admitted into the clerical office, and with Pamphilus,
a presbyter of distinction at that time in the Cæsarean church, he

---

* See lib. 3. c. 28.   † Eccles. Hist. book v. chap. 28.   ‡ Eusebius's.
§ Arius's letter to Eusebius, bishop of Nicomedia, will be found in Theodoret's
Eccles. Hist. lib. 1. c. 5. edit. *Val.* || Chap. 1. p. 2.

entered into the firmest friendship. Pamphilus was, as Photius relates, a Phœnician, born at Berytus, and scholar of Pierius, a presbyter of the Alexandrian church. Who, since he was animated with
the most singular attachment to sacred literature, and was with the
utmost zeal collecting all the books, especially Origen's, of the ecclic-
siastic writers, founded a very celebrated school and library at Cæsarea, of which school Eusebius seems to have been the first master.
Indeed, it is affirmed* by Eusebius, that Apphianus, who suffered
martyrdom in the thira year of the persecution, had been instructeo
by him in the sacred Scriptures, in the city of Cæsarea. From that
time Eusebius's intimacy with Pamphilus was so great, and his attention to him, as his inseparable companion till his death such, that
from this attachment he acquired the name of Pamphilus. Neither
did that attachment terminate with the death of the latter, but survived
with the former, who ever mentioned his deceased friend in the most
respectful and affectionate manner; this, indeed, is exemplified by the
three books, eulogized by St. Jerome, and written by Eusebius, concerning the life of Pamphilus, and by many passages in his Ecclesiastic History, and in his account of the martyrs of Palestine. In
his Second Book, also, against Sabellius, written by Eusebius, after
the Nicene Council, he frequently commends Pamphilus, though he
suppresses his name. In the commencement of that discourse, Eusebius observes, "I think that my ears are as yet affected by the memory of that blessed man; for I seem to be yet hearing him utter that
devout word, 'the only begotten Son of God,' a phrase he constantly
employed; for it was the remembrance of the only begotten to the
glory of the unborn Father. Now we have heard the apostle commanding that presbyters ought to be honoured with a double honour,
those especially who have laboured in the word and doctrine." And
at page 29, he thus again speaks of his friend: "With these things
from the memory of that blessed man, I am not elated, but wish I
could so speak, as if, together with you, I were always hearing from
him. And the words now cited may be pleasing to him, for it is the
glory of good servants to speak truth concerning the Lord, and it is
the honour of those fathers, who have taught well, if their doctrines
be repeated."† Some, it is true, "may insinuate, that these were

* In his book concerning the martyrs of Palestine.

† Again, in the same book, p. 37: "These words we always heard from that
blessed man, for they were often thus spoken by him."

phrases, the creatures of his lips, and no proof of the feelings of his heart. I remember, however, in what a satisfactory manner, I have heard with you, his solemn asseveration, that there was not one thing on his tongue and another in his heart." Shortly after, he says : " But now on account of the memory and honour of this our father, so good, so laborious, and so vigilant for the church, let these facts be briefly stated by us. For we have not mentioned yet his fami y, his education or learning, nor narrated the other incidents of his life, and its *leading or principal object.*"* These passages in Eusebius were pointed out to us by the most learned Franciscus Ogerius. Hence it may be satisfactorily inferred, that it was not any family alliance, but the bond of amity that connected Eusebius with Pamphius. Eusebius, though he mentions Pamphilus so frequently, and boasts so highly of his friendship, yet never speaks of him as a relative. The testimony of Eusebius alone is sufficient to decide that Pamphilus, though his friend, was not his kinsman. Since in the close of his Seventh Book of Ecclesiastic History, where he is making mention of Agapius, bishop of Cæsarea, he says : " In his time, we became acquainted with Pamphilus, a most eloquent man, and in his life and practices truly a philosopher,† and in the same church, ennobled with the honour of the presbytery." Since

---

* " Propositum" is the word employed by Valesius, doubtless in that acceptation in which its precise sense is so easily appreciated by the classic reader in Horace, Car. lib. iii. ode iii. line i. " Justum et tenacem *propositi* virum, non civium ardor prava jubentium, non vultus instantis tyranni mente quatit solidà," &c. Should not Christians have, universally, a far more vivid perception of this beautiful picture of mind than heathens ? St. Paul had ; see Philip. chap. iii. ver 13 & 14.

† The term philosopher, in the modern sense in which it is commonly understood, by no means expresses the precise meaning of the word ϲιλοϲοϲοϲ, here used by Eusebius. By Isocrates, it is frequently employed to express an eloquent per son, or teacher of eloquence. Its *generic* sense is a *lover of wisdom.* Wisdom by the Sophists, was of course confined to their own doctrines. But according to the sense in which Josephus and other Grecian writers employed the word ϲιλοϲοϲοϲ, the *lover of wisdom,* seems not to be searching for wisdom, either in the doctrines of the Sophists, or in the Cartesian vortices, but *in the volumes of inspired truth.* This character, then, is equivalent to what in modern language is called a *theologian,* in which sense, I have no doubt, Eusebius is here to be understood. Hence Pamphilus was a character not only devoted to the attainment of that *wisdom,* which is developed in the sacred code, but his life and practices were such as to recommend it to others; consequently, a true theologian.—*Translator.*

.hen, Eusebius attests that Pamphilus was then first known to him, it is sufficiently evident, that family alliance was not the tie that connected them.

In these times occurred that most severe persecution of the Christians, which was begun by Diocletian, and by his successors continued unto the tenth year. During this persecution, Eusebius, at that time being a presbyter of the church of Cæsarea, abode almost constantly in that city, and by continual exhortations, instructed many persons in order to martyrdom. Amongst whom was Apphianus, a noble youth, whose illustrious fortitude in martyrdom is related in Eusebius's book concerning the martyrs of Palestine. In the same year Pamphilus was cast into prison, where he spent two whole years in bonds. During which time, Eusebius by no means deserted his friend and companion, but visited him continually, and in the prison wrote, together with him, five books in defence of Origen ; but the sixth and last book of that work, he finished after the death of Pamphilus.—That whole work was by Eusebius and Pamphilus dedicated* to Christian confessors,† living in the mines of Palestine. In the time of this persecution, on account, probably, of some urgent affairs of the church, Eusebius went to Tyre. During his residence there, he witnessed ‡ the glorious martyrdom of five Egyptian Christians ; and afterwards, on his arrival in Egypt and Thebais, the persecution then prevailing there, he § beheld the admirable constancy of many martyrs of both sexes. Some have insinuated that Eusebius, to exempt himself in this persecution, from the troubles of a prison, sacrificed to idols ; and that this was objected against him, as will be hereafter related, by the Egyptian bishops and confessors, in the synod at Tyre. But we doubt not that this is false, and that it was a calumny forged by the ene-

* This is affirmed by Photius in his Bibliotheca, chap. 118.

† Though the word here employed by Valesius, is *confessores*, yet there cannot be the least doubt, that the characters to whom he alludes were very different from those which a more recent application of the term might intimate. Confessores were simply persons that had confessed and acknowledged openly, during the time of the persecution, that they were Christians, and would not, to save either their lives or property, deny their Master or his sacred cause. They were decided cha racters, tenaces propositi. This term was employed by Valesius, who lived in ar age of the church when its use was popular.

‡ Eusebius informs us of this in his Eighth Book, chap. 7.

§ This he relates in the ninth chapter of the same Book.

mies of Eusebius. For had a crime so great been really committed by him, how could he have been afterwards appointed bishop of Cæsarea? How is it likely that he should, *in this case*, have been invited by the Antiochians to undertake the episcopate of their city? And yet Cardinal Baronius has seized on that as certain and undoubted, which by his enemies, for litigious purposes, was objected against Eusebius, but never confirmed by the testimony of any one. At the same time, a book was written by Eusebius against Hierocles. For Hierocles of Nicomedia, about the beginning of the persecution, when the Christian churches were everywhere harassed, in the city of Nicomedia, published, as an insult to a religion then assailed *by all its enemies*, two* books against the Christian faith. In which books he asserted, that Apollonius Tyaneus performed more and greater things† than Christ. These impious assertions, Eusebius answered in a very short book, as if he regarded the man and his cause of little consequence.

Agapius, bishop of Cæsarea during this interval, being dead, the persecution subsiding, and peace being restored to the church, Eusebius, by common consent, succeeds to the episcopal dignity at Cæsarea. Others represent Agricola, who subscribed to the synod of Ancyra, at which he was present in the 314th year of the Christian era, to be the successor of Agapius. This is affirmed by Baronius in his Annals‡ and Blondellus.§ The latter writes, that Eusebius undertook the administration of the church of Cæsarea, after the death of Agricola, about the year 315. But these subscriptions of the bishops extant only in the Latin collections of the canons, seem in our judgment to be entitled to little credit. For they occur not either in the Greek copies, or in the Latin versions of Dionysius Exiguus, Berides, Eusebius,‖ enumerating the bishops of the principal dioceses, where the persecution began and raged, ends with the mention of Agapius bishop of Cæsarea; who, he observes, laboured much, during that persecution, for the good of his own church. The necessary inference, therefore, is, that Agapius must have been bishop until the end of the persecution. But Eusebius was elevated to the

---

* Which he termed φιλαληθεις.

† No word for "*miracles*" occurs in the text of Valesius.

‡ Ad. annum Christi, 314.

§ In his Apology pro Sententià Hieronymi. c. 19. *Val.*

‖ In the 7th Book of his Ecclesiactic Hist. chap. 32.

episcopal function immediately after that persecution. For after peace was restored to the church, Eusebius* and other prelates being invited by Paulinus bishop of Tyre, to the dedication of a cathedral. Eusebius made there a very eloquent oration. Now this happened before the rebellion of Licinius against Constantine, in the 315th year of the Christian era, about which period Eusebius wrote those celebrated books concerning *Evangelic Demonstration and Preparation.* And these books were certainly written before the Nicene Synod, since they are expressly mentioned in his Ecclesiastic History, which was written, as proved in our Annotations, before that council.

Meanwhile, Licinius, who managed the government in the eastern parts, excited by sudden rage, began to persecute the Christians, especially the prelates, whom he suspected of showing more favour, and of offering up more prayers for Constantine than for himself. Constantine, however, having defeated him in two battles by land and sea, compelled him to surrender, and restored peace to the Christians of the eastern countries.

A disturbance, however, far more grievous, arose at that time, amongst the Christians themselves. For since Arius, a presbyter of the city of Alexandria, would in the church, publicly advance some new and impious tenet relative to the Son of God, and notwithstanding repeated admonition by Alexander the bishop, persisted, he and his associates in this heresy, were at length expelled. Highly resenting this, Arius sent letters with a sketch of his own faith to all the bishops of the neighbouring cities, in which he complained, that since he asserted the same doctrines that the rest of the eastern prelates maintained, he had been unjustly deposed by Alexander. Many bishops imposed on by these artifices, and powerfully excited by Eusebius of Nicomedia, who openly favoured the Arian party, wrote letters in defence of Arius to Alexander bishop of Alexandria, entreating him to restore Arius to his former rank in the church. Our Eusebius was one of their number, whose letter written to Alexander is extant in the acts of the seventh Oecumenical Synod, which we have inserted amongst the testimonies† of the ancients. The

---

° As we are informed in the tenth book of his Ecclesiastic Hist. *Val.* See chap. 4, where Eusebius has inserted this oration.

† Of these, Valesius, after his account of Eusebius's life and writings, presents a collection made by himself, both for and against Eusebius. *q. v.*

example of Eusebius of Cæsarea, was soon followed by Theodotius
and Paulinus, the one bishop of Laodicea, the other of Tyre, who
interceded with Alexander for Arius's restoration. Of which letter,
since Arius boasted on every occasion, and by the authority of such
eminent men, drew many into the participation of his heresy, Alexander was compelled to write to the other eastern bishops, that the
justice of the expulsion of Arius and his associates might be understood. Two letters of Alexander's are yet extant; the one to Alexander bishop of Constantinople, in which the former complains of
three Syrian bishops, who, agreeing with Arius, had more than ever
inflamed that contest, which they ought rather to have suppressed.
These three, as may be learned from Arius's letter to Eusebius bishop
of Nicomedia, are Eusebius, Theodotius, and Paulinus. The other
letter of Alexander's, written to all the bishops throughout the world,
Socrates records in his first book.* To these letters of Alexander's,
almost all the eastern bishops subscribed, amongst whom the most
eminent were Philogonius bishop of Antioch, Eustathius of Beræa,
and Macarius of Jerusalem.

The bishops who favoured the Arian party, especially Eusebius of
Nicomedia, imagining themselves to be severely treated in Alexander's letters, devoted themselves with much greater acrimony to the
defence of Arius. For our Eusebius of Cæsarea, together with Pa-
trophilus, Paulinus, and other Syrian bishops, merely voted that
liberty to Arius might be granted of holding, as a presbyter, assemblies in the church, subject notwithstanding to Alexander the bishop,
and of imploring for reconciliation and church fellowship. The
bishops disagreeing thus amongst themselves, some favouring the
party of Alexander, and others that of Arius, the contest became sin-
gularly aggravated ; to remedy this, Constantine, from all parts of the
Roman world, summoned to Nicæa, a city of Bythinia, a general
synod of bishops, such as no age before had seen. In this greatest and
most celebrated council, our Eusebius was not one of either party.
For he both had the first seat on the right hand, and in the name of
the *whole* synod addressed the emperor Constantine, who sat on a
golden chair, between the two rows of the opposite parties. This is
affirmed by Eusebius himself in his Life† of Constantine, and by

---

* Chap. 6.

† In his preface to the first book concerning the life of Constantine, and in his
third book of the same work, chap. ii.

Sozomen* in his Ecclesiastic History. Afterwards, when there was a considerable contest amongst the bishops, relative to a creed or form of faith, our Eusebius proposed a formula, at once simple and ortho dox, which received the general commendation both of the bishops and of the emperor himself. Something, notwithstanding, seeming to be wanting in the creed, to confute the impiety of the new opinion, the fathers of the Nicene Council, determined that these words, " Very God of very God, begotten not made, being of one sub- stance with the Father," should be added. They also annexed anathemas against those who should assert that the Son of God was made of things not existing, and that there was a time when he ex- isted not. At first, indeed, our Eusebius refused to admit the term " consubstantial,"† but when the import of that word was explained to him by the other bishops, he consented, and as he himself relates in his letter‡ to his diocess at Cæsarea, subscribed to the creed. Some affirm that it was the necessity of circumstances, or the fear of the emperor, and not the conviction of his own mind, that compelled Eusebius to subscribe to the Nicene Council. Of some, present at the synod, this might be believed, but this we cannot think of Euse- bius bishop of Cæsarea. After the Nicene Council, too, Eusebius al- ways condemned§ those who asserted that the Son of God was made of things not existing. Athanasius likewise affirms the same con- cerning him, who though he frequently mentions that Eusebius sub- scribed to the Nicene Council, nowhere intimates that he did that in dissimulation. Had Eusebius subscribed to that Council, not accord- ing to his own mind, but fraudulently and in pretence, why did he afterwards send the letter we have mentioned to his diocess at Cæsarea, and therein ingenuously profess that he had embraced that faith which had been published in the Nicene Council ?

After that Council, the Arians through fear of the emperor, were, for a short time quiet. But by artfully ingratiating themselves into the favour of the prince, they resumed boldness, and began by every

---

* In the first book of that work, chap. 19.

† ·Ομοουσιος, consubstantial, of the same substance, or of the same essence, co-es- sential.

‡ See this letter in Socrates, book i. chap. 8.

§ This is evident from his books against Marcellus, particularly from the 9th and 10th chapters of his first book, De Ecclesiasticâ Theologiâ.

method and device, to persecute the Catholic prelates.* Their first
attack fell on Eustathius, bishop of the city of Antioch, eminent both
for the glory of his confession, and for the rank he sustained amongst
the advocates of the Nicene faith. Eustathius was, therefore, accused
before the emperor of maintaining the Sabellian impiety, and of slan-
dering Helena Augusta, the emperor's mother. A numerous assembly
of bishops was convened in the city of Antioch, in which Eusebius
of Nicomedia, the çhief and ring-leader of the whole faction, presided.
In addition to the accusation advanced at this assembly by Cyrus
bishop of the Beræans, against Eustathius, of maintaining the impious
doctrine of Sabellius, another† is devised against him of incontinency,
and he is therefore expelled from his diocese. On this account, a
very impetuous tumult arose at Antioch. The people divided into
two factions, the one requesting that the episcopacy of the Antiochian
church might be conferred on Eusebius of Cæsarea, the other, that
Eustathius their bishop might be restored, would have resorted to
measures of violence, had not the fear and authority of the emperor
and judges prevented it. The sedition being at length terminated, and
Eustathius banished, our Eusebius, though entreated both by the
people, and the bishops that were present, to undertake the administration of the church at Antioch, nevertheless refused. And, when
the bishops by letters written to Constantine, had acquainted him
with their own vote, and with the suffrages of the people, Eusebius
wrote his letters also to that prince, and Eusebius's resolution is
highly commended in the emperor's answer.

Eustathius, having been in this manner deposed, which occurred, as
remarked in our annotations‡ in the year 330, the Arians turned the violence of their fury on Athanasius; and in the prince's presence they
complained first of his ordination ; secondly, that he had exacted§ the
impost of a linen garment from the provincials ; thirdly, that he had

* " *Catholicos Antistites*" are the words of Valesius ; but, doubtless, to be understood here, as signifying, not the prelates of the Arian, or of any other seceding
party, but of the orthodox church *universally*, according to the meaning of the term
catholicus, universal.

† The story is given in Theodoret's Eccles. Hist. Book i. chap. 21. edit. *Vales.*

‡ See Life of Constantine, book 3, chap. 59, note e.

§ This calumny, the Meletians, instigated by Eusebius of Nicomedia, invented ;
as Athanasius tells us in his Apology to Constantine. See his works, *tom.* 1,
p. 778. Edit. Paris, 1627.

broken a sacred cup; and lastly, that he had murdered one Arsenius, a bishop. Constantine, wearied with these vexatious litigations, appointed a council in the city of Tyre, and directed Athanasius the bishop to proceed there, to make his defence. In that synod, Eusebius bishop of Cæsarea, whom Constantine had desired should be present, sat amongst others, as judge. Potamo bishop of Heracleopolis, who had come with Athanasius the bishop and some Egyptian prelates, seeing him sitting in the council, is said to have addressed him in these words: "Is it fit, Eusebius, that you should *sit*, and that the innocent Athanasius should *stand* to be judged by you? Who can endure this? Were you not in custody with me, during the time of the persecution? And I truly, in defence of the truth, lost an eye; but you are injured in no part of your body, neither did you undergo martyrdom, but are alive and whole. In what manner did you escape out of prison, unless you promised to our persecutors that you would commit the detestable* thing? And perhaps you have done it." This is related by Epiphanius, in the heresy of the Meletians. Hence it appears, that they are mistaken who affirm, that Eusebius had sacrificed to idols, and that he had been convicted of the fact in the Tyrian synod. For Potamo did not attest that Eusebius had sacrificed to idols, but only that he was dismissed out of prison safe and whole; a circumstance that favoured the malevolent surmise of Potamo. It was, however, evidently possible that Eusebius might have been dismissed from confinement in a manner very different from that of Potamo's insinuation. From the words of Epiphanius, it seems to be inferred that Eusebius bishop of Cæsarea presided at this synod; for he adds, that Eusebius being previously affected in hearing the accusation against him by Potamo, dismissed the council. Yet by other writers we are informed, that not Eusebius bishop of Cæsarea, but Eusebius of Nicomedia, presided at the Tyrian synod.†

After that council, all the bishops who had assembled at Tyre, re paired, by the emperor's orders, to Jerusalem, to celebrate the conse

---

* That is, to sacrifice to idols.

† Is it not a possible case that both presided? viz., First, Eusebius of Cæsarea, until the insult he sustained in the disparagement of his character by Potamo's insinuation. Feeling then, that his character stood arraigned by that insinuation, that he judged it expedient either to dismiss the council, or at least to leave it to the presidential jurisdiction of one less objectionable to Potamo, viz., to Eusebius of Nicomedia.

cration of the great church, which Constantine in honour of Christ had erected in that place. There our Eusebius graced the solemnity, by the several sermons he delivered. And when the emperor, by very strict letters, had summoned the bishops to his own court, that in his presence they might give an account of their fraudulent and litigious conduct towards Athanasius, our Eusebius, with five others, went to Constantinople, and furnished that prince with a developement of the whole transaction. Here also, in the palace, he delivered his tricennalian oration, which the emperor heard with the utmost joy, not so much on account of any praises to himself, as on account of the praises of God, celebrated by Eusebius throughout the whole of that oration. This oration was the second delivered by Eusebius in that palace.* For he had before made an oration there, concerning the sepulchre of our Lord, which the emperor heard standing; nor could he, though repeatedly entreated by Eusebius, be persuaded to sit in the chair placed for him,† alleging that it was fit that discourses concerning God should be heard standing.

How dear and acceptable our Eusebius was to Constantine, may be known both from the facts we have narrated, as well as from many other circumstances. For he both received many letters from him, as may be seen in the books already mentioned, and was not unfrequently sent for to the palace, where he was entertained at table, and honoured with familiar conversation. Constantine, moreover, related to our Eusebius, the vision of the cross seen by him when on his expedition against Maxentius; and showed to him, as Eusebius informs‡ us, the labarum§ that he had ordered to be made to represent the likeness of that cross. Constantine also, committed to Eusebius, since he knew him to be most skilful in Biblical knowledge, the care and superintendency of transcribing copies‖ of the Scriptures, which he wanted for the accommodation of the churches he had built at Constantinople. Lastly, the book concerning the Feast of Easter, dedicated to him by our Eusebius, was a present to Constantine, so acceptable, that he ordered its immediate translation into Latin; and by letter entreated Eusebius, that he would communicate, soon as

---

* According to his own testimony, in his fourth Book, concerning the Life of Constantine, chap. 46.

† As Eusebius relates in the 33d chapter of the Life of Constantine.

‡ Life of Constantine, lib. 1. c. 28 & 30.   § An imperial standard.

‖ Life of Constantine, lib. 4. c. 34 & 35.

possible, works of this nature, with which he was engaged, to those concerned in the study of sacred literature.

About the same time, Eusebius dedicated a small book to the emperor Constantine, in which was comprised his description of the Jerusalem church, and of the gifts that had been consecrated there. —Which book, together with his tricennalian oration, that he had placed at the close of his Life of Constantine, is not now extant. At the same time, Eusebius wrote five books against Marcellus; of which the three last, De Ecclesiasticâ Theologiâ, he dedicated to Flaccillus bishop of Antioch. Flaccillus entered on that bishopric, a little before the synod of Tyre, which was convened in the consulate of Constantius and Albinus, A. D. 335. It is certain that Eusebius, in his First Book* writes in express words, that Marcellus had been deservedly condemned by the church. Now Marcellus was first condemned in the synod held at Constantinople, by those very bishops that had consecrated Constantine's church at Jerusalem, in the year of Christ 335, or, according to Baronius, 336. Socrates,† indeed, acknowledges only three books written by Eusebius against Marcellus, namely, those entitled, "De Ecclesiasticâ Theologiâ;" but the whole work by Eusebius, against Marcellus, comprised Five Books. The last books written by Eusebius, seem to be the four on the life of Constantine; for they were written after the death of that emperor, whom Eusebius did not long survive, since he died about the beginning of the reign of Constantius Augustus, a little before the death of Constantine Junior, which happened, according to the testimony of Socrates' Second ‡ Book, when Acindynus and Proculus were consuls, A. D. 340.

We cannot admit, what Scaliger § has affirmed, that Eusebius's books against Porphyry, were written under Constantius, the son of Constantine the Great, especially since this is confirmed by the testimony of no ancient writer. Besides, in what is immediately after asserted by Scaliger, that Eusebius wrote his three‖ last books of the Evangelic Demonstration, against Porphyry, there is an evident error. St. Jerome says, indeed, that Eusebius in three volumes, (that is, in

---

* De Ecclesiasticâ Theologiâ, chap. 14.

† Eccles. Hist. book 2. chap. 20: where see note k.

‡ Chap. 4 & 5.

§ In his Animadversions on Eusebius, page 250, last edit.

‖ Namely, the Eighteenth, Nineteenth, and Twentieth.

the Eighteenth, Nineteenth, and Twentieth,) answered Porphyry, who in the Twelfth and Thirteenth of those books which he published against the Christians, had attempted to confute the book of the prophet Daniel. St. Jerome,* however, does not mean, as Scaliger thought, Eusebius's Books on Evangelic Demonstration, but the books he wrote against Porphyry, entitled, according to Photius's Bibliotheca, περι ελιγχου και 'απολογιας, *Refutation and Defence.* We are also persuaded that Eusebius wrote these books after his Ecclesiastic History; because Eusebius, though on other occasions he usually refers to his own works, does not in the Sixth Book† of his Eccle siastic History, where he quotes a notorious passage from Porphyry,‡ make any mention of the books he wrote against him.

We avail ourselves of the present opportunity to make some re marks relative to Eusebius's Ecclesiastic History, the chief subject of our present labour and exertions. Much, indeed, had been written by our Eusebius, both against Jews and Heathens, to the edification of the orthodox and general church, and in confirmation of the verity of the Christian faith, nevertheless, amongst all his books, his Ecclesiastic History deservedly stands pre-eminent. For before Eusebius, many had written in defence of Christianity, and had, by the most satisfactory arguments, refuted the Jews on the one hand and the Heathens on the other, but not one, before Eusebius, had delivered to posterity a history of ecclesiastic affairs. On which account, therefore, because Eusebius, not only was the first to show this example, but has transmitted to us, what he undertook, in a state so complete and perfect, he is entitled to the greater commendation. Though many, it is true, induced by his example, have, since his time, furnished accounts of ecclesiastic affairs, yet they have not only uniformly commenced their histories from the times of Eusebius, but have left him to be the undisputed voucher of the period of which he yet re mains the exclusive historian, and consequently he only is entitled to the epithet of the father of ecclesiastic history.

By what preliminary circumstances Eusebius was led to this his chef-d'œuvre, it is not difficult to conjecture. Having in his Chronological Canons accurately stated the time of the advent and passion of Jesus Christ, the names of the several bishops that had presided in the four principal churches, and of the eminent characters therein,

---

* In his preface to his Commentary on Daniel.
† Chap. 19.   ‡ From Porphyry's third book against the Christians.

and having also detailed an account of the successive heresies and persecutions, he was, as it were, led by insensible degrees to write a history specially on ecclesiastic affairs, to furnish a full developement of what had been but briefly sketched in his Chronological Canons. This, indeed, is expressly confirmed by Eusebius in his preface* to that work; where he also implores the forbearance of the candid reader, on account of his work being less circumstantial, consequent on his travelling in a path before untrod, and his being precluded from the intimations on that subject of any previous writer. Though this, it is true, in the view of some, may appear not so much an apology, as an indirect device of acquiring praise.

Though it is evident from Eusebius's own testimony, that he wrote his Ecclesiastic History, after his Chronological Canons, it is remarkable that the twentieth year† of Constantine is a limit common to both those works. Nor is it less singular, that, though the Nicene Council was held in that year,‡ yet no mention is made of it in either work. But in his Chronicle, at the fifteenth year of Constantine, we read that " Alexander is ordained the nineteenth bishop of the Alexandrian church, by whom Arius the presbyter being expelled, joins many to his own impiety. A synod, therefore, of three hundred and eighteen bishops, is convened at Nice, a city of Bithynia, who by their agreement on the term ὁμοουσιος, (consubstantial, or co-essential) suppressed all the devices of the heretics." It is sufficiently evident that these words were not written by Eusebius, but by St. Jerome, who in Eusebius's Chronicle inserted many passages of his own. For, not to mention that this reference to the Nicene Council is inserted in a place with which it has no proper connexion, who could believe that Eusebius would thus write concerning Arius, or should have inserted the term ὁμοουσιος in his own Chronicle; which word, as we shall hereafter state, was not satisfactory to him. Was it likely that Eusebius should, in the Chronicle, state that three hundred and eighteen bishops were present at the Nicene synod, and in his Third§ Book on the Life of Constantine, say expressly that something more than two hundred and fifty sat in that council ? We doubt not, however, that the Ecclesiastical History was not completely finished by Eusebius till some years after the council at Nice. As Dionysius of

---

* Book 1. chap. 1.   † i. e. A. D. 325.

‡ On Constantine's Vicennalia, that is, on the twentieth year of his empire.

§ Chap. 8.

Halicarnassus, in his Comparison of Herodotus and Thucydides, had
long since intimated to the writers of histories, the propriety of terminating their narratives at the consummation of some illustrious
event, Eusebius had, therefore, it is likely, resolved to close his history with that peace, which after Diocletian's persecution shone, as
he observes, like a light from heaven upon the church; on this account, probably, he avoided mentioning the Nicene synod, lest he
should be compelled to commence a narrative of renewed litigation,
and that too of bishops one amongst another. Now what event
more illustrious could have been desired by Eusebius, than that repose, which after a most sanguinary persecution, had been restored
to the Christians by Constantine; when the persecutors, and Licinius
being every where extinct, not a fear of past afflictions could exist.
This epoch, therefore, rather than that of the Nicene council, afforded the most eligible limit to his Ecclesiastical History. For in that
synod, the contentions seemed not so much appeased as renewed;
and that not through any fault of the synod itself, but by the perti-
nacity of those who refused to acquiesce in the very salutary decrees
of that venerable assembly.

Having said thus much relative to the life and writings of Euse
bius, it remains to make some remarks in reference to the soundness
of his religious faith and sentiments. Let not the reader, however,
here expect from us a defence, nor even any opinion of our own, but
rather the judgment of the church and of the ancient fathers concerning him. Wherefore, certain points shall be here premised, as preliminary propositions, relying on which, we may arrive at the greater
certainty relative to the faith of Eusebius. As the opinions of the
ancients concerning Eusebius, are various, since some have termed
him a Catholic, others a heretic, others a διγλωττον,* a person of a
double tongue, or wavering faith, it is incumbent on us to inquire to
which opinion we should chiefly assent. Of the law it is an invariable rule, to adopt, in doubtful cases, the more lenient opinion as
the safer alternative. Besides, since all the westerns, St. Jerome ex-
cepted, have entertained honourable sentiments relative to Eusebius,
and since the Gallican church has enrolled† him in the catalogue of
saints, it is questionless preferable to assent to the judgment of our

* See Socrates, lib. 1. c. 23.

† As may be learned from Victorius Aquitanus, the Martyrology of Usuardus,
und from others.

fathers, than to that of the eastern schismatics. In short, whose authority ought to be more decisive in this matter than that of the bishops of Rome ? But Galesius, in his work on the Two Natures, has recounted our Eusebius amongst the catholic writers, and has quoted two authorities out of his books. Pope Pelagius,* too, terms him the most honourable amongst historians, and pronounces him to be free from every taint of heresy, notwithstanding he had highly eulogized heretical Origen. Some, however, may say, that since the easterns were better acquainted with Eusebius, a man of their own language, a preference should be given, in this case, to their judgment. Even amongst these, Eusebius does not want those, Socrates† and Gelasius Cyzicenus‡ for example, who entertained a favourable opinion concerning him. But if the judgment of the Seventh Oecumenical Synod be opposed to any inclination in his favour, our answer is ready. The faith of Eusebius was not the subject of that synod's debate, but the worship of images. In order to the subversion of which, when the opponents that had lately assembled in the imperial city, had produced evidence out of Eusebius's letter to Constantia, and laid the greatest stress thereon, the fathers of the Seventh Synod, to invalidate the authority of that evidence, exclaimed that Eusebius was an Arian. But this was done merely casually, from the impulse of the occasion, and hatred of the letter, not advisedly, or from a previous investigation of the charge. They produce some passages, it is true, from Eusebius, to insinuate that he was favourable to the Arian hypothesis ; but they avoid all discrimination between what Eusebius wrote prior to the Nicene Council, and what he wrote afterwards, which, questionless, ought to have been done as essential to a just decision relative to Eusebius's faith. In short, nothing written by Eusebius before that synod is fairly chargeable in this respect, against him. Eusebius's letter to Alexander, containing his intercession with that prelate for Arius, was of course, written before that council. The affirmation, therefore, of the fathers of the Seventh Synod, notwithstanding it has the semblance of the highest authority, seems rather to have the character of temerity and premature judgment, than to be the verdict of a synod derived from a judicial investigation of the cause. The Greeks may assume the

* In Epist. Tertiâ ad Eliam Aqueleiensem et alios Episcopos Istri.
† See his Defence of him, in book 2. chap. 21.
‡ De Synod. Nicænâ, book 2. chap. 1.

liberty to think as they please concerning Eusebius, and to term him
an Arian, or a favourer of that heresy ; but who can patiently endure
St. Jerome, who, not content with calling him heretic and Arian, frequently terms him the ring-leader of that faction ? Can he be justly
termed a ring-leader of the Arians, who, after the Nicene Council,
always condemned their opinions ? Let his books De Ecclesiasticà
Theologiâ be perused, which he wrote against Marcellus long after
the Nicene Council ; and we shall find what we have affirmed, that
he condemned those who asserted that the Son of God was made of
things not existing ; and that there was a time when he existed not.
Athanasius, likewise, in his letter relative to the decrees of the Nicene
Council, attests the same fact concerning Eusebius, in the following
words : " In this, truly, he was unfortunate : that he might clear himself,
however, of the imputation, he ever afterwards opposed the Arians,
particularly since their denial of the pre-existence of the Son of God
applied equally to his conception or incarnation." With this testimony, too, Eusebius was favoured by Athanasius, notwithstanding
the personal differences between them. But St. Jerome, who had no
cause of enmity against Eusebius, who had profited so liberally by
his writings, who had translated his Chronological Canon, and his
Book de Locis Hebraicis, into Latin, brands, notwithstanding, Eusebius with a calumny, which even his most malignant enemies never
fastened on him. The reason of this we cannot conjecture, except
it is, that St. Jerome, in consequence of his enmity to Origen, persisted in an unqualified persecution of all that maintained his opinions,
particularly Eusebius.

On the other hand, we do not conceal the fact, that Eusebius,
though he cannot be deservedly esteemed a ring-leader of the Arian
faction, yet after the Nicene Council, was perpetually conversant with
the principals of that party, and, together with them, opposed the
catholic bishops, as Eustathius, and Athanasius, the most strenuous
advocates for the adoption of the term 'ομοουσιος. Though Eusebius
always asserted the eternity of the Son of God, against the Arians,
yet in his disapproval of that word,* he seems censurable. It is certain that he never made use of that term, either in his books against
Marcellus, or in his orations against Sabellius. Nay, in his Second
Book against Sabellius, he expressly declares, that since that word is
not in the Scriptures, it is not satisfactory to him. On this occasion,

* Viz. 'ομοουσιος.

he speaks to the following effect: "As not inquiring into truths which admit of investigation, is indolence, so prying into others, where the scrutiny is inexpedient, is audacity. Into what truths ought we then to search? Those which we find recorded in the Scriptures. But what we do not find recorded there, let us not search after. For had the knowledge of them been incumbent on us, the Holy Spirit would doubtless have placed them there." Shortly after, he says: "Let us not hazard ourselves in such a risk, but speak safely; and let not any thing that is written be blotted out." And in the end of his oration, he thus expresses himself: "Speak what is written, and the strife will be abandoned." In which passages, Eusebius, no doubt, alludes to the word ὁμοούσιος.

Finally, we now advert to the testimonies of the ancients concerning Eusebius. Here one thing is to be observed, namely, however various the opinions of men have been, relative to the accuracy of the religious sentiments of Eusebius, all however, have unanimously esteemed him as a person of the most profound learning. To this we have to mention one solitary exception, Joseph Scaliger, who within the memory of our fathers, impelled by the current of temerity, and relish for vituperation, endeavoured to filch from Eusebius those literary honours, which even his adversaries never dared to impugn. Scaliger's words,* we have inserted amongst the testimonies of the ancients, not as any proof of our value of his judgment on this point, but for the accommodation of those desirous of knowing them, and with the design that his unwarrantable detraction might meet with the exposure it deserved; who having resolved to write a commentary on the Chronological Canon of Eusebius, does not hesitate to arraign St. Jerome himself, because he speaks of Eusebius as a most learned character. On Scaliger's opinion, we had at first determined to bestow a more ample refutation; but this we shall defer, until more leisure on the one hand, or a more urgent claim on the part of the reader, on the other, shall again call our attention to the subject.

* See Scaliger's Elench. Trihæres. chap. 27; and book 6 de Emend. Temp. chap. 1, about the end: and his Animadversions on Eusebius's Chronicle, page 8.

PREFACE BY THE TRANSLATOR.

WHEN the proposition was started, to issue a new translation of the present work, the question no doubt frequently arose, *Cui bono?* Have we not ecclesiastical histories enough, and do not these give us all the information that we can reasonably expect, presented too in a form and style which is not likely to be surpassed by any age? Many may here have thought of the judicious and learned Mosheim, or of the popular Milner, some perhaps of the voluminous Schrœckh, and Fleury,* whose researches into primitive ages have condensed the labours of their predecessors. Some, indeed, who, in distinct and separate works, have confined their histories to the three first centuries of the church, as Mosheim in his Commentary de Rebus Christianis ante Constantinum, Walchii Historia Ecclesiastica Novi Testamenti. and others of less notoriety, might seem to preclude the necessity of any additional aids, or of recurring to the fountains whence they drew. But whatever be the superiority of modern ecclesiastical history, however justly it may represent the times recorded, it cannot give us the spirit of these times without the authors from which it is derived. It cannot, therefore, supersede the necessity of examining the same ground in the express statement of an original or primitive writer.

It will not, therefore, be pronounced an indifference to the superior literature of our own age, when we hold up to view a production of ages long passed away. Every age has its distinctive features, its advantages as well as defects; ours may, without arrogance, claim the character of more systematic precision in every department of learning. It has been reserved for this age, under Providence, by whose operations the human mind has attained an unprecedented expansion, to reduce the accumulated materials of

* Schrœckh has written an Ecclesiastical History in forty-two octavo, and Fleury in twenty quarto volumes; the former in German. the latter in French.

the past, to their correlative positions, to compress them into space
that brings them more within our grasp, and by rejecting the
superfluous, and digesting the essential, to enable us to traverse
the vast ground of human attainment with pleasure and profit.

The author, however, whose history is here presented to the
English reader, in order to be duly estimated, must not be measured by a standard like this. To be appreciated, he must be
measured by his own times. Neither are we to expect of him
the condensed proportions, the judicious selections, and the comprehensive distribution of materials, that mark the productions
of the scientific historian; nor was it the intention of our author.
If we may be allowed to judge from the work itself, his object
appears more like furnishing the materials, which himself or the
future historian should handle with a more masterly hand or a
more enlarged view. The work, therefore, abounds with extracts from the writers that flourished in the early ages of the
church, in which our author presents either a striking event, ex·
pressions of sentiments or doctrine, to illustrate the religious aspect of times and places, and by the express testimony of another,
perhaps often obviates the odium which would devolve upon his
own narrative. Hence the history contains rather accounts of
particular churches, than a history of the church generally, and
is more like detached incidents scattered in memoirs of the individuals that successively rise and pass away before us.

Our author, as the first that professedly entered the ground, has
been justly called the father of ecclesiastical history. Priority gives
him a just claim to the title. If his performance be examined by
all the tests, which would be applied to the scientific historians
this praise would indeed be awarded to a prominent name of
modern date. But Eusebius is the first, and the only historian
of the church bordering on primitive times. No just parallel
therefore can be drawn between the Ecclesiastical History here
translated, and the scientific labours of the present day. The
business of the modern historian, is to survey, with comprehensive
eye, to digest, to reduce to proper dimensions, and with a skilful
hand to mould, his materials into the form of pleasing yet faithful
narration; that of the primitive historian, was rather to trans-

cribe what was most important from the existing documents of the day.

Our author has the praise even from the hypercritical Scaliger of being a man who had made extensive use of the historical sources of his day. *Si eruditissimus vocandus*, says he, *qui multa legit, sane nemo illi hanc laudem invidere potest.* This writer does not, indeed, allow him all the qualifications of an historian, to use his own words, *judicium cum multa lectione*, but the selections that he has left to posterity are nevertheless invaluable. He was at least faithful to his purpose, by culling, as he himself expresses it, (ως αν εκ λογικων λειμωνων) the appropriate extracts from ancient writers.

In making this selection, we have only to regret that he did not give us more of the distinguished writers of those ages, and thus supplied, in some measure, the loss of their works. In the testimony thus preserved, however, we have a body of evidence, both to the existing events of the day, and to the truth of those Scriptures which, without the formality of a regular system of proof, carries its conviction to the mind. Whether this testimony appeared in a plain or polished style, whether simple or embellished, the great object of our author is the evidence that it furnishes, and which therefore he gives us, as one who, by the advantages of his situation, whilst Christianity was yet in the freshness of its morning sun, could arrest and seize some of its fleeting images, ere they were erased from the memory of man.

And in order to let these images appear, Eusebius with his testimony must be suffered to speak for himself. His history, independently of its practical utility and its literary store, is unquestionably the most interesting and the most important work that appeared in the first ages of the church. A work adapted to all ages and classes, to furnish materials of reflection to the man of letters, to supply the retired Christian with examples of unreserved devotion and sacrifice to duty, and to furnish all, some original views of primitive times, at the hand of one who may be pronounced a primitive man.

In undertaking the present work, the translator was influenced by a firm persuasion of its utility, and the necessity of a new ver sion. A more general circulation of primitive works, whether by copious extracts, or by entire translations, appears to be one of the best means at least, of giving a primitive tone to modern Christianity. And though we might not conceive ourselves bound to acknowledge every thing as biblical, merely because it was primitive, yet were it possible that we could ascertain the real state of Christianity in every respect as it was then, doubtless it would prove a salutary check upon many of our errors.*

To show that we are not singular on this subject, we here give the sentiments of a foreign journal, which will never be regarded as enthusiastic by those who are at all acquainted with its character. " Independently of the importance of studying the fathers with respect to doctrine and ecclesiastical history, and even with respect to exegesis, the perusal of their writings serves, among other objects, to awaken and excite religious views and ideas in the minds of the young, much more than any course of instruction, however logically exact, and in accordance with the rules of hermeneutics. And we are convinced that the excessive abuse that has been of late made of manuals, journals, magazines, &c., for clergymen, which for the last twenty years, and longer, has been the order of the day in many places, and by which the spirit of young clergymen has been warped and perverted to indolence and carelessness, would not have made such inroads, if, together with the Holy Scriptures, which should unquestionably form the basis of every discourse, the study of the fathers had also been zealously encouraged."†

It was well observed by a modern philosopher, that if every age had had its Aristotle, philosophy would long since have reached its climax ; and we may observe with regard to ecclesi-

---

* The importance of a more general acquaintance with the opinions and doctrines prevalent in the church, before the Council of Nice, is obvious. No attempt, however, has as yet been made to bring them into such general circulation, that all could have and read them, laity as well as clergy. With a view to supply this defect, among others, the translator has projected a publication to appear periodically, embracing copious extracts from the fathers on doctrine, and dissertations in reference to the Archæology of Christianity, with the title *Repertory of Primitive Theology.* See the Prospectus of this publication.

† Hall. Allgem. Lit. Zeitung. No. 10. 1817.

astical history, that if every period in primitive times had had
its Eusebius, we should, besides his own, be in possession of an
amount of ecclesiastical information at this day, that would sub-
serve the most salutary purposes. What our author, however,
has secured from the wrecks of time, only leaves us room to re
gret what we have not. As to the matter, therefore, which
the history of Eusebius embraces, no apology is necessary for
presenting this to the public. It belongs to the archœology of
Christianity; and therefore, to Christians at least must appear in
an interesting light.

As to the manner in which this is presented, various opinions
will doubtless prevail. The critic will form his opinion of Eusebius from the original, and there he will perceive what cannot
always be made to appear in a translation. One thing will strike
him on the first survey, that the style of an ecclesiastical writer,
three centuries after the birth of Christ, is far different from the
style that prevailed three centuries before, and that the Greek
authors, in the age of Constantine, are not the authors of the age
of Alexander. Our Eusebius is not without his beauties, but
they are so rarely scattered, that we can hardly allow him an
eminent rank, as a writer, although his subject may be offered
as his apology. His use of words is sometimes without sufficient
precision, which subjects him occasionally to ambiguity, and his
sentences are sometimes so involved as to require the hand of
critical dissection. His periods, too, are sometimes of enormous
length, and by their copious fulness incline much to the pleonastic
and hyperbolical. We are not here to expect the uniform suavity
of an Herodotus, the terse brevity of a Thucydides, though we
may occasionally meet with features that would not be overlooked as elegant even in these fathers of history. From the
great variety of authors that he quotes, our author indeed, could
not aim at the same kind of excellence, neither are his quota-
tions from others like those of Plutarch, Diodorus Siculus, and
others, for the mere purpose of embellishment or illustration, but
for positive information; and, therefore, they assume all the sim
plicity of a plain reference to authority. In a work so unosten-
tatious, it would be absurd to measure our author by a standard

he never adopted, as a production, which like those of the fathers of history, should contend for the prize as a literary performance. The only part of the work that could perhaps aspire to this honour, is contained in the last book, where he is altogether the panegyrist, and where he has left us, perhaps, what may be regarded as one of his most elaborate, if not one of his happiest performances as an orator.

Whether the present translator has succeeded in presenting his author to the public in a costume that shall appear worthy of the original, must be left to the judgment of others. He is not so confident, as to presume his labour is here immaculate, and a more frequent revision of the work may suggest improvements which have thus far escaped him. Some allowances are also due to a work like this, which may not obtain in those of a different description. The translator does not stand upon the same ground as one who renders a work of elegance and taste, from profane antiquity. The latter leaves more scope for the display of genius and taste. The great object of the former is to give a faithful transcript of his author's statement, that the reader may derive, if possible, the same impression that he would from the original, in case it were his vernacular language. He is not at liberty to improve his author, whatever may be the occasional suggestions of elegance or taste, for there is scarcely any such improvement but what involves the fidelity of the version. The more experienced reader and critic may, perhaps, discover instances where the translator might perhaps have been more easy, without sacrificing much of the meaning; and the present version is not without passages where perhaps a little liberty might have obviated an apparent stiffness in the style. But the translator has some times preferred the latter, to what appeared a sacrifice of the sense.*

The office of a translator, like that of a lexicographer, is an ungrateful office. Men who have no conception of the requisites for such a task, who measure it by the same rough standard

---

* Among some of the apparent anomalies of the translation, may perhaps be numbered many of the passages from Scripture. It will be recollected these are translated from our author, who quotes the Alexandrian version.

that they do a piece of manual labour, are apt to suppose he has nothing to do but to travel on from word to word, and that it amounts at last to scarcely more than a transcription of what is already written in his own mind. In the estimate which is thus made, there is little credit given, for the necessary adaptation of the style and phraseology to that of the original. No allowance for that degree of judgment, which the interpreter must constantly exercise in order to make his version tell what its original says. And yet, with all this, there is generally discrimination enough to mark what may be happily expressed; but by a singular perversion, such merit is sure to be assigned to the original work, whilst the defects are generally charged to the account of the translator. Some, ignorant of the limits of the translator's office, even expect him to give perfection to his author's deficiencies, and if he fails in this, he is in danger of having them heaped upon himself.

To preclude any unwarrantable expectations, the translator does not pretend to more in the present work, than to give a faithful transcript of the sense of his author. Occasionally, he thinks he has expressed that sense with more perspicuity than his original, and wherever the ambiguity seemed to justify it, it has been done, not with a view to improve his author, but to prevent mistaking his meaning.

The present version is from the accurate Greek text published by Valesius,* a learned civilian of the Gallican church. The most noted Latin versions besides that of Valesius, are those of Rufinus, Musculus, Christophorson, and Grinæus. Curterius also published a translation, but it is rather a revision of Christophorson.

Stroth among the Germans,† and Cousin among the French appear to be the latest that have given versions in the modern languages. The first translation in English was made by Hanmer, 1584, which passed through five editions. A translation by T. Shorting was published more than a century afterwards, and

* The best edition of Valesius is that published at Cambridge by Reading—the edition used in the present work.

† There is also an abridged translation in German, in Rœsler's Bibliothek der Kirchenvæter

this last, with the exception of an abridgment by Parker, is the best translation hitherto extant in the English language.

The present translator originally contemplated merely a revision or improvement of the last English version, but a slight examination will satisfy any one, that such labour would be equivalent to that of an original translation itself, whilst it could at best present little better than a mutilated aspect. The present, therefore, is a version entirely new. It has been finished in the midst of other vocations, and the author expected to have brought it to a state of readiness, for the press, before or about the beginning of the past winter. At the commencement of the work he anticipated a period of leisure, which would have enabled him to meet this expectation fully. But this period of expected leisure was absorbed by care and solicitude, amid sickness in his family, whilst his own health was but little calculated for the necessary effort.

It was one of the translator's original intentions to make the work more useful by the addition of many notes. Eusebius admits of a constant commentary, and there are some parts of the work, which besides mere illustration, require a separate discussion. Valesius has interspersed notes, which are more extensive than the whole work. They are mostly verbal criticisms, and refer to the various readings of the Greek text, and as such have but little interest for the general reader. Whoever wishes to consult these, will find the most of them translated in Shorting's Eusebius. The few notes that are scattered through the following pages, are by the present translator. He was diverted from his original plan of commenting on his author, partly by an apprehension of swelling the work; chiefly however, by a conviction that the time under existing circumstances would be better employed in a more diligent revision, and lastly, because he contemplates a prosecution of the author's historical works, in which abundant room and materials will be furnished for this purpose. In the mean time, the work is committed to the hands of the public, and in the quaint but expressive words of the oldest English translator of Eusebius: "If aught be well done, give the praise to God, let the pains be the translator's, and the profit the reader's."—*Hanmer.*

CONTENTS.

xxxiii

THE
ECCLESIASTICAL HISTORY
OF
EUSEBIUS PAMPHILUS.

BOOK I.

CHAPTER I.

Subject of the present work.

As it is my purpose to record the successions of the holy apos
tles, together with the times since our Saviour, down to the present, to recount how many and important transactions are said to
have occurred in ecclesiastical history, what individuals in the
most noted places eminently governed and presided over the
church, what men also in their respective generations, whether
with or without their writings, proclaimed the divine word; to
describe the character, times and number of those who, stimulated by the desire of innovation, and advancing to the greatest
errors, announced themselves leaders in the propagation of false
opinions, like grievous wolves, unmercifully assaulting the flock
of Christ ; as it is my intention, also, to describe the calamities
that swiftly overwhelmed the whole Jewish nation, in consequence
of their plots against our Saviour; how often, by what means
and in what times, the word of God has encountered the hostility
of the nations; what eminent persons persevered in contending
for it through those periods of blood and torture, beside the martyrdoms which have been endured in our own times: and after all,
to show the gracious and benign interposition of our Saviour;
these being proposed as the subjects of the present work, I shall
go back to the very origin and the earliest introduction of the
dispensation of our Lord and Saviour the Christ of God.

13

But here, acknowledging that it is beyond my power to present the work perfect and unexceptionable, I freely confess it will crave indulgence, especially since, as the first of those that have entered upon the subject, we are attempting a kind of trackless and unbeaten path. Looking up with prayer to God as our guide, we, trust indeed, that we shall have the power of Christ as our aid, though we are totally unable to find even the bare vestiges of those who may have travelled the way before us; unless, perhaps, what is only presented in the slight intimations, which some in different ways have transmitted to us in certain partial narratives of the times in which they lived; who, raising their voices before us, like torches at a distance, and as looking down from some commanding height, call out and exhort us where we should walk, and whither direct our course with certainty and safety. Whatsoever, therefore, we deem likely to be advantageous to the proposed subject, we shall endeavour to reduce to a compact body by historical narration. For this purpose we have collected the materials that have been scattered by our predecessors, and culled, as from some intellectual meadows, the appropriate extracts from ancient authors. In the execution of this work we shall be happy to rescue from oblivion, the successions, if not of all, at least of the most noted apostles of our Lord, in those churches which even at this day are accounted the most eminent; a labour which has appeared to me necessary in the highest degree, as I have not yet been able to find that any of the ecclesiastical writers have directed their efforts to present any thing complete in this department of writing. But as on the one hand I deem it highly necessary, so also I believe it will appear no less useful, to those who are zealous admirers of historical research. Of these matters, indeed, I have already heretofore furnished an epitome in my chronological tables, but in the present work I have undertaken a more full narrative. As I said above, I shall begin my treatise with that dispensation, and that doctrine of the divinity which in sublimity and excellence surpasses all human invention, viz. that of our Saviour Christ. And indeed, whoever would give a detail of ecclesiastical history to posterity, is necessarily obliged to go back to the very origin of the dispensation of Christ, as it is from him, indeed, that we derive our very epithet, a dispensation more divine than many are disposed to think.

CHAPTER II.

Summary view of the pre-existence and Divinity of our Lord and Saviour Jesus Christ.

As the mode of existence in Christ is twofold, the one resembling the head of the body, indicating his divinity; the other compared to the feet, by which he, for the sake of our salvation, assumed that nature which is subject to the same infirmities with ourselves; hence our account of the subsequent matter may be rendered complete and perfect, by commencing with the princi pal and most important points in his history. By this method, at the same time, the antiquity and the divine dignity of the Christian name will be exhibited to those who suppose it a recent and foreign production, that sprung into existence but yesterday, and was never before known.

No language, then, is sufficient to express the origin, the dignity, even the substance and nature of Christ. Whence even the divine Spirit in the prophecies says, " who will declare his generation?" For as no one hath known the Father, but the Son, so no one on the other hand, can know the Son fully, but the Father alone, by whom he was begotten. For who but the Father hath thoroughly understood that Light which existed before the world was—that intellectual and substantial wisdom, and that living Word which in the beginning was with the Father, before ill creation and any production visible or invisible, the first and only offspring of God, the prince and leader of the spiritual and immortal host of heaven, the angel of the mighty council, the agent to execute the Father's secret will, the maker of all things with the Father, the second cause of the universe next to the Father, the true and only Son of the Father, and the Lord and God and King of all created things, who has received power, and

dominion with divinity itself, and power and honour from the
Father. All this is evident from those more abstruse passages in
reference to his divinity, "In the beginning was the word, and
the word was with God, and the word was God." "All things
were made by him, and without him nothing was made." This,
too, we are taught by the great Moses, that most ancient of all
the prophets, when under the influence of the divine Spirit, he describes the creation and arrangement of all things, he also informs
us that the Creator and maker of the universe yielded to Christ,
and to none but to his divine and first begotten word, the formation of all subordinate things, and communed with him respecting the creation of man. "For," says he, "God said let us make
man according to our image and according to our likeness." This
expression is confirmed by another of the prophets, who, discoursing
of God in his hymns, declares, "He spake, and they were made; he
commanded, and they were created." Where he introduces the
Father and maker as the Ruler of all, commanding with his sovereign nod, but the divine word as next to him, the very same that is
proclaimed to us, as ministering to his Father's commands. Him
too, all that are said to have excelled in righteousness and piety,
since the creation of man; Moses, that eminent servant of God,
and Abraham before him, the children of the latter, and as many
righteous prophets as subsequently appeared, contemplated with
the pure eyes of the mind, and both recognized and gave him the
worship that was his due as the Son of God. The Son himself,
however, by no means indifferent to the worship of the Father, is
appointed to teach the knowledge of the Father to all. The
Lord God, therefore, appeared as a common man to Abraham,
whilst sitting at the oak of Mamre. And he, immediately falling down, although he plainly saw a man with his eyes, nevertheless worshipped him as God, and entreated him as Lord. He
confesses, too, that he is not ignorant who he is in the words, "Lord,
the judge of all the earth, wilt not thou judge righteously?" For
as it were wholly unreasonable to suppose the uncreated and unchangeable substance of the Almighty God to be changed into
the form of a man, or to deceive the eyes of beholders with the
phantom of any created substance, so also it is unreasonable to

suppose that the Scriptures have falsely invented such things as these. " God and the Lord who is judge of the whole earth, and executeth judgment" appearing in the shape of man, who else can he be called, if it be not lawful to call him the author of the universe, than his only pre-existing word? Concerning whom also in the Psalms it is said, " He sent his word and healed them, and delivered them from their corruptions." Of Him, Moses obviously speaks as the second after the Father, when he says, " The Lord rained upon Sodom and Gomorrah brimstone and fire from the Lord." Him also again appearing to Jacob in the form of man, the sacred Scriptures call by the name of God, saying to Jacob, " Thy name shall no longer be called Jacob, but Israel shall be thy name, because thou hast prevailed with God." Whence also Jacob called the name of that place the vision of God, saying, " I have seen God face to face, and my soul has lived." To suppose these divine appearances the forms of subordinate angels and servants of God, is inadmissible ; since, as often as any of these appeared to men, the Scriptures do not conceal the fact in the name, expressly saying that they were called not God nor Lord, but angels, as would be easy to prove by a thousand references. Joshua also, the successor of Moses, calls him as the ruler of celestial angels and archangels, of supernal powers, and as the power and wisdom of God, intrusted with the second rank of sovereignty and rule over all, " the captain of the Lord's host," although he saw him only in the form and shape of man. For thus it is written : "And it came to pass when Joshua was by Jericho, that he lifted up his eyes, and looked, and behold there stood a man over against him, with his sword drawn in his hand, and Joshua went unto him, and said unto him, Art thou for us, or for our adversaries. And he said, Nay but as captain of the Lord's host am I now come. And Joshua fell on his face to the earth, and said unto him, What saith my Lord unto his servant? And the captain of the Lord's host, said unto Joshua, Loose thy shoe from off thy foot : for the place whereon thou standest is holy." Josh. v.

Here then you will perceive from the words themselves, that this is no other than the one that also communicated with Moses

Since the Scriptures in the same words, and in reference to the same one says, " When the Lord saw that he drew near to see. the Lord called to him from the midst of the bush, saying, Moses, Moses. And he answered, Here am I. But he said, Draw not nearer, loose thy shoes from off thy feet, for the place on which thou standest is holy ground. And he said to him, I am the God of thy fathers, the God of Abraham, the God of Isaac, and the God of Jacob."

That there is also a certain antemundane, living, and self-existing substance, ministering to the Father and God of all unto the formation of all created objects, called the word and the wisdom of God, besides the proofs already advanced, we may also learn from the very words of wisdom, speaking of herself in the clearest manner, through Solomon, and thus initiating us into her mysteries. Prov. viii. " I wisdom make my habitation with prudence and knowledge, and have called to understanding. By me kings reign and princes define justice. By me the great are magnified, and rulers subdue the earth." To which he subjoins the following: " The Lord created me in the beginning of his ways, for his works; before the world he established me, before the formation of the earth, before the waters came from their fountains, before the foundation of the mountains, before all hills, he brought me forth. When he prepared the heavens, I was present with him, and when he established the fountains under the heavens, I was with him, adjusting them. I was his delight; daily I exulted before him at all times, when he rejoiced that he had completed the world." That the divine word, therefore, pre-existed and appeared, if not to all, at least to some, has been thus briefly shown.

The reason, however, why this was not also proclaimed before in ancient times, to all men and all nations, as it is now, will appear from the following considerations. The life of men, in ancient times, was not in a situation to receive the doctrine of Christ, in the all-comprehensive fulness of its wisdom and its virtue. For immediately in the beginning, after that happy state, the first man, neglecting the Divine commands, fell into the present mortal and afflicted condition, and exchanged his former divine enjoyment for the present earth, subject to the curse. The descendants of this one, having filled our earth, and proved themselves much worse, excepting one here and another there, commenced a certain brutal and disorderly mode of life. They had neither city nor state, no arts or sciences, even in contemplation. Laws and justice, virtue and philosophy they knew not, even in name. They wandered lawless through the desert, like savage and fierce animals, destroying the intellectual faculty of man, and exterminating the very seeds of reason and culture of the human mind, by the excesses of determined wickedness, and by a total surrender of themselves to every species of iniquity.

Hence, at one time they corrupted each other by criminal intercourse; at another, they murdered; and at others, fed upon human flesh. Hence too, their audacity, in venturing to wage war with the Deity himself; and hence those battles of the giants, celebrated by all. Hence too, their attempts to wall up the earth against heaven, and by the madness of a perverted mind, to prepare an attack upon the supreme God himself. Upon these men, leading a life of such wickedness, the Omniscient God sent down inundations and conflagrations, as upon a forest scattered over the earth. He cut them down with successive famines and pestilence, with constant wars and thunderbolts, as if to suppress the dreadful and obdurate disease of the soul, with his more severe punishments. Then it was, when the excess of malignity had nearly overwhelmed all the world, like a deep fit of drunkenness overshadowing and beclouding the minds of men—then it was, that the first begotten wisdom of God, existing before all creatures, and the self-same pre-existing word, induced by his exceeding love of man, appeared at times to his servants, in visions of angels; at others, in his own person. As the salutary power of God, he was seen by one and the other of the pious in ancient times, in the shape of man, because it was impossible to appear in any other way. And as by these pious men, the seeds of godliness had been already scattered among the mass of mankind, and the whole nation that claimed its origin from those ancient Hebrews, continued

devoted to the worship of God—to these, therefore, as to a multi
tude still affected by former corrupt practices, he imparted,
through Moses, images and signs of a certain mystical Sabbath and
circumcision, and instructions in other spiritual principles, but did
not yet grant the privilege of an immediate initiation. But when
their law obtained celebrity, and like a fragrant odour was spread
abroad among all men; and by means of this law, the dispositions
of men, even among most of the gentiles, were improved by legis-
lators and philosophers every where, who softened their wild and
savage ferocity, so as to enjoy settled peace, friendship, and mutual intercourse; then it was, when men at length throughout the
whole world, and in all nations had been, as it were, previously prepared and fitted for the reception of the knowledge of the Father,
that he himself again appeared, the master of virtue, the minister
of the Father in all goodness; the divine and celestial word of God.
He appeared in a human body, in substance not differing from our
own nature, at the commencement of the Roman empire; performed and suffered such things as were to follow, according to
prophecy, viz. that man and God, the author of miraculous works,
would dwell in the world, and would be exhibited to all the nations as the teacher of that piety which the Father will approve.
In these prophecies, also, were foretold the extraordinary fact of
his birth, his new doctrine, and his wonderful works; as also the
manner of his death, his resurrection from the dead, and finally
his divine return to the heavens. The prophet Daniel, under the
influence of the divine Spirit, foreseeing his kingdom in the end,
was inspired thus to write and describe his vision, in adaptation to
human capacity, in the following language: "I beheld," said he,
"until the thrones were placed; and the Ancient of Days sat, and
his garment was white as snow, and the hair of his head was as
pure wool; his throne was a flame of fire, his wheels burning fire;
a river of fire rolled before him; thousand thousands ministered
unto him, and ten thousand thousands stood near him. He appointed judgment, and the books were opened." " And next, I beheld," says he, " and lo! one coming with the clouds as the Son of
Man, and he advanced as far as the Ancient of Days, and he was
brought into his presence. And to him was given the dominion,

and the glory, and the kingdom, and all people, tribes, tongues shall serve him. His power is an everlasting power, which shall not pass away; and his kingdom shall not be destroyed." These passages can evidently be referred to no one but to our Saviour, that God word* which was in the beginning with God; called the Son of God, by reason of his final appearance in the flesh. But having collected the prophetic declarations concerning our Saviour Jesus Christ, in distinct commentaries† on this subject, and having elsewhere digested whatever is revealed concerning him, in a more demonstrable form, what has been said upon the subject here may suffice for the present.

CHAPTER III.

The name Jesus, as also that of Christ, was both known and honoured from ancient times, by the inspired prophets.

It is now the proper place to show that the very name of Jesus, as also that of Christ, was honoured by the pious prophets of old. And first, Moses himself, having intimated how exceedingly august and illustrious the name of Christ is, delivering types and mystical images, according to the oracle which declared to him, "See that thou make all things according to the pattern which was shown thee on the mount,"—the same man whom, as far as it was lawful, he had called the high priest of God, the self-same he calls Christ.‡ And in this way, to the dignity of the priesthood, which surpasses with him, all superiority among men, as additional honour and glory, he attaches the name of Christ. Hence he evidently understood that Christ was a Being divine. The same Moses, under the divine Spirit, foreseeing also the epithet Jesus, likewise dignifies this with a certain distinguished privilege. For

---

* *God word.* The literal expression is retained here.

† *Commentaries.* Eusebius here refers to two other works of his, written before this history, his Preparation and Demonstration.

‡ *Christ.* Christ and Messiah, the same epithets in different languages, signify anointed, or the anointed one.

this name, which had never been uttered among men, before Moses, he applies first to him alone who, by a type and sign, he knew would be his successor after his death, in the government of the nation. His successor, therefore, who had not assumed the appellation Jesus,* (Joshua,) before this period, being called by his other name *Oshea*, which his parents had given, was called by Moses Jesus, (Jehoshua, Joshua.) Num. xiii. 17. This name, as an honourable distinction, far superior to any royal diadem, was conferred on Joshua, because Joshua the son of Nun bore a resemblance to our Saviour, as the only one after Moses, and the completion of that symbolical worship given through him, that should succeed him in a government of pure and undefiled religion. Thus Moses attaches the name of our Saviour Jesus Christ, as the greatest honour to two men, who, according to him, excelled all the rest in virtue and glory; the one to the high priest, the other to him that should have the government after him. But the prophets that lived subsequently to these times, also plainly announced Christ before by name; whilst at the same time they foretel the machinations of the Jews against him, and the calling of the Gentiles through him. Jeremiah bears testimony, speaking thus: "The breath† (the spirit,) before our face, Christ the Lord, was taken away in their destructions; of whom we said, under his shadow will we live among the nations." Lam. iv. 20. David also, fixed in astonishment, speaks of him as follows: "Why do the heathen rage, and the people imagine vain things? The kings of the earth stood up, and the rulers were gathered together against the Lord and against his Christ." To which he afterwards adds, in the person of Christ himself: "The Lord said to me, thou art my Son, this day have I begotten thee; ask of me, and I will give thee the *nations* for thine inheritance, and the uttermost parts of the earth for thy possession." Ps. ii.

* *Jesus.* By some corruption of the name of Joshua, Eusebius calls him Auses. Jesus is the Greek form, for the more Hebrew Joshua. The Septuagint invariably use the former, and in one instance it is retained in our English version. Heb. iv. 8.

† This passage from Jeremiah is rendered as the above from the Septuagint, as quoted by Eusebius. In our English version, the force of the allusion is not perceptible, and one might look in vain for the passage as rendered here; but the Hebrew fully admits the Greek version here given.

Nor was the name of Christ among the Hebrews, given solely as an honour to those that were dignified with the priesthood, in consequence of their being anointed with oil prepared for the purpose, as a sacred symbol; the same was done also to the kings, whom the prophets, after anointing them under a divine impulse, constituted certain typical Christs, as they themselves also were, the shadows of the royal and princely sovereignty of the only and true Christ, of that divine word which holds sovereignty over all. Moreover, we are also told respecting the prophets, that some were typical Christs, by reason of their unction; so that all these have a reference to the true Christ, the divine and heavenly word, the only high priest of all men, the only king of all creation, and the Father's only supreme Prophet of the prophets. The proof of this is evident, from the fact that none of those anciently anointed, whether priests, kings, or prophets, obtained such power with divine excellence as our Saviour and Lord Jesus, the only and true Christ, has exhibited. For these, although illustrious among their countrymen in dignity and honour, and for a long series of generations, never called their subjects after themselves by a similar epithet, Christians, and neither was there ever divine honour paid to any of these from their subjects; nor even after their death, was there ever so strong a disposition in any, as to be prepared to die for the honoured individual. And never was there so great a commotion among the nations of the earth, respecting any one then existing, since the mere force of the type could not act with such efficacy among them, as the exhibition of the reality by our Saviour. Though He received no badges and emblems of priesthood from any; though he did not even derive his earthly origin from a sacerdotal race, nor was raised to empire under the escort of guards; nor installed a prophet, like those of old; nor obtained a peculiar, or even any dignity among the Jews, yet notwithstanding all this, he was adorned by the Father with all these, not merely typical honours, but with the reality itself. Although He did not obtain then the same honours with those mentioned above, yet he is called Christ by a far superior claim; and as he is the only and the true Christ of God, he has filled the whole world with a name really august and sacred, the name of Christians. To those who are admitted among these, he no longer imparts mere types and similitudes, but undisguised virtues, and a heavenly life, in the doctrines of truth. He received an unction, not formed of material substances, but that which comports with Deity, the divine Spirit itself, by a participation of the uncreated divinity of the Father. This is shown by Isaiah, who seems to exclaim in the very person of Christ: "The spirit of the Lord is upon me, wherefore he hath anointed me, (he hath sent me) to proclaim glad tidings to the poor, to heal the broken hearted, to proclaim liberty to the captives, and the recovery of sight to the blind." And not only Isaiah but David also, addressing him, says, "Thy throne, O God, is from everlasting to everlasting. A sceptre of righteousness is the sceptre of thy kingdom. Thou hast loved righteousness and hated iniquity. Therefore hath God, thy God, anointed thee with the oil of gladness above thy fellows." In which words, he calls him God in the first verse; and in the second he ascribes to him the royal sceptre, and thus proceeding after the divine and royal power, in the third place, he represents him as Christ, anointed not by the oil of material substances, but by the divine oil of gladness. By this also, he shows his excellence and great superiority over those who, in former ages, had been anointed as typical images with the material substance. The same speaks of him in another place, thus: "The Lord said unto my Lord, sit thou at my right hand, until I make thine enemies thy footstool;" and a little after, "From the womb before the morning star did I beget thee; the Lord hath sworn and he will not repent, thou art a priest for ever after the order of Melchisedech." This Melchisedek is mentioned in the holy Scriptures, as a priest of the Most High God, not consecrated by any unction prepared of any material substance, and not even succeeding to the priesthood of the Jews, by any descent of lineage. Hence, Christ our Saviour is denominated, with the addition of an oath, Christ and priest after his own order, but not according to the order of those who *received* merely the badges and emblems. Hence, also, neither does history represent him anointed corporeally among the Jews, nor even as sprung from a tribe of the priesthood, but as coming into existence from God himself

before the morning star; that is, before the constitution of the
world, obtaining an immortal priesthood, subject to no infirmity
of age, to all endless ages. But the great and convincing evidence of that incorporeal and divine power in him, is the fact
that he alone, of all that have ever existed to the present day,
even now is known by the title of Christ, among all men over the
world; and with this title he is acknowledged and professed by
all, and celebrated both among Barbarians and Greeks. Even to
this day, he is honoured by his votaries throughout the world, as
a king; he is admired as more than a prophet, and glorified as the
only true high priest of God. In addition to all these, as the pre-
existing word of God, coming into existence before all ages, and
who has received the honours of worship, he is also adored as God;
but what is most remarkable, is the fact, that we who are consecrated to him, honour him not only with the voice and sound of
words, but with all the affections of the mind; so that we prefer giving a testimony to him, even to the preservation of our own lives.

CHAPTER IV.

*The religion announced by Christ among all nations, was neithe1
unexpected nor strange.*

THESE matters have thus been necessarily premised before our
history, that no one may suppose our Lord and Saviour Jesus
Christ was merely a new comer, on account of the date at which
he appeared among men, in the flesh. And now, that no one
may suppose his doctrine is new or strange, as if springing from
one of recent origin, and in no respect differing from the rest of
men, let us also briefly examine this point.

It is evident, that but a short time after the appearance of our
Saviour Jesus Christ had been made known to all men, a new
nation suddenly came into existence; a nation confessedly neither
small nor weak, nor situated in a remote corner of the earth, but
the most populous and the most religious of all, and so much the
more indestructible and invincible, as it has always had the power

of God as its support. This nation, appearing at the time appointed by inscrutable wisdom, is that which among all, is honoured with the name of Christ. One of the prophets, foreseeing with the eye of the spirit of God, that this people would arise, was so struck with amazement that he exclaimed: " Who hath heard such things as this? and who hath ever declared thus? hath the earth brought forth in a single day, and hath a nation been born at once?" The same prophet also gives some intimation of the name that would be introduced: " They who serve me shall be called by a new name, which shall be blessed upon the earth." And indeed, though we are evidently a new people, this new name also of Christians has lately become known to all nations. The practice, however, and the walk and conversation, the principles of piety prevalent among this people, have not been recently invented, but were established, we may say, by the Deity in the natural dictates of pious men of old, from the very origin of our race ; an assertion which we shall endeavour to prove, in the following manner.

That the nation of the Hebrews is not new, but honoured among all for its antiquity, is well known. The writings and literature of this nation concern ancient men, rare and few in number, but yet excelling in piety, righteousness, and every virtue. And indeed, even before the flood, there were some who were distinguished for their virtue; and after this others, both of the sons and posterity of Noah, among whom we would mention Abraham, celebrated by the Hebrews as the founder and progenitor of their nation. Should any one, beginning from Abraham, and going back to the first man, pronounce those who have had the testimony of righteousness, Christians in fact, though not in name, he would not be far from the truth. For as the name Christians is intended to indicate this very idea, that a man, by the knowledge and doctrine of Christ, is distinguished by modesty and justice, by patience and a virtuous fortitude, and by a profession of piety towards the one and only true and supreme God; all this was no less studiously cultivated by them than by us. They did not, therefore, regard circumcision, nor observe the Sabbath, neither do we; neither do we abstain from certain foods, nor regard other injunctions, which

Moses subsequently delivered to be observed in types and symbols, because such things as these do not belong to Christians. But
they obviously knew the Christ of God, as he appeared to Abraham, communed with Isaac, spoke to Jacob; and that he communed with Moses and the prophets after him, has already been
shown.

Hence you will find, also, these pious persons honoured with
the name of Christ, as in the following expression: " Touch not
my anointed ones (my Christs,) and do my prophets no harm."
Whence we should plainly suppose, that the first and most ancient religion known, that of those pious men that were connected with Abraham, is the very religion lately announced to all in
the doctrines of Christ. Abraham is said to have received the
command of circumcision, and yet long before this, was proved to
have received the testimony of righteousness through faith.
" Abraham," the Scriptures say, " believed, and it was imputed
unto him for righteousness." And, indeed, the divine communication was given to him from God, who appeared to him when
he bore this character before circumcision. And this was
Christ himself, the word of God announcing that all who should
come in future times should be justified in a similar way ; saying,
" and in thee shall be blessed all the nations of the earth." And
again, " when he shall become a great and mighty nation, in him
all the nations of the earth shall be blessed." We may obviously
understand this by its fulfilment in us ; for he indeed was justified
by his faith in Christ, the word of God that appeared to him ; and
having renounced the superstition of his fathers and the former
errors of his life, confessed the one supreme God, and served him
by deeds of virtue, and not by the service subsequently enjoined
in the law of Moses.

To him, then, being such, it was declared that all the tribes
and all the nations of the earth should be blessed in him. But
the course of piety which was pursued by Abraham, has appeared
thus far cultivated only by Christians, and that too by works
more efficacious than words. What, then, should prevent us
henceforth from acknowledging that there is one and the same
principle of life and conduct, the same course of piety common

.o us, who have come after Christ, with those pious men who lived in times long before? Whence it is evident that the reli‑ gion delivered to us in the doctrine of Christ is not a new nor a strange doctrine; but if the truth must be spoken, it is the first and only true religion. Thus much may suffice on this point.

CHAPTER V.

The times of our Saviour's manifestation among men.

AFTER the necessary preliminary to the Ecclesiastical History which we have proposed to write, it now remains that we com‑ mence our course, invoking God, the Father of the word, and Jesus Christ himself, our revealed Saviour and Lord, the heavenly word of God, as our aid and fellow-labourer in the narration of the truth. It was the forty-second year of the reign of Augustus, but the twenty-eighth from the subjugation of Egypt and the death of Antony and Cleopatra, which terminated the dynasty of the Ptolemies, when, according to prophetic prediction, our Lord and Saviour Jesus Christ was born in Bethlehem of Judea; the same year, when the first census was taken, and Quirinius* was governor of Syria.—This census is mentioned by Flavius Jo‑ sephus, the distinguished historian among the Hebrews, who also adds another account respecting the sect of the Galileans, which arose about the same time, of which also mention is made by our Luke in his book of Acts, in the following words—" After this man arose Judas of Galilee, in the days of the taxing (assessment), and drew away much people after him, he also preached; and all, even as many as obeyed him were dispersed." Acts v. 37. The aforesaid author agreeing with this statement in the 18th

* Quirinius.—This Quirinius is the same Cyrenius mentioned by St. Luke. The former is the original Roman name, the latter the Latin mode of transferring the name from the Greek. Had it been recollected that the Greek name was not the original, this proper name would not have been returned to its own language, in a form so disguised.

nook of his Antiquities, adds the following : " But Quirinius, who belonged to the senate, and having enjoying other offices, advanced through all the grades of office to the consulship, a man also of great dignity in other respects, by the appointment of Cesar, came to Syria, with a small force, and with judicial power over the people, to take a valuation of their property." A little after he says : " But Judas, the Gaulonite, sprung from the town called Gamala, together with Sadducus, a Pharisee, headed a revolt of the people, saying that the assessment had nothing else in view but manifest slavery ; and they exhorted the people to assert their liberty." He also writes in the second book of the history of the Jewish War, concerning the same man : " About this time a certain Judas of Galilee, stimulated the inhabitants to revolt, urging it as a reproach, that they endured paying tribute, and that they who had God for their master, suffered mortals to usurp the sovereignty over them." Thus far Josephus.

CHAPTER VI.

About the time of our Lord, agreeably to prophecy, those rulers ceased that had formerly governed the nation of the Jews by regular succession, and Herod was the first foreigner that reigned over them.

At the time that Herod was king, who was the first foreigner that reigned over the Jewish people, the prophecy recorded by Moses received its fulfilment, viz. " That a prince should not fail of Judah, nor a ruler from his loins, until he should come for whom it is reserved."* The same, he also shows, would be the expectation of the nations. The prediction was evidently not accomplished, as long as they were at liberty to have their own native rulers, which continued from the time of Moses down to the reign of Augustus. Under him, Herod was the first foreigner that obtained the government of the Jews. Since, as Josephus has writ-

* This celebrated passage we here give after the Septuagint, which Eusebius invariably quotes.

ten, he was an Idumean by the father's side, and an Arabian by the mother's. But, as Africanus, who is also no common writer, says, "They who have written more accurately respecting him, say that he was the son of Antipater, and that the latter was the son of a certain Herod of Ascalon, one of those called the ministers of the temple of Apollo, in that city. This Antipater, when a boy, having been taken prisoner by some Idumean robbers, lived with them, because his father being a poor man, was unable to pay his ransom. Thus growing up in their practices, he was afterwards befriended by Hyrcanus the high priest of the Jews. His son was that Herod that flourished in the times of our Saviour. The government of the Jews, therefore, having devolved on such a man, the expectation of the nations was now at hand, according to prophecy; because with him terminated the regular succession of governors and princes, from the time of Moses. For before their captivity and their transfer to Babylon, they were first governed by Saul and David as their kings; and before the kings, the government was administered by magistrates called judges, who came after Moses and his successor Joshua. After the return from the captivity of Babylon, they continued to retain the aristocratical form of government, together with an oligarchy. The high priests had then the direction of affairs, until Pompey, the proconsular general of the Romans, took Jerusalem by force of arms, and defiled the sacred places, entering the sanctuary of the temple. Aristobulus, who had been both king and high priest by regular succession until then, was sent with his children in chains to Rome, and the priesthood was given to his brother Hyrcanus, whilst the whole nation of the Jews was made tributary to the Romans from that time.

But Hyrcanus, who was the last of the high priests by succession, having been soon after taken prisoner by the Parthians, Herod, as I said before, had the government of the Jews conferred upon him by the senate of Rome and the emperor Augustus. About this time, the advent of Christ being nigh at hand, the expected salvation of the nations received its fulfilment, and was followed by the calling of the Gentiles, according to prophetic declarations. From this time also, the princes and rulers of Judah,

i. e. of the Jewish nation, ceasing, by a natural consequence, the priesthood, which had descended from a series of ancestors in the closest succession of kindred, was immediately thrown into confu- sion. Of this, you have the evidence of Josephus; who shows that when Herod was appointed king by the Romans, he no longer no- minated the chief priests from the ancient lineage, but conferred the honour upon certain obscure individuals. A course similar to that of Herod, in the appointment of the high priest, was pur- sued by Archelaus, his son; and next by the Romans, who, after him, took the government of the Jews into their own hands. The same Josephus shows that Herod was the first that locked up the sacred vesture of the high priest, and having se- cured it under his own private seal, no longer permitted the high priests to have it at their disposal. The same thing was done by Archelaus his successor, as also by the Romans. It may suffice then, to have said thus much, in proof of another prophecy, which has terminated in the appearance of our Saviour Jesus Christ. Most clearly indeed does the book of Daniel, expressly embracing a number of certain weeks, until the government of Christ, con- cerning which we have treated in another work, predict that after the termination of these, the sacred unction amongst the Jews should be totally abolished. And this is evidently proved to have been fulfilled at the time of our Saviour's birth. Let this be suffi- cient, however, as a necessary preliminary, to establish the truth in reference to the times.

CHAPTER VII.

On the discrepancy which is supposed to exist in the Gospels, re specting the genealogy of Christ.

As the genealogy of Christ is differently given to us by Mat- thew and Luke, and they are supposed by the generality to disa- gree in their statements; and as every believer, for want of know- ing the truth, has been led to apply some investigation to explain the passages, we may also subjoin the account which has come

down to us. We refer to the history which has been handed
down on these passages by Africanus, in an epistle to Aristides,
respecting the harmony of the genealogy of the gospels. After
having refuted the opinions of others as forced and fictitious, he
sets forth the account that he had ascertained himself, in the following words. " It was customary in Israel to calculate the
names of the generations, either according to nature, or accord
ing to the law; according to nature, by the succession of legitimate
offspring; according to the law, when another raised children to
the name of a brother who had died childless. For as the hope
of a resurrection was not yet clearly given, they imitated the promise which was to take place by a kind of mortal resurrection,
with a view to perpetuate the name of the person who had died.
Since then, there are some of those who are inserted in this gene-
alogical table, that succeed each other in the natural order of
father and son, some again that were born of others, and were ascribed to others by name, both the real and reputed fathers have
been recorded. Thus, neither of the gospels has made a false
statement, whether calculating in the order of nature, or according to law. For the families descended from Solomon, and those
from Nathan, were so intermingled, by substitutions in the place
of those who had died childless, by second marriages and the raising up of seed, that the same persons are justly considered, as in
one respect, belonging to the one of these, and in another respect
belonging to others. Hence it is, that both of these accounts being
true, viz. of those who were reputed fathers, and those who really
were fathers, they come down to Joseph with considerable intri-
cacy, it is true, but with great accuracy. That this, however,
may be made evident, I will state the series of generations. If
(in the genealogy of Matthew,) you reckon the generations from
David through Solomon, Matthan, who begat Jacob the father of
Joseph, is found to be the third from the end. But if, with Luke,
you reckon from Nathan the son of David, in like manner, Melchi,
whose son was Eli, the father of Joseph, will be found to be the
third. As Joseph, then, is our proposed object, we are to show
how it happened that each is recorded as his father; both Jacob
as deduced from Solomon, and Eli from Nathan; also, how it hap-

pened that these two, Jacob and Eli, were brothers; and moreover, how the fathers of these, Matthan and Melchi, being of different families, are proved to be the grandfathers of Joseph. Matthan and Melchi, having married in succession the same woman, had children, who were brothers by the same mother, as the law did not prohibit a widow, whether she became such by divorce, or by the death of her husband, to marry again. Matthan, therefore, who traces his lineage from Solomon, first had Jacob, by Estha, for this is her name as handed down by tradition. Matthan dying, and Melchi, who traces his descent from Nathan, though he was of the same tribe, but of another family, having as before said, married her, had a son Eli. Thus, then, we shall find the two of different families, Jacob and Eli, brothers by the same mother. Of these, the one Jacob, on the death of his brother, marrying his widow, became the father of a third, viz. Joseph; his son both by nature and calculation. Wherefore, it is written, Jacob begat Joseph. But according to the law, he was the son of Eli, for Jacob being his brother, raised up seed to him. Wherefore, the genealogy traced also through him, will not be rendered void, which, according to Matthew, is given thus—" but Jacob begat Joseph." But Luke, on the other hand, says, "who was the son, as was supposed, (for this he also adds,) the son of Joseph. the son of Eli, the son of Melchi." For it was not possible to express the legal genealogy more distinctly, so that he entirely omits the expression, " *he begat*," in a generation like this, until the end : having traced it back as far as Adam, " who was the son of God," he resolves the whole series by referring back to God. Neither is this incapable of proof, nor is it an idle conjecture. For the relatives of our Lord, according to the flesh, whether to display their own illustrious origin, or simply to show the fact, but at any rate adhering strictly to the truth, have also handed down the following accounts : That robbers of Idumea, attacking Ascalon. a city of Palestine, led Antipater away captive together with other booty, from the temple of Apollo, which was built close to the walls. He was the son of one Herod, a minister of the temple. The priest, however, not being able to pay the ransom for his son. Antipater was trained up in the practices of the Idumeans, and afterwards in great favour with Hyrcanus the high priest of Judea. He was subsequently sent by Hyrcanus on an embassy to Pompey, and having restored the kingdom to him, which had been invaded by Aristobulus, the brother of the latter, Antipater himself had the good fortune to be nominated the procurator of Palestine. Antipater, however, having been treacherously slain. by those who envied his good fortune, was succeeded by his son Herod. He was afterwards, by a decree of the senate, appointed king of the Jews, under Antony and Augustus. His sons were Herod and the other tetrarchs. These accounts of the Jews also coincide with those of the Greeks. But, as the genealogies of the Hebrews had been regularly kept in the archives until then, and also of those who referred back as far as the ancient proselytes; as for instance, to Achior the Ammonite, and Ruth the Moabitess, and to those that were intermixed with the Israelites at their departure from Egypt; and as the lineage of the Israelites contributed nothing to Herod's advantage, he was goaded by the consciousness of his ignoble extraction, and committed all these records of their families to the flames. Thinking that himself might appear of noble origin, by the fact that no one else would be able to trace his pedigree by the public records, back to patriarchs or proselytes, and to those strangers that were called georæ.* A few however of the careful, either remembering the names, or having it in their power in some other way, by means of copies, to have private records of their own, gloried in the idea of preserving the memory of their noble extraction. Of these were the above-mentioned persons, called desposyni,† on account of their affinity to the family of our Saviour. These coming from Nazara and Cochaba, villages of Judea, to the other parts of the world, explain-

---

* The word γιωραις, used here by Eusebius, is taken from the Septuagint, Exod. xii. 19. It is evidently a corruption of the Hebrew word גר, a stranger, and is interpreted by Theodoret, in loc. γιωραν τον προσηλυτην προσηγορευσε, he called the proselyte γιωρας, stranger.

† The word *desposynos* signifies, in general, one who belongs to a master; it is here applied according to the usage of the primitive church, to indicate the relatives of our Lord, as those who were the Lord's according to the flesh. Suidas explains the word ταις του δεσποτου ιστι.

ed the aforesaid genea..gy from the book of daily records, as faithfully as possible. Whether, then, the matter be thus or otherwise, as far as I and every impartial judge would say, no one certainly could discover a more obvious interpretation. And this, then, may suffice on the subject; for, although it be not supported by testimony, we have nothing to advance, either better or more consistent with truth. The gospel, altogether, states the truth." At the close of the same epistle, this writer, (Africanus,) adds the following: " Matthan, whose descent is traced to Solomon, begat Jacob, Matthan dying, Melchi, whose lineage is from Nathan, by marrying the widow of the former, had Eli. Hence, Eli and Jacob were brothers by the same mother. Eli dying childless, Jacob raised up seed to him, having Joseph, according to nature belonging to himself, but by the law to Eli. Thus, Joseph was the son of both." So far Africanus; and the lineage of Joseph thus being traced, Mary, also, at the same time, as far as can be, is evinced to be of the same tribe, since, by the Mosaic law, intermarriages among different tribes were not permitted. For the injunction is, to marry one of the same kindred, and the same family, so that the inheritance may not be transferred from tribe to tribe. And this may suffice, also, on the present point.

CHAPTER VIII.

Herod's cruelty against the infants, and his wretched end.

CHRIST, then, having been born, according to the prophecies, in Bethlehem of Judea, about the times that had been revealed, Herod was not a little alarmed at the intelligence. Having ascertained, on the inquiry of the eastern Magi, where the king of the Jews should be born, as they had seen his star, and this had been the cause of so long a journey to them, glowing with zeal to worship the infant as God; he was under great apprehensions, as supposing his own kingdom to be in danger. Having, therefore, inquired of the doctors of the law in the nation, where they expected Christ should be born, and ascertained the prophecy of

Micah, announcing that it would be in Bethlehem, in a single edict he orders the male infants from two years and below to be slain, both in Bethlehem and all its parts, according to the time that he had accurately ascertained from the Magi; thinking at all events, as seemed very probable, that he would carry off Jesus also, in the same destruction with those of his own age. The child, however, anticipated the snare, being carried into Egypt by his parents, who had been informed by the appearance of an angel of what was about to happen. These same facts are also stated in the sacred text of the gospel.

It is also worth while to observe the reward which Herod received for his criminal audacity against Christ and the infants; how, without the least delay, the Divine justice immediately overtook him; and even before his death, exhibited the prelude to those punishments that awaited him after death. It is not possible for me here, to relate in what ways he tarnished what was supposed to be the felicity of his reign, by the successive calamities of his family, the slaughter of his wife and children, and the rest of his kindred, allied to him by the closest and most tender relations. The whole subject of these particulars, which casts all the representations of tragedy into the shade, has been handled to its full extent in the histories written by Josephus. But to understand in what manner also, the chastisement of Heaven scourged him onwards to the period of death, it may not be less proper to hear the words of the same author, describing the end of his life, in the seventeenth book of his Antiquities, as follows: " But the disease of Herod became daily more virulent, God inflicting punishment for his crimes. For it was a slow fire, not only exhibiting to those who touched him a heat in proportion to the internal wasting of his body, but there was also an excessive desire and craving after food, whilst no one dared to refuse. This was attended with swellings of the intestines, and especially excessive pains of the colon. A moist and transparent humour also covered his feet. Similar also was the disease about the ventricle, so that the corruption causing worms in the lower part of the abdomen, there was an increased violence of breathing, which, of itself was very offensive; both on account of the disagreeable effluvia, and the rapidity of the respiration. He was also so convulsed in every part of his body, that it added an almost insuperable strength. It was said, therefore, by those who are conversant with divine things, and to whose wisdom it appertained to declare such things, that God inflicted this punishment upon the king on account of his great impiety."

These are the particulars which are stated by the aforesaid writer, in the book mentioned; and in the second book of his history, he gives very much the same account concerning him, in the following words: " Then the disease pervading his whole body, distracted it by various torments. For the fever became more intense, the itching of the whole surface was insupportable, and the pains of the lower abdomen were incessant. On his feet were swellings, as of one labouring with the dropsy. There was also an inflammation of the ventricle, and a putrefaction that generated worms. Beside this, a more violent breathing, and difficult respiration, and convulsions of all the limbs; so that they who referred to a divine agency, said that this disease was a punishment. But, though struggling with so many sufferings, he nevertheless clung to life, and did not relinquish the hope of deliverance, but was ever devising new remedies. Crossing the Jordan, therefore, he used the warm baths near Callirhoe. These flow into the lake Asphaltites, (Dead sea,) but by reason of their sweetness, they are also potable. As the physicians here deemed it necessary to use some soothing application, his whole body was bathed in tepid oil, in a bathing tub filled with oil for that purpose, when he was so overcome that his eyes began to break, and turn up like one dead. His servants then being alarmed and raising an outcry, he indeed returned to himself at the noise; but after that, despairing of recovery, he ordered about fifty drachms to be distributed to the soldiers, and considerable sums to be given to his generals and friends. Returning, he came to Jericho; where, being seized with despair, and now only threatening death himself, he proceeded to a crowning act of most nefarious character. He collected the distinguished men of every village from the whole of Judea, and commanded them to be shut up in what was called the Hippodrome. He then sent for Salome, his sister, and her husband Alexander. I know," said he, " that the Jews will rejoice at my death; but I may be lamented by means of others, and have splendid funeral rites, if you are willing to perform my commands. As soon as I have expired, surround these men that are now under guard with soldiers, as soon as possible, and slay them, that all Judea and every house, though against their will, may be compelled to weep at my death." And soon after, he adds, " again, he was so tortured, partly by the want of food and by a convulsive cough, that, overpowered by his pains, he contemplated anticipating his fate. Having taken an apple, he also demanded a knife, for he was accustomed to cut and eat it. Then, looking around, lest there should be any one to hinder him, he raised his right arm as if to strike himself." The same author, in addition to these, says, " that he slew another of his own sons before his death, being the third that had already been slain by his orders, and that immediately after this, he breathed out his life, not without excessive torture."

Such, then, was the end of Herod, who thus suffered the just punishment for the crimes that he committed in the murder of the children of Bethlehem, when he designed the destruction of our Saviour. After this, an angel appearing in a dream to Joseph, who was then in Egypt, directed him to return with the child and his mother, revealing to him that they were dead who had sought the life of the infant. To this account the Evangelist adds: " But he hearing that Archelaus reigned in Judea, in the place of Herod, his father, was afraid to go thither, and being warned in a dream, he retired into the parts of Galilee."

CHAPTER IX.

Of the times of Pilate.

THE same historian also agrees with the statements respecting the government of Archelaus after Herod's death; and relates in what manner he succeeded to the kingdom of the Jews, by the will of Herod, his father, and the confirmation of it by Cesar Augustus; as also, that he having lost his kingdom after ten years, his brothers Philip and Herod, the younger, together with Lysanias, had the government of their tetrarchies. The same author, in the eighteenth book of his Antiquities, says, "that about the twelfth year of the reign of Tiberius, (for he succeeded to the empire after Augustus, who had reigned fifty-seven years,) Pontius Pilate was appointed over Judea, and remained there upon the whole ten years, almost to the death of Tiberius. Hence the fraud of those persons is plainly proved, who lately, and at other times have given currency to certain spurious acts against our Saviour. In which the very time of the date proves the falsehood of the inventors. For in the fourth consulship of Tiberius, which was in the seventh year of his reign, those things are said to have occurred, which they have dared to say respecting his salutary suffering. At which time, indeed, it is plain, that Pilate was not yet appointed over Judea, if Josephus is to be credited, who plainly says, in the work already cited, that Pilate was appointed procurator of Judea, by Tiberius, in the twelfth year of his reign.

CHAPTER X.

The high priests of the Jews, under whom Christ promulgated his doctrines.

It was about the fifteenth year of the reign of Tiberius, according to the Evangelist, in the fourth year, that Pilate was procurator of Judea, when Herod, Lysanias, and Philip, as tetrarchs, held the government of the rest of Judea, when our Lord and Saviour Jesus Christ was in his thirtieth year, that he came to the baptism of John, and then made the beginning of promulgating his gospel. The holy Scriptures, moreover, relate that he passed the whole time of his public ministry under the high priests Annas and Caiaphas; intimating, that during the years of their priesthood, the whole time of his ministry was termi nated. For, beginning with the pontificate of Annas, and continuing after that of Caiaphas, the whole of this interval does not even give us four years. The rites, indeed, of the law, having been already abolished since that period, with it were also annulled the privileges of the priesthood, viz. of continuing it for life, and of hereditary descent. Under the Roman governors, however, different persons at different times were appointed as high priests, who did not continue in office more than a year. Josephus, indeed, relates that there were four high priests in succession from Annas to Caiaphas. Thus, in his book of Antiquities, he writes in the following manner: " Valerius Gratus, having put a period to the priesthood of Annas, promoted Ishmael, the son of Baphi, to the office; and, removing him also, not long after, he appointed Eleazar, the son of Annas, who had been high priest, to the office. After the lapse of a year, removing also him, he transfers the priesthood to Simon, the son of Camithus. But he, also, did not continue to hold the honour longer than a year, when he was succeeded by Josephus, surnamed Caiaphas." Hence the whole time of our Saviour's ministry is proved not to embrace four entire years; there being four high priests for four years, from Annas to the appointment of Caiaphas, each of which held the office a year respectively. Caiaphas, indeed, is justly shown, by the gospel narrative, to have been high priest in that year in which our Saviour's sufferings were finished. With which present observation, the time of Christ's ministry is also proved to agree. Our Lord and Saviour Jesus Christ, not very long after the commencement of his public ministry, elected the twelve, whom he called Apostles, by way of eminence over the rest of his disciples. He also appointed seventy others beside these, whom he sent, two and two, before him into every place and city whither he himself was about to go.

CHAPTER XI.

The testimonies respecting John the Baptist and Christ.

As it was not long before this that John the Baptist was be-headed by Herod the younger, the holy Scriptures record the fact, which is also confirmed by Josephus, who has expressly made mention of Herodias by name, and the circumstance of her being married to Herod, though she was the wife of his brother; Herod having first divorced his former lawful wife. She was a daughter of Aretas, king of Arabia Petræa. But having forced Herodias from her husband yet living, and on whose account also he slew John, he was involved in a war with Aretas for the disgrace inflicted on his daughter; in which war he relates that, when coming to battle, the army of Herod was completely destroyed; and that he suffered all this, on account of the crime that he committed against John. But the same Josephus, in this account, in which he confesses that John was a most righteous man, also bears testimony to what is recorded of him in the narratives of the gospels. He relates, also, that Herod lost his kingdom on account of the same Herodias, and that he was driven into exile with her, and condemned to dwell at Vienna, a city of Gaul. These facts are stated by him in the eighteenth book of his Antiquities, where in the same paragraphs, he also writes thus concerning John: " To some of the Jews, the army of Herod seemed to have been destroyed by God; who thus, with signal justice, avenged John, called the Baptist. For Herod slew him, a good man, and one who exhorted the Jews to the practice of virtue, and with the pursuit of righteousness and piety towards God, to receive baptism. For this baptism appeared to have been imparted to him for this object, not with the view to avoid a few trifling sins, but for the purification of the body, as far as the mind had been first purified by righteousness.

" And when many others flocked to him, for they were also much delighted with listening to his discourses, Herod, dreading the great confidence of men in him, lest, perhaps, he might stimulate them to a revolt, (for they seemed disposed to do any thing at his suggestion,) considered it much better, before any change should be attempted by him, to anticipate by destroying him; than after a revolution, when involved in difficulties, to repent when it was too late. In consequence of Herod's suspicions, therefore, he was sent in bonds to the aforesaid prison of Machærus, and there slain." After relating these things concerning John, Josephus in the same work, also makes mention of our Saviour in the following manner: "About the same time, there was a certain Jesus, a wise man, if indeed it is proper to call him a man. For he was a performer of extraordinary deeds; a teacher of men, that received his doctrine with delight; and he attached to himself many of the Jews, many also of the Greeks. This was Christ. Pilate having inflicted the punishment of the cross upon him, on the accusation of our principal men, those who had been attached to him before did not, however, afterwards cease to love him: for he appeared to them alive again on the third day, according to the holy prophets, who had declared these and innumerable other wonderful things respecting him. The race of the Christians, who derive their name from him, likewise still continues." When such testimony as this is transmitted to us by an historian who sprung from the Hebrews themselves, both respecting John the Baptist and our Saviour, what subterfuge can be left, to prevent those from being convicted destitute of all shame, who have forged the acts against them? This however, may suffice on this subject.

CHAPTER XII.

Of the disciples of our Lord.

THE names of our Saviour's apostles are sufficiently obvious to every one, from his gospels; but of the seventy disciples, no cata logue is given any where. Barnabas, indeed, is said to have been one of them, of whom there is distinguished notice in the Acts of the Apostles; and also in St. Paul's epistle to the Galatians. Sosthenes, who sent letters with Paul to the Corinthians, is said to have been one of these. Clement, in the fifth of his Hypoty-

poses or Institutions, in which he also mentions Cephas, of whom
Paul also says, that he came to Antioch, and "that he withstood
him to his face;"—says, that one who had the same name with
Peter the apostle, was one of the seventy; and that Matthias, who
was numbered with the apostles in place of Judas, and he who
had been honoured to be a candidate with him, is also said to have
been deemed worthy of the same calling with the seventy. They
also say that Thaddeus was one of them; concerning whom, I shall
presently relate a narrative that has come down to us. Moreover, if any one observe with attention, he will find more disciples
of our Saviour than the seventy, on the testimony of Paul, who says,
that "he appeared after his resurrection, first to Cephas, then to
the twelve, and after these to five hundred brethren at once." Of
whom, he says, "some are fallen asleep," but the greater part were
living at the time he wrote. Afterwards, he says, he appeared to
James; he, however, was not merely one of these disciples of our
Saviour, but he was one of his brethren. Lastly, when beside these,
there still was a considerable number who were apostles in imitation
of the twelve, such as Paul himself was, he adds, saying "afterwards he appeared to all the apostles."

This account may suffice respecting these apostles; but the
history of Thaddeus, already mentioned by us, was as follows.

CHAPTER XIII.

Narrative respecting the prince of Edessa.

THE divinity of our Lord and Saviour Jesus Christ, being famed
abroad among all men, in consequence of his wonder-working
power, attracted immense numbers, both from abroad and from
the remotest parts of Judea, with the hope of being cured of
their diseases and various afflictions. Agbarus, therefore, who
reigned over the nations beyond the Euphrates with great glory,
and who had been wasted away with a disease, both dreadful
and incurable by human means when he heard the name of Jesus frequently mentioned, and his miracles unanimously attested

by all, sent a suppliant message to him, by a letter-carrier, entreating a deliverance from his disease.   But, though he did not
yield to his call at that time, he nevertheless condescended to
write him a private letter, and to send one of his disciples to heal
his disorder; at the same time, promising salvation to him and all
his relatives.   And it was not long, indeed, before the promise
was fulfilled.   After the resurrection, however, and his return to
the heavens, Thomas, one of the twelve apostles, by a divine im
pulse, sent Thaddeus, who was also one of the seventy disciples
to Edessa, as a herald and evangelist of the doctrines of Christ
And by his agency all the promises of our Saviour were ful
filled.   Of this, also, we have the evidence, in a written an
swer, taken from the public records of the city of Edessa, then
under the government of the king.   For in the public registers
there, which embrace the ancient history and the transactions of
Agbarus, these circumstances respecting him are found still preserved down to the present day.   There is nothing, however,
like hearing the epistles themselves, taken by us from the archives,
and the style of it as it has been literally translated by us, from
the Syriac language ·

COPY OF THE LETTER WRITTEN BY KING AGBARUS, TO JESUS, AND
SENT TO HIM, AT JERUSALEM, BY ANANIAS, THE COURIER.

Agbarus, prince of Edessa, sends greeting to Jesus the excellent Saviour, who has appeared in the borders of Jerusalem.   I
have heard the reports respecting thee and thy cures, as performed
by thee without medicines and without the use of herbs.   For as it
is said, thou causest the blind to see again, the lame to walk, and
thou cleansest the lepers, and thou castest out impure spirits and
demons, and thou healest those that are tormented by long disease,
and thou raisest the dead.   And hearing all these things of thee, I
concluded in my mind one of two things: either that thou art
God, and having descended from heaven, doest these things, or else
doing them, thou art the son of God.   Therefore, now I have written
and besought thee to visit me, and to heal the disease with which
I am afflicted.   I have, also, heard that the Jews murmur against

thee, and are plotting to injure thee; I have, however, a very small but noble state, which is sufficient for us both."

This epistle, he thus wrote, whilst yet somewhat enlightened by the rays of divine truth. It is, also, worth the time to learn the epistle sent to him from Jesus, by the same bearer, which, though very brief, is yet very nervous, written in the following style:

THE ANSWER OF JESUS, TO KING AGBARUS, BY THE COURIER, ANANIAS.

Blessed art thou, O Agbarus, who, without seeing, hast believed in me. For it is written concerning me, that they who have seen me will not believe, that they who have not seen, may believe and live. But in regard to what thou hast written, that I should come to thee, it is necessary that I should fulfil all things here, for which I have been sent. And after this fulfilment, thus to be received again by Him that sent me. And after I have been received up, I will send to thee a certain one of my disciples, that he may heal thy affliction, and give life to thee and to those who are with thee."

To these letters there was, also, subjoined in the Syriac language: "After the ascension of Jesus, Judas, who is also called Thomas, sent him Thaddeus, the apostle, one of the seventy; who, when he came, remained at the house of Tobias, the son of Tobias. When the report was circulated concerning his arrival, and he became publicly known by the miracles which he performed, it was communicated to Agbarus, that an apostle of Jesus had came thither, as he had written. Thaddeus, therefore, began in the power of God to heal every kind of disease and infirmity; so that all were amazed. But when Agbarus heard the great deeds and miracles which he performed, and how he healed men in the name and power of Jesus Christ, he began to suspect that this was the very person concerning whom Jesus had written, saying, after I have been received up again, I will send to thee one of my disciples, who shall heal thy affliction. Having, therefore, sent for Tobias, with whom he staid, I have heard, said he, that a certain powerful man, who hath come from Jerusalem, is staying at thy house, and is performing many cures in the name of Jesus. He answered, Yea, my lord, a certain stranger has come, who hath lodged with me, and is performing many wonders. And he replied, Bring him to me. Tobias, then, returning to Thaddeus, said to him, Agbarus the king having sent for me, has told me to conduct thee to him, that thou mayest heal his disorder. And Thaddeus replied, I will go, since I have been sent with power, to him. Tobias, therefore, arose early the next day, and taking Thaddeus with him, came to Agbarus. When he came, his nobles were present, and stood around. Immediately on his entrance, something extraordinary appeared to Agbarus, in the countenance of the apostle Thaddeus; which Agbarus observing, paid him reverence. But all around were amazed; for they did not perceive the vision which appeared to Agbarus alone: he then asked Agbarus whether he were truly a disciple of Jesus the Son of God, who had said to him, I will send one of my disciples to thee, who will heal thy sickness, and will give life to thee and to all thy connexions? And Thaddeus answered, Since thou hast had great confidence in the Lord Jesus, who hath sent me, therefore, I am sent to thee. And, moreover, if thou believest in him, with increasing faith, the petitions of thy heart shall be granted thee, as thou believest. And Agbarus replied, So much did I believe in him that I had formed the resolution to take forces, in order to destroy those Jews who had crucified him, had I not been deterred from my purpose by a regard for the Roman empire. Thaddeus replied, Our Lord and God, Jesus the Christ, hath fulfilled the will of his Father, and having fulfilled it, was taken up again to his Father. Agbarus saith to him, I have believed both in him and in his Father. Then said Thaddeus, Therefore, I place my hand upon thee in the name of the same Lord Jesus. And this being done, he was immediately healed of the sickness and sufferings with which he was afflicted. And Agbarus was amazed, that just as he had heard respecting Jesus, so in very deed he received it through his disciple and apostle Thaddeus, who had healed him without any medicine and herbs, and not only him, but Abdas also, the son of Abdas, who was afflicted with the podagra. He also, approaching, fell down at his feet, and received his benediction, with the imposition of his hand, and was healed. Many

of the same city were also healed by the same apostle, who performed wonderful and great deeds, and proclaimed the word of
God. After this, said Agbarus, Thaddeus, thou doest these things
by the power of God, and we are filled with wonder. But, beside these things, I request thee, also, to inform me respecting the
coming of Jesus, how he was born, and as to his power, with what
power he performed these things which we have heard. And
Thaddeus answered, Now, indeed, I will not tell thee, since I have
been sent to proclaim the word abroad; but to-morrow assemble
all thy citizens, and before them I will proclaim the word of God,
and will sow among them the word of life, both respecting the
coming of Jesus, as he was, and respecting his mission, and for
what purpose he was sent by the Father; also, concerning the
power of his works, and the mysteries which he declared in the
world; by what power, also, he did these things, concerning his
new mode of preaching, his lowly and abject condition, his humiliation in his external appearance, how he humbled himself, and
died, and lowered his divinity; what things, also, he suffered from
the Jews; how he was crucified, and descended into hell, (hades,)
and burst the bars which had never yet been broken, and rose
again, and also raised with himself the dead that had slept for
ages. And how he descended alone, but ascended with a great
multitude to his Father. And how he sitteth at the right hand
of God and the Father, with glory, in the heavens; and how he
is about to come again with glory and power, to judge the living
and dead.—Agbarus, therefore, commanded his subjects to be
called early in the morning, and to hear the annunciation of
Thaddeus; and after this, he commanded gold and silver to be
given him; but he would not receive it, saying, If we have left
our own, how shall we take what belongs to others? These
things were done in the three hundred and fortieth year. Which
also, we have literally translated from the Syriac language, op-
portunely as we hope, and not without profit.

BOOK II.

PRELIMINARY.

WHATSOEVER particulars it was necessary for us to premise in this Ecclesiastical History, both respecting the divinity of the saving word and the antiquity of the doctrines which we teach, as also of the antiquity of that evangelical life which Christians lead, these particulars we have already discussed, together with the circumstances of his late appearance among men, of his sufferings, of the election of his apostles, and have exhibited the proofs in the condensed subjects of the preceding book. Let us now, also, examine the circumstances that followed his ascension, presenting some from the divine Scriptures, and others from such other documents to which we shall have occasion to refer.

CHAPTER I.

The course pursued by the Apostles after the ascension of Christ.

FIRST then, in the place of Judas the traitor, Matthias was chosen by lot, who, as was shown above, was also one of the disciples of the Lord. There were appointed also, with prayer and the imposition of hands, by the apostles, approved men, unto the office of deacons, for the public service; these were those seven of whom Stephen was one. He was the first, also, after our Lord, who at the time of ordination, as if ordained to this very purpose, was stoned to death by the murderers of the Lord. And thus he first received the crown answering to his name, of the victorious martyrs of Christ. Then also James, called the brother of our Lord, because he is also called the son of Joseph.

48

For Joseph was esteemed the father of Christ, because the Virgin being betrothed to him, "she was found with child by the Holy Ghost before they came together," as the narrative of the holy gospels shews. This James, therefore, whom the ancients, on account of the excellence of his virtue, surnamed the Just, was the first that received the episcopate of the church at Jerusalem. But Clement, in the sixth book of his Institutions, represents it thus: " Peter, and James, and John after the ascension of our Saviour, though they had been preferred by our Lord, did not contend for the honour, but chose James the Just as bishop of Jerusalem." And the same author, in the seventh book of the same work, writes also thus: " The Lord imparted the gift of knowledge to James the Just, to John and Peter after his resurrection, these delivered it to the rest of the apostles, and they to the seventy, of whom Barnabas was one. There were, however, two Jameses; one called the Just, who was thrown from a wing of the temple, and beaten to death with a fuller's club, and another, who was beheaded. Paul also makes mention of the Just in his epistles. " But other of the apostles," says he, " saw I none, save James the brother of our Lord." About this time also, the circumstances of our Saviour's promise, in reference to the king of the Osrhoenians, took place. For Thomas, under a divine impulse, sent Thaddeus as herald and evangelist, to proclaim the doctrine of Christ, as we have shown from the public documents found there.

When he came to these places, he both healed Agbarus by the word of Christ, and astonished all there with the extraordinary miracles he performed. After having sufficiently disposed them by his works, and led them to adore the power of Christ, he made them disciples of the Saviour's doctrine. And even to this day, the whole city of Edessa is devoted to the name of Christ; exhibiting no common evidence of the beneficence of our Saviour likewise to them. And let this suffice, as taken from the accounts given in ancient documents. But let us pass again to the Holy Scriptures. As the first and greatest persecution arose among the Jews after the martyrdom of Stephen, against the church of Jerusalem, and all the disciples except the twelve were scattered throughout Judea and Samaria; some, as the Holy Scriptures say, coming as far as Phœnice, and Cyprus, and Antioch, they were not yet in a situation to venture to impart the faith to the nations, and there-fore only announced it to the Jews. During this time, Paul also was yet laying waste the church, entering the houses of the be-lievers, dragging away men and women, and delivering them over to prison. Philip, also, one of those who had been ordained to the office of deacons, being among those scattered abroad, went down to Samaria. Filled with divine power, he first proclaimed the divine word to the inhabitants of that place. But so greatly did the divine grace co-operate with him, that even Simon Magus, with a great number of other men, were attracted by his dis-courses. But Simon had become so celebrated at that time, and had such influence with those that were deceived by his impos-tures, that they considered him the great power of God. This same Simon, also, astonished at the extraordinary miracles per-formed by Philip through the power of God, artfully assumed, and even pretended faith in Christ, so far as to be baptized; and what is surprising, the same thing is done even to this day, by those who adopt his most foul heresy. These, after the manner of their founder, insinuating themselves into the church, like a pestilential and leprous disease, infected those with the greatest corruption, into whom they were able to infuse their secret, irremediable, and destructive poison. Many of these, indeed, have already been expelled, when they were caught in their wickedness; as Simon himself, when detected by Peter, suffered his deserved punish-ment For as the annunciation of the Saviour's gospel was daily advancing, by a certain divine providence, a prince of the queen of the Ethiopians, as it is a custom that still prevails there to be governed by a female, was brought thither, and was the first of the Gentiles that received of the mysteries of the divine word from Philip. The apostle, led by a vision, thus instructed him and he, becoming the first fruits of believers throughout the world, is said to have been the first, on returning to his country, that proclaimed the knowledge of God and the salutary abode of our Saviour among men. So that, in fact, the prophecy obtained its fulfilment through him : " Ethiopia stretcheth forth her hands unto God." After this, Paul, that chosen vessel, not of men, nor through men, but by the revelation of Jesus Christ himself, and God the Father, who raised him from the dead, is appointed an apostle, being honoured with the call by a vision and voice of revelation from heaven.

CHAPTER II.

How Tiberius was affected, when informed by Pilate respecting Christ.

THE fame of our Lord's remarkable resurrection and ascension being now spread abroad, according to an ancient custom prevalent among the rulers of the nations, to communicate novel occurrences to the emperor, that nothing might escape him, Pontius Pilate transmits to Tiberius an account of the circumstances concerning the resurrection of our Lord from the dead, the report of which had already been spread throughout all Palestine.   In this account, he also intimated that he ascertained other miracles respecting him, and that having now risen from the dead, he was believed to be a God by the great mass of the people.   Tiberius referred the matter to the senate, but it is said they rejected the proposition, in appearance, because they had not examined into this subject first, according to an ancient law among the Romans, that no one should be ranked among the gods unless by a vote and decree of the senate; in reality, however, because the salutary doctrine of the gospel needs no confirmation and co-operation of men.

The senate of the Romans, therefore, having thus rejected the doctrine of our Saviour as it was announced, and Tiberius still continuing to hold the opinion he had before cherished, formed no unreasonable projects against the doctrine of Christ.   This is the testimony of Tertullian, a man who made himself accurately acquainted with the laws of the Romans, and, besides his eminence in other respects, was particularly distinguished among the eminent men of Rome, and in his Apology for the Christians in the Roman tongue, which is also translated into the Greek, to give his own words, writes after the following manner. " In order to give also an account of these laws from their origin, it was an ancient decree, that no one should be consecrated a god by the emperor, before it had been approved by the senate. Marcus Aurelius has done this, in reference to a certain idol, Alburnus, so that this evidence has been given in favour of our doctrine, that divine dignity is conferred among you by the decrees of men. Unless a god pleases men he is not made a god; and thus, according to this procedure, it is necessary that man should be propitious to the god. Tiberius, therefore, under whom the name of Christ was spread throughout the world, when this doctrine was announced to him from Palestine, where it first began, communicated with the senate, being obviously pleased with the doctrine; but the senate, as they had not proposed the measure, rejected it. But he continued in his opinion, threatening death to the accusers of the Christians; a divine providence infusing this into his mind, that the gospel having freer scope in its commencement, might spread every where over the world."

CHAPTER III.

How the Christian doctrine soon spread throughout the whole world.

Thus, then, under a celestial influence and co-operation, the doctrine of the Saviour, like the rays of the sun, quickly irradiated the whole world. Presently, in accordance with divine prophecy, the sound of his inspired evangelists and apostles had gone throughout all the earth, and their words to the ends of the world. Throughout every city and village, like a replenished barn floor, churches were rapidly found abounding, and filled with members from every people. Those who, in consequence of the delusions that had descended to them from their ancestors, had been fettered by the ancient disease of idolatrous superstition, were now liberated, by the power of Christ, through the teaching and miracles of his messengers. And, as if delivered from dreadful masters, and emancipated from the most cruel bondage, on the one hand renounced the whole multitude of gods and de-

mons, and on the other, confessed that there was only one true
God, the Creator of all things. This same God they now also
honoured with the rites of a true piety, under the influence
of that inspired and reasonable worship which had been planted
among men by our Saviour. But the gratuitous benevolence
of God, being now poured out also upon the rest of the nations,
Cornelius was the first of Cesarea in Palestine, who, with his
whole house, received the faith in Christ, through a divine vision
and the agency of Peter; as did also a great number of Greeks
at Antioch, to whom the gospel had been preached by those who
were scattered by the persecution of Stephen.

The church at Antioch, also, now flourishing and abounding in
members, and the greatest number of teachers coming hither
from Jerusalem, with whom were Barnabas and Paul, and many
other brethren with them, the epithet of Christians first sprung
up at that place, as from a grateful and productive soil. Agabus,
also, one of the assembled prophets, uttered a prediction respecting the impending famine, and Paul and Barnabas were delegated
to proceed to the relief of the necessities of the brethren.

CHAPTER IV.

*Caius (Caligula) after the death of Tiberius, appoints Agrippa
king of the Jews, after punishing Herod with perpetual exile.*

TIBERIUS died after having reigned about twenty-two years,
and Caius, receiving the empire next, immediately conferred the
Jewish government on Agrippa, appointing him king over the
tetrarchy both of Philip and Lysanias. To these, not long after,
he adds also the tetrarchy of Herod, after having inflicted the
punishment of perpetual exile upon Herod, together with his
wife Herodias, for their numerous crimes. This was the Herod
who was concerned in the passion of our Saviour. Josephus
bears testimony to these facts. During the reign of this emperor,
Philo became noted, a man most distinguished for his learning,
not only among very many of our own, but of those that came

from abroad. As to his origin, he was a descendant of the He
brews, inferior to none at Alexandria in point of dignity of family
and birth. As to the divine Scriptures, and the institutions of his
country, how greatly and extensively he laboured, his work
speaks for itself. And how well skilled in philosophy and the
liberal studies of foreign countries, there is no necessity to say,
since, as he was a zealous follower of the sect of Plato and Pythagoras, he is said to have surpassed all of his contemporaries.

CHAPTER V.

Philo was sent on an embassy to Caius, in behalf of the Jews.

THIS author has given us an account of the sufferings of the Jews
in the reign of Caius, in five books. He there also relates the
madness of Caius, who called himself a god, and was guilty of
innumerable oppressions in the exercise of his power. He mentions the miseries of the Jews under him, and the embassy which
he himself performed when sent to the city of Rome, in behalf
of his countrymen at Alexandria; how that when he pleaded before Caius, for the laws and institutions of his ancestors, he received nothing but laughter and derision in return, and had well
nigh incurred the risk of his life. Josephus also mentions these
things in the eighteenth book of his Antiquities, in these words :

" A sedition having also arisen between the Jews dwelling at
Alexandria and the Greeks, three chosen deputies are sent from
each of the factions, and these appeared before Caius. One of
the Alexandrian deputies was Apion, who uttered many slanders
against the Jews; among other things, saying, that they treated
the honours of Cesar with contempt, that whilst all others, as
many as were subject to the Roman empire, erected altars and
temples to Caius, and in other respects regarded him as a god,
they alone considered it disgraceful to raise statues to his honour,
and to swear by his name. Apion having thus uttered many and
severe charges by which he hoped that Caius would be roused, as
was very probable, Philo, the chief of the Jewish embassy, a man

illustrious in every respect, being the brother of Alexander, the Alabarch,* and not unskilled in philosophy, was well prepared to enter upon a defence against these charges. But he was precluded from this by Caius, who ordered him straightway to be gone, and as he was very much incensed, it was very evident that he was meditating some great evil against them. Philo departed, covered with insult, and told the Jews that were with him, they had good reason to console themselves, that although Caius was enraged at them, he was already in fact challenging God against himself." Thus far Josephus. And Philo himself, in the embassy which he describes, details the particulars of what was then done to him, with great accuracy. Passing by the greatest part of these, I shall only state those by which it will be made manifest to the reader, that these things happened to the Jews forthwith, and at no distant period, on account of those things which they dared to perpetrate against Christ. First, then, he relates, that in the reign of Tiberius, at Rome, Sejanus, who was then in great favour with Tiberius, had made every effort to destroy the whole nation of the Jews from the foundation, and that in Judea Pontius Pilate, under whom the crimes were committed against our Saviour, having attempted something contrary to what was lawful among the Jews respecting the temple at Jerusalem, which was then yet standing, excited them to the greatest tumults.

CHAPTER VI.

What evils overwhelmed the Jews, after their presumption against Christ.

AFTER the death of Tiberius, Caius having received the government, besides many other innumerable acts of tyranny against many, did not a little afflict the whole nation of the Jews particularly. We may soon learn this, from the declaration of the same

* *Alabarch.*] The Alabarch was the chief magistrate among the Jews at **Alexandria.**

author, in which he writes as follows : " So great was the caprice
of Caius in his conduct towards all, but especially towards the nation of the Jews. As he was excessively hostile to these, he appropriated their places of worship to himself in all the cities, beginning with those at Alexandria, filling them with his images and
statues. For having permitted it when others erected them of
their own accord, he now began to erect them by absolute command. But the temple in the holy city, which had been left untouched as yet, and been endowed with privileges as an inviolable
asylum, he changed and transformed into a temple of his own,
that it should be publicly called the temple of Caius the younger,
the visible Jupiter. (επιφανους Διος.) Many other and almost indescribable calamities, the same author relates, as happening to the
Jews of Alexandria, during the reign of the aforesaid emperor, in
his second book, to which he gave the title, ' On the Virtues.' Josephus also agrees with him, who likewise intimates that the calamities of the whole nation took their rise from the times of Pilate, and the crimes against our Saviour. Let us hear then, wh t
he also says in the second book of the Jewish War. " Pilate
being sent by Tiberias as procurator of Judea, at night carried
the covered images of Cæsar into the temple ; these are called
statues. The following day, this excited the greatest disturbance
among the Jews. For they that were near, were confounded at
the sight, as a contemptuous prostitution of their legal institutions ;
for they do not allow any image to be set up in their city." Comparing these accounts with the writings of the evangelists, you
will perceive, that it was not long before that *exclamation* came
upon them, which they uttered under the same Pilate, and by
which they cried again and again that they had no other king
but Cæsar. After this, the same historian records, that forthwith
another calamity overtook them, in these words : " But after these
things, he (i. e. Pilate,) excited another tumult, by expending the
public treasure which is called Corban, in the construction of an
aqueduct. This extended nearly three hundred stadia, (furlongs,
i. e. from the city.) The multitude were sorely grieved at it ; and
when Pilate came to Jerusalem, surrounding the tribunal, they
began to cry out against him. But having anticipated thei

tumult, he planted his armed soldiers against the multitude, and previously intermixed them, concealed under the same common dress with the people. He had also forbidden them to use their swords, but ordered them to strike the noisy with clubs. The signal he gave from the tribunal. The Jews being thus beaten, many of them perished in consequence of the blows, many also being trodden to death by their own countrymen in the flight. The multitude thus overawed by the misfortune of those slain, held their peace." The same writer mentions innumerable other commotions that were raised beside these, in Jerusalem itself; showing that from that time tumults, and wars, and plots of mischief, one after another, never ceased in the city and all Judea, until, last of all, the siege of Vespasian overwhelmed them. Thus, then, the divine justice overtook the Jews in this way, for their crimes against Christ.

CHAPTER VII.

How Pilate destroyed himself.

It is proper also, to observe, how it is asserted that this same Pilate, who was governor at our Saviour's crucifixion, in the reign of Caius, whose times we are recording, fell into such calamities that he was forced to become his own murderer, and the avenger of his own wickedness. Divine justice, it seems, did not long protract his punishment. This is stated by those Greek historians, who have recorded the Olympiads in order, together with the transactions of the times.

CHAPTER VIII.

The famine that happened in the reign of Claudius.

Caius, however, had not reigned four years, when he was succeeded by Claudius, in the sovereignty of the empire. In his reign there was a famine that prevailed over the whole world; an event, indeed, which has been handed down by historians very far from our doctrine; and by which the prediction of the prophet Agabus, recorded in the Acts of the Apostles, respecting the impending famine over the whole world, received its fulfilment. Luke, however, in the Acts, after stating the famine in the time of Claudius, and after recording how by means of Paul and Barnabas, the brethren at Antioch had sent to those of Judea, according to the ability of each one, also adds the following.

CHAPTER IX.

The martyrdom of the Apostle James.

" About this time, (it is manifest he means the reign of Claudius,) Herod the king prepared to afflict some of the church. But he slew James, the brother of John with the sword." Of this James, Clement adds a narrative worthy of note, in the seventh book of his Institutions, evidently recording it according to the tradition which he had received from his ancestors. He says, that the man who led him to the judgment seat, seeing him bearing his testimony to the faith, and moved by the fact, confessed himself a Christian. Both therefore, says he, were led away to die. On their way, he entreated James to be forgiven of him, and James considering a little, replied, " Peace be to thee," and kissed him ; and then both were beheaded at the same time. Then also, as the Scriptures say, Herod, at the death of James, seeing that the deed gave pleasure to the Jews, also attacks Peter, and having committed him to prison, had well nigh executed the same murderous intention against him, had he not been wonderfully delivered from his prison by an angel appearing to him at night, and thus liberated to proclaim the gospel. Such was the providence of God in behalf of Peter.

CHAPTER X.

Herod Agrippa persecuting the Apostles, immediately experienced the divine judgment.

THE consequences, however, of the king's attempts against the apostles, were not long deferred, but the avenging minister of divine justice soon overtook him after his plots against the apostles. As it is also recorded in the book of Acts, he proceeded to Cesarea, and there on a noted festival, being clad in a splendid and royal dress, he harangued the people from an elevation before the tribunal. The whole people applauding him for his harangue, as if it were the voice of a god, and not of man, the Scriptures relate, " that the angel of the Lord immediately smote him, and being consumed by worms, he gave up the ghost." It is wonderful to observe, likewise, in this singular event, the coincidence of the history given by Josephus, with that of the sacred Scriptures. In this he plainly adds his testimony to the truth, in the nineteenth book of his Antiquities, where he relates the miracles in the following words: " But he (i. e. Herod) had completed the third year of his reign over all Judea, and he came to the city of Cesarea, which was formerly called the tower of Strato. There he exhibited public shows in honour of Cesar, knowing it to be a kind of festival for his safety. At this festival was collected a great number of those who were the first in power and dignity throughout the province. On the second day of the shows, being clad in a robe all wrought with silver, of a wonderful texture, he proceeded to the theatre at the break of day. There, the silver irradiated with the reflection of the earliest sunbeams, wonderfully glittered, reflecting a terrific and awful brilliancy upon the beholders. Presently the flatterers raised their shouts in different ways ; such, however, as were not for his good, calling him a god, and imploring his clemency in such language as this: " We have feared thee thus far as a man, but henceforth we confess thee to be superior to the nature of mortals." The king did not either chide them, or disclaim the impious flattery. After a little while, raising him self, he saw an angel sitting above his head. This he immediately perceived was the cause of evils, as it had once been the cause of his successes. And he felt a pain through his heart, and a sud den pang seize his bowels, which began to torment him with great violence. Turning, then, to his friends, he said, " I, your god, am now commanded to depart this life, and fate will soon disprove your false assertions respecting me. He whom you have called an immortal, is now compelled to die, but we must receive our destiny as it is determined by God. Neither have we passed our life ingloriously, but in that splendour which is so much extolled." Saying this, he laboured much with the increase of pain. He was then carried with great haste into the palace, while the report spread throughout the people, that the king at all events would soon die. But the multitude with their wives and chil dren, after their country's custom, sitting in sackcloth, implored God in behalf of the king; all places were filled with lamentation and weeping. But the king, as he lay reclining in an elevated chamber, and looking down upon them falling prostrate to the ground, could not refrain from tears himself. At length, overpowered by the pain of his bowels, for four days in succession, he ended his life, in the fifty-fourth year of his age and seventh of his reign. He reigned, therefore, four years under Caius Cesar, had the tetrarchy of Philip three years, and received that of Herod in the fourth year, reigning subsequently three years under Claudius Cesar." Thus far Josephus: in which statement, as in others, so in this, I cannot but admire his agreement with the divine Scriptures. But if he should appear to any to differ, in regard to the epithet of the king; yet the time and the fact show that it was the same individual, whether it happened by an error in writing that the name was changed, or in consequence of a double name applied to him· such as was the case with many.

CHAPTER XI.

Concerning the impostor Theudas and his followers.

As Luke in the Acts, also introduces Gamaliel in the consultation respecting the apostles, saying, that at this time "arose
Theudas, who gave out that he was some one, but who was destroyed, and all that obeyed him were dispersed," let us now,
also. add the written testimony of Josephus respecting the same
circumstance. He relates, in the book already quoted, the following particulars. "While Fadus was procurator of Judea, a
certain impostor called Theudas persuaded the multitude to take
their possessions with them and follow him to the river Jordan.
For he said he was a prophet, and that the Jordan should be divided at his command, and afford them an easy passage through
it. And with such promises he deceived many. But Fadus did
not suffer them to enjoy their folly, but sent a troop of horsemen
against them, who, falling upon them unexpectedly, slew many
and took many alive; but having taken Theudas himself captive,
they cut off his head and carried it to Jerusalem." Besides this, he
also mentions the famine that took place under Claudius, as follows.

CHAPTER XII.

Helen, queen of the Osrhoenians.

About this time it happened that the great famine took place
in Judea, in which also queen Helen having purchased grain from
Egypt, with large sums, distributed to the needy. You will also
find this statement in accordance with that in the Acts of the
Apostles, where it is said, that according to the ability of the disciples at Antioch, they determined, each one, to send to the assistance of those in Judea. Which also they did, sending to the
elders by the hands of Barnabas and Paul. Of this same Helen,

mentioned by the historian, splendid monuments are still to be
seen in the suburbs of the city (Jerusalem) now called Ælia.
But she is said to have been queen of the Adiabeni.

CHAPTER XIII.

Simon Magus

THE faith of our Lord and Saviour Jesus Christ, having now
been diffused abroad among all men, the enemy of salvation devising some scheme of seizing upon the imperial city for himself,
brought thither Simon, whom we mentioned before. Coming to
the aid of his insidious artifices, he attached many of the inhabitants of Rome to himself, in order to deceive them. This is attested by Justin, who was one of our distinguished writers, not long
after the times of the apostles, concerning whom I shall say what
is necessary in the proper place. The reader may see for himself, in the first defence of our religion, addressed to Antonine,
where he writes thus: "And after the ascension of our Lord into
heaven, certain men were suborned by demons as their agents,
who said that they were gods. These were not only suffered to
pass without persecution, but were even deemed worthy of honours by you. Simon, a certain Samaritan of the village called
Githon, was one of the number, who, in the reign of Claudius Cesar, performed many magic rites by the operation of demons, was
considered a god, in your imperial city of Rome, and was honoured
by you with a statue as a god, in the river Tiber, (on an island,)
between the two bridges, having the superscription in Latin, *Si-
moni Deo Sancto*, which is, To Simon the Holy God; and nearly
all the Samaritans, a few also of other nations, worship him, con
fessing him as the Supreme God. A certain Helen also, is of this
class, who had before been a public prostitute in Tyre of Pheni-
cia, and at that time attached herself to Simon, and was called
the first idea that proceeded from him." Such is the testimony
of Justin, with which also Irenæus coincides in his first book
against Heresies, where he also subjoins an account of the impiety

and corrupt doctrine of the man, which it would be superfluous
for us to detail, as it is in the power of those who wish to learn
the origin, and the lives, and the false doctrines, not only of this
one, but likewise of all the heresiarchs respectively, as also of the
institutions and principles of all of them, treated at large in the
abovementioned book of Irenæus. Simon, however, we have understood to have taken the lead in all heresy; from whom also, down
to the present time, those that followed his heresy, still affected
the modest philosophy of the Christians, so celebrated for purity
of life among all. From this, however, they appeared again to
depart, and again to embrace the superstitions of idols, falling
down before the pictures and statues of this selfsame Simon, and
the aforesaid Helen with him; venturing to offer them worship by
incense, and sacrifices, and libations. Those matters which are
kept more secret by them than these, at the first mention of which
they say one would be astonished, and to use an oracular phrase
with them, would be confounded, they happen in truth to be so
full of amazement, and folly, and madness, such as they are, that
it is not only impossible to commit them to writing, but even to
utter them with the lips to modest men, on account of their excessive baseness and obscenity. For every vile corruption that
could either be done or devised, is practised by this most abominable heresy, of a sect that ensnare those wretched females who
are literally overwhelmed with every kind of vice.

CHAPTER XIV.

The preaching of Peter in the city of Rome.

SUCH was the wickedness of which that malignant power, the
enemy of all good, and the waylayer of human salvation, constituted Simon the father and author at this time, as if with a view
to make him a great and powerful antagonist to the divine purposes of our Saviour and his apostles. Nevertheless, that divine
and celestial grace which co-operates with its servants, by their
appearance and presence, soon extinguished the flame that had

been kindled by the wicked one, humbling and casting down through them, "every height that elevated itself against the knowledge of God." Wherefore, neither the conspiracy of Simon, nor that of any other one then existing, was able to effect anything against those apostolic times. For the declaration of the truth prevailed and overpowered all, and the divine word itself, now shining from heaven upon men, and flourishing upon earth, and dwelling with his apostles, prevailed and overpowered every opposition. Immediately the aforesaid impostor being smitten as to his mental eye, by a divine and supernatural brilliancy, as when, on a former occasion in Judea, he was convicted of his wickedness by the apostle Peter, he undertook a great journey from the east across the sea, and fled to the west, thinking that this was the only way for him to live according to his mind. Entering the city of Rome, by the co-operation of that malignant spirit which had fixed its seat there, his attempts were soon so far successful, as to be honoured as a god, with the erection of a statue by the inhabitants of that city. This, however, did not continue long; for immediately under the reign of Claudius, by the benign and gracious providence of God, Peter, that powerful and great apostle, who by his courage took the lead of all the rest, was conducted to Rome against this pest of mankind. He, like a noble commander of God, fortified with divine armour, bore the precious merchandize of the revealed light from the east to those in the west, announcing the light itself, and salutary doctrine of the soul the proclamation of the kingdom of God.

CHAPTER XV.

The Gospel according to Mark.

THE divine word having thus been established among the Romans, the power of Simon was soon extinguished and destroyed together with the man. So greatly, however, did the splendour of piety enlighten the minds of Peter's hearers, that it was not sufficient to hear but once, nor to receive the unwritten doctrine of the gospel of God, but they persevered in every variety of entreaties, to solicit Mark as the companion of Peter, and whose gospel we have, that he should leave them a monument of the doctrine thus orally communicated, in writing. Nor did they cease their solicitations until they had prevailed with the man, and thus become the means of that history which is called the Gospel according to Mark. They say also, that the apostle (Peter,) having ascertained what was done by the revelation of the spirit, was delighted with the zealous ardour expressed by these men, and that the history obtained his authority for the purpose of being read in the churches. This account is given by Clement, in the sixth book of his Institutions, whose testimony is corroborated also by that of Papias, bishop of Hierapolis. But Peter makes mention of Mark in the first epistle, which he is also said to have composed at the same city of Rome, and that he shows this fact, by calling the city by an unusual trope, Babylon; thus, " The church at Babylon, elected together with you, saluteth you, as also my son Marcus." 1 Pet. v. 13.

CHAPTER XVI.

Mark first proclaimed Christianity to the inhabitants of Egypt.

THE same Mark, they also say, being the first that was sent to Egypt, proclaimed the gospel there which he had written, and first established churches at the city of Alexandria. And so great a multitude of believers, both of men and women, were collected there at the very outset, that in consequence of their extreme philosophical discipline and austerity, Philo has considered their pursuits, their assemblies, and entertainments, and in short their whole manner of life, as deserving a place in his descriptions.

CHAPTER XVII.

The account given by Philo respecting the Ascetics of Egypt.

THE same author, in the reign of Claudius, is also said to have had familiar conversation with Peter at Rome, whilst he was proclaiming the gospel to the inhabitants of that city. Nor is this at all improbable; since the work of which we now speak, and which was subsequently composed by him at a late period, evidently comprehends the regulations that are still observed in our churches, even to the present time; but at the same time that he describes with the greatest accuracy, the lives of our ascetics, he evidently shows that he not only knew, but approved, whilst he extolled and revered the apostolic men of his day, who were sprung probably from the Hebrews; and hence, still continuing to observe their most ancient customs, rather after the Jewish manner. In the book that he wrote, " On a Contemplative Life, or those who lead a Life of Prayer," he avers indeed, that he would add nothing contrary to the truth, or of his own invention, in the history that he was about to write, where he says, that these persons are called Therapeutæ, and the women Therapeutrides.

Subjoining the reasons of such an appellation, he refers its origin either to the fact, that like physicians, by removing the evil affections, they healed and cured the minds of those that joined them, or to their pure and sincere mode of serving and worshipping the Deity. Whether Philo himself attached this name to them of his own accord, giving an epithet well suited to the manners of the people, or whether the founders really called themselves so from the beginning, as the name of Christians was not yet spread to every place, are points that need not be so accurately determined. He bears witness, however, that they renounced their property, saying, that " as soon as they commenced a philosophical life, they divested themselves of their property, giving it up to their relatives; then laying aside all the cares of life, they abandon the city and take up their abode in solitary fields and gardens, well knowing that the intercourse with persons of a different character is not only unprofitable but injurious." There were at this time, in all probability, persons who, under the influence of an inspired and ardent faith, instituted this mode of life in imitation of the ancient prophets. Wherefore, as it is recorded in the Acts of the Apostles, a book well authenticated, that all the associates of the apostles, after selling their possessions and substance distributed to all according to the necessity of each one, so that there was none in want among them. " For as many as had lands and houses, as this account says, selling them, brought the value of the property sold, and laid it at the apostles' feet, so as to distribute to each one according to his necessity." Philo giving his testimony to facts very much like these, in the same description superadds the following statement. " This kind of men is every where scattered over the world, for both Greeks and barbarians should share in so permanent a benefit. They abound, however, in Egypt, in each of its districts, and particularly about Alexandria.

" But the principal men among them from every quarter emigrate to a place situated on a moderate elevation of land beyond the lake Maria, very advantageously located both for safety and temperature of the air, as if it were the native country of the Therapeutæ." After thus describing what kind of habitations they have, he speaks thus of the churches in the place. " In every house there is a sacred apartment which they call the Semnæum, or Monasterium, where, retired from men, they perform the mysteries of a pious life. Hither they bring nothing with them, neither drink nor food, nor anything else requisite to the necessities of the body; they only bring the law and the inspired declarations of the prophets, and hymns, and such things by which knowledge and piety may be augmented and perfected." After other matters, he adds: " The whole time between the morning and evening, is a constant exercise; for as they are engaged with the sacred Scriptures, they reason and comment upon them, explaining the philosophy of their country in an allegorical manner. For they consider the verbal interpretation as signs indicative of a secret sense communicated in obscure intimations. They have also commentaries of ancient men, who, as the founders of the sect, have left many monuments of their doctrine in allegorical representations, which they use as certain models, imitating the manner of the original institution." These facts appear to have been stated by a man who, at least, has paid attention to those that have expounded the sacred writings. But it is highly probable, that the ancient commentaries which he says they have, are the very gospels and writings of the apostles, and probably some expositions of the ancient prophets, such as are contained in the epistle to the Hebrews and many others of St. Paul's epistles. Afterwards again, concerning the new psalms which they composed, he thus writes, " Thus they not only pass their time in meditation, but compose songs and hymns unto God, noting them of necessity with measure uncommonly serious, through every variety of metres and tunes." Many other things concerning these persons he writes in the same book. But these it appeared necessary to select, in order to present the peculiarities of their ecclesiastical discipline. But, if what has been said does not appear to any one to belong to the discipline of the gospel, but that it can also be applied to others besides those mentioned, let him at least be convinced by the subsequent declarations of the author, in which, if he is at all impartial, he adduces an irrefragable testimony on the same subject. For thus he writes: " But laying down temperance first as a kind of foundation in their minds, upon this they build the other virtues. For none of them is to bring food or drink before the setting of the sun, since they judge that philosophical exercises should be prosecuted in the light, but the necessities of the body in the dark Whence they assign the one to the day, and to the other a small portion of the night. But some of them do not remember their food for three days, when influenced by an uncommon desire of knowledge. And some are so delighted, and feast so luxuriously on the doctrines so richly and profusely furnished by wisdom, that they forbear even twice this time, and are scarcely induced to take necessary food even for six days." These declarations of Philo respecting those of our communion, we deem obvious and in disputable. But, should any one still be so hardy as to contradict, let him at least abandon his incredulity, by yielding to the more powerful demonstrations, which is to be found among none but in the religion of Christians, according to the gospel. Our author also says, that there were also females that meet with those of whom we speak, of whom the most are aged maidens, preserving their purity, not by necessity, as some of the priestesses among the Greeks, but rather by a voluntary determination, in consequence of that zealous desire of wisdom, in the earnest prosecution of which, they disregard the pleasures of the body; as they are desirous not of a mortal progeny but an immortal, which the heavenly mind alone is able to produce of itself." After a little, he also adds the following, with still greater stress. " But they expound the sacred writings by obscure, allegorical, and figurative expressions. For the whole law appears to these persons like an animal, of which the literal expressions are the body, but the invisible sense that lies enveloped in the expressions, the soul. This sense was first pre-eminently studied by this sect, discerning as through a mirror of names, the admirable beauties of the thoughts reflected." Why should we add to these their meetings, and the separate abodes of the men and the women in these meetings, and the exercises performed by them, which are still in vogue among us at the present day, and which, especially at the festival of our Saviour's passion, we are accustomed to pass in fasting and watching, and in the study of the divine word? All these the abovementioned author has accurately described and stated in his writings, and are the same customs that are observed by us alone, at the present day, particularly the vigils of the great festival,* and the exercises in them, and the hymns that are commonly recited among us. He states that whilst one sings gracefully with a certain measure, the others, listening in silence, join in singing the final clauses of the hymns; also, that on the abovementioned days, they lie on straw spread on the ground, and to use his own words, " they abstain altogether from wine, and taste no flesh. Water is their only drink, and the relish of their bread, salt and hyssop." Besides this, he describes the grades of dignity among those who administer the

---

* *The great festival.*] Our author here speaks of the passion week, called by the Greek fathers, the Great Week.

ecclesiastical services committed to them, those of the deacons and the presidencies of the episcopate as the highest. But, whosoever desires to have a more accurate knowledge of these things, may learn them from the history already cited; but that Philo, when he wrote these statements, had in view the first heralds of the gospel, and the original practices handed down from the apostles, must be obvious to all.

CHAPTER XVIII.

The books of Philo that have come down to us.

THIS author, who was copious in language, comprehensive in thought, sublime and elevated in his views of the sacred Scriptures, has made his exposition of the sacred books equally distinguished for variety of matter and manner. On the one hand he expounds the history of Genesis, in the books that he calls " Allegories of the Divine Laws," following the order of the book; and on the other, he forms particular divisions of the chapters, according to the subject of the Scriptures, with the objections and solutions; in which same books also he prefixes the tables of the questions and solutions both in Genesis and Exodus respectively There are also, besides these, treatises on certain problems particularly discussed, such as two " On Agriculture," and two " On Drunkenness," and some others distinguished by a different and peculiar title. Such as " On the things that a Sober Mind earnestly desires, and those which it execrates;" also, " On the Confusion of Tongues," and the treatise "On Flight and Discovery," and that " On Literary Convention," and "On the question, 'Who is Heir to things Divine?'" or, "On the Division of Things into equal and unequal." Moreover, the treatise on the three virtues, which Moses records with others. Beside these, there is one " On those whose Names are changed, and wherefore their Names have been changed;" in which he says, that he wrote also on the first and second covenant. There is also a work of the same author, "On Emigration, and on the Life of the Wise Man perfect in Righteousness;" or, "On the Unwritten Laws." Also, "On Giants," or "On the Immutability of God." And also, "On the Proposition, that Dreams, according to Moses, are sent by God"—five books. These are the books that have come down to us on Genesis, but on Exodus we are acquainted with the first five books of Questions and Solutions; also, that "On the Tabernacle," that also "On the Ten Commandments;" also, the first four treatises on the laws referring particularly to the summary heads of the ten commandments. Also, the treatise " On the Sacrifice of Animals, and the Forms of Sacrifices;" that also, " On the Rewards proposed in the Law to Good Men, and the Punishments and Curses to the Wicked." Besides all these, there are single books extant of the same author, as the treatises "On Providence," and the book composed by him " On the Jews," and " The Statesman." To this may be added "Alexander," or "On Irrational Animals evincing Reason." Beside these " On the Proposition that a Wicked Man is a Slave;" to this is subjoined the book, "That every good Man is free." After which he added the book " On a Contemplative Life, or the Devout," from which we have related the circumstances respecting the life of the apostolical men. Also, the interpretations of the Hebrew names in the law and prophets, is said to be the result of his industry. The same author, in the reign of Caius, coming to Rome, is said to have recited before the whole senate, in the reign of Claudius, what he wrote on the impiety of Caius, to which he humorously prefixed the title " On the Virtues." And the discourses were so much admired as to be deemed worthy of a place in the libraries. During this time also, Paul finishing his journey from Jerusalem, and thence round to Illyricum, Claudius expelled the Jews from Rome, at which time Aquila and Priscilla, with the other Jews that left Rome, went over into Asia. There they abode with the apostle, who was confirming those among whom churches had been already established by him. Of these facts we are also formed in the sacred book of the Acts.

CHAPTER XIX.

The calamity which befel the Jews at Jerusalem, on the day of the Passover.

WHILST Claudius held the government of the empire, it happened about the festival of the passover, that so great a sedition and disturbance took place at Jerusalem, that thirty thousand Jews perished of those alone who were crowded out of the gates of the temple, and thus trodden to death by one another. Thus the festival became a season of mourning and weeping to the whole nation and every family. This is almost literally the account given by Josephus. But Claudius appointed Agrippa, the son of Agrippa, king of the Jews, having deputed Felix procurator of all Samaria and Galilee, and also of the region situated beyond Jordan. He died after a reign of thirteen years and eight months, leaving Nero as his successor in the empire.

CHAPTER XX.

The deeds done at Jerusalem in the reign of Nero.

JOSEPHUS, in the twentieth book of his Antiquities, relates the sedition of the priests, which happened whilst Felix was governor of Judea, under the reign of Nero, in the following words:— " There arose also a sedition between the chief priests on the one hand, and the priests and the leaders of the people at Jerusalem on the other. Each one of them forming collections of the most daring and disaffected, became a leader, and when these met they encountered each other with invectives and stones. Amid these disturbances there was no one that would interpose to rebuke them, but all this was done with the greatest licentiousness, as in a state destitute of a ruler. So greatly also, was the shamelessness and audacity of the chief priests, that they dared to send forth their servants to the barns, to seize the tithes due to the priests; and thus it happened that those of the priests that were destitute, saw themselves perishing for want. Thus did the violence of the factions prevail over all manner of justice." The same author again relates, that about the same time there sprung up a certain species of robbers at Jerusalem, " who," says he, " in broad day-light, and in the midst of the city, slew those whom they met; but particularly at festivals, mixed with the multitude, and with short swords concealed under their garments, stabbed the more distinguished of the people. When these fell, the very murderers themselves took part in expressing their indignation with the bystanders, and thus by the credit which they had with all, they were not detected. And first, he says, that the high priest Jonathan was slaughtered by them; and after him, many were slain from day to day, so that the alarm itself was more oppressive, than the very evils with which they were assailed; whilst every one was in expectation of death, as in the midst of battle.

CHAPTER XXI.

The Egyptian mentioned in the Acts of the Apostles.

NEXT in order, after other matters, he proceeds in his narration. " But the Jews were afflicted with an evil greater than these, by the Egyptian impostor. Having come into the country, and assuming the authority of a prophet, he collected about thirty thousand that were seduced by him. He then led them forth from the desert to the Mount of Olives, determining to enter Jerusalem by force, and after subduing the Roman garrison, to seize the government of the people, using his followers as body guards. But Felix anticipated his attack by going out to meet him with the Roman military, and all the people joined in the defence; so that when the battle was fought, the Egyptian fled with a few, and the most of his followers were either destroyed or captured." This account is given by Josephus in the second book of his history; and it is worth while to subjoin also to this account respecting the Egyptian, also that which is mentioned in the Acts of the

Apostles. It was there said to Paul, by the centurion under Felix, when the multitude of the Jews raised a sedition against the apostle, " Art thou not indeed that selfsame Egyptian that excited and led away the thirty thousand assassins into the desert?" Such, however, were the events that happened under Felix.

CHAPTER XXII.

Paul, being sent prisoner from Judea to Rome, after his defence, was absolved from all crime.

FESTUS was sent by Nero as successor to Felix. Under him, Paul, after having pleaded his cause, was sent a prisoner to Rome. But Aristarchus was his companion, whom he also somewhere in his epistles calls his fellow-prisoner; and here Luke, that wrote the Acts of the Apostles, after showing that Paul passed two whole years at Rome as a prisoner at large, and that he preached the gospel without restraint, brings his history to a close. After pleading his cause, he is said to have been sent again upon the ministry of preaching, and after a second visit to the city, that he finished his life with martyrdom. Whilst he was a prisoner, he wrote his second epistle to Timothy, in which he both mentions his first defence and his impending death. Hear, on these points, his own testimony respecting himself. " In my former defence no one was present with me, but all deserted me. May it not be laid to their charge. But the Lord was with me, and strengthened me, that through me the preaching of the gospel might be fulfilled, and all the nations might hear it. And I was rescued out of the lion's mouth." He plainly intimates in these words, " On the former occasion he was rescued from the lion's mouth, that the preaching of the gospel might be accomplished," that it was Nero to which he referred by this expression, as is probable on account of his cruelty. Therefore he did not subsequently subjoin any such expression as, " he will rescue me from the lion's mouth," for he saw in spirit how near his approaching death was. Hence, after the expression, "and I was rescued from the lion's mouth," this also, " the Lord will rescue me from every evil work, and will save me unto his heavenly kingdom," indicating the martyrdom that he would soon suffer; which he more clearly expresses in the same epistle, " for I am already poured out, and the time of my departure is at hand." And indeed, in this second epistle to Timothy, he shows that Luke alone was with him when he wrote, but at his former defence not even he. Whence, it is probable, that Luke wrote his Acts of the Apostles about that time, continuing his history down to the time that he was with Paul. Thus much we have said, to show that the martyrdom of the apostle did not take place at that period of his stay at Rome when Luke wrote his history. It is indeed probable, that as Nero was more disposed to mildness in the beginning, that the defence of the apostle's doctrine would be more easily received; but as he advanced to such criminal excesses as to disregard all right, the apostles also, with others, experienced the effects of the measures pursued against them.

CHAPTER XXIII.

The martyrdom of James, who was called the brother of the Lord.

But the Jews, after Paul had appealed to Cæsar, and had been sent by Festus to Rome, frustrated in their hope of entrapping him by the snares they had laid, turn themselves against James, the brother of the Lord, to whom the episcopal seat at Jerusalem was committed by the apostles. The following were their nefarious measures also against him. Conducting him into a public place, they demanded that he should renounce the faith of Christ before all the people; but contrary to the sentiments of all, with a firm voice, and much beyond their expectation, he declared himself fully before the whole multitude, and confessed that Jesus Christ was the Son of God, our Saviour and Lord. Unable to bear any longer the testimony of the man, who, on account of his elevated virtue and piety was deemed the most just of men, they seized the opportunity of licentiousness afforded by the prevailing anarchy, and slew him. For as Festus died about this time in Judea, the province was without a governor and head. But, as to the manner of James's death, it has been already stated in the words of Clement, that he was thrown from a wing of the temple, and beaten to death with a club. Hegesippus also, who flourished nearest the days of the apostles, in the fifth book of his Commentaries gives the most accurate account of him, thus: " But James, the brother of the Lord, who, as there were many of this name, was surnamed the Just by all, from the days of our Lord until now, received the government of the church with the apostles. This apostle was consecrated from his mother's womb. He drank neither wine nor fermented liquors, and abstained from anima food. A razor never came upon his head, he never anointed with oil, and never used a bath. He alone was allowed to enter the sanctuary. He never wore woollen, but linen garments. He was in the habit of entering the temple alone. and was often found upon his bended knees, and interceding for the forgiveness of the people; so that his knees became as hard as camel's, in consequence of his habitual supplication and kneeling before God. And indeed, on account of his exceeding great piety, he was called the Just, and Oblias (or Zaddick and Ozleam) which signifies justice and protection of the people; as the prophets declare concerning him. Some of the seven sects, therefore, of the people, mentioned by me above in my Commentaries, asked him what was the door to Jesus? and he answered, ' that he was the Saviour.' " From which, some believed that Jesus is the Christ. But the aforesaid heresies did not believe either a resurrection, or that he was coming to give to every one according to his works; as many however, as did believe did so on account of James. As there were many therefore of the rulers that believed, there arose a tumult among the Jews, Scribes, and Pharisees, saying that there was danger, that the people would now expect Jesus as the Messiah. They came therefore together, and said to James, " We entreat thee, restrain the people, who are led astray after Jesus, as if he were the Christ. We entreat thee to persuade all that are coming to the feast of the passover rightly concerning Jesus; for we all have confidence in thee. For we and all the people bear thee testimony that thou art just, and thou respectest not persons. Persuade therefore the people not to be led astray by Jesus, for we and all the people have great confidence in thee. Stand therefore upon a wing of the temple, that thou mayest be conspicuous on high, and thy words may be easily heard by all the people; for all the tribes have come together on account of the passover, with some of the Gentiles also. The aforesaid Scribes and Pharisees, therefore, placed James upon a wing of the temple, and cried out to him, ' O thou just man, whom we ought all to believe, since the people are led astray after Jesus that was crucified, declare to us what is the door to Jesus that was crucified.' And he answered with a loud voice, ' Why do ye ask me respecting Jesus the Son of Man? He is now sitting in the heavens, on the right hand of great Power, and is about to come on the clouds of heaven.' And as many were confirmed, and gloried in this testimony of James, and said, Hosanna to the son of David, these same priests and Pharisees said to one another, ' We have done badly in affording such testimony to Jesus, but let us go up and cast him down, that they may dread to believe in him.' And they cried out, ' Oh, oh, Justus himself is deceived,' and they fulfilled that which is written in Isaiah, ' Let us take away the just, because he is offensive to us; wherefore they shall eat the fruit of their doings.' Is. iii. Going up therefore, they cast down the just man, saying to one another, ' Let us stone James the Just.' And they began to stone him, as he did not die immediately when cast down; but turning round, he knelt down saying, ' I entreat thee, O Lord God and Father, forgive them, for they know not what they do.' Thus they were stoning him, when one of the priests of the sons of Rechab, a son of the Rechabites, spoken of by Jeremiah the prophet, cried out saying, ' Cease, what are you doing? Justus is praying for you.' And one of them, a fuller, beat out the brains of Justus with the club that he used to beat out clothes. Thus he suffered martyrdom, and they buried him on the spot where his tombstone is still remaining, by the temple. He became a faithful witness, both to the Jews and Greeks, that Jesus is the Christ. Immediately after this, Vespasian invaded and took Ju-

dea." Such is the more ample testimony of Hegesippus, in which
he fully coincides with Clement. So admirable a man indeed was
James, and so celebrated among all for his justice, that even the
wiser part of the Jews were of opinion that this was the cause of
the immediate siege of Jerusalem, which happened to them for
no other reason than the crime against him. Josephus also has
not hesitated to superadd this testimony in his works: " These
things," says he, " happened to the Jews to avenge James the
Just, who was the brother of him that is called Christ, and
whom the Jews had slain, notwithstanding his pre-eminent justice." The same writer also relates his death, in the twentieth
book of his Antiquities, in the following words: " But Cesar having learned the death of Festus, sends Albinus as governor of Judea. But the younger Ananus, whom we mentioned before as obtaining the priesthood, was particularly rash and daring in his
disposition. He was also of the sect of the Sadducees, which are
the most unmerciful of all the Jews in the execution of judgment,
as we have already shown. Ananus, therefore, being of this character, and supposing that he had a suitable opportunity, in consequence of the death of Festus, and Albinus being yet on the
way, calls an assembly of the judges; and bringing thither the
brother of Jesus who is called Christ, whose name was James,
with some others, he presented an accusation against them, as if
they had violated the law, and committed them to be stoned as
criminals. But those of the city that seemed most moderate and
most accurate in observing the law, were greatly offended at this,
and secretly sent to the king, entreating him to send to Ananus
with the request not to do these things, saying that he had not
acted legally even before. Some also went out to meet him as
he came from Alexandria, and inform him that it was not lawful
for Ananus to summon the sanhedrim without his knowledge. Albinus, induced by this account, writes to Ananus in a rage, and
threatening that he would call him to an account. But king
Agrippa, for the same reason, took from him the priesthood, after
he had held it three months, and appointed Jesus the son of Dam-
mæus his successor. These accounts are given respecting James,
who is said to have written the first of the epistles general, (ca-

tholic;) but it is to be observed that it is considered spurious. Not many indeed of the ancients have mentioned it, and not even that called the epistle of Jude, which is also one of the seven called catholic epistles. Nevertheless we know, that these, with the rest, are publicly used in most of the churches.

CHAPTER XXIV.

Annianus was appointed the first bishop of Alexandria after Mark.

NERO was now in the eighth year of his reign, when Annianus succeeded the apostle and evangelist Mark in the administration of the church at Alexandria. He was a man distinguished for his piety, and admirable in every respect.

CHAPTER XXV.

The persecution under Nero, in which Paul and Peter were honoured with martyrdom in the cause of religion at Rome.

BUT Nero now having the government firmly established under him, and henceforth plunging into nefarious projects, began to take up arms against that very religion which acknowledges the one Supreme God. To describe, indeed, the greatness of this man's wickedness, is not compatible with our present object; and as there are many that have given his history in the most accurate narratives, every one may, at his pleasure, in these contemplate the grossness of his extraordinary madness. Under the influence of this, he did not proceed to destroy so many thousands with any calculation, but with such indiscriminate murder as not even to refrain from his nearest and dearest friends. His own mother and wife, with many others that were his near relatives, he killed like strangers and enemies, with various kinds of deaths. And, indeed, in addition to all his other crimes, this too was yet wanting to complete the catalogue, that he was the first of the emperors that displayed himself an enemy of piety towards the Deity. This fact is recorded by the Roman Tertullian, in language like the following: " Examine your records. There you will find that Nero was the first that persecuted this doctrine, particularly then when after subduing all the east, he exercised his cruelty against all at Rome. Such is the man of whom we boast, as the leader in our punishment. For he that knows who he was, may know also that there could scarcely be any thing but what was great and good, condemned by Nero." Thus Nero publicly announcing himself as the chief enemy of God, was led on in his fury to slaughter the apostles. Paul is therefore said to have been beheaded at Rome, and Peter to have been crucified under him. And this account is confirmed by the fact, that the names of Peter and Paul still remain in the cemeteries of that city even to this day. But likewise, a certain ecclesiastical writer, Caius by name, who was born about the time of Zephyrinus bishop of Rome, disputing with Proclus the leader of the Phrygian sect, gives the following statement respecting the places where the earthly tabernacles of the aforesaid apostles are laid. " But I can show," says he, " the trophies of the apostles. For if you will go to the Vatican, or to the Ostian road, you will find the trophies of those who have laid the foundation of this church. And that both suffered martyrdom about the same time, Dionysius bishop of Corinth bears the following testimony, in his discourse addressed to the Romans. ' Thus, likewise you, by means of this admonition, have mingled the flourishing seed that had been planted by Peter and Paul at Rome and Corinth. For both of these having planted us at Corinth, likewise instructed us; and having in like manner taught in Italy, they suffered martyrdom about the same time.' "* This testimony I have superadded, in order that the truth of the history might be still more confirmed.

---

* In this passage from Dionysius, Valesius has followed the text of Syncellus contrary to that commonly received. We give the passage according to the latter

CHAPTER XXVI.

*The Jews were afflicted with innumerable evils, and finally com-
menced a war with the Romans.*

JOSEPHUS, in his account of the great distresses that seized the
Jewish nation, relates also, in his writings, that beside many
others, vast numbers also of those that were of the first rank
among the Jews, were scourged with rods, and nailed upon the
cross at Jerusalem, by Florus. For he happened to be procurator
of Judea at the commencement of the war, in the twelfth year
of Nero's reign. "Then," says he, "throughout all Syria a tre
mendous commotion seized upon the inhabitants, in consequence
of the revolt of the Jews. Every where did the inhabitants of
the cities destroy the Jews without mercy. So that you could
see the cities filled with unburied corpses, and the dead bodies of
the aged mixed with those of children, and women not even
having the necessary covering of their bodies. The whole province, indeed, was filled with indescribable distresses. But greater still than the crimes already endured, was the anticipation
of those that threatened." Such is the statement of Josephus,
and such was the condition of the Jews at this time.

BOOK III.

CHAPTER I.

The parts of the world where Christ WAS PREACHED *by the Apostles.*

Such, then, was the state of the Jews at this time. But the holy apostles and disciples of our Saviour, being scattered over the whole world, Thomas, according to tradition, received Parthia as his allotted region; Andrew received Scythia, and John, Asia, where, after continuing for some time, he died at Ephesus. Peter appears to have preached through Pontus, Galatia, Bithynia, Cappadocia and Asia, to the Jews that were scattered abroad; who also, finally coming to Rome, was crucified with his head downward, having requested of himself to suffer in this way. Why should we speak of Paul, spreading the gospel of Christ from Jerusalem to Illyricum, and finally suffering martyrdom at Rome, under Nero? This account is given by Origen, in the third book of his exposition of Genesis.

CHAPTER II.

The first that presided over the church at Rome.

After the martyrdom of Paul and Peter, Linus was the first that received the episcopate at Rome. Paul makes mention of him in his epistle from Rome to Timothy, in the address at the close of the epistle, saying, " Eubulus and Prudens, and Linus, and Claudia, salute thee."

CHAPTER III.

Of the Epistles of the Apostles.

As to the writings of Peter, one of his epistles called the first. is acknowledged as genuine. For this was anciently used by the ancient fathers in their writings, as an undoubted work of the apostle. But that which is called the second, we have not, indeed. understood to be imbodied with the sacred books, ενδιαθηκον, yet as it appeared useful to many, it was studiously read with the other Scriptures. As to that work, however, which is ascribed to him, called "The Acts," and the "Gospel according to Peter," and that called "The Preaching and the Revelations of Peter," we know nothing of their being handed down as Catholic* writings. Since neither among the ancient nor the ecclesiastical writers of our own day, has there been one that has appealed to testimony taken from them. But as I proceed in my history, I shall carefully show with the successions of the apostles, what ecclesiastical writers in their times respectively made use of any of the disputed writings, and what opinions they have expressed, both respecting the incorporated (ενδιαθηκοι) and acknowledged writings, and also what respecting those that were not of this description. These, however, are those that are called Peter's epistles, of which I have understood only one epistle to be genuine, and admitted by the ancient fathers. The epistles of Paul are fourteen, all well known and beyond doubt. It should not, however, be concealed, that some have set aside the Epistle to the Hebrews, saying, that it was disputed, as not being one of St. Paul's epistles; but we shall in the proper place, also subjoin what has been said by those before our time respecting this epistle. As to what are called his acts, I have not even understood that they were among the works of undisputed authority. But as the same apostle in the addresses at the close of the Epis-

---

* *Catholic.*] The word here plainly means universally received; i. e. genuine, as it is happily rendered by Shorting.

tle to the Romans, has among others made mention also of
Hermes, of whom they say we have the book called Pastor, it
should be observed, that this too is disputed by some, on account
of whom it is not placed among those of acknowledged authority
('ομολογουμενοι.) By others, however, it is judged most necessary, especially to those who need an elementary introduction.
Hence we know that it has been already in public use in our
churches, and I have also understood by tradition, that some of
the most ancient writers have made use of it. Let this suffice
for the present, to show what books were disputed, what admitted by all in the sacred Scriptures.

CHAPTER IV.

The first successors of the Apostles.

THAT Paul preached to the Gentiles, and established churches
from Jerusalem and around as far as Illyricum, is evident both
from his own expressions, and from the testimony of Luke in the
book of Acts. And in what provinces Peter also proclaimed the
doctrine of Christ, the doctrine of the New Covenant, appears
from his own writings, and may be seen from that epistle we
have mentioned as admitted in the canon, and which he addressed to the Hebrews in the dispersion throughout Pontus, Galatia,
Cappadocia, Asia and Bithynia But how many and which of
these, actuated by a genuine zeal, were judged suitable to feed
the churches established by these apostles, it is not easy to say,
any farther than may be gathered from the writings of Paul.
For he, indeed, had innumerable fellow-labourers, or as he himself calls them, fellow-soldiers in the church. Of these, the
greater part are honoured with an indelible remembrance by him
in his epistles, where he gives a lasting testimony concerning
them. Luke also, in his Acts, speaking of his friends, mentions
them by name. Timothy, indeed, is recorded as having first received the episcopate at Ephesus, (εν Epheso παροικιας) as

Titus also, was appointed over the churches in Crete. But Luke, who was born at Antioch, and by profession a physician, being for the most part connected with Paul, and familiarly acquainted with the rest of the apostles, has left us in two inspired books, the institutes of that spiritual healing art which he obtained from them. One of these is his gospel, in which he testifies that he has recorded, "as those who were from the beginning eye-witnesses, and ministers of the word," delivered to him, whom also, he says, he has in all things followed. The other is his Acts of the Apostles, which he composed, not from what he had heard from others, but from what he had seen himself. It is also said, that Paul usually referred to his gospel, whenever, in his epistles he spoke of some particular gospel of his own, saying, "according to my gospel." But of the rest that accompanied Paul, Crescens is mentioned by him as sent to Gaul. Linus, whom he has mentioned in his Second Epistle to Timothy as his companion at Rome, has been before shown to have been the first after Peter, that obtained the episcopate at Rome. Clement also, who was appointed the third bishop of this church, is proved by him to have been a fellow-labourer and fellow-soldier with him. Beside, the Areopagite, called Dionysius, whom Luke has recorded in his Acts, after Paul's address to the Athenians, in the Areopagus, as the first that believed, is mentioned by Dionysius, another of the ancients, and pastor of the church at Corinth, as the first bishop of the church at Athens. But the manner and times of the apostolic succession shall be mentioned by us as we proceed in our course. Now let us pursue the order of our history.

CHAPTER V.

The last siege of the Jews after Christ.

AFTER Nero had held the government about thirteen years, Galba and Otho reigned about a year and six months. Vespasian, who had become illustrious in the campaign against the Jews,

was then proclaimed sovereign in Judea, receiving the title of em
peror from the armies there. Directing his course, therefore, immediately to Rome, he commits the care of the war against the
Jews, into the hands of his son Titus; for after the ascension of
our Saviour, the Jews, in addition to their wickedness against
him, were now incessantly plotting mischief against his apostles.
First, they slew Stephen by stoning him, next James the son of
Zebedee, and the brother of John, by beheading, and finally
James, who first obtained the episcopal seat at Jerusalem, after
the ascension of our Saviour, and was slain in the manner before
related. But the rest of the apostles who were harassed in innumerable ways, with a view to destroy them, and driven from
the land of Judea, had gone forth to preach the gospel to all na
tions, relying upon the aid of Christ, when he said, "Go ye, teach
all nations in my name." The whole body, however, of the
church at Jerusalem, having been commanded by a divine revelation, given to men of approved piety there before the war, removed from the city, and dwelt at a certain town beyond the
Jordan, called Pella. Here, those that believed in Christ, having
removed from Jerusalem, as if holy men had entirely abandoned
the royal city itself, and the whole land of Judea; the divine justice, for their crimes against Christ and his apostles, finally
overtook them, totally destroying the whole generation of these
evildoers from the earth. But the number of calamities which
then overwhelmed the whole nation; the extreme misery to which
particularly the inhabitants of Judea were reduced, the vast
numbers of men, with women and children that fell by the sword
and famine, and innumerable other forms of death; the numerous
and great cities of Judea that were besieged, as also the great
and incredible distresses that those experienced who took refuge
at Jerusalem, as to a place of perfect security; these facts, as
well as the whole tenor of the war, and each particular of its
progress, when finally, the abomination of desolation, according
to the prophetic declaration, stood in the very temple of God, so
celebrated of old, but which now was approaching its total down-
fal and final destruction by fire; all this, I say, any one that wishes
may see accurately stated in the history written by Josephus.

It may, however, be necessary to state, in the very words of this writer, how about three hundred thousand that flocked from all parts of Judea at the time of the passover, were shut up in Jerusalem as in a prison. For it was indeed just, that in those very days in which they had inflicted sufferings upon the Saviour and benefactor of all men, the Christ of God, destruction should overtake them, thus shut up as in a prison, as an exhibition of the divine justice. Passing by, then, the particular calamities which befel them, such as they suffered from the sword, and other means employed against them, I may deem it sufficient only to subjoin the calamities they endured from the famine. So that they who peruse the present history, may know in some measure, that the divine vengeance did not long delay to visit them for their iniquity against the Christ of God.

CHAPTER VI.

The famine which oppressed the Jews.

Let us, then, with the fifth book of Josephus's history again in our hands, go through the tragedy of events which then occurred. "It was equally dangerous," says he, "for the more wealthy to remain. For under the pretext of desertion, a man was slain for his wealth. But the madness of the rioters increased with the famine, and both kinds of misery were inflamed from day to day. Provisions were plainly nowhere to be had. Hence they burst into houses to search for food, and if they found any, they would scourge the owners as if they intended to deny they had it; but if they found none, they tortured them as if they had carefully concealed it. The bodies of the poor wretches, however, were evidence enough whether they had or had not. Some of them, therefore, that were yet sound in health, they supposed to have an abundance of food, but those that were wan and pallid they passed by; for it seemed absurd to kill men that were soon likely to die for want. Many secretly exchanged their property for a single measure of wheat, if they happened to be the more wealthy; of barley, if they were of the poorer sort. Then locking themselves in the most retired parts of their houses, some, from excessive hunger, eat the grain unprepared; others however, baked it according as necessity or fear directed. As to a table, there was none set any where; but taking the food from the fire, they tore it asunder yet crude and raw. Wretched indeed was the fare, and a lamentable sight it was, where the most powerful grasped after all, and the weaker were constrained to mourn. For famine surpasses all other evils, but it destroys nothing so effectually as shame; for that which would otherwise demand some regard, is contemned in this. Thus wives tore away the food from the very mouths of their husbands children from their parents, and what was most wretched of all, mothers from their infants; so that whilst their dearest children lay wasting in their arms, there was not shame enough to prevent them taking away the very drops that supported life. And even in doing this, they did not remain undiscovered; for whenever they saw a door locked, this was a sign that those within were taking food, and then immediately bursting open the doors they rushed in, and choked them, almost forcing the morsels out of their very throats. Old men were beaten that held back their food, and women were torn by the hair, if they concealed what they had in their hands. Nor was there any pity for gray hairs or for infants; but taking up the infants clinging to the morsels, they dashed them to the ground. But they were much more cruel to those who anticipated their entrance, and were devouring what they wished to seize, just as if they had been wronged by them. They also devised terrible modes of torture, to discover where there was any food. For by cruel devices to prevent every relief of nature, they caused the unhappy individual to suffer such torment,* that the very recital makes one shudder at what he would endure, before he confessed that he had one loaf of bread, or that he had a single handful of wheat concealed. The tormentors themselves, however, suffered no want; for it might have been some palliation, if necessity had compelled them thus. But they

---

* The passages that we have here thrown into one, are thus given by Vales us: ‘ Nam miseris hominibus ipsos quidem genitalium meatus ervis obturabant, podicem præacutis sudibus transfigebant."

did it with the view to exercise their ferocity and to provide for themselves for the following days. When any crept forth at night to the outposts of the Romans, for the purpose of collecting wild herbs and grass, these tormentors would go out to meet them, and when they seemed just to have escaped the hands of the enemy, the oppressors robbed them of whatever they brought. And very often, though they entreated them, and conjured them by the most awful name of God, to give them some part of that for which they had risked their lives, they notwithstanding gave them nothing. It was a happy circumstance yet, if in addition to robbery, they were not also slain." This same author, after a few particulars, also says: " But with the hope of egress, was cut off all hope of safety to the Jews; and the famine now penetrating deeply, was consuming the people by houses and families. The houses were filled with women and children that had thus perished; the byways with the dead bodies of old men. But the boys and young men, swelling up, tottered and reeled like shadows through the markets, and then falling down, lay wheresoever the malady had overtaken them. The sick were not even able to bury their dead, and those yet in health and strength were loth to do it, both on account of the number of the dead, and the uncertainty of their own fate. Many, indeed, fell down and died upon those they were burying; many went to the sepulchres, even before they were overtaken by the struggles of death. There was, however, neither weeping nor lamentation, but the famine prevailed over all affection. With tearless eyes did they who were yet struggling with death, look on those that had gone to rest before them. A deep silence and deadly gloom also pervaded the city. But more oppressive than all these, were the robbers that broke into the houses, now mere sepulchres, and spoiling the dead, and tearing off the garments of their bodies, they went off with a laugh. They would also try the points of their swords in the dead bodies, and some of thos   at were lying yet alive, they thrust through, in order to try the edge of their weapons. But those that prayed them the relief of their arm and sword, they contemptuously left to be destroyed by the famine; whilst those expiring died with their eyes fixed upon the temple, and left the factious to survive them. These, at first, not bearing the effluvia from the dead bodies, ordered them to be buried out of the public treasury; afterwards, when they were not able to continue this, they threw the bodies from the walls into the ditches below. As Titus went around these, and saw them filled with the dead, and the deep gore flowing around the putrid bodies, he groaned heavily, and raising his hands, called God to witness that it was none of his work." After some additional remarks, Josephus proceeds: "I cannot hesitate to declare what my feelings demand. I think that had the Romans lingered to proceed against these guilty wretches, the city would either have been swallowed up by the opening earth, or overwhelmed with a flood, or like Sodom, been struck with the lightning. For it bore a much more impious race than those who once endured such visitations. Thus, by the madness of these wretches, the whole people perished." In the sixth book, he also writes thus: "Of those that perished by the famine in the city, there fell an infinite number. The miseries that befel them were indescribable; for at every house, wherever there was a shadow of food, there was war. The nearest relatives contended with one another, to seize the wretched supports of life. There was no belief that hunger was the cause, even when they saw the dying; but the robbers would search them whilst yet breathing, lest any one should pretend that he was dying, whilst he concealed food in his bosom. But the robbers themselves, with their mouths wide open for want of food, roved and straggled hither and thither, like mad dogs, beating the doors as if they were drunk; and for want of counsel, rushing twice or thrice an hour into the same houses. Indeed, necessity forced them to apply their teeth to every thing, and gathering what was no food, even for the filthiest of irrational animals, they de.oured it, and did not abstain at last even from belts and shoes. They took off the hides from their shields and devoured them, and some used even the remnants of old straw as food; others gathered the stubble, and sold a very small weight of it for four Attic drachms.*   And why

Attic drachms.] The drachma was a coin of about-fifteen cents. Some make it more. Shorting, in his translation, has computed the four drachms to be half a pound sterling, and refers to his note on B. I. ch. viii. He there states very cor-

should we speak of the excessive severity of the famine displayed upon inanimate objects? I am going to relate a piece of wickedness, such as is not recorded either by Greeks or barbarians. It is horrid to relate, and incredible to hear. And indeed, lest I should appear to deal in marvellous stories, I would cheerfully pass by this occurrence, if I had not innumerable witnesses still living. I should also deserve but cold thanks from my country, if I should pass by in carelessness what she in reality did suffer. A woman that dwelt beyond the Jordan, named Maria, the daughter of Eleazar, of the village Bathezor, signifying the home of hyssop, distinguished for her family and wealth, having taken refuge at Jerusalem among the rest of the multitude, was shut up in the city with them. The tyrants had already robbed her of all her other possessions, as much as she had collected, and brought with her from beyond the river into the city. But as to the relics of her property, and whatever food she provided, the ruffians daily rushing in, seized and bore it away. A dreadful indignation overpowered the woman, and frequently reviling and cursing the robbers, she endeavoured by these means to irritate them against herself. But as no one either through resentment or pity would slay her, and she was weary of providing food for others, and there was now no probability of finding it any where; the famine now penetrated the very bowels and marrow, and resentment raged more violently than the famine. Urged by frenzy and necessity as her counsellors, she proceeded against nature herself. Seizing her little son, who was yet at her breast, she said, " wretched child! in the midst of war, famine, and faction, for what do I preserve thee? Our condition among the Romans, though we might live, is slavery. But even slavery is anticipated by famine, and the assassins are more cruel than either—come,

rectly. that four Attic drachms equal one ordinary shekel, and the shekel to be 2s. 6d. But by some unaccountable oversight, makes the four drachms equal to ten shillings! He appears to have substituted the value of the shekel for the drachm, as the reader will readily see. But what is still more surprising, this error has been transcribed by Reading in his accurate edition of Valesius. See Reading's edition in loc.

be thou food to me, fury* to the assassins, and a tale for men, the only one yet wanting to complete the miseries of the Jews." As she said this, she slew her son; then roasting him, she eat one half herself, and covering over the rest, she kept it. It was not long before the murderers came in, and perceiving the fumes of the execrable food, they threatened immediately to slay her if she did not produce what she had prepared. She answered she had reserved a fine portion of it for them, and then uncovered the relics of her son. Horror and amazement immediately seized them. They stood mute with the sight. "This is my own son," said she, "and the deed is mine. Eat, for I too have eaten, be not more delicate than a woman, nor more tender than a mother; but if you are so pious, and reject my offering, I have already eaten half, and let the rest remain for me." After this, they indeed, went trembling away, cowardly at least in this one instance, and yet scarcely yielding to the mother even this kind of food. Forthwith the whole city was filled with the dreadful crime, and every one placing the wickedness before his eyes, was struck with a horror as if it had been perpetrated by himself. Thenceforth the wretched people overcome with hunger, only strove to hasten death; and it was a happiness yet for those who died before they heard and saw miseries like these." Such then, was the vengeance that followed the guilt and impiety of the Jews against the Christ of God.

CHAPTER VII.

The Predictions of Christ.

To these accounts it may be proper to add the sure prediction of our Saviour, in which he foretold these very events as follows: " But wo to them that are with child and those that give suck in

---

* *Fury*, or *vengeance*.] The Erynnes or Furies, according to the belief of the ancients, were among the tormenting fiends of Tartarus.

those days; but pray that your flight be not in the winter, nor on the Sabbath. But there shall be then great distress, such as has not been from the beginning of the world until now, neither may be." The historian, adding up the whole number of those slain, says, that eleven hundred thousand perished by famine and the sword, and that the rest, the factious and robbers, mutually informing against each other after the capture, were put to death. Of the young men, the tallest, and those that were distinguished for beauty, were preserved for the triumph. Of the remaining multitude, those above seventeen were sent prisoners to labour at the mines in Egypt. But great numbers were distributed to the provinces, to be destroyed by the sword or wild beasts in the theatres. Those under seventeen were carried away to be sold as slaves. Of these alone, there were upwards of ninety thousand. All this occurred in this manner, in the second year of the reign of Vespasian, according to the predictions of our Lord and Saviour Jesus Christ, who by his divine power foresaw all these things as if already present at the time, who wept and mourned indeed, at the prospect, as the holy evangelists show in their writings. These give us the very words that he uttered, when he said to this same Jerusalem, " If thou didst know, even thou, in this thy day the things that belong to thy peace, but now they are hidden from thy eyes, for the days will come upon thee, and thy enemies shall cast a trench around thee, and shall encompass thee around, and shall every where shut thee in, and they shall level thee and thy children with the ground." Afterwards he speaks as if of the people—" For there shall be great distress upon earth, and wrath upon this people, and they shall fall by the edge of the sword, and they shall be carried away captive to all nations, and Jerusalem shall be trodden down by the nations, until the times of the nations shall be fulfilled." And again, " When ye shall see Jerusalem surrounded by armies, then know that her desolation has drawn near."

On comparing the declarations of our Saviour with the other parts of the historian's work, where he describes the whole war, how can one fail to acknowledge and wonder at the truly divine and extraordinary foreknowledge and prediction of our Saviour ?

Concerning the events, then, that befel the Jews after our Sa
viour's passion, and those outcries in which the multitude of the
Jews refused the condemnation of a robber and murderer,
but entreated that the Prince of Life should be destroyed, it is
superfluous to add to the statement of the historian.   Yet it may
be proper to mention, also, what things occurred that show the
benignity of that all-gracious Providence that had deferred their
destruction for forty years after their crimes against Christ. During which time the greater part of the apostles and disciples,
James himself, the first bishop there, usually called the brother
of our Lord, still surviving, and still remaining at Jerusalem, continued the strongest bulwark of the place.   Divine Providence
yet bearing them with long-suffering, to see whether by repentance for what they had done, they might obtain pardon and salvation; and beside this long-suffering, it also presented wonderful
prodigies of what was about to happen to those that did not repent; all which having been recorded by the historian already
cited, it well deserved to be submitted to the view of our readers.

CHAPTER VIII.

The signs that preceded the war.

TAKING, then, the work of this author, read for yourself the
account given by him in the sixth book of his history.   " The
wretched people," says he, " at this time were readily persuaded
to give credit to the impostors and liars against God, but they
neither believed nor paid regard to the significant and wonderful events that prognosticated the approaching desolation.   On
the contrary, as if struck with stupidity, and as if they had neither eyes nor understanding, they slighted the declarations of
God.   At one time, when a star very like a sword stood above
the city, as also a comet that continued to be seen a whole year,
at another, when before the rebellion and the commotions that
preceded the war, whilst the people were collected at the feast

of unleavened bread, on the eighth of the month of April, about the ninth hour of the night, so great a light shone around the altar and the temple, as to seem a bright day. And this continued for half an hour. To the ignorant this appeared a good omen, but by the scribes it was immediately judged to refer to the events that took place at the issue. At the same festival also, a cow struck by the priest for sacrifice, brought forth a lamb in the midst of the temple. The eastern gate also, of the inner temple, which was of brass and immense weight, and which at evening was scarcely shut by twenty men, and resting on ironbound hinges, and secured with bolts very deeply sunk in the ground, was seen in the sixth hour of the night to open of itself. But not many days after the feast, on the twenty-first of the month of Artimisium, (May) a wonderful spectre was seen, which surpasses all belief. And indeed, that which I am about to tell would appear a prodigy, were it not related by those who had seen it, and unless the subsequent miseries had corresponded to the signs. For before the setting of the sun there were seen chariots and armed troops on high, wheeling through the clouds around the whole region, and surrounding the cities. And at the festival called Pentecost, the priests entering the temple at night according to their custom, to perform the service, said they first perceived a motion and noise, and after this a confused voice saying, " let us go hence." But what follows is still more awful.

One Jesus the son of Ananias, a common and ignorant rustic, four years before the war, when the city was most at peace and well regulated, coming to the festival at which it was customary for all to make tabernacles at the temple, to the honour of God, suddenly began to cry out, " A voice from the east, a voice from the west, a voice from the four winds. A voice against Jerusalem and the temple, a voice against bridegrooms and brides, a voice against all people." This man went about crying through all the lanes, night and day. But some of the more distinguished citizens, being offended at the ominous cry, and enraged at the man, seized him, and scourged him with many and severe lashes. But without uttering a word for himself or privately to those present, he still persisted in the cries he had before uttered. The magistrates, therefore judging, what it really was, a more than ordinary divine movement in the man, conducted him to the Roman governor. Then, though he was scourged to the bone, he neither entreated nor shed a tear. But lowering his voice in as mournful a tone as was possible, he answered to every blow, " Alas, alas, for Jerusalem." The same historian relates a fact still more remarkable. He says, " that an oracular passage was found in the sacred writings, declaring that about this time a certain one proceeding from that region would obtain the sovereignty of the world. This prediction, he supposed, was fulfilled in Vespasian. He, however, did not obtain the sovereignty over the whole world, but only over the Romans. More justly, therefore, would it be referred to Christ, to whom it was said by the Father, " Ask of me, and I will give thee the heathen for thine inheritance, and the uttermost parts of the earth for thy possession." Of whom, indeed, at this very time, " the sound of the holy apostles went throughout all the earth, and their words to the ends of the world."

CHAPTER IX.

Of Josephus and the works he has left.

Since we have referred to this writer, it may be proper also to notice Josephus himself, who has contributed so much to the history in hand, whence and from what family he sprung. He shows this, indeed, in his own works, as follows. " Josephus the son of Mattathias, a priest of Jerusalem, who at first himself fought against the Romans, and at whose affairs he was afterward of necessity present," was a man most distinguished, not only among his own countrymen the Jews, but also among the Romans; so that they honoured him with the erection of a statue at Rome, and the books that he composed, with a place in the public library. He wrote the whole Antiquities of the Jews, in twenty books, and his history of the Jewish war in seven books, which he says were not only written in Greek, but also translated by him into his native tongue; in all which he is worthy of credit, as well as in other matters. There are also two other works of his that deserve to be read, viz. those on the Antiquity of the Jews. In these he also makes his reply to Apion, the grammarian, who had then written against the Jews; they contain also a refutation of others, who attempted to vilify the national peculiarities of the Jewish people. In the first of these works he gives us the number of the canonical books of the Scriptures called the Old Testament, such as are of undoubted authority among the Hebrews, setting them forth, as handed down by ancient tradition, in the following words.

CHAPTER X.

The manner in which Josephus mentions the Holy Scriptures.

" WE have not therefore among us innumerable books that disagree and contradict each other, but only two and twenty, embracing the record of all history, and which are justly considered divine compositions. Of these, five are the books of Moses, comprehending both the laws and the tradition respecting the origin of man, down to his own death. This time comprehends a space of nearly three thousand years. But from Moses until the death of Artaxerxes, who reigned after Xerxes king of Persia, the prophets after Moses wrote the events of their day in thirteen books. The remaining four, comprehend hymns to the praise of God, and precepts for the regulation of human life. From Artaxerxes until our own times, the events are all recorded, but they are not deemed of authority equal with those before them, because, that there was not an exact succession of the prophets. But it is evident from the thing itself, how we regard these books of ours. For in the lapse of so many ages. no one has dared either to add to them, or to take from them, or to change them, but it has been implanted in all Jews, from the very origin of the nation, to consider them as the doctrines of God, and to abide by them, and cheerfully to die for them if necessary." These declarations of this historian, I thought might be properly here subjoined. There is also another work, of no mean execution, by the same writer, "On the Supremacy of Reason," which, indeed, is entitled by some Maccabaicum, because it contains the conflicts of those Hebrews that contended manfully for the true religion, as is related in the books called Maccabees. And at the end of the twentieth book of his Antiquities, the same author intimates, that he had purposed to write four books on God, and his existence, according to the peculiar opinions of the Jewish nation; also on the laws, wherefore it is permitted by them to do some things whilst others are forbidden. Other subjects, he says, are also discussed by him in his works. In addition to these, it seems proper to subjoin also the expressions that he uses at the close of his Antiquities, in confirmation of the testimony that we have taken from him. For when he accuses Justus of Tiberias, who, like himself, attempted the history of his own times, and convicts him of not writing according to truth, after upbraiding him with many other misdemeanours, he also adds the following language : " I am not, however, afraid respecting my writings, as you are; but have presented them to the emperors themselves, as the facts occurred almost under their eyes. For I was conscious of adhering closely to the truth in my narration, and hence was not disappointed in expecting to receive their testimony. To many others, also, did I hand my history, some of whom were present at the war, as king Agrippa and some of his relatives. For the emperor Titus desired so much that the knowledge of these events should be communicated to the world, that with his own hand he wrote they should be published. And king Agrippa wrote sixty-two letters bearing testimony to their truth, of which Josephus subjoined two. But this may suffice respecting him. Let us now proceed to what follows in order.

CHAPTER XI.

Simeon ruled the church of Jerusalem after James.

AFTER the martyrdom of James, and the capture of Jerusalem,
which immediately followed, the report is, that those of the
apostles and the disciples of our Lord, that were yet surviving,
came together from all parts with those that were related to
our Lord according to the flesh. For the greater part of them
were yet living. These consulted together, to determine whom
it was proper to pronounce worthy of being the successor of
James. They all unanimously declared Simeon the son of Cleophas, of whom mention is made in the sacred volume, as worthy
of the episcopal seat there. They say he was the cousin german* of our Saviour, for Hegesippus asserts that Cleophas was
the brother of Joseph.

CHAPTER XII.

Vespasian commands the descendants of David to be sought.

IT was also said that Vespasian, after the capture of Jerusalem,
commanded all of the family of David to be sought, that no one
might be left among the Jews who was of the royal stock, and,
that in consequence another very violent persecution was raised
against the Jews.

* The word ανεψιον is here correctly rendered cousin german, by the mother's
side Valesius has incorrectly rendered *patruelis*, cousin german, by the father's
side. Mary the wife of Cleophas, and Mary the mother of our Lord, were sisters.
John xix. 25. Hence, Shorting has correctly observed, that Hegesippus calls
Joseph and Cleophas brothers, by reason of this matrimonial connexion. See his
note.

CHAPTER XIII.

Anencletus, the second bishop of Rome.

AFTER Vespasian had reigned about ten years, he was succeeded by his son Titus; in the second year of whose reign, Linus, bishop of the church at Rome, who had held the office about twelve years, transferred it to Anencletus. But Titus was succeeded by Domitian, his brother, after he had reigned two years and as many months.

CHAPTER XIV.

Avilius, the second bishop of Alexandria.

IN the fourth year of Domitian, Annianus, who was the first bishop of Alexandria, died, after having filled the office twenty-two years. He was succeeded by Avilius, who was the second bishop of that city.

CHAPTER XV.

Clement, the third bishop of Rome.

IN the twelfth year of the same reign, after Anencletus had been bishop of Rome twelve years, he was succeeded by Clement, who, the apostle, in his Epistle to the Philippians, shows, had been his fellow-labourer, in these words: "With Clement and the rest of my fellow-labourers, whose names are in the book of life."

CHAPTER XVI.

The Epistle of Clement.

OF this Clement there is one epistle extant, acknowledged as genuine, of considerable length and of great merit, which he wrote in the name of the church at Rome, to that of Corinth, at the time when there was a dissension in the latter. This we know to have been publicly read for common benefit, in most of the churches, both in former times and in our own; and that at the time mentioned a sedition did take place at Corinth, is abundantly attested by Hegesippus.

CHAPTER XVII.

The persecution of the Christians under Domitian.

DOMITIAN, indeed, having exercised his cruelty against many, and unjustly slain no small number of noble and illustrious men at Rome, and having, without cause, punished vast numbers of honourable men with exile and the confiscation of their property, at length established himself as the successor of Nero, in his hatred and hostility to God. He was the second that raised a persecution against us, although his father Vespasian had attempted nothing to our prejudice.

CHAPTER XVIII.

Of John the Apostle, and the Revelation.

IN this persecution, it is handed down by tradition, that the apostle and evangelist John, who was yet living, in consequence of his testimony to the divine word, was condemned to dwell on the island of Patmos. Irenæus, indeed, in his fifth book against the heresies, where he speaks of the calculation formed on the epithet of Antichrist, in the abovementioned revelation of John, speaks in the following manner respecting him. " If, however, it were necessary to proclaim his name, (i. e. Antichrist,) openly at the present time, it would have been declared by him who saw the revelation, for it is not long since it was seen, but almost in our own generation, at the close of Domitian's reign." To such a degree, indeed, did the doctrine which we profess, flourish, that even historians that are very far from befriending our religion, have not hesitated to record this persecution and its martyrdoms in their histories. These also, have accurately noted the time, for it happened, according to them, in the fifteenth year of Domitian. At the same time, for professing Christ, Flavia Domitilla, the niece of Flavius Clemens, one of the consuls of Rome at that time, was transported with many others, by way of punishment, to the island of Pontia.

CHAPTER XIX.

Domitian commands the posterity of David to be slain.

But when the same Domitian had issued his orders, that the descendants of David should be slain according to an ancient tradition, some of the heretics accused the descendants of Judas, as the brother of our Saviour, according to the flesh, because they were of the family of David, and as such, also, were related to Christ. This is declared by Hegesippus as follows.

CHAPTER XX.

Of the relatives of our Lord.

There were yet living of the family of our Lord, the grandchildren of Judas, called the brother of our Lord, according to the flesh. These were reported as being of the family of David, and were brought to Domitian by the Evocatus. For this emperor was as much alarmed at the appearance of Christ as Herod. He put the question, whether they were of David's race, and they confessed that they were. He then asked them what property they had, or how much money they owned. And both of them answered, that they had between them only nine thousand denarii,* and this they had not in silver, but in the value of a piece of land, containing only thirty-nine acres; from which they raised their taxes and supported themselves by their own labour. Then they also began to show their hands, exhibiting the hardness of their bodies, and the callosity formed by incessant labour on their hands, as evidence of their own labour. When asked also, respecting Christ and his kingdom, what was its nature, and when and where it was to appear, they replied, " that it was not a temporal nor an earthly kingdom, but celestial and angelic; that it would appear at the end of the world, when coming in glory he would judge the quick and dead, and give to every one according to his works." Upon which, Domitian despising them, made no reply; but treating them with contempt, as simpletons, commanded them to be dismissed, and by a decree ordered the persecution to cease. Thus delivered, they ruled the churches, both as witnesses and relatives of the Lord. When peace was established, they continued living even to the times of Trajan." Such is the statement of Hegesippus. Tertullian also has mentioned Domitian thus: " Domitian had also once attempted the same against him, who was, in fact, a limb of Nero for cruelty; but I think, because he yet had some remains of reason, he very soon suppressed the persecution, even recalling those whom he had exiled. But after Domitian had reigned fifteen years, and Nerva succeeded to the government, the Roman senate decreed, that the honours of Domitian should be revoked, and that those who had been unjustly expelled, should return to their homes, and have their goods restored. This is the statement of the historians of the day. It was then also, that the apostle John returned from his banishment in Patmos, and took up his abode at Ephesus, according to an ancient tradition of the church.

* The Roman denarius was about the value of a Greek drachma, each fifteen cents nearly.

CHAPTER XXI.

Cerdon, the third bishop of Alexandria.

AFTER Nerva had reigned a little more than a year, he was succeeded by Trajan. It was in the first year of his reign, that Cerdon succeeded Avilius in the church of Alexandria, after the latter had governed it thirteen years. He was the third that held
the episcopate there since Annianus. During this time, Clement
was yet bishop of the Romans, who was also the third that held
the episcopate there after Paul and Peter; Linus being the first
and Anencletus next in order.

CHAPTER XXII.

Ignatius, the second bishop of Antioch.

ON the death of Evodius, who was the first bishop of Antioch,
Ignatius was appointed the second. Simeon also was the second
after the brother of our Lord, that had charge of the church at
Jerusalem about this time.

CHAPTER XXIII.

Narrative respecting the Apostle John.

ABOUT this time also, the beloved disciple of Jesus, John the
apostle and evangelist, still surviving, governed the churches in
Asia, after his return from exile on the island, and the death of
Domitian. But that he was still living until this time, it may suffice to prove, by the testimony of two witnesses. These, as main
taining sound doctrine in the church, may surely be regarded as
worthy of all credit: and such were Irenæus and Clement of Alexandria. Of these, the former, in the second book against heresies,

writes in the following manner: "And all the presbyters of Asia, that had conferred with John the disciple of our Lord, testify that John had delivered it to them; for he continued with them until the times of Trajan." And in the third book of the same work, he shows the same thing in the following words: "But the church in Ephesus also, which had been founded by Paul, and where John continued to abide until the times of Trajan, is a faithful witness of the apostolic tradition." Clement also, indicating the time, subjoins a narrative most acceptable to those who delight to hear what is excellent and profitable, in that discourse to which he gave the title, "What Rich Man is saved?" Taking therefore the book, read it where it contains a narrative like the following: "Listen to a story that is no fiction, but a real history, handed down and carefully preserved, respecting the apostle John. For after the tyrant was dead, coming from the isle of Patmos to Ephesus, he went also, when called, to the neighbouring regions of the Gentiles; in some to appoint bishops, in some to institute entire new churches, in others to appoint to the ministry some one of those that were pointed out by the Holy Ghost. When he came, therefore, to one of those cities, at no great distance, of which some also give the name, and had in other respects consoled his brethren, he at last turned towards the bishop ordained, (appointed,) and seeing a youth of fine stature, graceful countenance, and ardent mind, he said, 'Him I commend to you with all earnestness, in the presence of the church and of Christ.' The bishop having taken him and promised all, he repeated and testified the same thing, and then returned to Ephesus. The presbyter taking the youth home that was committed to him, educated, restrained, and cherished him, and at length baptized him. After this he relaxed exercising his former care and vigilance, as if he had now committed him to a perfect safeguard in the seal of the Lord. But certain idle, dissolute fellows, familiar with every kind of wickedness, unhappily attach themselves to him, thus prematurely freed from restraint. At first they lead him on by expensive entertainments. Then going out at night to plunder, they take him with them. Next, they encourage him to something greater, and gradually becoming accustomed to their ways in his enterprising spirit, like an unbridled and powerful steed that has struck out of the right way, biting the curb, he rushed with so much the greater impetuosity towards the preci- pice. At length renouncing the salvation of God, he contemplated no trifling offence, but having committed some great crime, since he was now once ruined, he expected to suffer equally with the rest. Taking, therefore, these same associates, and forming them into a band of robbers, he became their captain, surpassing them all in violence, blood, and cruelty. Time elapsed, and on a cer- tain occasion they send for John. The apostle, after appointing those other matters for which he came, said, ' Come, bishop, return me my deposite, which I and Christ committed to thee, in the pre- sence of the church over which thou dost preside.' The bishop at first, indeed, was confounded, thinking that he was insidiously charged for money which he had not received; and yet he could neither give credit respecting that which he had not, nor yet dis- believe John. But when he said, ' I demand the young man, and the soul of a brother,' the old man, groaning heavily and also weeping, said, ' He is dead.' ' How, and what death?' ' He is dead to God,' said he. ' He has turned out wicked and abandoned, and at last a robber; and now, instead of the church, he has be- set the mountain with a band like himself.' The apostle, on hearing this, tore his garment, and beating his head with great lamentation, said, ' I left a fine keeper of a brother's soul! But let a horse now be got ready, and some one to guide me on my way.' He rode as he was, away from the church, and coming to the country, was taken prisoner by the outguard of the banditti. He neither attempted, however, to flee, nor refused to be taken; but cried out, ' For this very purpose am I come; conduct me to your captain.' He, in the meantime stood waiting, armed as he was. But as he recognised John advancing towards him, overcome with shame he turned about to flee. The apostle, however, pursued him with all his might, forgetful of his age, and crying out, ' Why dost thou fly, my son, from me, thy father; thy defenceless, aged father? Have compassion on me, my son; fear not. Thou still hast hope of life. I will intercede with Christ for thee. Should it be necessary, I will cheerfully suffer death for thee, as Christ for us. I will give my life for thine. Stay; believe Christ hath sent me.' Hearing this, he at first stopped with downcast looks. Then threw away his arms; then trembling, lamented bitterly, and embracing the old man as he came up, attempted to plead for himself with his lamentations, as much as he was able; as if baptized a second time with his own tears, and only concealing his right hand. But the apostle pledging himself, and solemnly assuring him, that he had found pardon for him in his prayers at the hands of Christ, praying, on his bended knees, and kissing his right hand as cleansed from all iniquity, conducted him back again to the church. Then supplicating with frequent prayers, contending with constant fastings, and softening down his mind with various consolatory declarations, he did not leave him as it is said, until he had restored him to the church. Affording a powerful example of true repentance, and a great evidence of a regeneration, a trophy of a visible resurrection."

CHAPTER XXIV.

The order of the Gospels.

THESE extracts from Clement may here suffice, both for the sake of the history and the benefit of the readers. Let us now also show the undisputed writings of the same apostle. And of these his gospel, so well known in the churches throughout the world, must first of all be acknowledged as genuine. That it is, however, with good reason, placed the fourth in order by the ancients, may be made evident in the following manner. Those inspired and truly pious men, the apostles of our Saviour, as they were most pure in their life, and adorned with every kind of virtue in their minds, but common in their language, relying upon the divine and wonderful energy granted them, they neither knew how, nor attempted to propound the doctrines of their master, with the art and refinement of composition. But employing only the demonstration of the divine Spirit, working with them, and the wonder-working power of Christ, displayed through them, they proclaimed the knowledge of the kingdom of heaven throughout the world. They bestowed but little care upon the study of style, and this they did, because they were aided by a co-operation greater than that of men. Paul, indeed, who was the most able of all in the preparations of style, and who was most powerful in sentiments, committed nothing more to writing than a few very short epistles. And this too, although he had innumerable mysterious matters that he might have communicated, as he had attained even to the view of the third heavens, had been taken up to the very paradise of God, and had been honoured to hear the unutterable words there. The other followers of our Lord were also not ignorant of such things, as the twelve apostles, and the seventy, together with many others; yet of all the disciples, Matthew and John are the only ones that have left us recorded comments, and even they, tradition says, undertook it from necessity. Matthew also having first proclaimed the gospel in Hebrew, when on the point of going also to other nations, committed it to writing in his native tongue, and thus supplied the want of his presence to them, by his writings. But after Mark and Luke had already published their gospels, they say, that John, who during all this time was proclaiming the gospel without writing, at length proceeded to write it on the following occasion. The three gospels previously written, having been distributed among all, and also handed to him, they say that he admitted them, giving his testimony to their truth; but that there was only wanting in the narrative the account of the things done by Christ, among the first of his deeds, and at the commencement of the gospel. And this was the truth. For it is evident that the other three evangelists only wrote the deeds of our Lord for one year after the imprisonment of John the Baptist, and intimated this in the very beginning of their history. For after the fasting of forty days, and the consequent temptation, Matthew indeed specifies the time of his history, in these words: " But hearing that John was delivered up, he returned from Judea into Galilee." Mark in like manner writes: " But after John was delivered up, Jesus came into Galilee?" And Luke, before he commenced the deeds of Jesus, in much the same way designates the time saying, "Herod thus added, yet this wickedness above all he had committed, and that he shut up John in prison." For these reasons the apostle John, it is said, being entreated to undertake it, wrote the account of the time not recorded by the former evangelists, and the deeds done by our Saviour, which they have passed by, (for these were the events that occurred before the imprisonment of John,) and this very fact is intimated by him, when he says, "this beginning of miracles Jesus made;" and then proceeds to make mention of the Baptist, in the midst of our Lord's deeds, as John was at that time "baptising at Ænon near Salim." He plainly also shows this in the words: "John was not yet cast into prison." The apostle, therefore, in his gospel, gives the deeds of Jesus before the Baptist was cast into prison, but the other three evangelists mention the circumstances after that event. One who attends to these circumstances, can no longer entertain the opinion, that the gospels are at variance with each other, as the gospel of John comprehends the first events of Christ, but the others, the history that took place at the latter part of the time. It is probable, therefore, that for these reasons John has passed by in silence the genealogy of our Lord, because it was written by Matthew and Luke, but that he commenced with the doctrine of the divinity, as a part reserved for him, by the divine Spirit, as if for a superior. Let this suffice to be said respecting the gospel of John. The causes that induced Mark to write his, have already been stated. But Luke also in the commencement of his narrative, premises the cause which led him to write, showing that many others, having rashly undertaken to compose a narration of matters that he had already completely ascertained, in order to free us from the uncertain suppositions of others, in his own gospel, he delivered the certain account of those things, that he himself had fully received from his intimacy and stay with Paul, and also, his intercourse with the other apostles. But this may suffice respecting these. At a more proper time we shall endeavour also to state, by a reference to some of the ancient writers, what others have said respecting the sacred books. But besides the gospel of John, his first epistle is acknowledged without dispute, both by those of the present day, and also by the ancients. The other two epistles, however, are disputed. The opinions respecting the revelation are still greatly divided. But we shall, in due time, give a judgment on this point, also from the testimony of the ancients.

CHAPTER XXV.

The sacred Scriptures acknowledged as genuine, and those that are not.

THIS appears also to be the proper place, to give a summary statement of the books of the New Testament already mentioned. And here, among the first, must be placed the holy quaternion of the gospels; these are followed by " The book of the Acts of the Apostles;" after this must be mentioned the epistles of Paul, which are followed by the acknowledged first Epistle of John, as also the first of Peter, to be admitted in like manner. After these, are to be placed, if proper, the Revelation of John, concerning which we shall offer the different opinions in due time. These, then, are acknowledged as genuine. Among the disputed books, although they are well known and approved by many, is reputed, that called the Epistle of James and Jude. Also the " Second Epistle of Peter," and those called " The Second and Third of John," whether they are of the evangelist or of some other of the same name. Among the spurious must be numbered, both the books called " The Acts of Paul," and that called " Pastor," and " The Revelation of Peter." Beside these, the books called " The Epistle of Barnabas," and what are called " The Institutions of the Apostles." Moreover, as I said before, if it should appear right, " The Revelation of John," which some, as before said, reject, but others rank among the genuine. But there are also some who number among these, the gospel according to the Hebrews, with which those of the Hebrews that have received Christ are particularly delighted These may be said to be all concerning which there is any dispute. We have, however, necessarily subjoined here a catalogue of these also, in order to distinguish those that are true, genuine, and well authenticated writings, from those others which are not only not imbodied in the canon, but likewise disputed, notwithstanding that they are recognized by most ecclesiastical writers. Thus we may have it in our power to know both these books, and those that are adduced by the heretics under the name of the apostles, such, viz., as compose the gospels of Peter, Thomas, and Matthew, and others beside them, or such as contain the Acts of the Apostles, by Andrew, and John, and others, of which no one of those writers in the ecclesiastical succession has condescended to make any mention in his works; and indeed, the character of the style itself is very different from that of the apostles, and the sentiments, and the purport of those things that are advanced in them, deviating as far as possible from sound orthodoxy, evidently proves they are the fictions of heretical men; whence they are to be ranked not only among the spurious writings, but are to be rejected as altogether absurd and impious. Let us now proceed to the continuation of our history.

CHAPTER XXVI.

Menander the impostor.

MENANDER, who succeeded Simon Magus, exhibited himself in his conduct an instrument of diabolical wickedness, not inferior to the former. He also, was a Samaritan, and having made no less progress in his impostures than his master, revelled in still more arrogant pretensions to miracles; saying that he was in truth the Saviour, once sent from the invisible worlds for the salvation of men; teaching also, that no one could overcome even the very angels that formed the heavens in any other way, than by being first initiated into the magic discipline imparted by him, and by the baptism conferred by him for this purpose. Of which, those who were deemed worthy would obtain perpetual immortality in this very life, being no more subject to death, but continuing here the same, would be exempt from old age, and be in fact immortal. This account may be easily confirmed from Irenæus; but Justin, in the same place where he mentions Simeon, also adds the narrative respecting this one as follows: "But we know that Menander who was a Samaritan of the village Caparattæa, becoming a disciple of Simeon, and likewise stimulated by the dæmons, came to Antioch, and deceived many by his magic arts. He persuaded those that followed him, that they should never die. And there are now some of his followers that make a profession of the same thing. It was indeed, a diabolical artifice, by means of such impostors assuming the title of Christians, to evince so much zeal in defaming the great mystery of piety by magic arts, and to rend asunder by these means the doctrines of the church respecting the immortality of the soul, and the resurrection of the dead. Those, however, who called these their Saviours, fell away from solid hope.

CHAPTER XXVII.

The Heresy of the Ebionites.

THE spirit of wickedness, however, being unable to shake some in their love of Christ, and yet finding them susceptible of his impressions in other respects, brought them over to his purposes. These are properly called Ebionites * by the ancients, as those who cherished low and mean opinions of Christ. For they considered him a plain and common man, and justified only by his advances in virtue, and that he was born of the Virgin Mary, by natural generation. With them the observance of the law was altogether necessary, as if they could not be saved, only by faith in Christ and a corresponding life. Others, however, besides these, but of the same name, indeed avoided the absurdity of the opinions maintained by the former, not denying that the Lord was born of the Virgin by the Holy Ghost, and yet in like

* The word *ebion*, in Hebrew, signifying poor, seems to allude either to the opinions or the condition of this sect.

manner, not acknowledging his pre-existence, though he was God, the word and wisdom, they turned aside into the same irreligion, as with the former they evinced great zeal to observe the ritual service of the law. These, indeed, thought on the one hand that all the epistles of the apostles ought to be rejected, calling him an apostate from the law, but on the other, only using the gospel according to the Hebrews, they esteem the others as of but little value. They also observe the Sabbath and other discipline of the Jews, just like them, but on the other hand, they also celebrate the Lord's days very much like us, in commemoration of his resurrection. Whence, in consequence of such a course, they have also received their epithet, the name of Ebionites, exhibiting the poverty of their intellect. For it is thus that the Hebrews call a poor man.

CHAPTER XXVIII.

Cerinthus the Heresiarch.

ABOUT the same time, we have understood, appeared Cerinthus, the leader of another heresy. Caius, whose words we quoted above, in " The Disputation" attributed to him, writes thus respecting him : " But Cerinthus, by means of revelations which he pretended were written by a great apostle, also falsely pretended to wonderful things, as if they were showed him by angels, asserting, that after the resurrection there would be an earthly kingdom of Christ, and that the flesh, i. e. men, again inhabiting Jerusalem, would be subject to desires and pleasures. Being also an enemy to the divine Scriptures, with a view to deceive men, he said that there would be a space of a thousand years for celebrating nuptial festivals." Dionysius also, who obtained the episcopate of Alexandria in our day, in the second book " On Promises," where he says some things as if received by ancient tradition, makes mention of the same man, in these words : " But it is highly probable that Cerinthus, the same that established the heresy that bears his name, designedly affixed the name (of John) to his own forgery. For one of the doctrines that he taught was, that Christ would have an earthly kingdom. And as he was a voluptuary, and altogether sensual, he conjectured that it would consist in those things that he craved in the gratification of appetite and lust; i. e. in eating, drinking, and marrying, or in such things whereby he supposed these sensual pleasures might be presented in more decent expressions; viz. in festivals, sacrifices, and the slaying of victims." Thus far Dionysius. But Irenæus, in his first book against heresies, adds certain false doctrines of the man, though kept more secret, and gives a history in his third book, that deserves to be recorded, as received by tradition from Polycarp. He says that John the apostle once entered a bath to wash; but ascertaining Cerinthus was within, he leaped out of the place, and fled from the door, not enduring to enter under the same roof with him, and exhorted those with him to do the same, saying, " let us flee, lest the bath fall in, as long as Cerinthus, that enemy of the truth, is within."

CHAPTER XXIX.

Nicolaus and his followers.

ABOUT this time, also, for a very short time, arose the heresy of those salled Nicolaites, of which also mention is made in the revelation of John. These boasted of Nicolaus as their founder, one of those deacons who with Stephen were appointed by the apostles to minister unto the poor. Clement of Alexandria, in the third book of his Stromata, relates the following respecting him, " Having a beautiful wife, and being reproached after the ascension of our Lord, with jealousy by the apostles, he conducted her into the midst of them, and permitted any one that wished to marry her. This they say was perfectly consistent with that expression of his, " that every one ought to abuse his own flesh " And thus those that adopted his heresy, following both

this example and expression literally, rush headlong into fornication without shame. I have ascertained, however, that Nicolaus
lived with no other woman than the one to whom he was married, but that his daughters continued in the state of virginity
to advanced life; that his son also remained uncorrupt. It
would appear, therefore, from these facts, that the introduction
of his wife into the midst of the apostles, on account of jealousy,
was rather the suppression of passion. And, therefore, abstinence
from those pleasures that are so eagerly pursued, was inculcated
by the expression, ' we ought to abuse the flesh.' For I do not
think, that according to the saying of our Lord, he wished to
serve two masters, the flesh and the Lord. They indeed say
that Matthew thus taught to fight against and to abuse the flesh,
not to give way to any thing for the sake of pleasure, and to cultivate the spirit by faith and knowledge." But it may suffice to
have said thus much concerning those who have attempted to
mutilate the truth, and which again became extinct, sooner than
said.

CHAPTER XXX.

The apostles that lived in marriage.

CLEMENT indeed, whose words we have just cited, after the
above mentioned facts, next gives a statement of those apostles
that continued in the marriage state, on account of those who set
marriage aside. " And will they," says he, " reject even the apostles ! Peter and Philip, indeed, had children, Philip, also gave his
daughters in marriage to husbands, and Paul does not demur in
a certain epistle to mention his own wife, whom he did not take
about with him, in order to expedite his ministry the better."
Since however, we have mentioned these, we shall not regret to
subjoin another history worthy of record, from the same author
continued in the seventh book of the same work, Stromateus.
" They relate," says he, " that the blessed Peter, seeing his own
wife led away to execution, was delighted, on account of her

calling and return to her country, and that he cried to her in a consolatory and encouraging voice, addressing her by name: "Oh thou, remember the Lord!" Such was the marriage of these blessed ones, and such was their perfect affection towards their dearest friends, and this account we have given in its proper place, as well adapted to the subject.

CHAPTER XXXI.

The death of John and Philip.

THE time and manner of the death of Paul and Peter, and also the place where their bodies were interred after their departure from this life, has already been stated by us. The time when John died, has also, in some measure, been mentioned, but the place of his burial is shown from the epistle of Polycrates, who was bishop of the church of Ephesus, which epistle he wrote to Victor, bishop of Rome, and at the same time makes mention of him (John) and the apostle Philip, and his daughters, thus: "For in Asia, also, mighty luminaries have fallen asleep, which shall rise again at the last day, at the appearance of the Lord, when he shall come with glory from heaven, and shall gather again all the saints. Philip, one of the twelve apostles who sleeps in Hierapolis, and his two aged virgin daughters. Another of his daughters, who lived in the holy Spirit, rests at Ephesus. Moreover, John, that rested on the bosom of our Lord, who was a priest that bore the sacerdotal plate, and martyr and teacher, he, also, rests at Ephesus." This may suffice as to their death; and in the dialogue of Caius, which we mentioned a little before, Proclus, against whom he wrote his disputation, coinciding with what we have already advanced concerning the death of Philip and his daughters, speaks thus: "After this there were four prophetesses the daughters of Philip at Hierapolis in Asia, whose tomb, and that of their father, are to be seen there." Such is his statement. But Luke, in the Acts of the Apostles, mentions the daughters of Philip, tarrying in Cesarea of Judea, and as endued with the gift of prophecy, in these words: "We came to Cesarea, and having entered the house of Philip the evangelist, one of the seven, we abode with him. But he had four virgin daughters that prophesied." But as we have thus set forth what has come to our knowledge respecting the apostles and the apostolical times, as also respecting the sacred books that they have left us, both the disputed writings, though publicly used by many in most of the churches, and those that are altogether spurious, and far removed from the correct doctrine of the apostles, let us now proceed to our history in order.

CHAPTER XXXII.

The martyrdom of Simeon, bishop of Jerusalem.

AFTER Nero and Domitian, we have also been informed, that in the reign of the emperor, whose times we are now recording, there was a partial persecution excited throughout the cities, in consequence of a popular insurrection. In this we have understood, also, that Simeon died as a martyr, who, we have shown, was appointed the second bishop of the church at Jerusalem. To this the same Hegesippus bears testimony, whose words we have already so often quoted. This author, speaking of certain heretics, superadds, that Simeon indeed, about this time having borne the accusation of Christian, although he was tortured for several days, and astonished both the judge and his attendants in the highest degree, terminated his life with sufferings like those of our Lord. But it is best to hear the writer himself, who gives the account as follows: "Of these heretics," says he, "some reported Simeon the son of Cleophas, as a descendant of David, and a Christian; and thus he suffered as a martyr, when he was an hundred and twenty years old, in the reign of the emperor Trajan, and the presidency of the consular Atticus. The same author says, that as search was made for the Jews that were of the tribe of David, his accusers, as if they were descended from this family, were taken in custody. One might reasonably assert that this Simeon was among the witnesses that bore testimony to what they had both heard and seen of our Lord, if we are to judge by the length of his life, and the fact that the gospels make mention of Mary the daughter of Cleophas, whose son Simeon was, as we have already shown. But the same historian says, that there were others, the offspring of one of those considered brothers of the Lord, whose name was Judas, and that these lived until the same reign after their profession of Christ, and the testimony under Domitian beforementioned. He writes thus: " There are also, those that take the lead of the whole church as martyrs, even the kindred of our Lord. And when profound peace was established throughout the church, they continued to the days of the emperor Trajan, until the time that the abovementioned Simeon, the relative of our Lord, being the son of Cleophas, was waylaid by the heresies, and also himself accused for the same cause, under Atticus, who was of similar dignity. After he was tormented many days, he died a martyr, with such firmness, that all were amazed, even the president himself, that a man of a hundred and twenty years should bear such tortures. He was at last ordered to be crucified." The same author, relating the events of the times, also says, that the church continued until then as a pure and uncorrupt virgin; whilst if there were any at all, that attempted to pervert the sound doctrine of the saving gospel, they were yet skulking in dark retreats; but when the sacred choir of apostles became extinct, and the generation of those that had been privileged to hear their inspired wisdom, had passed away, then also the combinations of impious error arose by the fraud and delusions of false teachers. These also, as there was none of the apostles left, henceforth attempted, without shame, to preach their false doctrine against the gospel of truth. Such is the statement of Hegesippus. Let us, however, proceed in our history

CHAPTER XXXIII.

Trajan forbids the Christians to be sought after.

So great a persecution was then commenced against our faith, in most places, that Plinius Secundus, one of the most distinguished governors, moved by the number of martyrs, communicated with the emperor respecting the multitudes that were put to death for their faith. At the same time he informed him, that as far as he had ascertained, they did nothing wicked or contrary to the laws; except that they rose with the morning sun, and sang a hymn to Christ as to a god. But that adultery, and murder, and criminal excesses like these, were totally abhorred by them; and that in all things they acted according to the laws. To this, Trajan in reply, issued a decree, the purport of which was, that no search should be made after those that were Christians, but when they presented themselves they should be punished. On this, the persecution in some measure seemed abated, in its extreme violence, but there were no less pretexts left for those that wished to harass us. Sometimes the people, sometimes the rulers of different places, would waylay us to ensnare us. So that without an obvious persecution, there were partial persecutions in the provinces, and many of the faithful endured martyrdoms of various kinds. We have taken the account from the Apology of Tertullian, in Latin, mentioned above, of which, the translation is as follows: " And indeed," says he, " we have found that the inquisition against us is prohibited. For Plinius Secundus, who was governor of the province, having condemned certain Christians, and deprived them of their dignity, was confounded by the great number, and in doubt what course he should pursue. He communicated, therefore, the fact to Trajan the emperor, saying, that with the exception they were not willing to sacrifice, he found nothing criminal in them. He stated also this, that the Christians arose with the sun, and sang to Christ as to a god; and that for the purpose of keeping their discipline, they prohibited adultery, murder, overreaching, fraud, and all crimes like them. To this, Trajan wrote in reply, that the Christians should not be inquired after, but when they presented themselves they should be punished." And such were the circumstances attending these events.

CHAPTER XXXIV.

Euarestus, the fourth bishop of the church at Rome.

IN the third year of the abovementioned reign, Clement, bishop of Rome, committed the episcopal charge to Euarestus, and departed this life, after superintending the preaching of the divine word nine years.

CHAPTER XXXV.

Justus, the third bishop of Jerusalem.

SIMEON also having died in the manner shown above, a certain Jew named Justus succeeded him in the episcopate of Jerusalem. As there were great numbers from the circumcision, that came over to the Christian faith at that time, of whom Justus was one.

CHAPTER XXXVI.

The epistles of Ignatius.

ABOUT this time flourished Polycarp in Asia, an intimate disciple of the apostles, who received the episcopate of the church at Smyrna, at the hands of the eyewitnesses and servants of the Lord. At this time, also, Papias was well known as bishop of the church at Hierapolis, a man well skilled in all manner of learning, and well acquainted with the Scriptures. Ignatius, also, who is celebrated by many even to this day, as the successor of Peter at Antioch, was the second that obtained the episcopal office there. Tradition says that he was sent away from Syria to Rome, and was cast as food to wild beasts, on account of his testimony to Christ. And being carried through Asia under a most rigid custody, fortified the different churches in the cities were he tarried, by his discourses and exhortations; particularly to caution them more against the heresies which even then were springing up and prevailing. He exhorted them to adhere firmly to the tradition of the apostles; which, for the sake of greater security, he deemed it necessary to attest by committing it to writing. When, therefore, he came to Smyrna, where Polycarp was, he wrote one epistle, viz. that to the church of Ephesus, in which he mentions its pastor Onesimus. Another, also, to the church in Magnesia, which is situated on the Meander, in which again he makes mention of Damas the bishop. Another, also, to the church of the Trallians, of which he states that Polybius was then bishop. To these must be added, the epistle to the church at Rome, which also contains an exhortation, not to disappoint him in his ardent hope, by refusing to endure martyrdom. Of these, it is worth while also to subjoin very short extracts, by way of specimen. He writes, therefore, in the following manner: " From Syria to Rome, I am contending with wild beasts by land and sea, by night and day, being tied to ten leopards, the number of the military band, who, even when treated with kindness, only behave with greater ferocity. But in the midst of these iniquities, I am learning. Yet I am not justified on this account. May I be benefited by those beasts that are in readiness for me, which I also pray may be quickly found for me, which also I shall entice and flatter to devour me quickly, and not to be afraid of me as of some whom they did not touch. But, should they perchance be unwilling, I will force them. Pardon me; I know what advantage it will confer. Now I begin to be a disciple. Nothing, whether of things visible or invisible, excites my ambition, as long as I can gain Christ. Whether fire, or the cross, the assault of wild beasts, the tearing asunder of my bones, the breaking of my limbs, the bruising of my whole body, let the tortures of the devil all assail me, if I do but gain Christ Jesus." This he wrote from the abovementioned city to the aforesaid churches. But after he had left Smyrna, he wrote an exhortation from Troas to those in Philadelphia, and particularly to Polycarp, who was bishop there, whom he designates as an apostolical man and as a good and faithful shepherd, commends the flock of Antioch to him, requesting him to exercise a diligent oversight of the church. Writing to the Smyrnians, he has also employed words respecting Jesus, I know not whence they are taken, to the following effect. " But I know and believe that he was seen after the resurrection, and that he said to those that came to Peter, ' take, handle me, and see that I am not an incorporeal spirit,' and they immediately touched him and believed." Irenæus, also, knew his martyrdom, and makes mention of his epistles, as follows: " As some one of our faith has said, who was condemned to the wild beasts, ' I am the food of God, and am ground by the teeth of wild beasts that I may be found pure bread.' " Polycarp also makes mention of these same epistles in the Epistle to the Philippians, that bears his name, in the following words: " I exhort you, therefore, all to yield obedience, and to exercise all the patience which you see with your own eyes, not only in the blessed martyrs Ignatius and Rufus, and Zosimus, but likewise in others of your fellow-citizens, as also in Paul and the other apostles, being persuaded that all these did not run in vain, but in faith and righteousness, and that they are gone to the place destined for them by the Lord, for whom also they suffered. For they did not love the world that now is, but him that died for us, and that was raised again by God." And afterwards he writes: " You have also written to me, both you and Ignatius, that if any one is going to Syria, he should carry your letters thither, which shall be done if I find a suitable opportunity, either by me or the one that I send on this errand to you. The epistles of Ignatius that were sent to us by him, I have sent you at your request, and they are appended to this epistle, from which you will be able to derive great benefit. for they comprise faith, and patience, and all edification pertaining to our Lord." Thus much respecting Ignatius. But he was succeeded in the episcopal office at Antioch by Heros

CHAPTER XXXVII.

The preaching evangelists that were yet living in that age.

Of those that flourished in these times, Quadratus is said to have been distinguished for his prophetical gifts. There were many others, also, noted in these times, who held the first rank in the apostolic succession. These, as the holy disciples of such men, also built up the churches where foundations had been previously laid in every place by the apostles. They augmented the means of promulgating the gospel more and more, and spread the seeds of salvation and of the heavenly kingdom throughout the world far and wide. For the most of the disciples at that time, animated with a more ardent love of the divine word, had first fulfilled the Saviour's precept by distributing their substance to the needy. Afterwards leaving their country, they performed the office of evangelists to those who had not yet heard the faith, whilst with a noble ambition to proclaim Christ, they also delivered to them the books of the holy gospels. After laying the foundation of the faith in foreign parts as the particular object of their mission, and after appointing others as shepherds of the flocks, and committing to these the care of those that had been recently introduced, they went again to other regions and nations, with the grace and co-operation of God. The holy Spirit also, wrought many wonders as yet through them, so that as soon as the gospel was heard, men voluntarily in crowds, and eagerly, embraced the true faith with their whole minds. As it is impossible for us to give the numbers of the individuals that became pastors or evangelists, during the first immediate succession from the apostles in the churches throughout the world, we have only recorded those by name in our history, of whom we have received the traditional account as it is delivered in the various comments on the apostolic doctrine, still extant.

CHAPTER XXXVIII.

The Epistle of Clement, and those that are falsely ascribed to him.

WE may mention as an instance what Ignatius has said in the epistles we have cited, and Clement in that universally received by all, which he wrote in the name of the church at Rome to that of Corinth. In which, after giving many sentiments taken from the Epistle to the Hebrews, and also, literally quoting the words, he most clearly shows that this work is by no means a late production. Whence it is probable that this was also numbered with the other writings of the apostles. For as Paul had addressed the Hebrews in the language of his country; some say that the evangelist Luke, others that Clement, translated the epistle. Which also appears more like the truth, as the epistle of Clement and that to the Hebrews, preserve the same features of style and phraseology, and because the sentiments in both these works are not very different. It should also be observed, that there is a second epistle ascribed to Clement; but we know not that this is as highly approved as the former, and know not that it has been in use with the ancients. There are also other writings reported to be his, verbose and of great length. Lately, and some time ago, those were produced that contain the dialogues of Peter and Apion, of which, however, not a syllable is recorded by the primitive church. For they do not preserve the pure impress of apostolic orthodoxy. The epistle, therefore, of Clement, that is acknowledged as genuine is evident. But sufficient has been said on the writings of Ignatius and Polycarp.

CHAPTER XXXIX.

The writings of Papias

THERE are said to be five books of Papias, which bear the title " Interpretation of our Lord's Declarations." Irenæus also,

makes mention of these as the only works written by him, in the
following terms: "These things are attested by Papias, who was
John's hearer and the associate of Polycarp, an ancient writer,
who mentions them in the fourth book of his works. For he has
written a work in five books." So far Irenæus. But Papias
himself, in the preface to his discourses, by no means asserts that
he was a hearer and an eye-witness of the holy apostles, but
informs us that he received the doctrines of faith from their intimate friends, which he states in the following words: "But I
shall not regret to subjoin to my interpretations, also for your
benefit, whatsoever I have at any time accurately ascertained
and treasured up in my memory, as I have received it from the
elders, and have recorded it in order to give additional confirma
tion to the truth, by my testimony. For I have never, like many,
delighted to hear those that tell many things, but those that teach
the truth, neither those that record foreign precepts, but those
that are given from the Lord, to our faith, and that came from
the truth itself. But if I met with any one who had been a
follower of the elders any where, I made it a point to inquire
what were the declarations of the elders. What was said by
Andrew, Peter or Philip. What by Thomas, James, John, Matthew, or any other of the disciples of our Lord. What was said
by Aristion, and the presbyter John, disciples of the Lord; for I
do not think that I derived so much benefit from books as from
the living voice of those that are still surviving." Where it is
also proper to observe the name of John is twice mentioned.
The former of which he mentions with Peter and James and
Matthew, and the other apostles; evidently meaning the evangelist. But in a separate point of his discourse he ranks the
other John, with the rest not included in the number of apostles, placing Aristion before him. He distinguishes him plainly
by the name of presbyter. So that it is here proved that the
statement of those is true, who assert there were two of the
same name in Asia, that there were also two tombs in Ephesus.
and that both are called John's even to this day; which it is
particularly necessary to observe. For it is probable that the
second, if it be not allowed that it was the first, saw the revela-

tion ascribed to John. And the same Papias, of whom we now speak, professes to have received the declarations of the apostles from those that were in company with them, and says also that he was a hearer of Aristion and the presbyter John. For as he has often mentioned them by name, he also gives their statements in his own works. These matters, I trust, have not been uselessly adduced. But it may be important also to subjoin other declarations to these passages from Papias, in which he gives certain wonderful accounts, together with other matters that he seems to have received by tradition. That the apostle Philip continued at Hierapolis, with his daughters, has been already stated above. But we must now show how Papias, coming to them, received a wonderful account from the daughters of Philip. For he writes that in his time there was one raised from the dead. Another wonderful event happened respecting Justus, surnamed Barsabas, who, though he drank a deadly poison, experienced nothing injurious through the grace of the Lord. This same Justus is mentioned in the book of Acts, after the resurrection, as the one over whom, together with Matthew, the holy apostles prayed, in order to fill up their number, by casting lots, to supply the place of Judas the traitor. The passage is as follows ; " And they placed two, Joseph, called Barsabas, who was surnamed Justus and Matthias. And having prayed, they said." The same historian also gives other accounts, which he says he adds as received by him from unwritten tradition, likewise certain strange parables of our Lord, and of his doctrine and some other matters rather too fabulous. In these he says there would be a certain millennium after the resurrection, and that there would be a corporeal reign of Christ on this very earth ; which things he appears to have imagined, as if they were authorized by the apostolic narrations, not understanding correctly those matters which they propounded mystically in their representations. For he was very limited in his comprehension, as is evident from his discourses ; yet he was the cause why most of the ecclesiastical writers, urging the antiquity of the man, were carried away by a similar opinion ; as, for instance, Irenaus, or any other that adopted such sentiments. He has also inserted in his work other accounts given by the abovementioned Aristion, respecting our Lord, as also the traditions of the Presbyter John, to which referring those that are desirous of learning them, we shall now subjoin to the extracts from him, already given, a tradition which he sets forth concerning Mark, who wrote the gospel in the following words: "And John the Presbyter also said this, Mark being the interpeter of Peter whatsoever he recorded he wrote with great accuracy, but not however, in the order in which it was spoken or done by our Lord, for he neither heard nor followed our Lord, but as before said, he was in company with Peter, who gave him such instruction as was necessary, but not to give a history of our Lord's discourses: wherefore Mark has not erred in any thing, by writing some things as he has recorded them; for he was carefully attentive to one thing, not to pass by any thing that he heard, or to state any thing falsely in these accounts." Such is the account of Papias, respecting Mark. Of Matthew he has stated as follows : " Matthew composed his history in the Hebrew dialect*, and every one translated it as he was able." The same author (Papias) made use of testimonies from the first epistle of John, and likewise from that of Peter. He also gives another history of a woman, who had been accused of many sins before the Lord, which is also contained in the gospel according to the Hebrews. And this may be noted as a necessary addition to what we have before stated.

* The author here, doubtless, means the Syro-Chaldaic, which is sometimes in Scripture, and primitive writers, called **Hebrew.**

BOOK IV.

CHAPTER I.

The bishops of Rome and Alexandria, in the reign of Trajan.

ABOUT the twelfth year of the reign of Trajan, the bishop of the church of Alexandria, who was mentioned by us a little before, departed this life. Primus was the fourth from the apostles to whom the functions of the office were there allotted. At the same time also, after Euarestus had completed the eighth year as bishop of Rome, he was succeeded in the episcopal office by Alexander, the fifth in the succession from Peter and Paul.

CHAPTER II.

The calamities of the Jews about this time.

BUT the doctrines of our Saviour, and the church flourishing from day to day, continued to receive constant accessions. But the calamities of the Jews also continued to grow with one accumulation of evil upon another. The emperor was now advancing into the eighteenth year of his reign, and another commotion of the Jews being raised, he destroyed a very great number of them. For in Alexandria and the rest of Egypt, and also in Cyrene, as if actuated by some terrible and tempestuous spirit, they rushed upon seditious measures against the Greeks of the same place. Having increased the insurrection to a great extent, they excited no inconsiderable war the following year, when Lupus was governor of all Egypt. And in the first conflict, indeed, it happened that they prevailed over the Greeks; who, retreating into Alexandria, took and destroyed the Jews that were found in the city,

But the Jews of Cyrene being deprived of their assistance, after laying waste the country of Egypt, also proceeded to destroy its districts, under their leader Lucuas. Against these the emperor sent Marcius Turbo, with foot and naval forces, besides cavalry. He, however, protracting the war a long time against them in many battles, slew many thousand Jews, not only of Cyrene, but also of Egypt that had joined them, together with their leader Lucuas. But the emperor suspecting that the Jews in Mesopotamia would also make an attack upon those there, ordered Lucius Quietus to clear the province of them, who also led an army against them, and slew a great multitude of them. Upon which victory, he was appointed governor of Judea by the emperor. These things are recorded by the Greek writers of the day, in nearly the same words.

CHAPTER III.

The authors that wrote in the defence of the faith, in the reign of Adrian.

But Trajan having held the sovereignty for twenty years, wanting six months, is succeeded in the imperial office by Ælius Hadrian. To him, Quadratus addressed a discourse, as an apology for the religion that we profess; because certain malicious persons attempted to harass our brethren. The work is still in the hands of some of the brethren, as also in our own, from which any one may see evident proof, both of the understanding of the man, and of his apostolic faith.

This writer shows the antiquity of the age in which he lived, in these passages: "The deeds of our Saviour," says he, " were always before you, for they were true miracles; those that were healed, those that were raised from the dead, who were seen, not only when healed and when raised, but were always present. They remained living a long time, not only whilst our Lord was on earth, but likewise when he had left the earth. So that some of them have also lived to our own times." Such was Quadratus.

Aristides, also, a man faithfully devoted to the religion we profess, like Quadratus, has left to posterity a defence of the faith, addressed to Adrian. This work is also preserved by a great number, even to the present day.

CHAPTER IV

The bishops of Alexandria and Rome, under the same emperor.

But in the third year of the same reign, Alexander, bishop of Rome, died, having completed the tenth year of his ministrations. Xystus was his successor; and about the same time Primus dying, in the twelfth year of the episcopate, was succeeded by Justus.

CHAPTER V.

The bishops of Jerusalem, from the period of our Saviour until these times.

We have not ascertained in any way, that the times of the bishops in Jerusalem have been regularly preserved on record, for tradition says that they all lived but a very short time. So much, however, have I learned from writers, that down to the invasion of the Jews under Adrian, there were fifteen successions of bishops in that church, all which, they say, were Hebrews from the first, and received the knowledge of Christ pure and unadulterated; so that, in the estimation of those who were able to judge they were well approved, and worthy of the episcopal office. For at that time the whole church under them, consisted of faithful Hebrews who continued from the time of the apostles, until the siege that then took place. The Jews then again revolting from the Romans, were subdued and captured, after very severe conflicts In the mean time, as the bishops from the circumcision tailed, it may be necessary now to recount them in order, from the first. The first, then, was James called the brother of our Lord; after whom, the second was Simeon, the third Justus, the fourth Zaccheus, the fifth Tobias, the sixth Benjamin, the seventh John, the eighth Matthew, the ninth Philip, the tenth Seneca, the eleventh Justus, the twelfth Levi, the thirteenth Ephres, the fourteenth Joseph, and finally, the fifteenth Judas. These are all the bishops of Jerusalem that filled up the time from the apostles until the abovementioned time, all of the circumcision. And Adrian being now in the twelfth year of his reign, Xystus, who had now completed the tenth year of his episcopate, was succeeded by Telesphorus the seventh in succession from the apostles. In the mean time, however, after the lapse of a year and some months, Eumenes succeeded, the sixth in order in the episcopate of Alexandria, his predecessor having filled the office eleven years.

CHAPTER VI.

The last siege of the Jews, under Adrian.

As the revolt of the Jews again proceeded to many and great excesses, Rufus, who was lieutenant-governor of Judea, having received an augmentation of forces from the emperor, and using their madness as a pretext, destroyed, without mercy, myriads of men, women, and children in crowds; and by the laws of war, he reduced their country to a state of absolute subjection. The Jews were then led on by one Barchochebas, signifying a star, but who was in other respects a murderer and robber. But by means of his assumed title, among a degraded race, now reduced to the condition of slaves, he pretended to many miracles, as if he were a light descending from heaven, whose object was to cheer them in their oppression. But in the eighteenth year of the reign of Adrian, when the war had reached its height at the city of Bitthera, a very strong fortress not very far from Jerusalem, the siege was continued for some time, and the revolters were driven to the last extreme by hunger and famine. The author of their madness had also suffered his just punishment, and the whole nation from that time were totally prohibited, by the decree and commands of Adrian, from even entering the country about Jerusalem, so that they could not behold the soil of their fathers even at a distance. Such is the statement of Aristo, of Pella. The city of the Jews being thus reduced to a state of abandonment for them, and totally stripped of its ancient inhabitants, and also inhabited by strangers; the Roman city which subsequently arose, changing its name, was called Elia, in honour of the emperor Ælius Adrian; and when the church was collected there of the Gentiles, the first bishop after those of the circumcision was Marcus.

CHAPTER VII.

Those who were considered leaders in false doctrine at this time.

As the churches now were reflecting the light like splendid luminaries throughout the world, and the faith of our Lord and Saviour Jesus Christ was spreading so as to embrace the whole human race, the malignant spirit of iniquity, as the enemy of all truth, and always the most violent enemy to the salvation of men, was now devising every species of machination against the church, as he had already before armed himself against it by former persecutions. When, however, cut off from those, he then waged a war by other methods, in which he employed the agency of wicked impostors as certain abandoned instruments and minions of destruction. Intent upon every course, he instigated these insidious impostors and deceivers, by assuming the same name with us (Christians) to lead those believers whom they happened to seduce to the depths of destruction, and by their presumption, also turn those that were ignorant of the faith, from the path that led to the saving truth of God. Hence a certain double-headed and double-tongued serpentine power, proceeding from that Menander whom we have already mentioned as the successor of Simon, produced two leaders of different heresies; Saturninus, a native of Antioch, and Basilides, of Alexandria. The former of these established schools of impious heresy in Syria, the latter in Egypt. Irenæus, indeed, states, that in most respects Saturninus held the same false doctrines with Menander, but that Basilides, under the pretext of matters too deep to be divulged, stretched his inventions to a boundless extent, in his astonishing fictions of impious heresy. But as there were at the time many ecclesiastical writers, who contended for the truth, and defended the doctrine of the apostles and the church, with more than common learning, so there were also some who, by publishing their writings, furnished preventives by he way against these heresies. Of these, the best refutation of Basilides that has come down to us, is that of Agrippa Castor, one of the most distinguished writers of that day. In this refutation he fully exposes the dreadful imposture of the man, and reveals his pretended mysteries. He says, that he composed twenty-four books upon the gospels, and that he mentions Barcabbas, and Barcoph, as prophets, and invents others for himself that never existed. That he also gave them certain barbarous names, in order to astonish those the more who are easily ensnared by such things as these. That he taught also, it was indifferent for those that tasted of things sacrificed to idols, and were betrayed unwarily to abjure the faith in times of persecution. Like Pythagoras, he enjoined, also, upon his followers a silence of five years. Other accounts similar to these are given by the abovementioned author, respecting Basilides, in which he ably exposes the fallacy of his heresy. Irenæus also writes, that Carpocrates was contemporary with these, who was also the father of another heresy, called the heresy of the Gnostics.

These did not, like the former, wish to retain the magic arts of Simon in secret, but thought that they should be made public. So that, as if it were something great and glorious, they boasted of preparations of love potions, and of tutelary and dream-exciting dæmons, and other similar magic rites. In accordance with these things, they also taught, that the basest deeds should be perpetrated by those that would arrive at perfection in the mysteries, or rather, that would reach the extent of their abomina-

tions. So that, as they were accustomed to speak, one could in
no other way escape the rulers of the world, unless by performing
his part of obscenity to all. By the aid of such coadjutors, it
happened, that the spirit of wickedness enslaved those that were
led astray by them to their own destruction; whilst to the unbelieving Gentiles, they afforded abundant scope to slander the truth
of God, as the report proceeding from them extended with its
infamy to the whole body of Christians. In this way it happened,
therefore, for the most part, that a certain impious and most
absurd suspicion was spread abroad among the unbelievers respecting us, as of those who had unlawful commerce with mothers
and sisters, and made use of execrable food. These artifices,
however, did not continue to advance far, as the truth nevertheless established itself, and in process of time shed abroad its
own light more and more. Indeed, the machinations of its enemies were almost immediately extinguished by the power of
truth; one sect rising after another, the first always passing
away, and one in one way, and another in another, evaporating
into speculations of many modes, and as many forms. But the
splendour of the universal and only true church constantly advanced in greatness and glory, always the same in all matters
under the same circumstances, and reflected its dignity, its sincerity, its freedom the modesty and purity of that divine life and
temper which it inculcates, to all nations, both Greeks and barbarians. At the same time with the above heresy, were extinguished, also, the aspersions upon our religion. For the doctrine
that we hold has alone survived, has prevailed over all, and been
universally acknowledged as surpassing all in dignity and gravity, in divine truths that evince a genuine and sound philosophy.
So that no one, down to the present time, has dared to af-
fix any calumny upon our faith, nor any such slander, such as
was formerly so eagerly applied by those that rose up against us.
Nevertheless, in those times the truth presented many champions that undertook its defence, not only by unwritten argumentation, but, also, by their written demonstrations against the prevailing heretical impieties.

CHAPTER VIII.

The ecclesiastical writers then flourishing.

AMONG these, Hegesippus holds a distinguished rank, many of whose writings we have already quoted, where we have given some things as he has delivered them from apostolic tradition. This author compiled, in five books, the plain tradition of the apostolic doctrine, in a most simple style of composition, and clearly shows the time in which he lived, where he writes respecting those that began to erect idols, as follows: "To whom they made cenotaphs and temples, as we see to this day. Among whom was Antinous, the slave of Adrian the emperor, to whose honour likewise games are celebrated, which has been done in our own days. For he (Adrian,) also built a city, called after Antinous, and instituted prophets." At this time also, Justin, a true lover of sound philosophy, whilst he yet continued exercising himself in the literature of the Greeks, likewise shows this very time in his apology to Antonine, as follows: "I do not think it out of place here, to mention Antinous of our own day, whom all, notwithstanding they know who and whence he was, yet affected to worship as a god." The same author adds this remark, speaking of the Jewish war: "And, indeed, in the Jewish war which has happened in our times, Barchochebas, the leader of the Jewish revolt, commanded the Christians alone to be led to severe and dreadful tortures, unless they would deny and blaspheme Christ Jesus." In the same work, also, showing his own conversion from the Greek philosophy to religion to be the effect of cool deliberation and judgment, and not without good reason, writes as follows: "For whilst I was delighted with the doctrines of Plato, and heard the Christians calumniated, but at the same time saw them intrepid at the prospect of death, and every thing deemed terrific, I reflected that it was impossible they should live devoted to vice and voluptuousness. For what lover of pleasure, or intemperate man, or what man deeming human flesh a delicacy, could embrace death in order to be deprived of the objects of his own desires; and would not rather strive to live always to escape the eye of the magistrate, and not inform against himself, in the expectation of certain death." The same author, moreover, relates, that Adrian having received letters from Serenius Granianus, the most illustrious proconsul, respecting the Christians, in which he states, that it did not appear just to put the Christians to death without a regular accusation and trial, merely to gratify the outcries of the populace ; and that he wrote back to Minucius Fundanus, proconsul of Asia, enjoining upon him to put no one to death, without an indictment and lawful accusation. Of this epistle, also, he (Justin,) adds a copy in the Latin tongue, in which it was written. He also premises the following explanation. " Although we have good cause, from the epistle of your most illustrious father, the emperor Adrian, to request of you as we requested of him, that the Christians should be regularly tried ; this we have requested, not so much because it was ordered by Adrian, as because we know that the object of our request is just. We have also subjoined a copy of Adrian's epistle, that you may know we declare the truth likewise in this. And here it follows." To this, the author adds the copy of the epistle, in the Latin tongue ; and we have translated it into the Greek, according to the best of our abilities, as follows.

CHAPTER IX.

The epistle of Hadrian, forbidding the Christians to be punished without trial.

" To Minucius Fundanus. I have received an epistle, written to me by the most illustrious Serenius Granianus, whom you have succeeded. I do not wish, therefore, that the matter should be passed by without examination, so that these men may neither be harassed, nor opportunity of malicious proceedings be offered to informers. If, therefore, the provincials can clearly evince their charges against the Christians, so as to answer before the tribunal, let them pursue this course only, but not by mere petitions, and mere outcries against the Christians. For it is far more proper, if any one would bring an accusation, that you should examine it. If any one, therefore, brings an accusation, and can show that they have done any thing contrary to the laws, determine it thus according to the heinousness of the crime. So that indeed, if any one should purpose this with a view to slander, investigate it according to its criminality, and see to it that you inflict the punishment." Such, then, is the copy of Adrian's letter.

CHAPTER X.

The bishops of Rome and Alexandria, in the reign of Antonine.

But this emperor (Adrian,) having finished his mortal career, after the twenty-first year of his reign, is succeeded by Antonine, called the Pious, in the government of the Romans. In the first year of this reign, and in the eleventh year of his episcopate, Telesphorus departed this life, and was succeeded in the charge of the Roman church by Hyginus. Irenæus, indeed, relates that Telesphorus was rendered illustrious by martyrdom; showing, at the same time, that under the abovementioned Roman bishop Hyginus, Valentinus the founder of a peculiar heresy, and Cerdon the leader in the errors propagated by Marcion, were both notorious at Rome. His statement is as follows.

CHAPTER XI.

The heresiarchs of these times.

" Valentine came to Rome under Hyginus, was in his prime under Pius, and lived until the time of Anicetus. But Cerdon, who preceded Marcion, and flourished under the episcopate of Hyginus the ninth in succession, coming to the church, and acknowledging his error, continued in this way, at one time secretly teaching his doctrines, at another renouncing them again, sometimes also, convicted of his perverse doctrines, kept aloof from assembling with the brethren." Such is the account of Irenæus in the third book against the heresies. In the first, however, he relates the following respecting Cerdon: " A certain man, however, by name Cerdon, who derived his first impulse from the fol lowers of Simon, and who made some stay at Rome, under Hyginus the ninth, that held the episcopate in succession from the apostles, taught that the God who had been proclaimed by the law and prophets, was not the Father of our Lord Jesus Christ, for the latter was revealed, the other was unknown; the former also, was just, but the other was good. Marcion, who was from Pontus, having succeeded Cerdon, augmented his school by uttering his blasphemies without a blush. But the same Irenæus, having most dexterously unravelled the bottomless abyss of the errors enveloped in the Valentinian heresy, laid bare the wickedness concealed in it, like a serpent lurking in his nest." Besides these, he says there was another (Marcus was his name,) about the same time, who was a most perfect adept in magic illusions; and he describes also, their profane rites of initiation, and their abominable mysteries, in the following language: " Some of them," says he, " prepare a nuptial bed, and they perform the mystery of initiation with certain forms addressed to the initiated. This, they say, is the spiritual marriage that has taken place with them, bearing form and resemblance to the marriages above. Some conduct them to water, and baptizing them, repeat these words, ' unto the name of the unknown Father of the universe, unto the truth the mother of all, unto Jesus, unto him that descended.' Others, again, repeated Hebrew names in order the better to confound the initiated." But Hyginus dying after the fourth year of his office, Pius received the episcopate, but at Alexandria Marcus was appointed the pastor, after Eumenes had filled the office thirteen years in all. Marcus also dying, after ten years of his ministrations, Celadin had charge of the church of Alexandria, and Pius dying at Rome in the fifteenth year of his episcopate, the church there was governed by Anicetus. At this time Hegesippus writes that he was at Rome and continued there until the episcopate of Eleutherus. But Justin was the most noted of those that flourished in those times, who, in the guise of a philosopher, preached the truth of God, and contended for the faith, also, in his writings. In a work that he wrote against Marcion, he mentions, that at the time he wrote, the man was yet living. He says that a certain Marcion from Pontus, who is now still teaching those that believe him, to think that there is another God greater than God the creator; that he by means of conjunction with dæmons, persuaded many throughout the whole world, to utter blasphemy, and to deny that the Creator of all things was the father of Christ; they asserted, also, that another who was greater than He, was the creator. But, as we said before, all the followers of these were called Christians, just as the name of philosophy is applied to philosophers, although they may have no opinions in common. To these he adds: " We have also written a work against all the heresies that have arisen, which we will give you to peruse if you wish." But this same Justin, after having contended with great success against the Greeks, addressed also other works, containing a defence of our faith, to the emperor Antonine, surnamed the Pious, and to the senate of Rome. He also had his residence at Rome, but he shows who and whence he was in the following extracts in his Apology.

CHAPTER XII.

The Apology of Justin, addressed to Antoninus.

" To the emperor Titus Ælius Adrian Antoninus Pius Cesar Augustus, and to Onesimus his son the philosopher, and to Lucius the natural son of Cesar the philosopher, and the adopted son of Pius, a votary of learning ; also, to the sacred senate and the whole Roman people, in behalf of those who of all nations are now unjustly hated and aspersed; I, Justin, the son of Priscus, the grandson of Bacchius of Flavia, the new city of Palestine, Syria.

being one of their number, present this volume and address." The same emperor was also addressed by others when the brethren in Asia were suffering under every kind of injury from the provincials, and honoured the people of Asia with an ordinance like the following.

CHAPTER XIII.

The Epistle of Antonine, to the assembly of Asia, respecting our doctrine.

THE emperor Cesar Marcus Aurelius Antoninus Augustus, Armenicus, Pontifex Maximus, Tribune of the people XV. Consul III., sends greeting, to the Assembly of Asia; 'I know, indeed, that the gods themselves will take care that such men as these shall not escape detection. For it would more properly belong to them to punish those that will not worship them, than to you. And whilst you drive them into a tumult, you only confirm them the more in their mind, by accusing them as impious. And thus, to them it would be more desirable when arraigned, to appear to die for their God, than to live. Whence, also, they may come off in triumph, when they yield up their lives in preference to a conformity with those things which you exact of them. But as to those earthquakes which have taken place and still continue, it is not out of place to admonish you who are cast down whenever these happen, and you compare your own deportment with theirs. They, indeed, become on these occasions so much the more cheerful towards God, but you, the whole of this time in which you seem not to have correct knowledge, neglect both the gods and other duties, especially the worship of the Immortal. But the Christians who worship Him, you expel and persecute to death. Respecting these, however, many of the governors of the provinces also wrote to our most divine father. To whom, also, he wrote in reply, not to trouble them at all, unless they appeared to make attempts against the Roman government. Many also have sent communications to me respecting them, to whom also, I wrote in reply, following the course pursued by my father. But if any still persevere in creating difficulties to any one of these because he is of this description (i. e. a Christian,) let him that is thus arraigned be absolved from crime, although he should appear to be such, but let the accuser be held guilty." This was published at Ephesus in the public convention of Asia. To these events Melito bears testimony, who was then bishop of Sardis, and well known at that time. This is clear from what he has said in that most excellent defence of our faith which he wrote and addressed to the emperor Verus.

CHAPTER XIV.

Circumstances related of Polycarp, an apostolic man.

ABOUT this time, when Anicetus was at the head of the Roman church, Irenæus says that Polycarp was yet living, and coming to Rome, had a conference with Anicetus, on a question respecting the day of the passover. He also gives another account of Polycarp, which should be added to what is already related respecting him. The story is taken from the third book of Irenæus against the heresies, and is as follows: " And Polycarp, a man who had been instructed by the apostles, and had familiar intercourse with many that had seen Christ, and had also been appointed bishop by the apostles in Asia, in the church at Smyrna, whom we also have seen in our youth, for he lived a long time, and to a very advanced age, when, after a glorious and most distinguished martyrdom, he departed this life. He always taught what he had learned from the apostles, what the church had handed down, and what is the only true doctrine. All the churches bear witness to these things, and those that have been the successors of Polycarp, to the present time, a witness of the truth much more worthy of credit, and much more certain than either Valentine or Marcion, or the rest of those perverse teachers. The same Polycarp, coming to Rome under the episcopate

of Anicetus, turned many from the aforesaid heretics to th
church of God, proclaiming the one and only true faith, that he
had received from the apostles, that, viz.. which was delivered
by the church. And there are those still living who heard him
relate, that John the disciple of the Lord went into a bath at
Ephesus, and seeing Cerinthus within, ran out without bathing,
and exclaimed, " let us flee lest the bath should fall in, as long as
Cerinthus, that enemy of truth, is within." And the same Polycarp, once coming and meeting Marcion, who said, " acknowledge us, " he, replied, " I acknowledge* the first born of Satan."
Such caution did the apostles and their disciples use, so as not
even to have any communion, even in word with any of those
that thus mutilated the truth, according to the declaration of
Paul: " An heretical man after the first and second admonition
avoid, knowing that such an one is perverse, and that he sins,
bringing condemnation upon himself." There is, also, an excellent epistle of Polycarp to the Philippians. From which those
that wish, and that have any concern for their salvation, may
perceive both the character of his faith, and the doctrine of the
truth." Such is the account of Irenæus. But Polycarp, in the
epistle to the Philippians, still extant, has made use of certain
testimonies taken from the first epistle of Peter. About this time
Antonine, surnamed the Pious, having completed the twenty-second year of his reign, was succeeded by Marcus Aurelius Verus, who is also called Antoninus, his son, together with his brother Lucius.

* It was customary in the primitive church to use this expression as a form of
salutation, particularly at the communion. I acknowledge thee, therefore, is the
same as " I salute thee."

CHAPTER XV.

The martyrdom of Polycarp, with others at Smyrna.

AT this time, as there were the greatest persecutions excited in Asia, Polycarp ended his life by martyrdom. But I consider it all-important also to record his end in this history, as it is handed down in writings still extant. There is, however, an epistle of the church which he superintended, to the churches of Pontus, which shows what befel him, in the following words: "The church of God at Smyrna, to that of Philomelius, and to all parts of the holy catholic, (universal church,) everywhere, mercy, peace, and the love of God the Father, and of our Lord Jesus Christ, be multiplied. We have written to you, brethren, the circumstances respecting the martyrs, and the blessed Polycarp, who as if sealing it with his martyrdom has also put a stop to the persecution." After these, before the account of Polycarp's death, they give the account of the other martyrs, and show what firmness they evinced against the tortures they endured. "For," say they, "those standing around, were struck with amazement, at seeing them lacerated with scourges, to their very blood and arteries, so that now the flesh concealed in the very inmost parts of the body, and the bowels themselves were exposed to view. Then they were laid upon conch shells from the sea, and on sharp heads and points of spears on the ground, and after passing through every kind of punishment and torment, were at last thrown as food to wild beasts. But they relate that Germanicus, a most noble youth, was particularly eminent as a martyr; who, strengthened by divine grace, overcame the natural dread of death implanted in us; although the proconsul was desirous of persuading him, and urged him from considerations of his youth, and entreated him, that as he was so very young and blooming he should take compassion on himself. He, however, hesitated not, but eagerly irritated the wild beast against him, all but forcing and stimulating him, that he might the sooner be freed from this unjust and lawless generation. On the glorious death

of this one, the whole multitude amazed at the courage of the
pious martyr, and at the fortitude of the whole race of Christians, began to cry out "Away with the wicked fellows, let Polycarp be sought." A very great tumult arising in consequence
of these outcries, a certain Phrygian, Quintus by name, who had
recently come from Phrygia, seeing the beasts and the additional
tortures threatened, was so overcome by fear and shaken in his
resolution, that he finally gave up his salvation. The contents of
the aforesaid epistle, show that this man had frowardly rushed
forward to the tribunal with others, and not in a modest retiring
manner; and yet when seized, he gave a manifest proof to all,
that it is not proper for those in this situation, to brave danger by
rushing blindly and rashly upon it. Thus far, however, respecting these. But the admirable Polycarp hearing these things, at first,
continued unmoved, preserving his firm and unshaken mind, and,
had determined to remain there in the city. But persuaded by the
entreaties of those around him, and exhorting him to leave the city
secretly, he went forth to a farm not far from it. There he staid
with a few friends, night and day, engaged in nothing but constant
prayer to the Lord, and imploring peace for all the churches
throughout the world. For this had always been his practice. In
this situation, three days before he was seized, in a vision at night,
and during prayer, the pillow under his head seemed to him suddenly to take fire, and thus to be consumed. On this, waking out
of his sleep, he immediately began to interpret the vision to those
present, almost foretelling the event that was about to take place,
and plainly declaring to those around him, that it would be necessary for him to give up his life in the flames for Christ's sake.
Those, however, that were in search of him, making every effort to
discover him, he was again constrained by the affection and love of
the brethren, to go away to another part of the country. Thither
the pursuers came upon him, not long after, and caught two boys
there, one of which they scourged in order to direct them to the
retreat of Polycarp. Entering upon him at a late hour of the
day, they found him, indeed, resting in an upper room, whence,
although he might easily have escaped to another house, he
would not, saying: "The Lord's will be done," and having

understood also that they were come, as it is said, he descended and addressed the men with a very cheerful and mild countenance, so that those who did not know him before, thought they beheld a miracle, as they beheld the advanced age of the man, the gravity and firmness of his countenance, and were surprised that so much zeal should be exercised to seize a venerable old man like this. He, however, without hesitation, ordered a table to be immediately prepared for the men; then requests them to partake of food largely, and begged of them only one hour, that he might pray undisturbed. As they gave him permission, he arose and prayed, so full of the grace of the Lord, that those present who heard him were amazed, and many of them now repented, that so venerable and pious a man should be put to death. Beside these things, the abovementioned epistle respecting him pursues the narrative as follows:

"But after he had ended praying, and had in this remembered all that had ever been connected with him, small and great, noble and obscure, and the whole catholic (universal) church throughout the world, when the hour come for him to go, they placed him upon an ass and conducted him to the city, it being a great Sabbath-day.* He was met by Herod, who was the irenarch,† and his father Nicetes; who, taking him into their vehicle, persuaded him to take a seat with them, and said, "For what harm is there in saying Lord Cesar, and to sacrifice, and thus save your life?" He, however, did not at first make any reply; but as they persevered, he said, "I shall not do what you advise me." Failing, therefore, to persuade him, they uttered dreadful language, and thrust him down from the car with great vehemence, so that as he descended from the car he sprained his thigh. But not at all moved from his purpose, as if nothing had happened, he eagerly went on, and was conducted to the stadium. But as there was so great an uproar in the place that not many could hear, a voice came from heaven to Polycarp as he entered the stadium: "Be strong, Polycarp, and contend manfully." No one saw who it

---

* The great Sabbath was the feast of unleavened bread, which immediately preceded the passover. See Beverege in Can. Apost.

† The irenarch, as the name implies, was an officer to preserve the public peace.

was that spoke; but the voice itself was heard by many of our brethren. When he was led forward, however, a great tumult arose among those that heard Polycarp was taken. At length, as he advanced, the proconsul asked him whether he was Polycarp, and he answering that he was, he persuaded him to renounce Christ, saying, " Have a regard for your age," and adding similar expressions, such as is usual for them to say, he said, " Swear by the genius of Cesar. Repent; say, Away with those that deny the gods." But Polycarp, with a countenance grave and serious, and contemplating the whole multitude that were collected in the stadium, beckoned with his hand to them, and with a sigh he looked up to heaven, and said, " Away with the impious." As the governor, however, continued to urge him, and said, " Swear, and I will dismiss you. Revile Christ;" Polycarp replied, " Eighty and six years have I served him, and he never did me wrong; and how can I now blaspheme my King that has saved me?" The governor still continuing to urge him, and again saying, " Swear by the genius of Cesar," said Polycarp, " If you are so vain as to think that I should swear by the genius of Cesar, as you say, pretending not to know who I am, hear my free confession. I am a Christian. But if you wish to learn what the doctrine of Christianity is, grant me a day and listen to me." The proconsul said, " Persuade the people." Polycarp replied, " I have thought proper to give you a reason; for we have been taught to give magistrates and powers appointed by God, the honour that is due to them, as far as it does not injure us; but I do not consider those the proper ones before whom I should deliver my defence. The proconsul said, " I have wild beasts at hand, I will cast you to these unless you change your mind." He answered, " Call them. For we have no reason to repent from the better to the worse, but it is good to change from wickedness to virtue." He again urged him. " I will cause you to be consumed by fire, should you despise the beasts, and not change your mind. Polycarp answered " You threaten fire that burns for a moment and is soon extinguished, for you know nothing of the judgment to come, and the fire of eternal punishment reserved for the wicked. But why do you delay? Bring what you wish." Saying these, and many otner similar declarations, he was filled with confidence and joy, and his countenance was brightened with grace. So that he not only continued undismayed at what was said to him, but on the contrary, the governor, astonished, sent the herald to proclaim in the middle of the stadium, " Polycarp confesses that he is a Christian." When this was declared by the herald, all the multitude, Gentiles and Jews dwelling at Smyrna, cried out, " This is that teacher of Asia, the father of the Christians, the destroyer of our gods; he that teaches multitudes not to sacrifice, not to worship." Saying this, they cried out, and asked Philip the Asiarch,* to let loose a lion upon Polycarp. But he replied, that he was not permitted, as he had already completed the exhibition of the chase in the amphitheatre. Then all cried out together, that Polycarp should be burnt alive. For it seemed necessary that the vision which he saw on his pillow should be fulfilled; when seeing it on fire whilst he prayed, he turned to those few faithful friends with him, and said prophetically, " I must be burnt alive." These things were executed, however, with such haste that they were no sooner said than done. The crowd, however, forthwith collected wood and straw from the shops and baths, especially the Jews, as usual, freely offered their services for this purpose. But when the pile was prepared, laying aside all his clothes, and loosing his girdle, he attempted also to take off his shoes, which he had not been in the habit of doing before, as he always had some one of the brethren, that were soon at his side, and rivalled each other in their services to him. For he had always been treated with great respect on account of his exemplary life even before his gray hairs. Presently the instruments prepared for the funeral pile were applied to him. As they were also on the point of securing him with spikes, he said, " let me be thus. For he that gives me strength to bear the fire, will also give me power without being secured by you with these spikes, to remain unmoved on the pile." They, therefore, did not nail him, but merely bound him to the stake. But he, closing his hands behind him.

* The Asiarchs were the priests of the assembly or common council of Asia, whose office, among others, was to exhibit the public shows in the amphitheatre.

and bound to the stake as a noble victim selected from the great flock, an acceptable sacrifice to Almighty God, said: "Father of thy well-beloved and blessed Son Jesus Christ, through whom we have received the knowledge of thee. The God of angels and powers, and all creation, and of all the family of the righteous, that live before thee, I bless thee that thou hast thought me worthy of the present day and hour, to have a share in the number of the martyrs and in the cup of Christ, unto the resurrection of eternal life, both of the soul and body, in the incorruptible felicity of the holy Spirit. Among whom may I be received in thy sight, this day, as a rich and acceptable sacrifice as thou the faithful and true God hast prepared, hast revealed and fulfilled. Wherefore, on this account, and for all things I praise thee, I bless thee, I glorify thee, through the eternal high priest, Jesus Christ, thy well-beloved Son. Through whom glory be to thee with him in the Holy Ghost, both now and for ever. Amen."

After he had repeated amen, and had finished his prayer, the executioners kindled the fire. And when it arose in great flames, we saw a miracle, those of us who were privileged to see it, and who, therefore, were preserved to declare the facts to others. For the flames presented an appearance like an oven, as when the sail of a vessel is filled with the wind; and thus formed a wall around the body of the martyr. And he was in the midst not like burning flesh, but like gold and silver purified in the furnace. We also perceived a fragrant odour, like the fumes of incense, or some other precious aromatic drugs. At length the wicked persecutors, seeing that the body could not be consumed by fire, commanded the executioner to draw near to him and to plunge his sword into him; and when he had done this, such a quantity of blood gushed forth that the fire was extinguished. So that the whole multitude were astonished that such a difference should be made between the unbelievers and the elect, of whom this one, bishop of the catholic church in Smyrna, was the most admirable, apostolical, and prophetical teacher of our times. For every word that he uttered, was either fulfilled or will yet be fulfilled. But that envious and malignant adversary, that wicked enemy of all the righteous, seeing the lustre of his martyrdom, and his uniform walk and conversation, and him now crowned with the crown of immortality, and bearing off the indisputable prize, had provided that not even his corpse could be obtained by us, though many of us eagerly wished it, so as to have communion with the sacred body. Some, therefore, secretly engaged Nicetas, the father of Herod and brother of Dalce, to go to the governor, so as not to give the body, lest, said they, abandoning him that was crucified, they should begin to worship this one. And this they said on the suggestion and urging of the Jews, who were also watching and looking out whilst we were preparing to take him from the fire. Not knowing, however, that we can never abandon Christ, who suffered for the salvation of those that are becoming saved from all the world, nor even worship any other. For him we worship as the Son of God; but the martyrs we deservedly love as the disciples and imitators of our Lord, on account of their exceeding love to their king and master. Of whom may we only become true associates and fellow-disciples. The centurion then seeing the obstinacy of the Jews, placed him in the middle, and burnt it according to the custom of the Gentiles. Thus, at last, taking up his bones, more valuable than precious stones, and more tried than gold, we deposited them where it was proper they should be. There, also, as far as we can, the Lord will grant us to collect and celebrate the natal day* of his martyrdom in joy and gladness, both in commemoration of those who finished their contest before, and to exercise and prepare those that shall hereafter." Such is the account respecting the blessed Polycarp, who, together with the twelve from Philadelphia, was crowned a martyr. Who, however, is rather mentioned alone by all, so that he is spoken of by the Gentiles in every place. Of such an end, then, was the admirable and apostolic Polycarp deemed worthy, according to the account which the brethren in Smyrna recorded in the epistle that we have quoted. In this same epistle, also, respecting him, other martyrdoms are also recorded, which took place in the same city,

---

* The martyrdom of Polycarp is here called his natal day, as his birthday for a better world.

and about the time of Polycarp's death. Among these, also, was Metrodorus, a follower of Marcion's error, but who appears to have been a presbyter, and who was committed to the flames. A very celebrated martyr of those times was Pionius. Those who feel inclined to know respecting him, we refer to that epistle that has been imbodied in the work on the ancient martyrs collected by us, in which is given a very full account of his particular confessions, of the freedom with which he spoke, of his defence of the faith before the people and rulers. Also his instructive exhortations; moreover his strong invitations to those that fell away under the temptation of persecution, the consolations which he presented to the brethren that came in to him in prison, what excruciating tortures he also endured besides, when he was secured with spikes, his firmness on the pile, and after all his extraordinary sufferings, his death. There are, also, records extant of others that suffered martyrdom in Pergamus, a city of Asia. Of these we mention only Carpus and Papylus, and a woman named Agathonice; who, after many and illustrious testimonies given by them, gloriously finished their course.

CHAPTER XVI.

How Justin, the philosopher, suffered martyrdom, asserting the doctrine of Christ.

ABOUT this time, the same Justin who was mentioned by us a little before, after having given a second defence of our doctrines to the abovementioned rulers, was crowned with divine martyrdom, at the insidious instigation of Crescens the philosopher, who was called a cynic, and emulated the life and manner indicated by the name he bore. After having frequently refuted him in discussion, in the presence of many hearers, he at length also bore away the palm of victory, in the truth which he asserted, by his own martyrdom. It is also plainly stated by the same excellent and most learned author, in the Apology already quoted that he predicted the issue just as it was about to happen in reference to himself, in the following words; "I also expect to be waylaid by some one of those whom I have named, and to be put to the rack, even by Crescens himself, that unphilosophical, and vainglorious opponent. For it seems not proper to call a man a philosopher, since he publicly attempts to contend against matters that he does not understand, as if Christians were infidels and wicked characters, merely for the purpose of captivating and gratifying the multitude. He has done all this under a strong delusion. For if he counteracts us without having read the doctrines of Christ, he is most iniquitous in his conduct, and much worse than common men, who for the most part are cautious in speaking and bearing a false testimony in matters that they do not understand ; and if when happening to read, he does not understand the sublimity in them, or if understanding, he does those things that may lead one to suspect he is not one of them, (i. e.) no Christian, he is so much the more base and nefarious, inasmuch as he is enslaved to vulgar applause and an absurd fear. And, indeed, when I proposed certain questions to him, in order to ascertain and convince him that he really was ignorant, I would beg leave to inform you, that I found this to be the case. And that you may know all that I here say is true, if these discussions have not yet reached you, I am prepared to repeat these interrogations in your presence. This, too, would be a work suited to your majesties. But if these questions of mine, and his answers are known to you, it is obvious to you, that he knows nothing of our doctrines, or if he knows, he does not declare them on account of his hearers ; so that, as I before said, he proves himself to be not a true lover of wisdom, a philosopher, but a lover of vainglory. He, indeed, does not even regard that excellent saying of Socrates, viz. "that no one is to be preferred to truth :" Thus far Justin. But that in consequence of his freedom against Crescens, he was brought to his end, is shown by Tatian, a man who at first, as a sophist, taught the various branches of literature among the Greeks, and obtained no small celebrity in them, and who left numerous monuments of his attainments in his works. This he relates in the book against the Greeks, thus :

" And that most excellent Justin, justly declared that the aforesaid persons were like robbers." Then after some comments on
these philosophers, he adds the following : " Crescens indeed,
who had nestled in the great city (Rome,) surpassed all in his
unnatural lust (παιδεραςια) and was also wholly enslaved to the
love of money. And he who advised others to despise death, was
nimself so much in dread of death, that he plotted death for Justin as a very great evil. Because that when proclaiming the
truth, he proved the philosophers gluttons and impostors." And
such was the cause that produced the martyrdom of Justin.

CHAPTER XVIII.

The martyrs mentioned by Justin in his books.

BUT the same author before his conflict makes mention of
others that suffered martyrdom before him, in his first Apology
In which he aptly introduces the following statement : " A certain
woman," says he, " had a husband that was intemperate. She
herself, had also previously led a dissolute life ; but after she
was made acquainted with the doctrines of Christ, she became
modest, and endeavoured to persuade her husband also to lead
a virtuous life, presenting to his mind the doctrines of Christianity, and the punishment of eternal fire awaited those that would
not live virtuously, and according to right reason. But he still
continuing in the same lascivious habits, wholly alienated his
wife's affections by his practices. Finally, the woman considering it wicked to live with one who, contrary to the law of nature and propriety, was intent upon every course to gratify his
lusts, contemplated a divorce. But when she was encouraged
by her friends, who advised her still to remain with him, as if
he might give hopes of a change of life, she did violence to herself and remained. Afterwards, however, her husband, who had
gone to Alexandria, was reported to be acting much worse.
Fearing, therefore, lest she should become a sharer in his un-
righteousness and impieties, if she continued united to him. and

should be his companion, she sent him what is called the bill of divorce, and was separated. This good and excellent husband, however, who ought to have rejoiced that his wife, who had formerly delighted in debauchery and all manner of vice, had now ceased from those deeds in which she had formerly been wantonly engaged with servants and hirelings, and that she now wished him, also, to cease from doing the same things, would not do thus, when she left him, but he brought an accusation against her, asserting that she was a Christian. And she delivered to you, the emperor, a petition, requesting that she might first be permitted to regulate her domestic affairs, and then, after the regulation of her affairs, she would make her defence in reference to the accusation. And this you granted. But he, who had formerly been the husband of the woman, not being able to say anything against her now, turned upon a certain Ptolemy, whom Urbicius had punished, and who had become her instructer in the principles of Christianity, in the following manner.

He had persuaded the centurion to seize Ptolemy his friend, and cast him in prison, and to ask him only this, whether he was a Christian? Ptolemy, who was a lover of truth, and averse to all deceit and falsehood, confessed himself a Christian; in consequence of which, he was cast into prison, and punished by the centurion in this way for a long time. At last, when the man came before Urbicius in like matter, only this one thing was asked, whether he was a Christian? And as he was conscious of deriving every happiness and blessing from the doctrine of Christ, he again professed the principles of celestial virtue.— For he that denies that he is a Christian, either denies, because he despises, or because he is conscious that he is unworthy of this religion, and a stranger to its excellency; and thus avoids the confession. Neither of these things can apply to the true Christian. Urbicius, however, having commanded him to be led forth, a certain Lucius, who was also a Christian, seeing the judgment so unjustly passed, says to Urbicius, " What charge is this, that you should punish one who is neither an adulterer, nor fornicator, nor a murderer, nor a thief, nor a robber; nor convicted, indeed, of any crime, but simply confessing the name of a Christian? O, Urbicius, you do not judge what becomes our pious emperor, nor the philosophic son of Cesar, nor the sacred senate." But without any other reply, he said to Lucius, " Thou appearest also to be one such as these," and as Lucius answered " by all means," he in like manner commanded him to be led forth. But he, (Lucius,) said, he thanked him; " for now," he added, " he was liberated from wicked masters, and was going to the good Father and king, even God. And a second and third coming up, were punished in the same way." To these Justin, next in order, adds the passages that we quoted above, where he says: " But I am now waiting to be waylaid by a 'ertain one of those called philosophers," &c.

CHAPTER XVIII

The books of Justin that have come down to us.

This Justin has left us many monuments of a mind well stored with learning, and devoted to sacred things, replete with matter profitable in every respect. To these we shall refer our studious readers, only indicating as we proceed, those that have come to our knowledge. There is a discourse of his, addressed to Antonine, surnamed the Pious, and his sons and the Roman senate, in defence of our doctrines. Another work, comprising a defence of our faith, which he addressed to the emperor of the same name, Antoninus Verus, the successor of the preceding, the circumstances of whose times we are now recording. Also, another book, against the Greeks, in which, dilating upon most of the questions agitated between us and the Greek philosophers, he also discusses the nature of dæmons; of which it is not necessary to add anything here. There is also another work, that has reached us, also against the Gentiles, to which he gave the title, " *Refutation.*" Besides these, also another, " *On the Sovereignty of God,*" which he establishes not only by the holy Scriptures, but also by references to the works of the Greeks. Moreover he wrote a work called *Psaltes*, (the psalmist,) another, also consisting of Remarks on the Soul, in which, after proposing various questions on the subject, he adds the opinions that prevailed among the Greek philosophers, which he also promises to disprove, and to give his own opinion in a separate work. He also wrote a dialogue against the Jews, which he held at Ephesus with Tryphon, the most distinguished among the Hebrews of the day. In this he shows how the Divine grace stimulated him to this discourse on the faith, what zeal also he had before evinced in the studies of philosophy, and what indefatigable research he had applied in the discovery of the truth. In this also he states respecting the Jews, how insidiously they plotted against the doctrine of Christ, and addresses the following words to Tryphon: " But you do not only continue impenitent for your evil deeds, but selecting chosen men, you sent them from Jerusalem to all the world, declaring that the infidel sect of Christians had made its appearance, and uttering all those falsehoods against us which those that know us not are accustomed to repeat. Thus you are the causes of iniquity not only to yourselves but to all others also." He writes also, that even down to his time, gifts of prophecy shone forth in the church; mentions also, the Revelation of John, plainly calling it the work of the apostle, and records also, certain prophetic declarations, in his discussion with Tryphon, and showing that the Jews had expunged them from the Scriptures. There are also many other works of his in the hands of many of our brethren. So valuable and worthy of study were these works esteemed by the ancients, that Irenæus quotes him often. This he does in the fourth book against heresies, adding the words: " And well does Justin, in his work against Marcion, say: ' I would not even believe the Lord himself, if he were to announce any other God but the Creator.' " And in the fifth book, he says: " And well did Justin say, that before the appearance of our Lord, Satan never ventured to blaspheme God, because he did not yet know his own condemnation." These we deemed necessary to state, in order to stimulate the studious likewise to the diligent perusal of these books. And thus much respecting Justin.

CHAPTER XIX.

Those that presided over the churches of Rome and Alexandria,
in the reign of Verus.

It was in the eighth year of the abovementioned reign, viz., that of Verus, that Anicetus, who had held the episcopate of Rome for eleven years, was succeeded by Soter; but at Alexandria, Celadion, who had presided over the church fourteen years, was succeeded by Agrippinus.

CHAPTER XX.

The bishops of Antioch.

At this time, also, Theophilus in the church of Antioch, was well known as the sixth in succession from the apostles. As Cornelius, who succeeded Heron, had been the fourth of those that presided there, and after him Eros, the fifth in order that held the episcopate.

CHAPTER XXI.

The ecclesiastical writers that flourished in these times.

About this time flourished Hegesippus, whom we quoted above. Also Dionysius, bishop of Corinth, and Pinytus, bishop of Crete. Moreover, Philip and Apollinaris and Melito. Musanus, also, and Modestus, and, lastly, Irenæus, whose correct views of the sound faith have descended to us in the works written by them, as they received it from apostolic tradition.

CHAPTER XXII.

Of Hegesippus, and those whom he mentions.

HEGESIPPUS, indeed, in the five books of commentaries that have come down to us, has left a most complete record of his own views. In these he states that he conversed with most of the bishops when he travelled to Rome, and that he received the same doctrine from all. We may also add what he says, after some observations on the Epistle of Clement to the Corinthians: " And the church of Corinth," says he, " continued in the true faith, until Primus was bishop there. With whom I had familiar conversation (as I passed many days at Corinth,) when I was on the point of sailing to Rome, during which time also, we were mutually refreshed in the true doctrine. After coming to Rome, I made my stay with Anicetus, whose deacon was Eleutherus. After Anicetus, Soter succeeded, and after him Eleutherus. In every succession, however, and in every city, the doctrine prevails according to what is declared by the law and the prophets and the Lord." The same author, also, treats of the beginnings of the heresies that arose about his time, in the following words: " But after James the Just had suffered martyrdom, as our Lord had for the same reason, Simeon, the son of Cleophas our Lord's uncle, was appointed the second bishop, whom all proposed, as the cousin of our Lord. Hence they called the church as yet a virgin, for it was not yet corrupted by vain discourses. Thebuthis made a beginning secretly to corrupt it, on account of his not being made bishop. He was one of those seven sects among the Jewish people. Of these, also, was Simeon, whence sprung the sect of Si- monians; also, Cleobius, from whom came the Cleobians; also, Dositheus, the founder of the Dositheans. From these also sprung the Gorthœonians, from Gorthœus, and the Masbothœans, from Masbotheus. Hence, also, the Menandrians, and Marcion- ists, and Carpocratians, and Valentinians, and Basilidians, and the Saturnilians, every one introducing his own peculiar opinions, one differing from the other. From these sprung the false Christs and false prophets and false apostles, who divided the unity of the church, by the introduction of corrupt doctrines against God and against his Christ." The same author also mentions in his history, the ancient heresies prevalent among the Jews, as follows: " There were also, different opinions in the circumcision among the children of Israel, against the tribe of Judah and the Messiah, viz., the Essenes, the Galileans, Hemerobaptists, the Masbothœans, the Samaritans, the Sadducees and Pharisees." He also speaks of many other matters, which we have in part already quoted, and introduced in their appropriate places. He also states some particulars from the gospel of the Hebrews and from the Syriac, and particularly from the Hebrew language, showing that he himself was a convert from the Hebrews. Other matters he also records as taken from the unwritten tradition of the Jews. And not only he, but Irenæus also, and the whole body of the ancients, called the Proverbs of Solomon, " Wisdom, comprehending every virtue." Also in discoursing on the books called Apocrypha, he relates that some of them were forged in his day, by some of the heretics. But it is now time to proceed to another.

CHAPTER XXIII.

Of Dionysius, bishop of Corinth, and his epistles.

AND first we must speak of Dionysius, who was appointed over the church at Corinth, and imparted freely, not only to his own people, but to others abroad also, the blessings of his divine labours. But he was most useful to all in the catholic epistles that he addressed to the churches. One of which is addressed to the Lacedæmonians, and contains instructions in the true religion, and inculcates peace and unity. One also to the Athenians, exciting them to the faith, and the life prescribed by the gospel, from which he shows that they had swerved, so that they had nearly fallen from the truth, since the martyrdom of Publius, then bishop, which happened in the persecutions of those times. He also makes mention of Quadratus, who was bishop after the martyrdom of Publius, bearing witness also that the church was again collected, and the faith of the people revived by his exertions. He states, moreover, that Dionysius the Areopagite, who was converted to the faith by Paul the apostle, according to the statement in the Acts of the Apostles, first obtained the episcopate of the church at Athens. There is also another epistle of his extant, addressed to the Nicomedians, in which he refutes the heresy of Marcion and adheres closely to the rule of faith. In an epistle to the church of Gortyna, and to the other churches in Crete, he commends their bishop Philip, for the numerous instances of fortitude that the church evinced under him, according to the testimony of all, whilst he cautions them against the perversions of the heretics. He also wrote to the church at Amastris, together with those at Pontus, in which he makes mention of Bacchylides and Elpistus, as those who urged him to write. He also adds some expositions of the sacred writings, where he intimates that Palmas was then bishop. He also recommends many things in regard to marriage, and the purity to be observed by those who enter this state, and enjoins upon the church to receive again kindly all that return again from any fall; whether of heresy or delinquency. Among them is also inserted an epistle to the Gnossians, in which he admonishes Pinytus, the bishop of the church, not to impose upon the brethren without necessity, a burden in regard to purity too great to be borne, but to pay regard to the infirmity of the great mass. To which Pinytus, writing in reply, admires and applauds Dionysius, but exhorts him at the same time to impart some time or other stronger food, and to feed the people under him with writings abounding in more perfect doctrine when he wrote again, so that they might not remain constantly nurtured with milky doctrine, and imperceptibly grow old, under a discipline calculated only for children. In which epistle, also, the correct views which Pinytus cherished, and his solicitude respecting the welfare of those that were committed to his care, also his learning and intelligence in divine matters is exhibited as in a most perfect image. There is yet another epistle ascribed to Dionysius, to the Romans, and addressed to Soter the bishop of that city, from which we may also subjoin some extracts, viz., from that part where he commends a practice of the Romans retained even to the persecution in our day, and writes as follows: "For this practice has prevailed with you from the very beginning, to do good to all the brethren in every way, and to send contributions to many churches in every city. Thus refreshing the needy in their want, and furnishing to the brethren condemned to the mines, what was necessary, by these contributions which ye have been accustomed to send from the beginning, you preserve, as Romans, the practices of your ancestors the Romans. Which was not only observed by your bishop Soter, but also increased, as he not only furnished great supplies to the saints, but also encouraged the brethren that came from abroad, as a loving father his children, with consolatory words." In this same letter he mentions that of Clement to the Corinthians, showing that it was the practice to read it in the churches, even from the earliest times. "To-day," says he, "we have passed the Lord's holy day, in which we have read your epistle. In reading which we shall always have our minds stored with admonition, as we shall, also, from that written to us before by Clement." Besides this, the same author writes respecting his own epistles as having been corrupted: "As the brethren," says he, "desired me to write epistles, I wrote them, and these the apostles of the devil have filled with tares, exchanging some things, and adding others, for whom there is a wo reserved. It is not, therefore, matter of wonder, if some have also attempted to adulterate the sacred writings of the Lord, since they have attempted the same in other works that are not to be compared with these." There is also another epistle attributed to this Dionysius, addressed to his most faithful sister Chrysophora, in which he writes what was suitable to her, and imparts also to her the proper spiritual food. And thus much respecting Dionysius.

CHAPTER XXIV.

Of Theophilus, bishop of Antioch.

THERE are three books containing the elements of the faith, addressed to Autolycus, which are ascribed to Theophilus, whom we have mentioned as bishop of Antioch. Another, also, which has the title, " Against the heresy of Hermogenis ;" in which he makes use of testimony from the Revelation of John, besides certain other catechetical works. And as the heretics, no less then, than at any other time, were like tares destroying the pure seed of the apostolical doctrines, the pastors of the churches every where hastened to restrain them as wild beasts from the fold of Christ. Sometimes they did it by their exhortations and admonitions to the brethren, sometimes more openly contending with the heretics themselves, by oral discussions and refutations, and then again confuting their opinions, by the most rigid proofs in their written works.

Theophilus, therefore, with others, also contended against these, as is manifest from a work of no mean character, written by him against Marcion, which, together with others that we have mentioned, is still preserved. He was succeeded by Maximinus, the seventh from the apostles in the church of Antioch.

CHAPTER XXV.

Of Philip and Modestus.

PHILIP, also, who we have seen from the words of Dionysius was bishop of the church at Gortyna, has written a very elaborate work against Marcion. Irenaeus, also, and Modestus, the last of whom beyond all others, has detected the error of the man, and exposed it to the view of all. Many others have also written, whose labours are carefully preserved by the brethren even to this day.

CHAPTER XXVI.

Of Melito, and the circumstances he records.

In these times, also flourished Melito, bishop of the church in
Sardis, and Apollinaris, the bishop of Hierapolis. Each of these
separately addressed discourses as apologies for the faith, to the
existing emperor of the Romans, already mentioned. Of these,
those that follow below, are those that have come to our knowledge. Of Melito, two works *On the Passover*, and those, *On the
Conduct of Life, and the Prophets.* One, *On the Church*, and another discourse, *On the Lord's-day.* One, also, *On the Nature of
Man*, and another *On his Formation.* A work *On the Subjection
of the Senses to Faith.* Besides these, a treatise *On the Soul, the
Body, and the Mind.* A dissertation also, *On Baptism;* one also,
On Truth, and Faith, and the Generation of Christ. His discourse
On Prophecy, and that *On Hospitality.* A treatise called *The Key,*
his works *On the Devil*, and *The Revelation of John.* The treatise
On the Incarnate God. And last of all, the discourse addressed
to Antonine. In the work on the passover, he shows the time
in which he wrote it, beginning with these words: " When Ser-
vilius Paulus was proconsul of Asia, says he, at which time Sagaris suffered martyrdom, there was much discussion in Laodicea, respecting the passover, which occurred at that time in its
proper season, and in which, also, these works were written."
This work is also mentioned by Clement of Alexandria, in his
own work on the passover, which, he says, he wrote on occasion
of Melito's work. But in the book addressed to the emperor, he
relates the following transactions against those of our faith, under
this emperor. " What, indeed, says he, never before happened,
the race of the pious is now persecuted, driven about in Asia, by
new and strange decrees. For the shameless informers, and
those that crave the property of others, taking occasion from the
edicts of the emperors, openly perpetrate robbery ; night and day
plundering those who are guilty of no crime." And afterwards
he says, " and if these things are done by your orders let them be

done at least in a proper way. For a just ruler should never form unjust decrees. We, indeed, cheerfully bear the reward of such a death, but we only urge upon you this request, that you yourself would first take cognisance of these plotters of mischief, and justly judge, whether they deserve death and punishment, or safety and security. But if this decree, and this unheard of ordinance, which ought not be tolerated even against barbarous enemies, have not proceeded from you, so much the more do we entreat you not to overlook us in the midst of this lawless plunder of the populace." After a few other remarks, he adds, " The philosophy which we profess, first indeed, flourished among the barbarians, but afterwards, when it grew up, also among the nations under your government; under the glorious reign of Augustus your ancestor, it became, especially to your reign, an auspicious blessing. For since that time, the Roman power has grown in greatness and splendour. Whose desired successor you have become, and will be, together with your son, if you preserve that philosophy which has been nurtured with the empire, which commenced its existence with Augustus, and which also your ancestors did honour, with other religions ; and one of the greatest evidences, that our doctrine flourished, to the advantage of a reign so happily begun, is this : that there has nothing disastrous occurred to the empire, since the reign of Augustus ; on the contrary, all things have proceeded splendidly and gloriously according to the wishes of all. Nero, and Domitian, alone, stimulated by certain malicious persons, showed a disposition to slander our faith. From whom it has happened, also, that this falsehood respecting Christians has been propagated by an absurd practice of waylaying and informing. But your pious fathers corrected what was done by the ignorance of those, by frequently reproving many in writing, as many as dared to attempt any innovations against those of our religion. Your grandfather Adrian, evidently wrote, among others, to Fundanus the proconsul of Asia. But your father, also, when you held the government with him, wrote to the cities, forbidding any strange movements against us. Among these were the ordinances to the Larisseans, to the Thessalonians, and Athenians, and all the Greeks. But as you cherish the same opinion on these matters with those, and, indeed, have still more benevolent and more philosophical views, we are so much the more confident you will do what we entreat." This passage is given in the discourse beforementioned. But in the selections made by him, the same writer in the beginning of his preface, gives a catalogue of the books of the Old Testament acknowledged as canonical. This we have thought necessary to give here, literally as follows:

" Melito sends, greeting, to his brother Onesimus, as you have frequently desired in your zeal for the Scriptures, that I should make selections for you, both from the law and the prophets, respecting our Saviour, and our whole faith; and you were, moreover, desirous of having an exact statement of the Old Testament, how many in number, and in what order the books were written, I have endeavoured to perform this. For I know your zeal in the faith, and your great desire to acquire knowledge, and that especially by the love of God, you prefer these matters to all others, thus striving to gain eternal life. When, therefore, I went to the east, and came as far as the place where these things were proclaimed and done, I accurately ascertained the books of the Old Testament, and send them to thee here below. The names are as follows: Of *Moses, five books, Genesis, Exodus, Leviticus, Numbers, Deuteronomy. Jesus Nave, Judges, Ruth.* Four of *Kings.* Two of *Paralipomena,* (Chronicles,) *Psalms of David, Proverbs of Solomon,* which is also called Wisdom, *Ecclesiastes, Song of Songs, Job.* Of prophets, *Isaiah, Jeremiah.* Of the twelve prophets, one book. *Daniel, Ezekiel, Esdras.* From these I have, therefore, made the selections which I have divided into six books." Thus much of Melito's writings.

CHAPTER XXVII.

Of Apollinaris bishop of Hierapolis.

ALTHOUGH there are many works of Apollinaris preserved by many, those that have reached us are the following: An Apology, addressed to the abovementioned emperor, and *five books against the Greeks.* Two *books on Truth, two also against the Jews,* and those that he afterwards wrote *against the Heresy of the Phrygians,* which was revived not long after. Then, indeed, also began as it were to spring up, the sect of Montanus, who, with his false prophetesses, laid the foundation of their errors. Thus much, however, may suffice, also, concerning this author.

CHAPTER XXVIII.

Of Musanus and his works.

MUSANUS, also, whom we have mentioned among the foregoing authors, is said to have written a very elegant work addressed to certain brethren, who had swerved from the truth to the heresy of the Encratites, which had even then made its appearance, and which introduced a singular and pernicious error into the world. The founder of this singularity is said to have been Tatianus.

CHAPTER XXIX.

The heresy of Tatianus.

HE is the same whose words we adduced before in reference to the excellent Justin, mentioning that he was also the disciple of that martyr. This is shown by Irenæus, in the first book against heresies, where he writes both respecting the man and against his heresy : " Those," says he, " that sprung from Sa-

turninus and Marcion, called the Encratites, proclaimed absti
nence from marriage, setting aside the original design of God,
and tacitly censuring him that made male and female for the
propagation of the human race. They also introduced the abstinence from things called animate with them, displaying in-
gratitude to God who made all things. They also deny the salvation of our first parents. And this has been but lately discovered
by them, a certain Tatian being the first that taught the horrible
doctrine. This man, who had been a hearer of Justin, as long
as he was in company with him, exhibited nothing like this, but
after his martyrdom, having apostatized from the church, and
elated with the conceit of a teacher, and vainly puffed up as if
he surpassed all others, he established a peculiar characteristic
of his own doctrine, by inventing certain invisible Æons, similar
to those of Valentinus. Marriage, also, he asserted, with Marcion
and Saturninus, was only corruption and fornication. And he
also devised arguments of his own against the salvation of Adam."
Thus far Irenæus then. A little after, however, a certain man
by the name of Severus, having strengthened the abovementioned heresy, became the cause of another sect, called after himself,
the Severians. These indeed, make use of the law and prophets
and gospels, giving a peculiar interpretation to the passages of
the sacred writings, but abuse Paul the apostle, and set aside his
epistles; neither do they receive the Acts of the Apostles. But
their chief and founder Tatianus, having formed a certain body
and collection of gospels, I know not how, has given this the title,
Diatessaron, that is the gospel by the four, or the gospel formed
of the four; which is in the possession of some even now. It
is also said that he dared to alter certain expressions of the apostles, in order to correct the composition of the phrase. He has
also left a great multitude of writings, of which the most noted
among all, is that work against the Greeks, in which, as he records ancient times, he proves Moses and the prophets are more
ancient than all the celebrated writers among the Greeks. This
book, indeed, appears to be the most elegant and profitable of all
his works. And so much for these.

CHAPTER XXX.

Of Bardesanes, the Syrian, and the works of his extant.

UNDER the same reign, also, as heresies abounded in the country between the rivers (Mesopotamia,) lived one Bardesanes; a man of very great abilities, and a powerful disputant in the Syriac tongue. This man composed dialogues against Marcion and certain others of different opinions, and committed them to writing in his native language, together with many other works. These were translated from the Syriac into the Greek, by his friends; for as a powerful assertor of the word, he had many followers. Among these there is a most able dialogue *On Fate*, addressed to Antonine. Many others also, he is said to have written on occasion of the persecution which then arose. He was at first indeed a disciple of Valentine, but afterwards, rejecting his doctrine, and having refuted most of his fictions, he appeared somehow to himself to have returned again to the more correct opinion. But he did not entirely wipe away the filth of his old heresy. About this time, also, died Soter, bishop of the church at Rome.

BOOK V.

PRELIMINARY

Soter, bishop of Rome, died, after having held the episcopate eight years. He was succeeded by Eleutherus the twelfth in order from the apostles. It was also the seventeenth year of the reign of the emperor Antoninus Verus, when a more violent persecution having broken out against our brethren, in certain parts, occasioned by insurrections in the cities, it is probable that innumerable martyrs obtained the crown of eminence in the conflict, from the events that happened in a single nation. These, as worthy of imperishable remembrance, were also handed down to posterity in historical records. The full account of these is given in our history of martyrs, comprising not only historical narrative, but that which may contribute to edification. But whatsoever may have a reference to our present purpose, I shall here select for the present. Others, indeed, that compose historical narratives, would record nothing but victories in battle, the trophies of enemies, the warlike achievements of generals, the bravery of soldiers, sullied with blood and innumerable murders, for the sake of children and country and property. But our narrative embraces that conversation and conduct which is acceptable to God. The wars and conflicts of a most pacific character, whose ultimate tendency is to establish the peace of the soul. Those, also, that have manfully contended for the truth, rather than for their country, and who have struggled for piety rather than their dearest friends. Such as these our narrative would engrave on imperishable monuments. The firmness of the champions for the true religion, their fortitude in the endurance of innumerable trials, their trophies erected over dæmoniacal agency, and their victories over their invisible antagonists, and the crowns that have been placed upon all these, it would proclaim and perpetuate by an everlasting remembrance.

168

CHAPTER I.

The number and sufferings of those that suffered for the faith in Gaul.

GAUL was the place where the arena was prepared for the abovementioned conflict. Of these the two distinguished capitals are celebrated as surpassing all the rest, viz., Lyons and Vienna. Through both of these the river Rhone passes, traversing the whole region with a mighty stream. The account, however, of the martyrs, was sent by the most illustrious churches there, to those of Asia and Phrygia, by whom the events that took place among them, are related in the following manner—I will subjoin their own declarations: "The servants of Christ dwelling at Lyons and Vienna, in Gaul, to those brethren in Asia and Phrygia, having the same faith and hope with us, peace and grace and glory from God the Father and Christ Jesus our Lord." Then, premising some other matters, they commence their subject in the following words:

"The greatness, indeed, of the tribulation, and the extent of the madness exhibited by the heathen against the saints, and the sufferings which the martyrs endured in this country, we are not able fully to declare, nor is it, indeed, possible to describe them. For the adversary assailed us with his whole strength, giving us already a prelude, how unbridled his future movements among us would be. And, indeed, he resorted to every means, to accustom and exercise his own servants against those of God, so that we should not only be excluded from houses, and baths, and markets, but every thing belonging to us was prohibited from appearing in any place whatever. But the grace of God contended for us, and rescued the weak, and prepared those who, like firm pillars, were able through patience, to sustain the whole weight of the enemy's violence against them. These coming in close conflict, endured every species of reproach and torture. Esteeming what was deemed great, but little, they hastened to Christ, showing in reality, " that the sufferings of this time are not worthy to

be compared with the glory that shall be revealed in us." And
first, they nobly sustained all the evils that were heaped upon
them by the populace, clamours, and blows, plundering and robberies, stonings and imprisonments, and whatsoever a savage
people delight to inflict upon enemies. After this they were
led to the forum, and when interrogated by the tribune, and
the authorities of the city, in the presence of the multitude,
they were shut up in prison until the arrival of the governor.
Afterwards, they were led away to be judged by him, from
whom we endured all manner of cruelty. Vettius Epagathus,
one of the brethren, who abounded in the fulness of the love
of God and man, and whose walk and conversation had been
so unexceptionable though he was only young, shared in the
same testimony with the elder Zacharias. He had walked,
therefore, in all the commandments and righteousness of the Lord
blameless, and with alacrity in kind offices to man, abounding in
zeal for God, and fervent in spirit. As he was of this high character, he could not bear to see a judgment so unjustly passed
against us, but gave vent to his indignation, and requested also,
that he should be heard in defence of his brethren, whilst he
ventured to assert that there was nothing either at variance with
religion or piety among us. At this, those around the tribunal
cried out against him, for he was a man of eminent standing.
Nor did the governor allow a request so just and so properly
made, but only asked whether he also were a Christian? He
confessed in as clear a voice as possible, and he, too, was transferred to the number of martyrs, being publicly called the advocate of the Christians. But he had the paraclete, (advocate,)
within him, viz., the spirit more abundant than Zacharias, which,
indeed, he displayed by the fulness of his love; glorying in the
defence of his brethren, and to expose his own life for theirs. He
was, indeed, a genuine disciple of Christ, following the Lamb
whithersoever he would go. After this, the others were also set
apart, and the first martyrs endured their sufferings with promptness and alacrity, most cheerfully finishing the confession of
martyrdom. They appeared, indeed, unprepared and inexpe-
rienced, and yet so weak as to be incapable of bearing the in

tensity of the mighty contest. Of these, indeed, about ten also fell away, causing great sorrow and excessive grief to our brethren, and damping the ardour of those who had not yet been taken. These, however, although they endured all manner of affliction, nevertheless were always present with the martyrs, and never left them. Then, indeed, we were all struck with great fear, on account of the uncertainty of their holding out in the profession, not indeed dreading the tortures inflicted, but looking at the end, and trembling lest they should apostatize. Those, indeed, that were worthy to fill up the number of the martyrs, were seized from day to day, so that all the zealous members of the two churches, and those by whose exertions the church had been there established, were collected. Some domestics that were heathen, belonging to our brethren, were also seized as the governor had publicly commanded search to be made for all of us. But these, at the instigation of Satan, fearing the tortures which they saw the saints suffering, and the soldiers beside this urging them, charged us with feasts of Thyestes,* and the incests of Oedipus,† and such crimes as are neither lawful for us to speak nor to think ; and, such, indeed, as we do not even believe were committed by men. These things being spread abroad among the people, all were so savage in their treatment of us, that, if before some had restrained themselves on account of some affinity, they then carried their cruelty and rage against us to a great excess. Then was fulfilled the declaration of our Lord, " that the day would come when every one that slayeth you will think he is doing God a service." The holy martyrs, after this, finally endured tortures, beyond all description ; Satan striving with all his power, that some blasphemy might be uttered by them. Most violently did the collective madness of the mob, the governor and the soldiers rage against the holy deacon of Vienna, and against Maturus, a new convert, indeed, but a noble champion of the faith. Also, against Attalus, a native of Pergamus, who was a pillar and foundation of the church there. Against

* Thyestes, according to the heathen mythology, ate part of his own son, whom his brother Atreus, to revenge the crime committed against himself, had slain.

† Oedipus, in ignorance, slew his father Laius, and married his mother Jocasta

Blandina, also, in whom Christ made manifest, that the things that appear mean and deformed and contemptible among men, are esteemed of great glory with God, on account of love to him, which is really and powerfully displayed, and glories not in mere appearance. For whilst we were all trembling, and her earthly mistress, who was herself one of the contending martyrs, was apprehensive lest through the weakness of the flesh she should not be able to profess her faith with sufficient freedom, Blandina was filled with such power, that her ingenious tormentors who relieved and succeeded each other from morning till night, confessed that they were overcome, and had nothing more that they could inflict upon her. Only amazed that she still continued to breathe after her whole body was torn asunder and pierced, they gave their testimony that one single kind of the torture inflicted was of itself sufficient to destroy life, without resorting to so many and such excruciating sufferings as these.

But this blessed saint, as a noble wrestler, in the midst of her confession itself renewed her strength, and to repeat, " I am a Christian, no wickedness is carried on by us," was to her rest, refreshment and relief from pain. But Sanctus himself, also nobly sustaining beyond all measure and human power, the various torments devised by men, whilst the wicked tormentors hoped that by the continuance and the greatness of the tortures, they would get to hear something from him that he ought not to say, withstood them with so much firmness, that he did not even declare his name, nor that of his nation, nor the city whence he was, nor whether he was a slave or a freeman, but to all the questions that were proposed, he answered in the Roman tongue, " I am a Christian." For this he confessed instead of his name, his city, his race, and instead of every thing. No other expression did the heathen hear from him. Whence, also, an ambitious struggle in torturing arose between the governor and the tormentors against him ; so that when they had nothing further that they could inflict, they at last fastened red hot plates of brass to the most tender parts of his body. But he continued unsubdued and unshaken, firm in his confession, refreshed and strengthened by the celestial fountain of living water that flows from Christ. But

the corpse itself was evidence of his sufferings, as it was one continued wound, mangled and shrivelled, that had entirely lost the
form of man to the external eye. Christ suffering in him exhibited wonders ; defeating the adversary, and presenting a kind of
model to the rest, that there is nothing terrific where the love of
the Father, nothing painful where the glory of Christ prevails.
For when the lawless tormentors tortured the martyr again
during the day, and supposed that whilst the wounds were
swollen and inflamed, if they applied the same torments, they
would subdue him, as if he would not then be able to bear even
the touch of the hand, or else, that dying under his tortures he
would strike a terror into the rest, not only was there no appearance like this, but, beyond all human expectation, the body raised
itself, and stood erect amid the torments afterwards inflicted, and
recovered the former shape and habit of the limbs ; so that his
second tortures became, through the grace of Christ, not his
torment, but his cure. But the devil also led forth a certain
Biblias to punishment, who was one of those that had renounced
the faith, thinking that he had already swallowed her, was anxious
to increase her condemnation by blasphemy, and constraining her
as a frail and timid character, easily overpowered, to utter impieties against us. But in the midst of the torture she repented
and recovered herself, and as if awaking out of a deep sleep, was
reminded by the punishment before her, of the eternal punishment in hell. And accordingly she contradicted the blasphemers
in her declarations. " How," said she, " could such as these devour
children, who considered it unlawful even to taste the blood of
irrational animals ?" After that, she professed herself a Christian,
and was added to the number of martyrs. But as all the tortures
of the tyrants were defeated by Christ, through the patience of the
martyrs, the devil devised other machinations ; among these were
their confinement in prison, in a dark and most dismal place ;
their feet also stretched in the stocks,* and extended to the fifth
hole, and other torments, which the enraged minions of wicked-

* The instrument of punishment here mentioned was a piece of timber, with five
pair of holes cut at certain distances apart. The feet were put into these and secured
with cords and fetters.

ness, especially when stimulated by the influence of Satan, are accustomed to inflict upon the prisoners. Numbers of them were, therefore, suffocated in prison, as many, viz., as the Lord would have to depart, thus showing forth his glory. Some of them, indeed, had been cruelly tormented, so that it appeared they could scarcely live, though every means were applied to recover them. Though confined in prison, devoid of all human aid, they were strengthened by the Lord, and filled with power from him both in body and mind, and even stimulated and encouraged the rest. But the new converts and those that were recently taken, whose bodies were not exercised in trials, did not bear the oppression of incarceration, but died within the prison.

But the blessed Pothinus, who had faithfully performed the ministrations of the episcopate at Lyons, and who was past his ninetieth year, and very infirm in body; who, indeed, scarcely drew his breath, so weak was he in body at the time; yet in the ardour of his soul, and his eager desire for martyrdom, he roused his remaining strength, and was himself also dragged to the tribunal. Though his body, indeed, was already nearly dissolved, partly by age and partly by disease, yet he still retaining his life in him, that Christ might triumph by it. When carried by the soldiers to the tribunal, whither the public magistrates accompanied him, as if he were Christ himself, and when all the mob raised every outcry against him, he gave a noble testimony. When interrogated by the governor, who was the God of the Christians, he said, " If thou art worthy, thou shalt know." After this, he was unmercifully dragged away and endured many stripes, whilst those that were near abused him with their hands and feet in every possible way, not even regarding his age. But those at a distance, whatsoever they had at hand, every one hurled at him, all thinking it would be a great sin and impiety if they fell short of wanton abuse against him. For they supposed they would thus avenge their own gods. Thus, scarcely drawing breath, he was thrown into prison, and after two days he there expired. A wonderful interposition of God was then exhibited, and the boundless mercy of Christ clearly displayed a thing that had rarely happened among brethren, but by no means beyond the reach of the skill of Christ. For those that had fallen from the faith on the first seizure, were also themselves imprisoned, and shared in the sufferings of the rest. Their renunciation did them no good at this time, but those that confessed what they really were, were imprisoned as Christians; no other charge being alleged against them. But these, at last, were confined as murderers and guilty culprits, and were punished with twice the severity of the rest. The former, indeed, were refreshed by the joy of martyrdom, the hope of the promises, the love of Christ, and the spirit of the Father ; but the latter were sadly tormented by their own conscience. So that the difference was obvious to all in their very countenances, when they were led forth. For the one went on joyful, much glory and grace being mixed in their faces, so that their bonds seemed to form noble ornaments, and, like those of a bride, adorned with various golden bracelets, and impregnated with the sweet odour of Christ, they appeared to some anointed with earthly perfumes. But the others, with downcast look, dejected, sad, and covered with every kind of shame, in addition to this, were reproached by the heathen as mean and cowardly, bearing the charge of murderers, and losing the honourable, glorious, and life-giving appellation of Christians. The rest, however, seeing these effects, were so much the more confirmed, and those that were taken immediately, confessed, not even admitting the thought suggested by diabolical objections. Introducing some further remarks, they again proceed : " After these things their martyrdom was finally distributed into various kinds ; for platting and constituting one crown of various colours and all kinds of flowers, they offered it to the Father. It was right, indeed, that these noble wrestlers, who had sustained a diversified contest, and had come off with a glorious victory, should bear away the great crown of immortality. Maturus, therefore, and Sanctus, and Blandina, and Attalus, were led into the amphitheatre to the wild beasts, and to the common spectacle of heathenish inhumanity, the day for exhibiting the fight with wild beasts being designedly published on our account. Maturus, however, and Sanctus, again passed through all the tortures in the amphitheatre, just as if they had suffered nothing at all before, or rather as those who in many trials before had defeated the adversary, and now contending for the crown itself, again as they passed, bore the strokes of the scourge* usually inflicted there, the draggings and lacerations from the beasts, and all that the madness of the people, one here and another there, cried for and demanded; and last of all the iron chair, upon which their bodies were roasted, whilst the fumes of their own flesh ascended to annoy them. The tormentors did not cease even then, but continued to rage so much the more, intending if possible to conquer their perseverance. They could not, however, elicit or hear anything from Sanctus, besides that confession which he had uttered from the beginning."

These two, therefore, in whom life for the most part had remained through the mighty conflict, were at last despatched. On that day, they were made an exhibition to the world, in place of the variety of gladiatorial combats. Blandina, however, was bound and suspended on a stake, and thus exposed as food to the assaults of wild beasts, and as she thus appeared to hang after the manner of the cross, by her earnest prayers she infused much alacrity into the contending martyrs. For as they saw her in the contest, with the external eyes, through their sister, they contemplated Him that was crucified for them, to persuade those that believe in him, that every one who suffers for Christ, will for ever enjoy communion with the living God. But as none of the beasts then touched her, she was taken down from the stake, and remanded back again to prison to be reserved for another contest; so that by gaining the victory in many conflicts, she might render the condemnation of the wily serpent, irrefragable, and though small and weak and contemptible, but yet clothed with the mighty and invincible wrestler Christ Jesus, might also encourage her brethren. Thus she overcame the enemy in many trials, and in the conflict received the crown of immortality. But Attalus himself, being vehemently demanded by the populace, as he was a distinguished character, came well prepared for the conflict, conscious as he was of no

---

* The punishment here inflicted, was much like what is called *running the gantlet*. The hunters stood in a long line, and as the martyrs passed, each one inflicted a stroke with a scourge upon the naked body.

evil done by him, and as one who had been truly exercised in Christian discipline, and had always been a witness of the truth with us. When led about in the theatre, with a tablet before him, on which was written in Latin, " This is Attalus the Christian," and the people were violently incensed against him, the governor learning that he was a Roman, ordered him to be remanded back again to prison with the rest, concerning whom he had written to Cesar, and was now awaiting his determination. But he (Attalus) in the meantime was neither idle nor unprofitable to them, but, by their patient endurance, the immeasurable mercy of Christ was manifested. For by means of those that were yet living, were things dead made to live. And the martyrs conferred benefits upon those that were no martyrs, (i. e. upon those that had fallen away.) Much joy was also created in the Virgin Mother, (the church,) for those whom she had brought forth as dead she recovered again as living. For by means of these the greater part of those that fell away, again retraced their steps, were again conceived, were again endued with vital heat, and learned to make the confession of their faith. And now living again, and strengthened in their faith, they approached the tribunal, where that God that willeth not the death of the sinner, but inviteth all to repentance, sweetly regarding them, they were again interrogated by the governor. For as Cesar had written that they should be beheaded, but if any renounced the faith these should be dismissed ; at the commencement of the fair which is held here, which indeed is attended by an immense concourse of people from all nations, the governor led forth the martyrs, exhibiting them as a show and public spectacle to the crowd. Wherefore, he also examined them again, and as many as appeared to have the Roman citizenship, these he beheaded. The rest he sent away to the wild beasts. But Christ was wonderfully glorified in those that had before renounced him, as they then, contrary to all suspicion, on the part of the Gentiles, confessed. And these indeed, were separately examined, as if they were soon to be dismissed ; but as they confessed, they were added to the number of the martyrs. Those, however, who had never any traces of the faith, nor any conception of the marriage garment, nor any thought of the fear of God, remained without, who, as the sons of perdition, blasphemed the way by their apostacy. All the rest, however, were attached to the church, of whom, when examined, a certain Alexander was found to be one, a Phrygian by birth, and physician by profession. Having passed many years in Gaul, and being well known for his love of God and his freedom in declaring the truth, for he was not destitute of apostolical grace, he stood before the tribunal, and by signs encouraged them to a good confession, appearing to those around the tribunal as one in the pains of childbirth. The mob, however, chagrined that those who had before renounced the faith were again confessing, cried out against Alexander, as if he had been the cause of this. And when the governor urged and asked him who he was, and he replied that he was a Christian, in his rage he condemned him to the wild beasts, and accordingly on the following day, he entered the arena with Attalus. For the governor to gratify the people, also gave up Attalus a second time to the beasts.

Thus, enduring all the torments that were invented as punishment in the amphitheatre, and after sustaining the arduous conflict, these were likewise finally despatched. As to Alexander, he neither uttered a groan nor any moaning sound at all, but in his heart communed with God; and Attalus, when placed upon the iron chair, and the fumes from his roasting body arose upon him, said to the multitude in Latin: " Lo this is to devour men, what you are doing. But as to us, we neither devour men nor commit any other evil." And when asked what was the name of God, he answered, God has no name like a man. After all these, on the last day of the shows of gladiators, Blandina was again brought forth, together with Ponticus, a youth about fifteen years old. These were brought in every day to see the tortures of the rest. Force was also used to make them swear by their idols; and when they continued firm, and denied their pretended divinity, the multitude became outrageous at them, so that they neither compassionated the youth of the boy nor regarded the sex of the woman. Hence they subjected them to every horrible suffering, and led them through the whole round of torture, ever and anon striving to force them to swear, but were unable to effect it. Ponticus, indeed, encouraged by his sister, so that the heathen could see that she was encouraging and confirming him, nobly bore the whole of these sufferings, and gave up his life. But the blessed Blandina, last of all, as a noble mother that had animated her children, and sent them as victors to the great King, herself retracing the ground of all the conflicts her children had endured, hastened at last, with joy and exultation at the issue, to them, as if she were invited to a marriage feast, and not to be cast to wild beasts. And thus, after scourging, after exposure to the beasts, after roasting, she was finally thrown into a net and cast before a bull, and when she had been well tossed by the animal, and had now no longer any sense of what was done to her by reason of her firm hope, confidence, faith, and her communion with Christ, she too was despatched. Even the Gentiles confessed, that no woman among them had ever endured sufferings as many and great as these. But not even then was their madness and cruelty to the saints satisfied; for these fierce and barbarous tribes, stimulated by the savage beast Satan, were in a fury not easily to be assuaged, so that their abuse of the bodies assumed another novel and singular aspect. Not abashed when overcome by the martyrs, but evidently destitute of all reason, the madness both of the governor and the people, as of some savage beast, blazed forth so much the more, to exhibit the same unjust hostility against us. That the Scriptures might be fulfilled, " He that is unjust let him be unjust still, and he that is righteous let him be righteous still." Rev. xxii. 11. For those that were suffocating in the prison, they cast to the dogs, carefully watching them night and day, lest any should be buried by us, and then also cast away the remains left by the beasts and the fire, howsoever they had either been mangled or burnt. They also guarded the heads of the others, together with the trunks of their bodies, with military watches, for many days in succession, in order to prevent them from being buried. Some, indeed, raged and gnashed their teeth against them, anxious to find out some better way of punishment. Others, again, laughed at and insulted them, extolling their idols, and imputing to them the punishment of the martyrs. But others, more moderate, and who in some measure appeared to sympathize, frequently upbraided them, saying, " where is their God, and what benefit has their religion been to them, which they preferred to their own life?" Such was the variety of disposition among the Gentiles, but among our brethren, matters were in great affliction for want of liberty to commit the bodies to the earth. For neither did the night avail us for this purpose, nor had money any effect to persuade, nor could any prayers or entreaties move them. But they guarded them in every possible way, as if it were a great gain, to prevent them from burial. To these, they afterwards add other accounts, saying : " The bodies of the martyrs after being abused in every possible manner, and thus exposed to the open air for six days, were at length burned and reduced to ashes by the wretches, and finally cast into the Rhone that flows near at hand, that there might not be a vestige of them remaining on the land. These things they did as if they were able to overcome God, and destroy their resurrection, ($\pi\alpha\lambda\iota\gamma\gamma\epsilon\nu\epsilon\sigma\iota\alpha\nu$) as they themselves gave out, ' that they might not have any hope of rising again, in the belief of which, they have introduced a new and strange religion, and contemn the most dreadful punishments, and are prepared to meet death even with joy. Now we shall see, whether they will rise again ; and whether their god is able to help them, and rescue them out of our hands.' "

CHAPTER II.

Those that had fallen away, kindly restored, by the pious martyrs.

Such were the occurrences that befel the churches of Christ under the abovementioned emperor, from which it is easy to conjecture what was the probable course of things in the remaining provinces. It may be well here to add to these accounts, other extracts from the same epistle, in which the moderation and benevolence of these martyrs whom we have mentioned, is recorded in the following words : " They were also so zealous in their imitation of Christ, who, though in the form of God, thought it not robbery to be equal with God," that though they were esteemed in the same light, and had neither once nor twice, but frequently, endured martyrdom, and had been again taken away from the beasts to prison, and had brands, and scars, and wounds spread over them, they did not proclaim themselves martyrs, for it did not become us to apply this name to them; but if any one of us, either by letter or in conversation, called them martyrs, they seriously reproved us. For they cheerfully yielded the title of martyr to Christ, the true and faithful martyr, (witness) the first begotten from the dead, the prince of divine life. They also made mention of those martyrs that had already departed, and said: "They now are martyrs whom Christ has thought worthy to be received in their confession, setting the seal to their martyrdom, (testimony,) by the issue. But we are but indifferent and mean confessors, and with tears did they entreat the brethren, that they should offer up incessant prayers, that they might be made perfect. They exhibited, indeed, the power of martyrdom in fact, exercising much freedom in declaring themselves to all people, and manifested their noble patience and fearless intrepidity; but the name of martyrs, (witnesses) they declined receiving from the brethren, filled as they were with the fear of God." Again, after a little, they say, "They humbled themselves under the mighty hand, by which they are now highly exalted. Then, however, they pleaded for all, they accused none, they absolved all, they bound none, and prayed for those that were so bitter in their hostility, like Stephen, that perfect martyr. 'Lord impute not this sin to them.' But if he prayed for those that stoned him, how much more for the brethren." And again they say, after mentioning other matters, "This was their greatest conflict against him, (the devil,) on account of the genuine character of their love, that the beast being choaked and throttled might be forced to return alive again (to vomit up) those whom he had already thought to have swallowed. For they did not arrogate any superiority over the backsliders: but in those things wherein they themselves abounded; in this they supplied those that were deficient, exercising the compassion of mothers, and pouring forth many prayers, to the Father on their account. They implored life, and he gave it to them, which they also shared with their neighbours; coming off victorious over all, to God: always lovers of peace, they always recommended peace, and with peace they departed to God. Not leaving grief to their mother, (the church,) no discord or dissensions to the brethren, but joy and peace, unanimity and love. This account may be profitably added, respecting the love of these blessed brethren towards those that fell away, on account of those also, who after these events, unsparingly exercised an inhuman and merciless disposition towards the members of Christ.

CHAPTER III.

The vision that appeared to Attalus the martyr, in a dream.

THE same epistle of the abovementioned martyrs, also contains another account worthy of record, which no one could regret to be presented to the knowledge of our readers. It is as follows: " A certain Alcibiades, who was one of these (martyrs,) and who had led a hard and rough kind of life, partook of no food usually eaten, but merely bread and water. When cast into prison, and he attempted to lead the same kind of life, it was revealed to Attalus, after the first conflict which he finished in the amphitheatre, that Alcibiades did not do well in not making use of the creatures of God, and affording an example of offence to others. Alcibiades, therefore, in obedience to this, partook of all kinds of food, and gave thanks to God; for neither were they destitute of divine grace, but the divine spirit was their counsellor." But let this suffice concerning these. Now as Montanus, and Alcibiades,* and Theodotus, in Phrygia, then first began to be esteemed by many for their gifts, (as there were many other wonderful powers of divine grace, yet exhibited even at that time in different churches,) they created the belief with

---

* This is a different Alcibiades from the one beforementioned.

many, that they also were endued with prophecy. And as there was a dissension in consequence of these men, the brethren in Gaul again presented their own pious and correct judgment also concerning these, and published several letters of the martyrs that had been put to death among them. These they had written whilst yet in prison, and addressed to the brethren in Asia and Phrygia. And not only to these but likewise to Eleutherus, who was then bishop of Rome, negotiating as it were for the peace of the churches.

CHAPTER IV.

The martyrs commend Irenaus in their epistle.

But these same martyrs recommending also Irenæus, who was then a presbyter of the church at Lyons, to the bishop of Rome beforementioned, bear abundant testimony in his favour, as the following extracts show : " We pray and desire, father Eleutherus, that you may rejoice in God in all things and always. We have requested our brother and companion Irenæus to carry this epistle to you, and we exhort you to consider him as commended to you as a zealous follower of the testament (covenant) of Christ. For if we knew that any place could confer righteousness upon any one, we would certainly commend him among the first as a presbyter of the church, the station that he holds." Why should we here transcribe the list of those martyrs given in the abovementioned epistle, of whom some were made perfect by decapitation, some cast to be devoured by wild beasts, and others again fell asleep in prison. Why repeat the number of confessors still living ? For whoever wishes to learn these, can more easily obtain the fullest account by consulting the epistle itself, which, as I said, has been inserted by us in our collection of martyrs. But such were the events that happened under Antonine.

CHAPTER V.

God sent rain from heaven to Marcus Aurelius, the emperor, at the prayers of our brethren.

But it is said that Marcus Aurelius Cesar, the brother of the former, when about to engage in battle with the Germans and Sarmatians, and his army was suffering with thirst, was greatly at a loss on this account. Then, however, those soldiers that belonged to the Melitine legion, as it was called, by a faith which has continued from that time to this, bending their knees upon the earth whilst drawn up in battle array against the enemy, according to our peculiar custom of praying, entered into prayer before God. And as this was a singular spectacle to the enemy, a still more singular circumstance is reported to have happened immediately; that the lightning drove the enemy into flight and destruction, but that a shower came down and refreshed the army of those that then called upon God, the whole of which was on the point of perishing with thirst. This history is related also by historians who are strangers to our doctrine, who, however, took an interest in the writings of those whom we have mentioned; but it is also stated by our own writers, whilst the wonderful event is also added by historians who differ from our faith, but who do not admit that this happened at the prayers of our brethren. But the fact is handed down on record by our brethren, as lovers of truth, in a plain and undisguised manner. Of these we might mention Apollinaris, who says that from that time the legion at whose prayers the wonder took place, received an appellation appropriate to the event, from the emperor, being called the *fulminea*, or thundering legion. Tertullian also might be cited as a suitable witness of these things, in the Apology that he addressed to the Roman senate for the faith, the work which has been already mentioned by us, in which he confirms the history with greater and more powerful proof, where he writes as follows: " There are epistles of the most learned emperor Marcus still extant, in which he himself bears testimony that when his army was ready to perish for want of water, it was saved by the prayers of the Christians;" he says also, " that the same emperor threatened death to those that attempted to accuse us." To which he also adds, " What kind of laws are those which the wicked, unjust, and cruel put in force against us alone? which neither Vespasian observed, although be conquered the Jews, which Trajan in part annulled; forbidding that the Christians should be hunted up; which not even Adrian, though very inquisitive in all matters, nor he that was surnamed the Pious, confirmed." But every one may place these to what account he pleases. Let us proceed to the order of our history. Pothinus having died with the other martyrs of Gaul, in the ninetieth year of his age, he was succeeded by Irenæus in the episcopate of the church at Lyons. We have understood he was a hearer of Polycarp in his youth. This writer has inserted the succession of the bishops in his third book against the heresies, where he reviews the catalogue down to Eleutherus, whose times we are now examining, as he laboured with him in the production of this work, writing as follows.

CHAPTER VI.

Catalogue of the bishops of Rome.

" THE blessed apostles having founded and established the church, transmitted the office of the episcopate to Linus. Of this Linus, Paul makes mention in his Epistles to Timothy. He was succeeded by Anencletus, and after him Clement held the episcopate, the third from the apostles. Who, as he had seen the blessed apostles, and had been connected with them, might be said to have the doctrine of the apostles still sounding in his ears, and what they delivered before his eyes. And not only he, but many others were still left, who had been taught by the apostles. In the times of this Clement, there was no little dissension among the brethren at Corinth, on occasion of which the church at Rome wrote a considerable Epistle to the Corinthians, confirming them in peace, and renewing their faith and the doctrine they had lately received from the apostles. After a little, he subjoins: "But this Clement was succeeded by Euarestus, and Euarestus by Alexander. Xystus followed as the sixth from the apostles, after whom was Telesphorus, who also illustriously suffered martyrdom, then came Hyginus, and after him Pius. He was followed by Anicetus, and as he was succeeded by Soter, the twelfth from the apostles in the episcopate now is Eleutherus, in the same order and the same doctrine (or succession*) in which the tradition of the apostles in the church and the promulgation of the truth has descended to us."

CHAPTER VII.

Miracles were performed in those times by the believers.

THESE accounts are given by Irenæus in those five books of his, to which he gave the title of "Refutation and Overthrow of False Doctrine." In the second book of the same work, he also shows that even down to his times, instances of divine and miraculous power were remaining in some churches. "So far are they," says he, "from raising the dead, as the Lord raised, and as the apostles by means of prayer, for even among the brethren frequently in a case of necessity when a whole church united in much fasting and prayer, the spirit has returned to the ex-animated body, and the man was granted to the prayers of the saints." And again, he says, after other observations: "But if they say that our Lord also did these things only in appearance, we shall refer them back to the prophetic declarations, and shall show from them that all those things were strictly foretold, and were done by him, and that he alone is the Son of God. Wherefore, also, those that were truly his disciples, receiving grace from him, in his name performed these things for the benefit

* The word succession, in the parenthesis, is adopted by Valesius as the correct reading.

or the rest of men, as every one received the free gift from him. Some, indeed, most certainly and truly cast out dæmons, so that frequently these persons themselves that were cleansed from wicked spirits believed and were received into the church. Others have the knowledge of things to come, as also visions and prophetic communications; others heal the sick by the imposition of hands, and restore them to health. And, moreover, as we said above, even the dead have been raised and continued with us many years. And why should we say more? It is impossible to tell the number of the gifts which the church throughout the world received from God, and the deeds performed in the name of Jesus Christ, that was crucified under Pontius Pilate, and this too every day for the benefit of the heathen, without deceiving any, or exacting their money. For as she has received freely from God, she also freely ministers." In another place the same author writes: " As we hear many of the brethren in the church who have prophetic gifts, and who speak in all tongues through the spirit, and who also, bring to light the secret things of men for their benefit, and who expound the mysteries of God." These gifts of different kinds also continued with those that were worthy until the times mentioned.

CHAPTER VIII.

The statement of Irenæus respecting the sacred Scriptures.

SINCE we have promised in the outset of our work to give extracts occasionally when we refer to the declarations of the ancient presbyters and historians of the church, in which they have transmitted the traditions that have descended to us respecting the sacred Scriptures, among these Irenæus was one. Let us now give his words, and first of all what he has said of the holy gospels: " Matthew, indeed," says he, " produced his gospel written among the Hebrews in their own dialect, whilst Peter and Paul proclaimed the gospel and founded the church at Rome.

After the departure of these, Mark, the disciple and interpreter of Peter, also transmitted to us in writing what had been preached by Peter. And Luke, the companion of Paul, committed to writing the gospel preached by him, i. e. Paul. Afterwards John the disciple of our Lord, the same that lay upon his bosom, also published the gospel, whilst he was yet at Ephesus in Asia." This is what this author says in the third book of the work already mentioned; and in the fifth, he thus descants on the Revelation of John and the calculation of antichrist's name: " As matters are thus, and the number is thus found in all the genuine and ancient copies, and as they who saw John attest, reason itself shows that the number of the name of the beast is indicated by the Greek letters which it contains." And a little further on he speaks of the same John: " We, therefore," says he, " do not venture to affirm any thing with certainty respecting the name of antichrist. For were it necessary that his name should be clearly announced to the present age, it would have been declared by him who saw the revelation. For it has not been long since it was seen, but almost in our own generation, about the end of Domitian's reign." These are what he states respecting the Revelation. He also mentions the First Epistle of John, extracting many testimonies from it: he also mentions the First Epistle of Peter. And he not only knew, but also admitted the book called Pastor, in these words: " Well is it said in that work which declares, ' first of all believe that there is one God, who created and arranged all things,' " &c.

He also quotes some expressions from the Wisdom of Solomon, almost in these words: " The vision of God is productive of immortality, but immortality makes us to be next to God." He also mentions the commentaries of a certain apostolical presbyter, whose name he has passed by in silence; he also adds his expositions of the sacred Scriptures. He moreover makes mention of Justin Martyr and Ignatius, taking some testimony also from the works written by these. He also promises in a separate work to refute some of the writings of Marcion. Hear also what he has written respecting the translation of the holy Scriptures by the seventy. " God," says he, " became man, and the Lord himsel' saved us, giving us the sign of the Virgin. But not as some say, that now presume to interpret the Scriptures. 'Behold a young woman shall conceive and bear a son,' as Theodotian of Ephesus and Aquila of Pontus, have translated, both of them Jewish proselytes. Whom the Ebionites following, assert that Jesus was begotten of Joseph." After a little, he adds: " For before the Romans established their empire, whilst yet the Macedonians had possession of Asia, Ptolemy the son of Lagus being ambitious to adorn the library established by him in Alexandria, with the works of all men, as many as were worthy of being studied, requested of the inhabitants of Jerusalem to have their works translated into the Greek; but as they were yet subject to the Macedonians, they sent seventy of their elders that were best skilled in the Scriptures, and in both languages, to Ptolemy, and thus Providence favoured his design. But as he wished them to make the attempt separately, and apprehensive, lest by concert they might conceal the truth of the Scriptures by their interpretation, therefore separating them from one another, he commanded all to write the same translation. And this he did in all the books. Assembling therefore in the same place, in the presence of Ptolemy, and each of them comparing their respective versions, God was glorified, and the Scriptures were recognised as truly divine, as all of them rendered the same things, in the very same expressions, and the same words, from the beginning to the end. So that the Gentiles present knew that the Scriptures were translated by a divine inspiration. Neither was it any thing extraordinary that God should have done this, who, indeed, in the captivity of the people under Nebuchadnezzar, when the Scriptures had been destroyed, and the Jews returned to their country after seventy years, subsequently in the times of Artaxeres king of the Persians he inspired Esdras the priest, of the tribe of Levi, to compose anew all the discourses of the ancient prophets, and to restore to the people the laws given by Moses." Thus far Irenæus.

CHAPTER IX.

The bishops under Commodus.

ANTONINUS having held the empire nineteen years, Commodus received the government. In his first year Julian undertook the superintendance of the churches of Alexandria, after Agrippinus had filled the office twelve years.

CHAPTER X.

Of Pantænus the philosopher.

ABOUT the same time, the school of the faithful was governed by a man most distinguished for his learning, whose name was Pantænus. As there had been a school of sacred learning established there from ancient times, which has continued down to our own times, and which we have understood was held by men able in eloquence, and the study of divine things. For the tradition is, that this philosopher was then in great eminence, as he had been first disciplined in the philosophical principles of those called stoics. But he is said to have displayed such ardour, and so zealous a disposition, respecting the divine word, that he was constituted a herald of the gospel of Christ to the nations of the east, and advanced even as far as India. There were even there yet many evangelists of the word, who were ardently striving to employ their inspired zeal after the apostolic example, to increase and build up the divine word. Of these Pantænus is said to have been one, and to have come as far as the Indies. And the report is, that he there found his own arrival anticipated by some who there were acquainted with the gospel of Matthew, to whom Bartholomew, one of the apostles, had preached, and had left them the gospel of Matthew in the Hebrew, which was also preserved until this time. Pantænus, after many praiseworthy deeds, was finally at the head of the Alexandrian school, commenting on the treasures of divine truth, both orally and in his writings.

CHAPTER XI.

Clement of Alexandria.

At this time, also, flourished Clement, at Alexandria, of the same name with him who anciently presided over the church of Rome, and who was a disciple of the apostles. This Clement was devoted to the study of the same Scriptures with Pantænus, and in his Institutions expressly mentions the latter by name as his teacher. He also appears to me to designate this same one in the first book of his Stromata, when he points out the most distinguished of the apostolic succession, which he had received from tradition, in the following words: " These books," says he, " were not fabricated as a work of ostentation, but they are treasured up by me as a kind of commentaries for my old age, and an antidote to forgetfulness, as a natural image and sketch of those efficacious and inspired doctrines which I was honoured to have from those blessed and truly excellent men. Of these, the one was Ionicus in Greece, but the other in Magna Græcia; the one of them being a Syrian, the other a native of Egypt. Others, however, there were, living in the east; and of these, one was from Assyria, another of Palestine, a Hebrew by descent. The last that I met with was the first in excellence. Him I found concealed in Egypt; and, meeting him there, I ceased to extend my search beyond him, as one who had no superior in abilities. These, indeed, preserved the true tradition of the salutary doctrine, which, as given by Peter and James, John and Paul, had descended from father to son. Though there are few like their fathers, they have, by the favour of God, also come down to us to plant that ancient and apostolic seed likewise in our minds."

CHAPTER XII.

The bishops of Jerusalem.

At this time also, Narcissus, who is celebrated among many even at this day, was noted as bishop of Jerusalem, being the fifteenth in succession since the invasion of the Jews under Hadrian. Since this event, we have shown that the church there consisted of Gentiles after those of the circumcision, and that Marcus was the first bishop of the Gentiles that presided there. After him, Cassianus held the episcopal office; after him followed Publius, then Maximus; these were followed by Julian, then Caius; after him Symmachus, and another Caius; and then another Julian, who was followed by Capito, and Valens and Dolichianus. Last of all Narcissus, the thirtieth in regular succession from the apostles.

CHAPTER XIII.

Of Rhodo, and the dissension occasioned by Marcion, which he records.

About this time, also, Rhodo, a native of Asia, being instructed, as himself says, by Tatian, with whom we have already become acquainted, and having written various other books, among the rest, also combatted the heresy of Marcion. This, he says, was split into various opinions in his time; and describing those that occasioned the decision, he also accurately refutes the perverse doctrines devised by each of them. Hear him in his own words: "Hence," says he, "they are also divided among themselves, as they maintain a doctrine that cannot stand. For from this herd arose Apelles, who, assuming a gravity of deportment, and presuming upon his age, professed to believe but one principle, and that the prophetic declarations proceeded from an adverse spirit. He was deluded, however, by the responsive oracular answers of a certain virgin under demoniacal influence, and whose name was Philumena. But others, as the Mariner Marcion himself, introduced two principles, to which sect belong Potitus and Basilicus. These following that wolf of Pontus (Marcion), and, like the former, unable to find the division of things, sunk into licentiousness, and roundly asserted, without any proof, that there were two principles. Others, again, declining from them to a still greater error, established not only two but three natures.' Of these, the chief and leader was Syneros, as those that established his school say. But the same author writes, that he also had some conference with Apelles. " For," says he, " the old man Apelles, when he came into conversation with us, was refuted in many of his false assertions. Hence, he also said, that one ought not to examine doctrine, but that each one should continue as he believed. For he asserted, that those who trusted in him that was crucified would be saved, if they were only found engaged in good works. But he asserted, that the most obscure of all things was, as we before said, the question respecting the Deity." For he said there was one principle, as our doctrine asserts: then, after advancing the whole of his opinion, he subjoins the following: " When I said to him, ' how do you prove this? or, how can you say there is one principle? I wish you to explain,' he said, ' that the prophecies refuted themselves, because they uttered nothing that was true. For they are inconsistent and false, and contradict themselves. But said, that he did not, however, know there was only one principle, he was only moved to adopt this opinion.' Then conjuring him to speak the truth, he swore that he did speak the truth, and said he did not understand how there could be a God without being produced, but that he believed it. On learning this, I laughed, and reproved him; because whilst he asserted that he was a teacher, he knew not how to establish that which he taught."

In the same work which he addressed to Callistion, he confesses that he himself was taught by Tatian at Rome, and says, also, that a book of questions had been written by Tatian, in which Tatian, having promised that he would explain what was hidden and obscure in the sacred writings; Rhodon himself promises that he would give solutions to these questions in a work of his own. There is also a commentary of his extant, on the Hexahemeron. But this same Apelles uttered innumerable impieties against the law of Moses, and in many works he reviled the sacred Scriptures, using no small exertions, as it seems, to refute and overturn them. Thus far, however, respecting these

CHAPTER XIV.

The false prophets of the Phrygians.

But, as the enemy of the church of God is the great adversary of all goodness, the promoter of evil, and omits no method of plotting against men, he was active again in causing new heresies to spring up against the church. Some of these crept like venomous reptiles over Asia and Phrygia, pretending that Montanus was the Paraclete,* but that the two women who followed him, Priscilla and Maximilla, were prophetesses of Montanus.

CHAPTER XV.

Of the schism of Blastus, at Rome.

OTHERS there were that flourished at Rome, at the head of whom was Florinus, who falling from his office as a presbyter of the church, Blastus was very nearly involved in the same fall

---

* *Paraclete*, the epithet of the holy Spirit, occurring in St. John's gospel. It is the Greek derivative, signifying *Comforter* or *Advocate*. Other false teacher besides Montanus, have either assumed or had this epithet applied to them; among these, the impostor Mahomet is not the least noted. In the gospel of Barnabas, this name, by a mere change of the vowels, is περικλυτος, *the most glorious*, instead of παρακλητος. As this expresses the meaning of Mahomet's name, this gospel o Barnabas is much valued, at least among the African Mahometans. See the Coran, Sur. LXI.

with him. These, also, drawing away many of the church, seduced them into their opinions, each one endeavouring separatelᵛ
to introduce his own innovations respecting the truth

CHAPTER XVI.

The affairs of Montanus, and his false prophets.

AGAINST the abovementioned heresy of the Cataphrygians,
that power which is the defender of the truth, raised up a powerful weapon and antagonist in Apollinaris of Hierapolis, whom
we mentioned before, and many other eloquent men with him
there. Of whom, also, most abundant matter has been left us
for our history. A certain one of them, in the very beginning
of his work against them (the Cataphrygians,) first intimates
that he would meet and refute them by open argument. For
thus he commences his work: " As for a long and very considerable time, O beloved Avircius Marcellus, I have been
urged by thee to write a discourse against the heresy which
is called after Miltiades, I have been somehow too much in
doubt until now, not indeed, for want of argument to refute the
false doctrine, or to bear witness to the truth, but fearing and
apprehensive, lest, perhaps, I should appear to any to give any
new injunctions, or to superadd any thing to the doctrine of the
New Testament, to which it is impossible that any thing should
be added or diminished, by one who has resolved to live according to the gospel. Lately, however, having been at Ancyra, a
city of Galatia, and having understood that the church in Pontus
was very much agitated by this new prophecy, as they call it,
but which, as shall be shown, with divine assistance, deserves
rather the name of false prophesy, I discoursed many days in
the church, both respecting these matters and others that were
proposed by them. So that the church, indeed, rejoiced and
was strengthened in the truth ; but the adversaries were put to
flight, and the opponents were cast down. But as the presbyters
of the place requested that we should leave some comment of

those things that we said, in opposition to the opponents of the truth, Zoticus Otrenus also being present, who was our fellow-presbyter ; this, indeed, I did not perform, but I promised writing hither, and to send it as soon as possible, if the Lord permitted." Such, and other matters, he states in the beginning of his work, premising the cause of the mentioned heresy, as follows: "Their combination, therefore, and the recent heretical severance of theirs from the church, had for its origin the following cause :— There is said to be a certain village of Mysia in Phrygia, called Ardaba. There, they say, one of those who was but a recent convert, Montanus by name, when Cratus was proconsul in Asia, in the excessive desire of his soul to take the lead, gave the adversary occasion against himself. So that he was carried away in spirit, and wrought up into a certain kind of frenzy and irregular ecstasy, raving, and speaking, and uttering strange things, and proclaiming what was contrary to the institutions that had prevailed in the church, as handed down and preserved in succession from the earliest times. But of those that hap-pened then to be present, and to hear these spurious oracles, some being indignant, rebuked him as one under the influence of dæmons and the spirit of delusion, and who was only exciting disturbances among the multitude. These bore in mind the distinction and the warning given by our Lord, when he cau-tioned them to be vigilantly on their guard against false prophets. Others again, as if elated by the holy spirit, and the gift of grace, and not a little puffed up, and forgetting the distinction made by our Lord, challenged this insidious, flattering, and seducing spirit being themselves captivated and seduced by him ; so that they could no longer restrain him to keep silence. Thus, by an ar-tifice, or rather by a certain crafty process, the devil having devised destruction against those that disobeyed the truth, and thus excessively honoured by them, secretly stimulated and fired their understandings, already wrapt in insensibility, and wander-ing away from the truth. For he excited two others, females, and filled them with the spirit of delusion, so that they also spake like the former, in a kind of extatic frenzy, out of all season. and in a manner strange and novel, whilst the spirit of evi con-

gratulated them, thus rejoicing and inflated by him, and continu
ed to puff them up the more, by promises of great things. Sometimes pointedly and deservedly, directly condemning them that
he might appear also disposed to reprove them. Those few that
were deceived were Phrygians; but the same inflated spirit
taught them to revile the whole church under heaven, because it
gave neither access nor honour to this false spirit of prophecy.
For when the faithful held frequent conversations in many
places throughout Asia for this very purpose, and examined
their novel doctrines, and pronounced them vain, and rejected
them as heresy, then indeed they were expelled and prohibited
from communion with the church." After relating these facts
in the beginning of his work, and introducing the refutation of
their error in the body of the work, he adds the following remarks in the second book, respecting their end : " Therefore,"
says he, " since they call us slayers of the prophets, because we
did not promptly receive their talkative prophets, saying, ' these
were those whom the Lord promised to send to the people.' " Let
them answer us in the name of God, O friends, which of these
who began prating from Montanus and his women, is there that
suffered persecution, or was slain by the evil doers? None. Not
even one of them has been seized and crucified for the name (of
Christ.) None at all. Not one of their women was ever scourged
in the synagogues of the Jews, or stoned. No, never.

Montanus and Maximilla indeed, are said to have died
another death than this, for at the instigation of that mischievous
spirit, the report is, that both of them hung themselves, not indeed
at the same time, but at the particular time of each one's death,
as the general report is ; and thus they died and terminated their
life like the traitor Judas. Thus, also, the general opinion is, that
Theodotus, one of the first that was carried away by their prophecy, as it was called, and who became a kind of patron of the
delusion, as if he should at some time be taken up and received into
the heavens, and who falling into trances, gave himself up to the
spirit of deception, was finally tossed by him like a quoit in the
air, and thus miserably perished. They say this happened as
we have stated. But, my friend, we do not presume to know

anything certain of these matters, unless we had seen them. For perhaps both Montanus and Theodotus, and the abovementioned woman, may have died in this way, or they may not." He mentions also in the same book, that the holy bishops of that time attempted to refute the spirit in Maximilla, but were prevented by others who manifestly co-operated with the spirit. His statement is as follows: " And let not, as is said in the same work of Asterius Urbanus, let not the spirit of Maximilla say, 'I am chased like a wolf from the flock, I am no wolf. I am utterance, spirit, and power.' But let him show the power in the spirit effectually, and prove it. And let him by the spirit face those that were present at the time, to examine and argue with the babbling spirit, men who were eminent, and bishops of the church, Zoticus of Comana, Julian of Apamea, whose tongues the followers of Themison bridled and prevented them from refuting the false and seducing spirit."

In the same work, after stating other matters in refutation of the false predictions of Maximilla, he likewise indicates the time that he wrote this, and mentions also, her declarations in which she foretold that there would be wars and political convulsions. The falsity of which is evinced by him as follows: " And has not," says he, " the falsehood of this been made obvious? For it is now more than thirteen years since the woman died, and neither has there been a partial nor a general war, but rather, by the mercy of God, continued peace to the Christians." This he writes in the second book. I shall also subjoin some extracts from the third book, in which he speaks as follows, against those who boasted that there were many of their number that had suffered martyrdom: " But," says he, " since they are at a loss what to reply to the refutation of their errors, they attempt to take refuge to their martyrs, saying they have many martyrs, and that this is one sure evidence of the power of that spirit which they call prophetical. But this, as it appears, is nothing the more true on that account. For some of the other heresies also have a vast number of martyrs, but neither do we the more on that account agree with them, nor acknowledge that they have truth on their side. Indeed, they who are called Marcionites, say that they had vast numbers that were martyrs for Christ. But they do not confess Christ in truth." And a little after, he adds: "Hence, whenever those that are called martyrs by the church, on account of enduring martyrdom for the true faith, happen to fall in with those called martyrs of the Phrygian heresy, they always separate from them and undergo death, having no communion with them, because they do not assent to the spirit of Montanus and the women, and that all this is true, and happened in our own times at Apamea on the Menander, is manifest from those who suffered martyrdom with Caius and Alexander of Eumenia."

CHAPTER XVII.

Of Miltiades and his works.

In the same work he also makes mention of the historian Miltiades, who also wrote a book against the same heresy. After quoting some passages from them, he adds: "As I found these statements in one of their works against another work written by our brother Alcibiades, in which he demonstrates the impropriety of a prophet's speaking in ecstasy. This work I have abridged." After stating other matters, he enumerates those who had prophesied under the New Testament. Among these he mentions one Ammias and Quadratus. "But the false prophet," says he, "is carried away by a vehement ecstasy, accompanied by want of all shame and fear. Beginning, indeed, with a designed ignorance, and terminating, as beforesaid, in involuntary madness. They will never be able to show that any of the Old or any of the New Testament, were thus violently agitated and carried away in spirit. Neither will they be able to boast that Agabus, or Judas, or Silas, or the daughters of Philip, or Ammias in Philadelphia, or Quadratus, or others that do not belong to them, ever acted in this way." Again, after a little, he says: "If after Quadratus and Ammias in Philadelphia, the women that followed Montanus succeeded in the gift of prophecy,

let them show us what women among them succeeded Montanus
and his women. For the apostle shows that the gift of prophecy
should be in all the church until the coming of the Lord, but they
can by no means show any one at this time, the fourteenth year
from the death of Maximilla." Thus far of this author. But
the Miltiades mentioned by him has left other monuments of his
study in the holy Scriptures, both in the works that he wrote
against the Greeks, and those against the Jews. Both treatises
are composed in two separate volumes. He has, moreover, written a work against the philosophers of the age, in favour of the
philosophy which he embraced.

CHAPTER XVIII.

*Apollonius also refutes the Phrygian heresy, and those whom he
has mentioned.*

But the heresy of the Phrygians, as it was called, still continuing to prevail in Phrygia, Apollonius undertook to refute it in a
particular work which he wrote; on the one hand correcting their
false predictions in reference to what they said, and on the other
describing the life that those led who were its founders. Hear him
in his own words respecting Montanus: "But who," says he, "is
this new teacher? His works and his doctrines sufficiently show
it. This is he that taught the dissolutions of marriage, he that
imposed laws of fasting, that called Pepuza and Tymium, little
places in Phrygia, a Jerusalem, in order to collect men from
every quarter thither; who established exactors of money, and
under the name of offerings, devised the artifice to procure presents; who provided salaries for those that preached his doctrine,
that it might grow strong by gormandizing and gluttony." Thus
far concerning Montanus; and further on he writes concerning
his prophetesses: "We show, therefore," says he, "that these
same leading prophetesses, as soon as they were filled with the
spirit, abandoned their husbands. How then can they utter this
falsehood, who call Prisca a virgin?" He afterwards proceeds

again: " Does it not appear to you that the Scripture forbids any prophet to receive gifts and money? When, therefore, I see a prophetess receiving both gold and silver, and precious garments, how can 1 fail to reject her?" Again, further on, respecting a certain one of their confessors, he says : " Moreover, Themison, who was completely clad in a most plausible covetousness, who could not bear the great characteristic of confession, but threw aside bonds and imprisonment for the abundance of wealth, and though it became him to walk humbly, boasted as a martyr, and dared to imitate the apostles by drawing up a certain catholic epistle, to instruct those who had a better faith than himself, to contend for doctrines of empty sound, and to utter impieties against the Lord and his apostles and the holy church." Again, speaking of others that are honoured among them as martyrs, he writes thus : " But not to speak of many, let the prophetess tell us the circumstances of Alexander, who called himself a martyr, with whom she feasted, the same too that is adored by numbers; whose robberies and other crimes, for which he was punished, it is not for us to tell, but which are preserved in the public records. Which of them forgives another his sins? Does the prophetess forgive the martyr his robberies? or the martyr forgive the prophetess her avarice? Although the Lord has said, ' lay not up for yourselves gold or silver, nor two coats,' these, in direct opposition, have committed great crimes in regard to the possession of things thus prohibited. For we shall show, that those that are called martyrs and prophets among them, have derived pecuniary gain, not only from the wealthy, but from the poor, and from widows and orphans, and if they have any confidence (of innocence) in this, let them stand and settle these matters with us; so that if they are convicted, they may abandon their misdemeanours hereafter.

" The fruits of a prophet must be examined ; for by its fruits the tree is known. But that those who wish may understand the circumstances respecting this Alexander, he was tried by Æmilius Frontinus, the proconsul (of Asia) at Ephesus, not for the name (of Christian), but for the robberies which he dared to commit, as he had already been a transgressor.—

Then, however, pretending to the name of the Lord, he was liberated, after he had spread his errors among the faithful there. But the church of the place whence he sprung would not receive him, because he was a robber. Those, however, that wish to learn his history, can consult the public archives of Asia. And yet the prophet professed to be totally ignorant of having lived with him many years; but by refuting him, through him, we also overturn the pretensions of the prophet. The same thing could be shown in many others, and if they have the courage let them undergo the test of argument." In another part of the same work, he adds the following, respecting their boasted prophets: " If," says he, " they deny that their prophets took presents, let them at least acknowledge, that, if they should be proved to have received them, they are no prophets. And of these matters we will furnish a thousand proofs. But it is necessary that all the fruits of a prophet should be examined. Tell me, does a prophet dye (his hair)? Does a prophet stain (his eyelids)? Does a prophet delight in ornament? Does a prophet play with tablets and dice? Does he take usury? Let them first acknowledge these things, whether they are right or not; and I will show that they have been done by them."

This same Apollonius relates, in the same work, that it was forty years from the time that Montanus undertook his pretended prophecy down to the period when he wrote his work. And again he says, that Zoticus, who was also mentioned by the former historian, when Maximilla was pretending to utter prophecies at Pepuza, attempted to interfere and reason with the spirit by which she was stimulated, but was hindered by those that followed her opinions. He mentions, also, a certain Thraseas among the martyrs of the times, and also that it was handed down by tradition, that our Saviour commanded his disciples not to depart from Jerusalem for twelve years. He quotes, also, the Revelations of John as testimony; and relates, also, that a dead man was raised by the divine power, through the same John, at Ephesus. Many other matters he also states; by which he abundantly refutes the error of the abovementioned heresy.—These are the matters stated by Apollonius.

CHAPTER XIX.

The opinion of Serapion respecting the heresy of the Phrygians

SERAPION, who is said about this time to have been the bishop of the church of Antioch, after Maximinus, has also made mention of the writings of Apollinaris against the same heresy. In a private letter, which he wrote to Caricus and Ponticus, he mentions him, and also refutes his heresy in the following words: " But that you may also see, that the influence of this lying party of a new prophecy, as it is called, is abominated by all the brethren in the world, I have also sent you the epistle of Claudius Apollinaris, that most blessed bishop of Hierapolis in Asia." In this same epistle of Serapion are also given the subscriptions of several bishops. Of whom one wrote as follows: " I, Aurelius Cyrenius, a witness, wish you health." Another, as follows: " Ælius Publius Julius, bishop of Debeltum, a colony of Thrace, as sure as God lives in the heavens, the blessed Sotas, in Anchialus, wished to cast out the dæmon from Priscilla, and the hypocrites would not suffer him." The signatures of many other bishops who bear witness to the facts, are given in their own hand in this epistle. And such are the statements referring to these.

CHAPTER XX.

The writings of Irenæus against the schismatics at Rome.

BUT Irenæus composed various epistles in opposition to those that attempted to disfigure the sound institutions of the church at Rome. One addressed to Blastus, On Schism. One to Florinus, On Sovereignty, or on the truth that God is not the author of evil: for the latter appeared to maintain this opinion. On whose account, as he was again on the point of being carried away by the Valentinian delusion, Irenæus also wrote the treatise on the Ogdoad, or the number eight; in which book he also shows that he was the first that received the original succession from the apostles. There, also, at the close of the work, we found a most delightful remark of his, which we shall deem incumbent on us also to add to the present work. It is as follows: "I adjure thee, whoever thou art, that transcribest this book, by our Lord Jesus Christ, and by his glorious appearance, when he shall come to judge the quick and dead, to compare what thou last copied, and to correct it by this original manuscript, from which thou hast carefully transcribed. And that thou also copy this adjuration, and insert it in the copy." These things may be profitably read in his works, and we hope with equal profit have been related by us, that we may have these ancient and truly holy men, as the noblest examples before us. In that epistle, indeed, which we have already mentioned, and which Irenæus addressed to Florinus, he again speaks of his intimacy with Polycarp. "These doctrines," says he, "O Florinus, to say the least, are not of a sound understanding. These doctrines are inconsistent with the church, and calculated to thrust those that follow them into the greatest impiety. These doctrines, not even the heretics out of the church ever attempted to assert. These doctrines were never delivered to thee by the presbyters before us, those who also were the immediate disciples of the apostles. For I saw thee when I was yet a boy in the lower Asia with Polycarp, moving in great splendour at court, and endeavourning by all means to gain his esteem. I remember the events of those times much better than those of more recent occurrence. As the studies of our youth growing with our minds, unite with it so firmly that I can tell also the very place where the blessed Polycarp was accustomed to sit and discourse ; and also his entrances, his walks, the complexion of his life and the form of his body, and his conversations with the people, and his familiar intercourse with John, as he was accustomed to tell, as also his familiarity with those that had seen he Lord. How also he used to relate their discourses, and what things he had heard from them concerning the Lord. Also concerning his miracles, his doctrine, all these were told by Polycarp, in consistency with the holy Scriptures, as he had received them from the eyewit nesses of the doctrine of salvation. These things, by the mercy of God, and the opportunity then afforded me, I attentively heard, noting them down, not on paper, but in my heart; and these same facts I am always in the habit, by the grace of God, to recall faithfully to mind. And I can bear witness in the sight of God, that if that blessed and apostolic presbyter had heard any such thing as this, he would have exclaimed, and stopped his ears, and according to his custom, would have said: "O good God, unto what times hast thou reserved me, that I should tolerate these things." He would have fled from the place in which he had sat or stood, hearing doctrines like these. From his epistles, also, which he wrote to the neighbouring churches, in order to confirm them, or to some of the brethren in order to admonish or to exhort them, the same thing may be clearly shown." Thus far Irenæus.

CHAPTER XXI.

The martyrdom of Apollonius, at Rome.

About the same period, in the reign of Commodus, our circumstances were changed to a milder aspect, as there was peace by the grace of God prevailing in the churches throughout the whole world. Then also the salutary doctrine brought the minds of men from every race on earth, to the devout veneration of the Supreme God. So that now, many of those eminent at Rome for their wealth and kindred, with their whole house and family, yielded to their salvation. But this was not to be easily borne by the adversary of all good, that dæmon who in his own nature is envy itself: for he again prepared for action, and commenced plotting various devices against us. He led to the tribunal Apollonius, one of the faithful at that day, renowned for his learning and wisdom, by stimulating a certain man, well calculated to be his minister for such a purpose, to bring accusation against him. But this miserable instrument, entering upon the charge out of season, when such informers were not suffered to

live according to the imperial edict, his limbs were immediately broken, after Perennis the judge had pronounced the sentence.   But this most approved and divinely favoured martyr, as
the judge earnestly desired and entreated him to give an account
of himself before the senate, delivered a most eloquent defence
of the faith for which he was suffering, in the presence of all,
terminated his life, by decapitation, according to the decree of the
senate; as there was a law of long standing with them, that those
who had once been led to trial, and that would by no means
change their purpose, should not be dismissed.   But the declarations of this martyr before the judge, and the answers that he
gave to the questions of Perennis, and his whole defence before
the senate, whoever wishes to know, may learn from the narratives of ancient martyrs collected by us.

CHAPTER XXII.

The bishops that flourished at this time.

In the tenth year of the reign of Commodus, Eleutherus, who
had held the episcopate for thirteen years, was succeeded by
Victor.   In this year, also, Julianus, who had the episcopal
charge of the churches at Alexandria ten years, was succeeded
by Demetrius.   At this time, also, was yet living the abovementioned Serapion, bishop of Antioch, and the eighth in succession
from the apostles.   At Cesarea, in Palestine, Theophilus presided;
and Narcissus, who was mentioned before, had yet at the same
time the administration of the church in Jerusalem.   Bacchyllus
was then also bishop of Corinth, in Greece, and Polycrates of the
church at Ephesus, and many others besides these, as is probable,
were prominent.   We have only given the names of those whose
orthodoxy has descended to us on record.

CHAPTER XXIII.

*The question then agitated respecting the passover.**

THERE was a considerable discussion raised about this time, in consequence of a difference of opinion respecting the observance of the paschal season. The churches of all Asia, guided by a remoter tradition, supposed that they ought to keep the fourteenth day of the moon for the festival of the Saviour's passover, in which day the Jews were commanded to kill the paschal lamb; and it was incumbent on them, at all times, to make an end of the fast on this day, on whatever day of the week it should happen to fall. But as it was not the custom to celebrate it in this manner in the churches throughout the rest of the world, who observe the practice that has prevailed from apostolic tradition until the present time, so that it would not be proper to terminate our fast on any other but the day of the resurrection of our Saviour. Hence there were synods and convocations of the bishops on this question; and all unanimously drew up an ecclesiastical *decree*, which they communicated to all the churches in all places, that the mystery of our Lord's resurrection should be celebrated on no other day than the Lord's-day; and that on this day alone we should observe the close of the paschal fasts. There is an epistle extant even now, of those who were assembled at the time; among whom presided Theophilus, bishop of the church in Cesarea, and Narcissus, bishop of Jerusalem. There is also another epistle extant on the same question, bearing the name of Victor.

---

* Our English word *passover*, happily, in sound and sense, almost corresponds to the Hebrew פסח, of which it is a translation. Exod. xii. 27. The Greek pascha, formed from the Hebrew, is the name of the Jewish festival, applied invariably in the primitive church to designate the festival of the Lord's resurrection, which took place at the time of the passover. Our word, Easter, is of Saxon origin, and of precisely the same import with its German cognate *Ostern*. The latter is derived from the old Teutonic form of auferstehn, auferstehung, *i. e.* resurrection. The name Easter, as expressive of meaning, is undoubtedly preferable to pascha or passover, but the latter was the primitive name.

An epistle, also, of the bishops in Pontus, among whom Palmas. as the most ancient, presided; also, of the churches of Gaul, over whom Irenæus presided. Moreover, one from those in Osrhoene, and the cities there. And a particular epistle from Bacchyllus, bishop of the Corinthians; and epistles of many others, who, advancing one and the same doctrine, also passed the same vote. And this, their unanimous determination, was the one already mentioned.

CHAPTER XXIV.

The dissension of the churches in Asia.

THE bishops, however, of Asia, persevering in observing the custom handed down to them from their fathers, were headed by Polycrates. He, indeed, had also set forth the tradition handed down to them, in a letter which he addressed to Victor and the church of Rome. " We," said he, " therefore, observe the genuine day; neither adding thereto nor taking therefrom. For in Asia great lights have fallen asleep, which shall rise again in the day of the Lord's appearing, in which he will come with glory from heaven, and will raise up all the saints; Philip, one of the twelve apostles, who sleeps in Hierapolis, and his two aged virgin daughters. His other daughter, also, who having lived under the influence of the Holy Ghost, now likewise rests in Ephesus. Moreover, John, who rested upon the bosom of our Lord; who also was a priest, and bore the sacerdotal plate * ($\pi\varepsilon\tau\alpha\lambda o\nu$), both a martyr and teacher. He is buried in Ephesus; also Polycarp of Smyrna, both bishop and martyr. Thraseas, also, bishop and martyr of Eumenia, who is buried at Smyrna. Why should I mention Sagaris, bishop and martyr, who rests at Laodicea. Moreover, the blessed Papirius; and Melito, the eunuch, whose walk and conversation was altogether under the

---

* The sacerdotal plate here mentioned, is not to be understood of the Jewish priesthood, for John had no connexion with that. It is probable that he, with others, wore a badge like his, as the priests of a better covenant.

influence of the Holy Spirit, who now rests at Sardis, awaiting the episcopate from heaven, when he shall rise from the dead. All these observed the fourteenth day of the passover according to the gospel, deviating in no respect, but following the rule of faith. Moreover, I, Polycrates, who am the least of all of you, according to the tradition of my relatives, some of whom I have followed. For there were seven, my relatives bishops, and I am the eighth; and my relatives always observed the day when the people (*i. e.* the Jews) threw away the leaven. I, therefore, brethren, am now sixty-five years in the Lord, who having conferred with the brethren throughout the world, and having studied the whole of the sacred Scriptures, am not at all alarmed at those things with which I am threatened, to intimidate me. For they who are greater than I, have said, ' we ought to obey God rather than men.' " After this, he also proceeds to write concerning all the bishops that were present, and thought the same with himself: " I could also mention," says he, " the bishops that were present, whom you requested to be summoned by me, and whom I did call. Whose names, did I write them, would present a great number. Who, however, seeing my slender body, consented to the epistle, well knowing that I did not bear my gray hairs for nought, but that I did at all times regulate my life in the Lord Jesus." Upon this, Victor, the bishop of the church of Rome, forthwith endeavoured to cut off the churches of all Asia, together with the neighbouring churches, as heterodox, from the common unity. And he publishes abroad by letters, and proclaims, that all the brethren there are wholly excommunicated. But this was not the opinion of all the bishops. They immediately exhorted him, on the contrary, to contemplate that course that was calculated to promote peace, unity, and love to one another.

There are also extant, the expressions they used, who pressed upon Victor with much severity. Among these also was Irenæus, who, in the name of those brethren in Gaul over whom he presided, wrote an epistle, in which he maintains the duty of celebrating the mystery of the resurrection of our Lord, only on the day of the Lord. He becomingly also admonishes Victor,

not to cut off whole churches of God, who observed the tradition
of an ancient custom.   After many other matters urged by him,
he also adds the following :   " For not only is the dispute respecting the day, but also respecting the manner of fasting.   For some
think, that they ought to fast only one day, some two, some more
days; some compute their day as consisting of forty hours night
and day ; and this diversity existing among those that observe it,
is not a matter that has just sprung up in our times, but long ago
among those before us, who perhaps not having ruled with sufficient strictness, established the practice that arose from their
simplicity and inexperience.   And yet with all, these maintained
peace, and we have maintained peace with one another; and
the very difference in our fasting establishes the unanimity in our
faith."   To these he also adds a narrative, which I may here
appropriately insert.   It is as follows: " And those presbyters
who governed the church before Soter, and over which you now
preside, I mean Anicetus and Pius, Hyginus with Telesphorus
and Xystus, neither did themselves observe, not did they permit
those after them to observe it.   And yet, though they themselves
did not keep it, they were not the less on peace with those from
churches where it was kept, whenever they came to them; although to keep it then was so much the more in opposition to
those who did not.*   Neither at any time did they cast off any
merely for the sake of the form.   But those very presbyters before thee, who did not observe it, sent the eucharist† to those of
churches who did.   And when the blessed Polycarp went to
Rome, in the time of Anicetus, and they had a little difference
among themselves likewise respecting other matters, they immediately were reconciled, not disputing much with one another
on this head.   For neither could Anicetus persuade Polycarp not
to observe it, because he had always observed it with John the

---

* The meaning of this passage, if it has any obscurity, is, that the act of observing
and celebrating, was a more decided attitude of opposition in the very face of the
church that did not observe the festival at this time.   And that the western church
bore with this, is here adduced as proof of the love and unity prevailing in the
churches.

† The bishops were accustomed at Easter to send the eucharist to one another

disciple of our Lord, and the rest of the apostles, with whom he associated; and neither did Polycarp persuade Anicetus to observe, who said that he was bound to maintain the practice of the presbyters before him. Which things being so, they communed with each other; and in the church, Anicetus yielded to Polycarp, out of respect no doubt, the office of consecrating, and they separated from each other in peace, all the church being at peace; both those that observed and those that did not observe, maintaining peace. And this same Irenæus, as one whose character answered well to his name, being in this way a peacemaker, exhorted and negociated such matters as these for the peace of the churches. And not only to Victor, but likewise to the most of the other rulers of the churches, he sent letters of exhortation on the agitated question.

CHAPTER XXV.

All agree to one opinion respecting the passover.

THE bishops indeed of Palestine, whom we have just mentioned, Narcissus and Theophilus, and Cassius with them, the bishop of the church at Tyre, and Clarus of Ptolemais, and those that came together with them, having advanced many things respecting the tradition that had been handed down to them by succession from the apostles, regarding the passover, at the close of the epistle, use these words: " Endeavour to send copies of the epistle through all the church, that we may not give occasion to those whose minds are easily led astray. But we inform you also, that they observe the same day at Alexandria, which we also do; for letters have been sent by us to them, and from them to us, so that we celebrate the holy season with one mind and at one time."

CHAPTER XXVI.

The elegant works of Irenæus that have come down to us.

BESIDES the works and epistles of Irenæus abovementioned, there is a certain very brief and most important discourse by him *On Knowledge*, against the Greeks; another also, which he dedicated to his brother named Marcion, as a proof of the apostolic preaching; a book also of various disputes, in which he mentions the Epistle to the Hebrews; and the book called the Wisdom of Solomon, quoting certain passages from them. These are the works of Irenæus that have come down to us. But after Commodus had ended his reign in the thirteenth year, and Pertinax had held the government not quite six months, Severus was created emperor, and ruled the state.

CHAPTER XXVII.

The works of others that flourished at the time.

NUMEROUS works, indeed, of ancient ecclesiastical writers are still preserved by many, the monuments of a virtuous industry. Those which we would select of them, might be the commentaries of Heraclitus *On the Apostle;* the works of Maximus, also, on that question so much agitated among the heretics, *The Origin of Evil;* also, *On the Creation of Matter.* Also, the works of Candidus *On the Hexaemeron.** And Apion's work on the same subject. Sextus, also, *On the Resurrection,* and a certain other treatise of Arabianus, with many others, of whom, as we have no data, we can neither insert the times nor any extracts in our history. Innumerable others there also are, that have come down to us, even the names of whom it would be impossible to give. All of these were orthodox and ecclesiastical writers as

---

* The Greek name, designating the six days of the creation.

the interpretation which each gives of the sacred Scriptures shows; yet they are not known to us, because the works them selves do not give their authors.

CHAPTER XXVIII.

Those that followed the heresy of Artemon, in the beginning. Their character and conduct; and their attempt at corrupting the Scriptures.

In a work written by a certain one of these authors against the heresy of Artemon, which Paul of Samosata again attempted to revive among us, there is a narrative well adapted to the history we are now investigating. This writer, not long since, in refuting the heresy mentioned, which asserts that Christ is a mere man, since its leaders wish to boast as if it were the ancient doctrine, besides many other arguments that he adduces in refutation of their impious falsehood, he gives the following account: " For they assert," says he, " that all those primitive men and the apostles themselves, both received and taught these things as they are now taught by them, and that the truth of the gospel was preserved until the times of Victor, who was the thirteenth bishop of Rome from Peter. But that from his successor Zephyrinus, the truth was mutilated. And perchance what they say might be credible, were it not that the holy Scriptures contradict them; and then, also, there are works of certain brethren older than Victor's times, which they wrote in defence of the truth, and against the heresies then prevailing. I speak of Justus and Miltiades, and Tatian and Clement, and many others, in all which the divinity of Christ is asserted. For who knows not the works of Irenæus and Melito, and the rest, in which Christ is announced as God and man? Whatever psalms and hymns were written by the brethren from the beginning, celebrate Christ the word of God, by asserting his divinity. How then could it happen, that since the doctrine of the church has been proclaimed for so many years, that those until the times of Victor, preached the gospel after this manner? And how are they so devoid of shame to utter these falsehoods against Victor, well knowing that Victor excommunicated that currier Theodotus, the leader and father of this God-denying apostacy, as the first one that asserted Christ was a mere man. For had Victor entertained the sentiments which their impious doctrine promulgates, how could he have expelled Theodotus, the inventor of this heresy?" Thus much with respect to Victor. But after this author had superintended the church, Zephyrinus was appointed his successor about the ninth year of the reign of Severus. The same author that composed the book already mentioned respecting the founder of this heresy, also adds an account of another event that occurred in the times of Zephyrinus, in these words: "I shall remind many of the brethren of a fact," says he, "that happened in our days, which, had it happened in Sodom, I think would have led them to reflection. There was a certain Natalius, who lived not in remote times, but in our own. This man was seduced on a certain occasion by Asclepiodotus, and another Theodotus, a moneychanger. Both of these were disciples of Theodotus the currier, the first that had been excommunicated by Victor, then bishop, as before said, on account of this opinion or rather insanity. Natalius was persuaded by them to be created a bishop of this heresy, with a salary from them of one hundred and fifty denarii a month. Being connected, therefore, with them, he was frequently brought to reflection by the Lord in his dreams. For the merciful God and our Lord Jesus Christ, would not that he who had been a witness of his own sufferings, should perish, though he was out of the church. But as he paid but little attention to these visions, being ensnared both by the desire of presiding among them, and that foul gain which destroys so many, he was finally lashed by holy angels, through the whole night, and was thus most severely punished; so that he arose early in the morning, and putting on sackcloth and covered with ashes, in great haste, and bathed in tears, he fell down before Zephyrinus the bishop, rolling at the feet not only of the clergy but even of the laity, and thus moved the compassionate church of Christ with his tears. And, although he implored their clemency with much earnestness, and pointed to the strokes of the lashes he had received, he was at last scarcely admitted to communion." To this, we will also add other extracts from the same writer respecting this sect: "The sacred Scriptures," says he, "have been boldly perverted by them; the rule of the ancient faith they have set aside, Christ they have renounced, not inquiring what the holy Scriptures declared, but zealously labouring what form of reasoning may be devised to establish their impiety. And should any one present a passage of divine truth, they examined first whether a connected or disjoined form of syllogism* can be formed from it. But they abandon the holy Scriptures for the study of geometry,† as being of the earth they talk of the earth, and know not him that cometh from above. Euclid, therefore, is industriously measured‡ by them. Aristotle and Theophrastus, are also admired, and as to Galen, he is even perhaps worshipped by some. But as to these men who abuse the acts of the unbelievers, to their own heretical views, and who adulterate the simplicity of that faith contained in the holy Scriptures, by the wily arts of impious men; where is the necessity of asserting that they are not right in the faith? For this purpose they fearlessly lay their hands upon the holy Scriptures, saying that they have corrected them. And that I do not say this against them

* Logicians call the syllogisms here spoken of, hypothetical and disjunctive. In the former, the premises are supposed; in the latter, they are separated by a disjunctive conjunction, whence their names.

† The author whose words are here quoted, plays upon the word *geometry*, in its original. The word literally means earth or land-measuring. The science appears to owe its origin to the necessity of frequently measuring the lands in Egypt, after the inundations of the Nile; and when reduced to its more abstract principles, it still continued to bear its original name. The author here quoted seems to reprove, in these men, an absorbing devotedness to a science, the study of which is doubtless a powerful auxiliary in disciplining the human mind, independently of its practical utility. It was considered so important a preparatory discipline among the ancients, that the words ουδεις αγεωμετρητος ωδι εισελθη were written over the gates of their philosophical schools.

‡ *Measured.*] Another play upon the word *geometry*, the force of which is entirely lost in a translation. The author had already hinted that this was only an earthly study; and now he sarcastically remarks, Euclid is *earth* measured by them.

without foundation, whoever wishes may learn; for should any one collect and compare their copies one with another, he would find them greatly at variance among themselves. For the copies of Asclepiodotus will be found to differ from those of Theodotus. Copies of many you may find in abundance, altered, by the eagerness of their disciples to insert each one his own corrections, as they call them, i. e. their corruptions. Again, the copies of Hermophilus do not agree with these, for those of Appollonius are not consistent with themselves. For one may compare those which were prepared before by them, with those which they afterwards perverted for their own objects, and you will find them widely differing. But what a stretch of audacity this aberration indicates, it is hardly probable themselves can be ignorant. For either they do not believe that the holy Scriptures were uttered by the holy Spirit, and they are thus infidels, or they deem themselves wiser than the holy Spirit, and what alternative is there but to pronounce them dæmoniacs? For neither can they deny that they have been guilty of the daring act, when the copies were written with their own hand, nor did they receive such Scriptures from those by whom they were instructed in the elements of the faith; nor can they show copies from which they were transcribed. But some of them did not even deign, or think it worth while, to mutilate the Scriptures, but directly denying the law and the prophets by their lawless and impious doctrine, under the pretext of grace, they sunk down to the lowest depths of perdition." But let this suffice on this subject.

BOOK VI.

CHAPTER I.

The persecution under Severus.

BUT when Severus raised a persecution against the churches, there were illustrious testimonies given by the combatants of religion in all the churches every where. They particularly abounded in Alexandria, whilst the heroic wrestlers from Egypt and Thebais were escorted thither as to a mighty theatre of God, where, by their invincible patience under various tortures and modes of death, they were adorned with crowns from heaven. Among these was Leonides, said to be the father of Origen, who was beheaded, and left his son behind yet very young. His early predilection for the divine word, as instructed by his father, it is not out of place here briefly to state, so much the more especially as his fame is celebrated by many.

CHAPTER II.

The education of Origen, from his earliest youth.

ONE might, indeed, say much in attempting to write the life of the man at school, for the subject respecting him would require a particular and separate work. Nevertheless, for the present, we shall endeavour by abridging the most of the materials, as briefly as possible to relate some few events respecting him, and adduce the facts from certain epistles and histories which have come down to our own day, by those of his familiar friends who are yet living. The life of Origen, indeed, appears to me worthy of being recorded, even from his tender infancy. It was

217

in the tenth year of the reign of Severus, when Alexandria and the rest of Egypt was under the government of his viceroy Lætus, and the churches there were under the episcopal administration of Demetrius, the successor of Julian, that the kindled flame of persecution blazed forth mightily, and many thousands were crowned with martyrdom.

It was then, too, that the love of martyrdom so powerfully seized the soul of Origen, though yet an almost infant boy, that he advanced so close to encounter danger, and was eager to leap forward and rush upon the conflict. And indeed, there had been now but little wanting, and the termination of his life had not been far off, unless the heavenly providence of God for the benefit of vast numbers, had, by means of his mother, interposed an impediment to his eager desire. She, indeed, at first, implored and entreated him to spare a mother's tenderness regarding him, but seeing him only the more vehemently bent upon it, as he understood that his father was taken and kept a prisoner, and he was wholly borne away by the desire of becoming a martyr, his mother concealed his clothes in order to compel him to remain at home. But when he saw that there was no other course for him to pursue, as his great zeal was far beyond his years, he could not remain inactive, but sent to his father a most encouraging letter on martyrdom, in which he encourages him, saying, "take heed, (father) not to change thy mind on account of us." This may serve as the first specimen that we mention of Origen's shrewdness, and his genuine devotedness to piety. For he had even then made no little progress in the doctrine of faith, as he had been conversant with the holy Scriptures even when a child. He had been considerably trained in them by his father, who, besides the study of the liberal sciences, had also carefully stored his mind with these. First of all, therefore, before he studied the Grecian literature, he led him to frequent exercise in the study of sacred things, appointing him to commit and repeat some passages every day; and these things were not unwillingly done by the child, but studies most cheerfully performed with great diligence. So that it was not sufficient for him merely to read what was simple and obvious in the sacred

books, but he sought also what was beyond this, into the deeper
senses of the text, and was busily employed in such speculations
even at that age ; so that he gave his father trouble, by his questions what forsooth the passage of the inspired Scriptures should
mean. He, indeed, to appearance, rebuked him to his face, telling him not to inquire into things beyond his age, nor to search
beyond the obvious meaning of Scriptures. But he, greatly delighted in his own mind, gave most hearty thanks to Almighty
God, the author of all good, that he had honoured him to be the
father of such a child. And they say, that frequently, when
standing over his sleeping boy, he would uncover his breast, and
as a shrine consecrated by the divine Spirit, he reverently kissed
it and congratulated himself upon his favoured offspring. These
and other similar circumstances are related of Origen when yet
a boy. But now, as his father had ended his days a martyr, he is
left in this bereaved condition with his mother and younger
brothers, in number six, when he was yet in his seventeenth year.
And as his father's property was forfeited to the imperial treasury, he was reduced with his relatives to great straits for the
necessaries of life. But he was honoured with a provision from
God. For he found a kind reception and retreat with a certain
lady of great wealth and distinction ; but who at the same time
patronized a certain celebrated man who was an advocate of the
heretics then existing in Alexandria. This man was a native of
Antioch, and was taken home by the lady as an adopted son, and
was treated with the greatest kindness by her. But as Origen
thus necessarily associated with him, he thenceforth gave him
strong specimens of his orthodox faith. As great numbers not
only of heretics but ours also, induced by the apparent eloquence
of the man, collected to hear this Paul, for that was his name,
he could never be induced to join with him in prayer, observing
even from a boy that rule of the church, and as he himself says,
somewhere, abominating the inculcation of heretical doctrines.
But as he had been instructed by his father in Greek literature,
and after his death devoted himself more ardently to the sole
study of literature, so that he acquired a tolerable acquaintance
with philology, he devoted himself not long after his father's

death to this study, and young as he was, he thus acquired sufficient to supply his necessary wants in abundance.

CHAPTER III.

When a very young man he preached the Gospel.

But whilst he was thus engaged with his school where he
abode, as he somewhere states, and there was no one at Alexandria that applied himself to give instruction in the principles of the
faith, but all driven away by the threatening aspect of persecution,
some of the Gentiles came to him with a mind to hear the word of
God. The first of whom, he states, was Plutarch; who, after a
life of piety, was also crowned with divine martyrdom. The
second was Heraclas, the brother of Plutarch, who, indeed, having
given abundant proof of a life of retired contemplation and dis
cipline, was deemed worthy of the episcopate of Alexandria after
Demetrius. But he was in his eighteenth year when he conducted
the school for elementary instruction in the faith, in which also
he made great proficiency under the persecutions of Aquila governor of Alexandria; where, also, he obtained a celebrated
name with all the believers, on account of that cordiality and
promptness which he exhibited to all the martyrs, whether known
to him or not. For not only was he with them when in bonds,
nor only until the last of their trial at the tribunal; but, even
after this, when led away to die, he conversed freely with these
holy martyrs, and advanced in the face of danger. So, that as he
boldly proceeded, and with great freedom saluted the brethren
with a kiss, the infuriate multitude who stood around had more
than once almost overwhelmed him (with stones), had he not this
once experienced the helping hand of God, and wonderfully escaped. But this same celestial grace, at one time and another,
again and again, and indeed no one can tell how often, in consequence of his great zeal for the doctrine of Christ, and his fear-
lessness, as often protected him in danger. So great, indeed, was

the hostility of the unbelievers to him, that they formed themselves into companies, to station soldiers about the house where he abode, on account of the numbers that were instructed by him in the principles of the faith. But the persecution against him daily blazed forth with such virulence, that the whole city of Alexandria could no longer contain him, as he removed from house to house, driven about in every direction, on account of the great number of those that had been brought over by him to the true faith, since also his daily actions afforded admirable specimens of a conduct resulting from a sound philosophy. For, " as his doctrine, say they, so was his life; and as his life, so also was his doctrine." Wherefore, also, with the divine assistance, he induced numbers to imitate him. But when he saw a greater number of pupils coming, the instruction of them having been committed to him entirely by Demetrius the bishop of the church, he thought that to teach literature exclusively* was inconsistent with the study of divine truth, and without delay abandoned the school of philosophy, as useless, and an obstruction to his sacred studies. Then, also, with a becoming consideration that he might not stand in need of aid from others, he disposed of whatsoever works he had formerly written on ancient works, and composed with great elegance and taste, and was content with receiving four oboli † the day from the purchaser. Many years he continued to lead this life of philosophy,‡ completely removing all the incentives to youthful passions from him, during the whole day

---

* *Literature exclusively.*] We have added the word exclusively as the obvious meaning. Origen could not, without great inconsistency, consider the business of literary instruction as hostile to the study of divine things, nor does this appear to have been his opinion. But the exclusive occupation of such a teacher in his relative situation was incompatible with a higher duty. We have also rendered γραμματικοι λογοι, contrary to our predecessors, by the terms *literature* and *philology*. Others render *grammar*, but seem to have overlooked the fact, that the terms, beside the grammatical study of a language, also comprehended the whole compass of philology and the belles lettres.

† *Oboli.*] The obolus was a small coin, about two or three cents in value.

‡ *Philosophy.*] Our author uses this word, when applied to the primitive Christians, in a practical sense, indicating the austerity of life and self-denial which they exercised.

undergoing no trifling amount of laborious exercise, and at night devoting himself the most of the time to the study of the holy Scriptures, and restraining himself, as far as possible, by a most rigid and philosophical life. Sometimes he was exercised in the discipline of fasting; then, again, at night, he limited his times for sleep, which, in consequence of his great zeal, he never enjoyed on his bed, but upon the bare ground. But, most of all, he thought that the evangelical precepts of our Saviour should be observed, in which he exhorts that we should not have two coats, nor make use of shoes, nor pass our time in cares for the future. But indulging, also, an ardour greater than his years, he persevered in cold and nakedness; and advancing to the greatest extremes of poverty, astonished, most of all, his nearest friends. Many, indeed, that wished to impart to him some of their means, were grieved on account of the laborious toil that he endured for the sake of inspired truth. He did not, however, relax in his perseverance. He is said, indeed, to have walked the ground for many years without any shoes; and also to have abstained from the use of wine and other food not necessary for sustenance, many years. So that now he was greatly in danger of subverting and destroying his constitution.* But in presenting such specimens of his ascetic life to the beholders, he naturally induced many of his visiters to pursue the same course; so that now many, both of the unbelieving heathen, and some of the learned, and even philosophers of no mean account, were prevailed upon to adopt his doctrine. Some of these, also, having been deeply imbued by him, with the sound faith in Christ deeply implanted in the soul, were also eminent in the midst of the persecution then prevailing; so that some were taken, and finished their course by martyrdom.

---

* The word used here is θωραξ, the *chest*.

CHAPTER IV.

The number of his catechumens that suffered martyrdom.

Of these, then, the first was that Plutarch, mentioned above, at whose martyrdom when led away to die, the same Origen of whom we are now speaking, being present with him to the last of his life, was nearly slain by his own countrymen, as if he were the cause of his death. But the providence of God preserved him likewise then. But after Plutarch, the second of Origen's disciples that was selected, was Severus, who presented in the fire, a proof of that unshaken faith which he had received. The third that appeared as martyr from the same school, was Heraclides; and the fourth, after him, was Heron: both of these were beheaded. Besides these, the fifth of this school that was announced a champion for religion, was another Severus, who, after a long series of tortures, is said to have been beheaded. Of women, also, Herais, who was yet a catechumen, and, as Origen himself expresses it, after receiving her baptism by fire, departed this life.

CHAPTER V.

Of Potamiæna.

But, among these, Basilides must be numbered the seventh; he who led away the celebrated Potamiæna to execution, concerning whom many traditions are still circulated abroad among the inhabitants of the place, of the innumerable conflicts she endured for the preservation of her purity and chastity, in which indeed she was eminent. For, besides the perfections of her mind, she was blooming also in the maturity of personal attractions. Many things are also related of her fortitude in suffering for faith in Christ; and, at length, after horrible tortures and pains, the very relation of which makes one shudder, she was, with her mother

Macella, committed to the flames. It is said, indeed, that the
judge, Aquila by name, after having applied the severest tortures
to her on every part of her body, at last threatened that he
would give her body to be abused by the gladiators; but that she,
having considered the matter a little, after being asked what she
would determine, made such a reply as made it appear that she
uttered something deemed impious with them. Immediately,
therefore, receiving the sentence of condemnation, she was led
away to die by Basilides, one of the officers in the army. But
when the multitude attempted to assault and insult her with
abusive language, he, by keeping off, restrained their insolence;
exhibiting the greatest compassion and kindness to her. Perceiving the man's sympathy, she exhorts him to be of good cheer,
for that after she was gone she would intercede for him with her
Lord, and it would not be long before she would reward him for
his kind deeds towards her. Saying this, she nobly sustained
the issue; having boiling pitch poured over different parts of her
body, gradually by little and little, from her feet up to the crown
of her head. And such, then, was the conflict which this noble
virgin endured. But not long after, Basilides, being urged to
swear on a certain occasion by his fellow-soldiers, declared that
it was not lawful for him to swear at all; for he was a Christian,
and this he plainly professed. At first, indeed, they thought that
he was thus far only jesting; but as he constantly persevered
in the assertion, he was conducted to the judge, before whom,
confessing his determination, he was committed to prison. But
when some of the brethren came to see him, and inquired the
cause of this sudden and singular resolve, he is said to have declared, that Potamiæna, indeed for the three days after her martyrdom, standing before him at night, placed a crown upon his
head, and said that she had entreated the Lord on his account,
and she had obtained her prayer, and that ere long she would
take him with her. On this, the brethren gave him the seal *
in the Lord; and he, bearing a distinguished testimony to the

---

* Our author here means baptism, which, in the primitive church, was sometimes thus figuratively called.

Lord, was beheaded. Many others, also, of those at Alexandria, are recorded as having promptly attached themselves to the doctrine of Christ in these times; and this by reason of Potamiæna, who appeared in dreams, and exhorted many to embrace the divine word. But of these let this suffice.

CHAPTER VI.

Clement of Alexandria.

CLEMENT having succeeded Pantænus in the office of elementary instruction, had charge of it until this time; so that Origen, whilst yet a boy, was one of his pupils. Clement, in the first book of the work that he wrote, called Stromata, gives us a chronological deduction of events down to the death of Commodus. So that it is evident these works were written in the reign of Severus, whose times we are now recording.

CHAPTER VII.

The historian Judas.

AT this time, also, another historian, discoursing on the seventy weeks of Daniel, extends his chronology down to the tenth year of the reign of Severus, who also thought that the appearance of antichrist, so much in the mouths of men, was now fully at hand. So mightily did the agitation of persecution, then prevailing, shake the minds of many.

CHAPTER VIII.

The resolute act of Origen

WHILST at this time Origen was performing the office of an elementary instructor at Alexandria, he also carried a deed into effect, which would seem, indeed, rather to proceed from a youthful understanding not yet matured; at the same time, however, exhibiting the strongest proof of his faith and continence. For understanding this expression, " There are eunuchs who have made themselves such (who have acted the eunuch) for the sake of the kingdom of heaven," in too literal and puerile a sense, and at the same time thinking that he would fulfil the words of our Saviour, whilst he also wished to preclude the unbelievers from all occasions of foul slander, it being necessary for him, young as he was, to converse on divine truth not only with men but with females also, he was led on to fulfil the words of our Saviour by his deeds, expecting that it would not be known to the most of his friends. But it was impossible for him, much as he wished it, to conceal such an act. And when it was at last ascertained by Demetrius, the bishop of the church there, well did he admire the courage of the deed; and perceiving the ardour, and the soundness of his faith, he immediately exhorts him to cherish confidence; and at this time, indeed, urges him the more to continue in his work of instruction. Such, indeed, was his conduct then. But not long after this, the same Demetrius, seeing him doing well, great and illustrious, and celebrated among all, was overcome by human infirmity, and wrote against him to the bishops throughout the world, and attempted to traduce what he had done as a most absurd act. Then, as the most distinguished bishops of Palestine, and those of Cesarea and Jerusalem, judged Origen worthy of the first and highest honour, they ordained him to the presbytery by the imposition of hands. He advanced, therefore, at this time, to great reputation, and obtained a celebrity among all men, and no little renown for his virtue and wisdom; but Demetrius, though he had no other charge to urge than that act which was formerly done by him when but a boy, raised a violent accusation against him. He attempted, also, to involve those in his accusations who had elevated him to the presbytery. These things were done a long time after. But Origen performed, without fear, his labours of instruction at Alexandria, night and day, to all that came; devoting the whole of his leisure incessantly to the study of divine things, and to those that frequented his school. In the meanwhile, Severus, having held the government about eighteen years, was succeeded by his son Antoninus. At this time, one of those that had courageously endured the persecution, and who, by the providence of God, had been preserved after the persecution, was Alexander, who we have already shown was bishop of the church at Jerusalem, and had been deemed worthy of this episcopate, on account of his distinguished firmness in his confession of Christ during the persecution. This happened whilst Narcissus was yet living.

CHAPTER IX.

The miracle of Narcissus.

MANY miracles are attributed to Narcissus by his countrymen, as they received the tradition handed down from the brethren. Among these they relate a wonderful event like the following. About the great watch of the passover, they say, that whilst the deacons were keeping the vigils the oil failed them; upon which all the people being very much dejected, Narcissus commanded the men that managed the lights to draw water from a neighbouring well, and to bring it to him. He having done it as soon as said, Narcissus prayed over the water, and then commanded them in a firm faith in Christ, to pour it into the lamps. When they had also done this, contrary to all natural expectation, by an extraordinary and divine influence, the nature of the water was changed into the quality of oil, and by most of the brethren a small quantity was preserved from that time until our own, as a specimen of the wonder then performed. They relate also many

other matters worthy of note respecting the life of this man.
Among these, such as the following. Certain fellows not being
able to endure the firm and constant character of his life, fearing
also lest they should be taken and punished for the numerous
crimes of which they were conscious, endeavoured to anticipate
him, by plotting an artifice against him.* They gave currency
therefore to a foul slander against him. Then, in order to make
the hearers believe, they confirmed their accusations with oaths;
and one of them swore that he might perish with fire; another that
his body might be wasted with a miserable and foul disease; a
third that he should be deprived of his eyes; but notwithstanding
their oaths, none of the faithful heeded them, on account of the
well known continent and virtuous life which Narcissus had always led. Unable, however, to endure the wickedness of these
men, and having besides already long before embraced a life of contemplation, he ran away from the body of the church, and continued many years concealed in deserts and trackless wilds. But the
omnipotent eye of justice did not remain inactive in the midst of
these things; but soon descended with his judgments upon the
impious wretches, and bound them with the curses they had
invoked. The first indeed, in consequence of a light spark falling upon his habitation without any apparent cause, was burnt
with his whole family. The next was forthwith covered with
the disease which he had imprecated upon himself, from the extremity of his feet to the top of his head. But the third, perceiving the events of the former two, and dreading the inevitable
judgment of the all-seeing God, confessed indeed to all the
slander which had been concocted in common among them. But
he was so wasted with excessive grieving, and so incessantly diffused with tears, that at last both his eyes were destroyed. And
these suffered the punishment due to their calumnies.

---

* The meaning is, that Narcissus was so rigid in his discipline, that these slanderers could not bear his uniform and exemplary life, whilst they were also afraid
of detection and punishment for their own crimes.

CHAPTER X.

The bishops in Jerusalem.

NARCISSUS having retired from the world, and no one knowing whither he had gone, it seemed proper to the bishops of the neighbouring churches, to proceed to the ordination of another bishop. Dius was his name, who, after presiding over the church a short time, was succeeded by Germanio, and he by Gordius, in whose times Narcissus appearing again as one raised from the dead, was entreated by the brethren to undertake the episcopate again; all admiring him still more, both for his retired life, and his philosophy, and above all on account of the punishment inflicted by God upon his slanderers.

CHAPTER XI.

Of Alexander.

BUT as on account of his extreme age, he was now no longer able to perform the duties of his office, by a divine dispensation revealed in a dream at night, the abovementioned Alexander, who was bishop of another church, was called to the office at the same time with Narcissus. Influenced by this, as if an oracle from God had commanded him, he performed a journey from Cappadocia, where he was first made bishop, to Jerusalem, in consequence of a vow and the celebrity of the place. Whilst he was there, most cordially entertained by the brethren, who would not suffer him to return home, another revelation also appeared to them at night, and uttered a most distinct communication to those that were eminent for a devoted life. This communication was, that by going forth beyond the gates, they should receive the bishop pointed out to them by God. Having done this, with the common consent of the bishops of the neighbouring churches, they constrain him to stay among them. Alexander, indeed, himself in his particular epistles to the Antinoites, which are still preserved among us, makes mention of the episcopal office as shared by himself with Narcissus, in the following words, at the end of the epistle: "Narcissus salutes you, the same who before me held the episcopate here, and is now colleagued with me in prayers, being now advanced to his hundred and tenth year, and who with me exhorts you to be of one mind." Such, then, were these events.   But Serapion dying at Antioch, he was succeeded by Asclepiades; he also, was distinguished among the confessions* in the persecution.   His consecration is also mentioned by Alexander, who writes to the inhabitants of Antioch thus: "Alexander, a servant and prisoner of Jesus Christ, sends, greeting, in the Lord, to the blessed church at Antioch, in the Lord.   The Lord has made my bonds easy and light during the time of my imprisonment, since I have ascertained, that by divine Providence, Asclepiades, who in regard to his faith is most happily qualified, has undertaken the trust of the episcopate of your holy church."   This same epistle intimates, that he sent it by Clement, writing at the end of it, as follows: "This epistle, my brethren, I have sent to you by Clement, the blessed presbyter, a man endued with all virtue, and well approved, whom you already know, and will learn still more to know; who, also, coming hither, by the providence and superintendence of the Lord, has confirmed and increased the church of God."

* The primitive church, as is evident from our author, distinguished a confession from martyrdom.   The former implied all sufferings and trials for the sake of religion, except the loss of life.   The latter was attended with this also.   Hence, the latter was regarded as the highest grade of confession, and as such the martyr, in contradistinction to the confessor, was said to be perfected.   The expression, therefore, to be perfected, often occurs in our author, in the sense of being put to death. This remark will explain the expression as it occurs sometimes in the book of martyrs.

CHAPTER XII.

Serapion, and the writings ascribed to him.

SERAPION, however, it is probable, has left many monuments of his application to learning, which are preserved by others; but only those that are addressed to Domninus have come down to us. He was one of those that had fallen away from the faith, at the time of the persecution, and relapsed into Jewish superstition. Those epistles, also, that he addressed to Pontus and Caricus, ecclesiastical writers, and many others to others. There is also another work composed by him on the gospel of Peter, as it is called; which, indeed, he wrote to refute the false assertions which it contains, an account of some in the church of Rhosse,* who by this work were led astray to perverted doctrines. From which it may be well to add some brief extracts, by which it may be seen what he thought of the book :—

" We, brethren," says he, " receive Peter and the other apostles as Christ himself. But those writings which falsely go under their name, as we are well acquainted with them, we reject, and know also, that we have not received such handed down to us. But when I came to you, I had supposed that all held to the true faith; and as I had not perused the gospel presented by them under the name of Peter, I said, ' If this be the only thing that creates difference among you, let it be read;' but now having understood, from what was said to me, that their minds were enveloped in some heresy, I will make haste to come to you again; therefore, brethren, expect me soon. But as we perceived what was the heresy of Marcianus, we plainly saw that he ignorantly contradicted himself, which things you may learn from what has been written to you. For we have borrowed this gospel from others, who have studied it, that is, from the successors of those who led the way before him, whom we call Docetæ, (for most opinions have sprung from this sect.) And in this we have discovered many things, superadded to the sound faith of our Sa-

* Rhosse was a town of Cilicia. Plutarch calls it Orossus.

viour; some also, attached that are foreign to it, and which we have also subjoined for your sake." Thus far of the works of Serapion.

CHAPTER XIII.

The works of Clement.

OF Clement there are, in all, eight books extant, called Stromata,* to which he has prefixed the following title: " Stromata of Commentaries, by Titus Flavius Clement, on the Knowledge of the True Philosophy."

Equal in number to these, are the books that go under the title of Hypotyposes, or Institutions. In these, he also mentions Pantænus by name, as his teacher, giving the opinions that he expressed, and traditions that he had received from him. There is also a book of exhortation, addressed by him to the Greeks. Also, one entitled the Pædagogue, and another with the title, " What Rich Man may be saved." A work also on the Passover. Discussions also on Fasting and Detraction. An Exhortatation also, to Patience, or an Address to the New Converts. (Neophytes.) A work also, with the title, Ecclesiastical Canon, or an Address to the Judaizing (Christians,) which he dedicated to the abovementioned bishop Alexander. In these Stromata, he has not only spread out† the divine Scriptures (made a spreading), but he also quotes from the Gentiles where he finds any useful remark with them, elucidating many opinions held by the multitude both among the Greeks and barbarians. Moreover, he refutes the false opinions of the heresiarchs. He also, reviews a great

---

* The Greek word *stromateus*, which Clement prefixed as the title to each of his books, means a covering, or hangings for a table, or couch, mostly of various colours. It also signified, in later times, the bag in which the beds and covers were tied up. The former, however, gave rise to the use of it as a title for books of various contents. Hence, they were miscellanies. The plural of this word is stromates, or stromateis, to avoid which we use the synonymous stromata.

† Our author here plays upon the title Stromateus, giving us by the way to understand what was meant by the word, viz., a variegated covering spread out.

point of history, in which he presents materials of great variety of learning. With all these he intermixes the opinions of philosophers; whence, in all probability, he took the title Stromata, as corresponding to the materials (of his book.) In these he also makes use of testimony from the Antilegomenoi, the disputed Scriptures; also from that book called the Wisdom of Solomon, and that of Jesus the son of Sirach; also the Epistle to the Hebrews, that of Barnabas, and Clement, and Jude. He mentions also the work of Tatian against the Greeks; Cassian, also, who wrote a history of the times in chronological order. Moreover, he mentions the Jewish authors Philo, and Aristobulus, Josephus, and Demetrius, and Eupolemus, as all of these in their works prove, that Moses and the Jewish nation are much older than the earliest origin of the Greeks. The works of this writer here mentioned, also abound in a great variety of other learning. In the first of these he speaks of himself as being the next that succeeded the apostles, and he promises in his works also, to write a commentary on Genesis; also in his treatise on the Passover, he acknowledges that for the benefit of posterity, he was urged by his friends to commit to writing those traditions that he had heard from the ancient presbyters. He mentions, also, Melito and Irenæus, and others, some of whose narratives he also gives.

CHAPTER XIV.

The books that Clement mentions.

In the work called Hypotyposes, to sum up the matter briefly he has given us abridged accounts of all the canonical Scriptures, not even omitting those that are disputed, (The Antilegomenoi,) I mean the book of Jude, and the other general epistles. Also the epistle of Barnabas, and that called the revelation of Peter. But the Epistle to the Hebrews he asserts was written by Paul, to the Hebrews, in the Hebrew tongue; but that it was carefully translated by Luke, and published among the Greeks. Whence, also, one finds the same character of style and of phraseology in the epistle, as in the Acts. "But it is probable that the title, Paul the Apostle, was not prefixed to it. For as he wrote to the Hebrews, who had imbibed prejudices against him, and suspected him, he wisely guards against diverting them from the perusal, by giving his name." A little after this he observes: "But now as the blessed presbyter used to say, 'since the Lord who was the apostle of the Almighty, was sent to the Hebrews, Paul by reason of his inferiority, as if sent to the Gentiles, did not subscribe himself an apostle of the Hebrews; both out of reverence for the Lord, and because he wrote of his abundance to the Hebrews, as a herald and apostle of the Gentiles.'" Again, in the same work, Clement also gives the tradition respecting the order of the gospels, as derived from the oldest presbyters, as follows: "He says that those which contain the genealogies were written first; but that the gospel of Mark was occasioned in the following manner: 'When Peter had proclaimed the word publicly at Rome, and declared the gospel under the influence of the spirit; as there was a great number present, they requested Mark, who had followed him from afar, and remembered well what he had said, to reduce these things to writing, and that after composing the gospel he gave it to those who requested it of him. Which, when Peter understood, he directly neither hindered nor encouraged it. But John, last of all, perceiving that what had reference to the body in the gospel of our Saviour, was sufficiently detailed, and being encouraged by his familiar friends, and urged by the spirit, he wrote a spiritual gospel.'" Thus far Clement. But again, the abovementioned Alexander mentions both Clement and Pantænus, in a certain epistle to Origen, as men with whom he was familiarly acquainted. Thus he writes: "For this, thou knowest was the divine will, that the friendship which has existed between us from our ancestors, should remain unshaken, rather that it should grow warmer and firmer. For we well know those blessed fathers, that have trod the path before us, and to whom we ere long shall go. Pantænus, that truly blessed man, my master, also the holy Clement, who was both my master and benefactor, and whoever there may be like them, by whom I have become acquainted with thee, my Lord and brother surpassing all." Such is the complexion of these matters. But Adamantius, for this too was Origen's name, whilst Zephyrinus, at this time, was bishop of the church of Rome, says that he also came to Rome, being desirous of seeing the very ancient church of Rome. After no long stay, he returned to Alexandria, and there fulfilled the duties of an instructor, with the greatest diligence, in which he was also encouraged by Demetrius who was then bishop, and who earnestly counselled him to labour cheerfully for the benefit of the brethren.

CHAPTER XV.

Of Heraclas.

BUT when he saw that he was not adequate at the same time to the more intense study of divine things, and to the interpretation of the Scriptures, and in addition to the instruction of the catechumens, who scarcely allowed him even to draw breath, one coming after another from morning till night, to be taught by him, he divided the multitude, and selected Heraclas, one of his friends, who was devoted to the study of the Scriptures, and in other respects also a most learned man, not unacquainted with philosophy, and associated him with himself in the office of instruction. To him, therefore, he committed the elementary initiation of those that were yet to be taught the first beginning, or rudiments, but reserved for himself lecturing to those that were more familiar with the subject.

CHAPTER XVI.

The great study which Origen devoted to the holy Scriptures.

BUT so great was the research which Origen applied in the investigation of the holy Scriptures, that he also studied the Hebrew language; and those original works written in the Hebrew and in the hands of the Jews, he procured as his own. He also investigated the editions of others, who, besides the seventy, had published translations of the Scriptures, and some different from the well known translations of Aquila, Symmachus and Theodotion, which he searched up, and traced to I know not what ancient lurking places, where they had lain concealed from remote times, and brought them to the light. In which, when it was doubtful to him from what author they came, he only added the remark that he had found this translation at Nicopolis near Actium, but this other translation in such a place. In the Hexapla, indeed, of the Psalms, after those four noted editions he adds, not only a fifth, but a sixth, and seventh translation, and in one it is remarked that it was discovered at Jericho, in a tub, in the times of Antonine the son of Severus. Having collected all these versions, and divided them by punctuation into their proper members, and arranged them opposite one another in parallel columns, together with the Hebrew texts, he left us those copies of the Hexapla which we now have. In a separate work he also prepared an edition of Aquila and Symmachus, and Theodotion, together with the Septuagint, in what is called the Tetrapla.

CHAPTER XVII.

Of the translator Symmachus.

OF these translators it should be observed that Symmachus was an Ebionite; but the heresy of the Ebionites as it is called, asserts that Christ was born of Joseph and Mary, and supposes him to be a mere man, and insists upon an observance of the law too much after the manner of the Jews, as we have already seen in a previous part of our history. There are also commentaries of Symmachus still extant, in which he appears to direct his remarks against the gospel of Matthew, in order to establish this heresy. But Origen remarks that he received these with interpretations of others, from one Juliana, who, he also said, derived them by inheritance from Symmachus himself.

CHAPTER XVIII.

Of Ambrose.

ABOUT this time also, Ambrose, who had favoured the heresy of Valentinus, being convinced by the truth as maintained by Origen, and as if illuminated by a light beaming on his mind, became attached to the sound doctrine of the church. Many others, also, induced by the celebrity of Origen's learning, came to him from all parts, to make trial of the man's skill in sacred literature. Many also of the heretics, and of distinguished philosophers not a few, were among his diligent hearers, deriving instructions from him, not only in divine things but also in those which belonged to foreign philosophy. As many as he saw endowed with abilities, he also taught the philosophical branches, such as geometry, arithmetic, and other preparatory studies; and then advancing them to the opinions in vogue among the philosophers, and explaining their writings, he commented and speculated upon each, so that he was celebrated as a great philosopher even among the Greeks. He also instructed many of the more common people in the liberal studies, asserting frequently that they would receive no small advantage from these in understanding the holy Scriptures; whence also he considered the studies of political and philosophical matters particularly necessary for himself.

CHAPTER XIX.

The accounts given of Origen by others.

BUT the Gentile philosophers, themselves, among the Greeks who flourished in the age of Origen, bear witness to his proficiency in these studies, in whose works we find frequent mention made of the man; at one time quoting his own words, at another referring their own labours to his judgment as to a master. Why should we say this, when even Porphyry, who was our contemporary, wrote books against us, and attempted to slander the sacred writings; when he mentioned those that had expounded them, and when unable to urge any opprobrious censure against the doctrines, for want of argument, he turned to reviling, and to slander especially the commentators, among whom he is particularly fierce against Origen, saying that he knew him when he was a young man. But, in fact, without knowing it, he commends the man; saying some things in confirmation of the truth when he could not do otherwise, and in other matters uttering falsehoods where he thought he would not be detected. Sometimes he accuses him as a Christian, and sometimes he admires and describes his proficiency in the branches of philosophy. Hear his own words: "But some," says he, "ambitious rather to find some solution to the absurdities of the Jewish writings, instead of abandoning them, have turned their minds to expositions, inconsistent with themselves, and inapplicable to the writings; and which, instead of furnishing a defence of these foreigners, only give us encomiums and remarks in their praise. For boasting of what Moses says plainly in his writings, as if they were dark and intricate propositions, and attaching to them divine influence, as if they were oracles replete with hidden mysteries; and in their vanity pretending to great discrimination of mind, they thus produce their expositions."

Then, again, he says: "But let us take an example of this absurdity, from the very man whom I happened to meet when I was very young, and who was very celebrated, and is still celebrated by the writings that he has left; I mean Origen, whose glory is very great with the teachers of these doctrines. For this man having been a hearer of Ammonius, who had made the greatest proficiency in philosophy among those of our day, as to knowledge, derived great benefit from his master, but with regard to a correct purpose of life, he pursued a course directly opposite. For Ammonius, being a Christian, had been educated among Christians by his parents, and when he began to exercise his own understanding, and apply himself to philosophy, he immediately changed his views, and lived according to the laws. But Origen, as a Greek, being educated in Greek literature, declined to this barbarian impudence. To which, also, betaking himself, he both consigned himself and his attainments in learning, living like a Christian, and swerving from the laws; but in regard to his opinions, both of things and the Deity, acting the Greek, and intermingling Greek literature with these foreign fictions. For he was always in company with Plato, and had the works also of Numenius and Cranius, of Apollophanes and Longinus, of Moderatus and Nicomachus, and others whose writings are valued, in his hands. He also read the works of Chæremon, the stoic, and those of Cornutus. From these he derived the allegorical mode of interpretation usual in the mysteries of the Greeks, and applied it to the Jewish Scriptures."

Such are the assertions made by Porphyry, in the third book of his works, against the Christians, in which he asserts the truth respecting the study and great learning of the man, but also plainly asserts a falsehood (for what would not a man do writing against Christians?) when he says that he went over from the Greeks to the Christians, and that Ammonius apostatised from a life of piety to live like the heathen. For the doctrine of Origen, and his Christian instruction, he derived from his ancestors, as our history has already shown; and Ammonius continued to adhere unshaken, to the end of his days, to the unadulterated principles of the inspired philosophy. This is evident, from the labours of the man that are extant, in his written works, and that establishes his reputation with most men, even at the present day. As, for instance, that work with the title, "The Harmony of Moses and Jesus," and whatsoever others are found among the learned. Let these, therefore, suffice to evince both the calumnies of the false accuser, and also the great proficiency of Origen in the branches of Grecian literature. Respecting this, he defends himself, in an epistle, against the allegations of some who censured him for devoting so much study to these, writing, as follows: " But," says he, " when I had devoted myself wholly to the word, and my fame went abroad concerning my proficiency, as I was sometimes visited by heretics, sometimes by those who were conversant with the studies of the Greeks, especially those that were pursuing philosophy, I was resolved to examine both the opinions of the heretics, and those works of the philosophers which pretend to speak of truth. This we have also done, in imitation of Pantænus, by whom so many have been benefited before us, and who was not meanly furnished with erudition like this. In this I have also followed the example of Heraclas, who has now a seat in the presbytery of Alexandria, who I have found persevered five years with a teacher of philosophy before I began to attend to these studies. Wherefore, also, as he had before used a common dress, he threw it aside, and assuming the habit of philosophers, he retains it even until now. He also still continues to criticise the works of the Greeks with great diligence." These remarks were made by Origen, when he defended himself for his application to the study of the Greeks.

About the same time, also, whilst he was staying at Alexandria, a soldier arriving, handed a letter both to Demetrius, the bishop of the place, and to the prefect of Egypt, from the governor of Arabia; the purport of which was that he should send Origen to him, in all haste, in order to communicate to him his doctrine. Wherefore he was sent by them. But, ere long, having finished the objects of his visit, he again returned to Alexandria. Some time after, however, when a considerable war broke out in the city, he made his escape out of the city; and not thinking it would be safe to stay in Egypt, came to Palestine, and took up his abode in Cesarea. There he was also requested by the bishops to expound the sacred Scriptures publicly in the church, although he had not yet obtained the priesthood by the imposition of hands. This might also be shown, from what was written to Demetrius respecting him, by Alexander bishop of Jerusalem, and Theoctistus bishop of Cesarea, who defended him in the following manner :*—" He has added (.. *e.* Demetrius) to his letter, that this was never before either heard or done, that laymen should deliver discourses in the presence of the bishops. I know not how it happens that he is here evidently so far from the truth. For,

---

* Demetrius is here addressed, by way of respect, in the third person.

ındeed, wheresoever there are found those qualified to benefit the brethren, these are exhorted by the holy bishops to address the people. Thus at Laranda, Euelpis was exhorted by Neon, and at Iconium, Paulinus by Celsus, and at Synada, Theodore by Atticus, our blessed brethren. It is also probable, that this has happened in other places, but we know not that it has." In this way the selfsame Origen was honoured, when yet a young man, not only by his own familiar friends, but also by bishops abroad. But Demetrius, recalling him by letter, and urging his return to Alexandria, by sending members and deacons of the church, he returned and pursued the accustomed duties of his occupation.

CHAPTER XX.

The works of the writers of the day still extant.

MANY learned men of the church also flourished in these times, of whom we may easily find epistles, which they wrote to one another, still extant. These have been also preserved for us in the library of Ælia, which was built by Alexander, who was bishop there. From this we have also been able to collect materials for our present work. Of these Beryllus has left us, together with epistles and treatises, also different kinds of works written with elegance and taste. But he was bishop of Bostra in Arabia. Hippolytus, also, who was bishop of another church, has left us some works. There is beside, a discussion that has come down to us, of Caius, a most learned man, held at Rome in t e times of Zephyrinus, against Proclus, who contended for the Phrygian heresy. In which, whilst he silences the rashness and daring of his opponents in composing new books, (*i. e.* of Scripture,) he makes mention of only thirteen epistles, not reck oning that to the Hebrews with the rest; as there are, even to this day, some of the Romans who do not consider it to be the work of the apostles.

CHAPTER XXI.

The bishops that were noted at this time.

ANTONINE reigned seven years and six months, and was succeeded by Macrinus; and he, after the lapse of a year, was succeeded by another Antonine, in the sovereignty of Rome. In the
first year of the latter, Zephyrinus the bishop of Rome, departed this life, after having charge of the church eighteen years.
He was succeeded in the episcopate by Callisthus, who survived
him five years, and left the church to Urbanus. After these the
government of Rome was held by the emperor Alexander, Antonine having lived only four years from the commencement of
his reign. At this time also, Philetas succeeds Asclepiades in
the church of Antioch. But Mamæa, the emperor's mother, a
woman distinguished for her piety and religion, when the fame
of Origen had now been every where spread abroad, so that it
also reached her ears, was very eager both to be honoured with
a sight of the man, and to make trial of his skill in divine things
so greatly extolled. Therefore, whilst staying at Alexandria, she
sent for him by a military escort. With her he staid some time,
exhibiting innumerable matters calculated to promote the glory
of the Lord, and to evince the excellence of divine instruction,
after which he hastened back again to his accustomed engagements.

CHAPTER XXII.

The works of Hippolytus, that have reached us.

AT the same time, Hippolytus, who composed many other
treatises, also wrote a work on the passover. In this he traces
back the series of times, and presents a certain canon comprising
a period of sixteen years, on the Passover, limiting his computation of the times to the first year of the emperor Alexander.

But the remaining works written by him, that have come dowr to us, are the following: *On the Hexaemeron, On the Works after the Hexaemeron, To Marcion, On the Canticles, On parts of Eze-kiel, On the Passover, Against all the Heresies.* You will also find many others still preserved by many.

CHAPTER XXIII.

Origen's zeal, and his elevation to the priesthood.

FROM this time, however, Origen began his Commentaries on the sacred Scriptures, to which he was particularly urged by Ambrose, who presented innumerable incentives, not only by verbal exhortation. but by furnishing the most ample supplies of all necessary means; for he had more than seven amanuenses, when he dictated, who relieved each other at appointed times. He had not fewer copyists, as also girls, who were well exercised in more elegant writing. For all which, Ambrose furnished an abundant supply of all the necessary expense. And, indeed he, for his own part, evinced an inexpressible zeal in the study of the sacred Scriptures, by which also he particularly stimulated Origen to write his Commentaries. Whilst this was the state of things, Urban, who had been bishop of Rome eight years, was succeeded by Pontianus. At Antioch, Philetus was succeeded by Zebinus. At this time Origen, being compelled by some necessary affairs of the church, went to Greece by way of Palestine, where he received the ordination to the priesthood, at Cesarea, from the bishops of that country. The matters that were agitated upon this in reference to him, and the decisions of the bishops of the churches, in consequence of these movements, and whatsoever other works he wrote in the prime of his life, to advance the divine word, as it demands a separate treatise, we have suf-ciently stated in the second book of the work we have writtcn in his defence.

CHAPTER XXIV.

The expositions he gave at Alexandria.

To these it might be necessary, perhaps, to add, that in the sixth book of his exegetical works on the gospel of John, he shows that the first five were composed by him whilst yet at Alexandria. But of the whole work on this gospel, only twenty-two books have come down to us. But in the ninth book on Genesis, for there are twelve in all, he not only shows that the eight preceding ones were written at Alexandria, but also, his commentaries on the first five and twenty Psalms. Moreover, those on Lamentations, of which five books have reached us, in which he also makes mention of his books on the resurrection. But these are two in number. Likewise, the works on the Principles were written before his removal from Alexandria, and also those entitled Stromata, in number ten, he composed in the same city during the reign of the emperor Alexander, as is shown by his own notes, fully written out before the books.

CHAPTER XXV.

His review of the collective Scriptures.

In his exposition of the first Psalm, he has given a catalogue of the books in the sacred Scriptures of the Old Testament, as follows: "But it should be observed that the collective books, as handed down by the Hebrews, are twenty-two, according to the number of letters in their alphabet." After some further remarks, he subjoins: "These twenty-two books, according to the Hebrews, are as follows, 'That which is called Genesis, but by the Hebrews, from the beginning of the book, Bresith, which means, in the beginning. Exodus, Walesmoth,* which means,

---

* We have here given the Hebrew pronunciation according to Origen's Greek, which differs sometimes from the common pronunciation; allowance must also be made for the pronunciation of the Greek itself.

these are the names. Leviticus, Waikra, and he called. Numbers, Anmesphekodlim. Deuteronomy, Elle haddabarim, that is, these are the words. Jesus the son of Nave, in Hebrew, Joshue ben Nun. Judges and Ruth, in one book, with the Hebrews, which they call Sophetim. Of Kings, the first and second, one book, with them called Samuel, the called of God. The third and fourth of Kings, also in one book with them, and called, Wahammelech Dabid,* which means, and king David. The first and second book of the Paralipomena, contained in one volume with them, and called Dibre Hamaim, which means the words, *i. e.* the records of days. The first and second of Esdras, in one, called Ezra, *i. e.* an assistant. The book of Psalms, sepher Thehillim. The Proverbs of Solomon, Misloth. Ecclesiastes, Coheleth. The Song of Songs, Sir Hasirim. Isaiah, Iesaia. Jeremiah, with the Lamentations, and his Epistle, in one, Jeremiah. Daniel, Daniel. Ezekiel, Jeezkel. Job, Job. Esther, also with the Hebrews, Esther. Besides these, there are, also, the Maccabees, which are inscribed Sarbeth sarbane el.' "

These, then, are the books that he mentions in the book mentioned above. But in the first book of his Commentaries on the gospel of Matthew, following the Ecclesiastical Canon, he attests that he knows of only four gospels, as follows : " As I have understood from tradition, respecting the four gospels, which are the only undisputed ones in the whole church of God throughout the world. The first is written according to Matthew, the same that was once a publican, but afterwards an apostle of Jesus Christ, who having published it for the Jewish converts, wrote it in the Hebrew. The second is according to Mark, who composed it, as Peter explained to him, whom he also acknowledges as his son in his general Epistle, saying, ' The elect church in Babylon, salutes you, as also Mark my son.' And the third, according to Luke, the gospel commended by Paul, which was

---

* *David* is here written with a ?, and we have given it according to our usual Greek pronunciation. But Origen appears to have pronounced the *beta* as *v;* as also the Septuagint, who, in several instances give the name Α???, from the Hebrew, where it would be impossible to suppose they had the sound of *b.* Some of the older grammarians, as Clenardus, follow the same pronunciation.

246 ECCLESIASTICAL HISTORY.

written for the converts from the Gentiles, and last of all the
gospel according to John. And in the fifth book of his Commentaries on John, the same author writes as follows: " But he
being well fitted to be a minister of the New Testament, Paul, I
mean a minister not of the letter but of the spirit; who, after
spreading the gospel from Jerusalem and the country around as
far as Illyricum, did not even write to all the churches to which
he preached, but even to those to whom he wrote he only sent a
few lines. But Peter, upon whom the church of Christ is built,
against which the gates of hell shall not prevail, has left one
epistle undisputed. Suppose, also, the second was left by him,
for on this there is some doubt. What shall we say of him who
reclined upon the breast of Jesus, I mean John? who has left
one gospel, in which he confesses that he could write so many
that the whole world could not contain them. He also wrote the
Apocalypse, commanded as he was, to conceal, and not to write
the voices of the seven thunders. He has also left an epistle
consisting of very few lines; suppose, also, that a second and third
is from him, for not all agree that they are genuine, but both together do not contain a hundred lines." To these remarks he
also adds the following observation on the Epistle to the Hebrews, in his homilies on the same: " The style of the Epistle
with the title, ' To the Hebrews,' has not that vulgarity of diction which belongs to the apostle, who confesses that he is but
common in speech, that is in his phraseology. But that this
epistle is more pure Greek in the composition of its phrases,
every one will confess who is able to discern the difference of
style. Again, it will be obvious that the ideas of the epistle are
admirable, and not inferior to any of the books acknowledged to
be apostolic. Every one will confess the truth of this, who attentively reads the apostle's writings." To these he afterwards
again adds: " But I would say, that the thoughts are the apos
tle's, but the diction and phraseology belong to some one who has
recorded what the apostle said, and as one who noted down at his
leisure what his master dictated. If then, any church considers
this epistle as coming from Paul, let it be commended for this,
for neither did those ancient men deliver it as such without

cause. But who it was that really wrote the epistle, God only knows. The account, however, that has been current before us is, according to some, that Clement who was bishop of Rome wrote the epistle; according to others, that it was written by Luke, who wrote the gospel and the Acts. But let this suffice on these subjects.

CHAPTER XXVI.

Heraclas succeeds to the episcopate of Alexandria.

But this was the tenth year of the abovementioned reign (of Alexander,) in which Origen, after removing from Alexandria to Cesarea, left his school for catechetical instruction there in the charge of Heraclas. But ere long Demetrius, the bishop of the church of Alexandria, died, having performed the duties of the office, upon the whole, forty-three years. He was succeeded by Heraclas. About this time also flourished Firmilianus bishop of Cesarea in Cappadocia.

CHAPTER XXVII.

How the bishops regarded him.

This bishop was so favourably disposed towards Origen, that he then called him to the regions in which he dwelt, to benefit the churches; at another time, he went to visit him in Judea, and passed some time with him there, for the sake of improvement in things divine. Moreover Alexander, the bishop of Jerusalem, and Theoctistus, bishop of Cesarea, attending him the whole time nearly like pupils their master, allowed him alone to perform the duties of expounding the sacred Scriptures, and other matters that pertain to the doctrines of the church.

CHAPTER XXVIII.

The persecution under Maximinus.

BUT the emperor Alexander being carried off after a reign of thirteen years, was succeeded by Maximinus, who, inflamed with hatred against the house of Alexander, consisting of many believers, raised a persecution, and commanded at first only the heads of the churches to be slain, as the abettors and agents of evangelical truth. It was then that Origen wrote his book on Martyrdom, which he dedicated to Ambrose and Protoctetus a presbyter of the church at Cesarea, because both of these encountered no common danger in the persecution. In which also it is said that these men were pre-eminent for (persevering in) their confession, as Maximinus did not reign longer than three years. Origen has assigned the time of this persecution, both in the twenty-second book of his Commentaries on John, and in different epistles.

CHAPTER XXIX.

Of Fabianus, who was remarkably appointed bishop of Rome by a divine communication.

GORDIAN succeeded Maximinus in the sovereignty of Rome, when Pontianus who had held the episcopate six years, was succeeded by Anteros in the church of Rome; he also is succeeded by Fabianus, after having been engaged in the service about a month. It is said that Fabianus had come to Rome with some others from the country, and staying there in the most remarkable manner, by divine and celestial grace, was advanced to be one of the candidates for the office. When all the brethren had assembled in the church, for the purpose of ordaining him that should succeed in the episcopate, though there were very many eminent and illustrious men in the expectation of many, Fabianus being present, no one thought of any other man. They relate, further, that a dove suddenly flying down from on high, sat upon his head, exhibiting a scene like that of the holy Spirit once descending upon our Saviour in the form of a dove. Upon this the whole body exclaimed, with all eagerness and with one voice, as if moved by the one spirit of God, that he was worthy; and without delay they took and placed him upon the episcopal throne. At the same time Zebinus, bishop of Antioch, dying, was succeeded in the government (of the church,) by Babylas, and at Alexandria, Demetrius held the episcopate forty-three years, and was succeeded in the office by Heraclas. But in the catechetical school there, he was succeeded by Dionysius, who was also one of Origen's pupils.

CHAPTER XXX.

The pupils of Origen.

WHILST Origen was attending to his accustomed duties at Cesarea, many frequented his school, not only of the residents of the place, but also innumerable others from abroad, who left their country in order to attend his lectures. Of these the most noted whom we know is Thedorus, known also by the name of Gregory, and so celebrated among the bishops of our day; also his brother Athenodorus. Origen, seeing them excessively wrapt in the prosecution of the studies of the Greeks and Romans, infused into them the love of philosophy, and induced them to exchange their former zeal for the study of divine things. But after being with him five years, they made such improvement in the divine oracles, that both, though very young, were honoured with the episcopate in the churches of Pontus.

CHAPTER XXXI.

Cf Africanus.

At this time, also, flourished Africanus, who wrote tne books with the title Cesti. There is an epistle of his extant, addressed to Origen, in which he intimates his doubts on the history of Susannah, in Daniel, as if it were a spurious and fictitious composition. To which Origen wrote a very full answer. Other works of the same Africanus that have reached us, are his five books of Chronography, a most accurate and laboured performance. In these, he says that he had gone to Alexandria, on account of the great celebrity of Heraclas, the same that we have already shown was advanced to the episcopate there, and who was, also, very eminent for his skill in philosophical studies, and the other sciences of the Greeks. Another epistle of the same Africanus is also extant, addressed to Aristides, on the supposed discrepancy between Matthew and Luke in the genealogy of Christ. In this he most clearly establishes the consistency of the two evangelists, from an account which had been handed down from his ancestors, which, in its proper place, we have already anticipated in the first book of the work we have in hand.

CHAPTER XXXII.

The Commentarie s that Origen wrote in Palestine

About this time, also, Origen composed his Commentary on Isaiah, as also on Ezekiel. Of the former, thirty books * have come down to us as far as the third part of Isaiah, until (the chapter beginning) the vision of the beast in the desert. On

---

* The word τοµος, from which we get *tome*, properly signifies a section; and as the sections of a work were sometimes on different scrolls, hence they were called books, volumes, and τοµοι.

Ezekiel there are twenty-five books, which are all that he wrote upon this prophet. But when he came to Athens, he, indeed, finished his Commentaries on Ezekiel, but also commenced his Notes on the Song of Solomon, and advanced there as far as the fifth book. But on his return to Cesarea, he also brought these to a close, in number ten. Why should we, however, give a minute statement of the man's labours, a performance, in itself, that would require a separate and distinct work? And, indeed, this has already been done by us in our life of Pamphilus, that holy martyr of our day, in which, after exhibiting the great zeal of Pamphilus, we also subjoin the catalogues of the library collected by him, of the works written by Origen and other ecclesiastical writers. By which any one that wishes may most satisfactorily learn what works of Origen have come down to us.

CHAPTER XXXIII.

The error of Beryllus.

BERYLLUS, who was mentioned a little before, as bishop of Bostra in Arabia, perverting the doctrine of the church, attempted to introduce certain opinions that are foreign to Christian faith, daring to assert that our Lord and Saviour did not exist in the proper sense of existence, before his dwelling among men; neither had he a proper divinity, but only that divinity which dwelt in him from the Father. As the bishops had many examinations and discussions on this point with the man, Origen, who was also invited together with the rest, at first entered into conversation with him, in order to ascertain what opinion the man held. But when he understood what he advanced, after correcting his error, by reasoning and demonstration, he convinced him, and thus recovered him to the truth in doctrine, and brought him back again to the former sound opinion. There are also works still extant, both of Beryllus and the synod that was held on his account, containing the questions put to him by Origen, and the discussions held in his church, together with all that was done there. Innumerable other facts are reported by our elder brethren, which I have thought proper to pass by, as having no reference to the objects of the present work; but whatsoever it was necessary to select of matters concerning him, these may be collected from that defence of him which we and Pamphilus, that holy martyr of our times, have written, which work we performed jointly, in order to obviate the malevolence of some.

CHAPTER XXXIV.

Of Philip Cesar.

GORDIANUS had held the government of Rome six years, when he was succeeded by Philip, together with his son Philip. It is said that, as a Christian, on the day of the last vigil of the passover, he wished to share with the multitude in the prayers of the church, but was not permitted by the existing bishop to enter before he had confessed his sins, and numbered himself with those who were referred to transgressors, and had space for repentance. For otherwise he would never be received by him, unless he first did this, on account of the many crimes which he had committed. The emperor is said to have obeyed cheerfully, and exhibited a genuine and religious disposition in regard to his fear of God.

CHAPTER XXXV.

Dionysius succeeds Heraclas in the episcopate.

IN the third year of this reign also, Heraclas dying, after an episcopate of sixteen years, was succeeded by Dionysius in the supervision of the church of Alexandria.

CHAPTER XXXVI.

Other works written by Origen.

THEN also, as was to be expected, our religion spreading more and more, and our brethren beginning to converse more freely with all, Origen, who they say was now more than sixty years of age, and who from long practice had acquired the greatest facility in discoursing, permitted his discourses to be taken down by ready writers, a thing which he had never allowed before. At this time, also, he composed in eight books a reply to that work written against us by Celsus the Epicurean, bearing the title, " The True Doctrine," and the twenty-five books on Matthew's gospel, those also on the twelve apostles, of which we have found only twenty-five. There is also an epistle of his extant, addressed to the emperor Philip, and another to his wife Severa; several others also to different persons. Of these as many as we have been able to collect, scattered in the hands of different individuals, we have reduced to certain distinct books, in number exceeding one hundred. But he also wrote to Fabianus bishop of Rome, and to many others of the bishops of churches respecting his orthodoxy; and of these you have the proofs in the sixth book of our Apology for the man.

CHAPTER XXXVII.

The dissension of the Arabians.

BUT about this time, also, other men sprung up in Arabia as the propagators of false opinions. These asserted, that the human soul, as long as the present state of the world existed, perished at death and died with the body, but that it would be raised again with the body at the time of the resurrection. And as a considerable council was held on account of this, Origen being again requested, likewise here discussed the point in question with so much force, that those who had been before led astray, completely changed their opinions.

CHAPTER XXXVIII.

The heresy of the Helcesaites.

ANOTHER error also sprung up about this time, called the heresy of the Helcesaites, which, however, was almost stifled in its birth. But it is mentioned by Origen, in his public lecture on the eighty-second Psalm : " A certain one, says he, came recently with a great opinion of his abilities, to maintain that ungodly and wicked error of the Helcesaites, which has but lately appeared in the churches. The mischievous assertions of this heresy, I will give you, that you may not be carried away with it. It sets aside certain parts of the collective Scriptures, and it makes use of passages from the Old Testament, and from the gospels. It rejects the apostle altogether. It asserts, also, to deny (Christ) is indifferent, and that one who has made up his mind, in case of necessity will deny with his mouth, but not in his heart. They also produce a certain book, which they say fell from heaven : and that whoever has heard and believed this, will receive remission of sins ; a remission different from that given by Christ." And such is the account respecting these.

CHAPTER XXXIX.

The persecution of Decius.

PHILIP, after a reign of seven years, was succeeded by Decius, who, in consequence of his hatred to Philip, raised a persecution against the church, in which Fabianus suffered martyrdom, and was succeeded as bishop of Rome by Cornelius. —In Palestine, however, Alexander, bishop of Jerusalem, was again brought before the tribunal of the governor, at Cesarea, and after an eminent perseverance in his profession, though crowned with the hoary locks of venerable age, he was cast into prison.   After giving a splendid and illustrious testimony at the governor's tribunal, and expiring in prison, he was succeeded by Mazabanes as bishop of Jerusalem.   But Babylas, like Alexander, dying in prison at Antioch, after his confession, the church there was governed by Fabius.   But the number and greatness of Origen's sufferings there during the persecution, and the nature of his death, when the spirit of darkness drew up his forces, and waged a war with all his arts and power against the man, and assailed him particularly beyond all that were then assaulted by him; the nature and number of bonds which the man endured on account of the doctrine of Christ, and all his torments of body, the sufferings also which he endured under an iron collar, and in the deepest recesses of the prison, when for many days he was extended and stretched to the distance of four holes on the rack; besides the threats of fire, and whatsoever other sufferings inflicted by his enemies he nobly bore, and finally the issue of these sufferings, when the judge eagerly strove with all his might to protract his life (in order to prolong his sufferings,) and what expressions after these he left behind replete with benefit to those needing consolation, all this the many epistles of the man detail with no less truth than accuracy:

CHAPTER XL.

What happened to Dionysius.

I shall now subjoin the occurrences that befel Dionysius, from his epistle to Germanus, where, speaking of himself, he gives the following account : " But I speak before God, and he knows that I lie not; it was never by my own counsel, nor without divine intimation, that I projected my flight.   But before the persecution of Decius, Sabinus, at the very hour, sent Frumentarius to search for me.   And I indeed, staid at home about four days, expecting the arrival of Frumentarius.   But he went about examining all places, the roads, the rivers, the fields, where he suspected that

I would go or lie concealed. But he was smitten with blindness, not being able to find the house, for he could not believe that I would remain at home when persecuted. Four days had scarcely elapsed when God ordered me to remove, and opened the way for me in a most remarkable manner. I and my domestics, and many of my brethren, went forth together. And that this happened by the providence of God, was shown by what followed, and in which, perhaps, we were not unprofitable to some." After this, he shows the events that befel him after his flight, adding the following : " But about sunset, being seized, together with my company, by the soldiers, I was led to Taposiris. But Timothy, by the providence of God, happened not to be present, nor even seized. But coming afterwards, he found the house deserted, and servants guarding it, and us he found reduced to slavery." After other remarks, he observes : " And what was the manner of this divine interposition of his ? For the truth shall be told. A certain man of the country met Timothy flying, and much disturbed, and when he was asked the cause of his haste, he declared the truth. When he heard it, he went his way, for he was going to a marriage festival, (as it is the custom with them on these occasions to keep the whole night,) and when he entered he told it to those that were present at the feast. These, forthwith, with a single impulse, as if by agreement, all arose, and came as quick as possible in a rush upon us, and as they rushed they raised a shout. The soldiers that guarded us immediately took to flight, and they came upon us, lying as we were upon the bare bedsteads. I indeed, as God knows, supposed them at first to be robbers, who had come to plunder and pillage. Remaining, therefore, on my bed, naked as I was, only covered with a linen garment, the rest of my dress I offered them as it lay beside me. But they commanded me to rise and to depart as quick as possible. Then, understanding for what purpose they had come, I began to cry out, beseeching and praying them to go away and to let us alone. But if they wished to do us any good, to anticipate those that had led me away, and to cut off my head. When I thus cried out, as my companions and partners in all my distresses well know, they attempted to raise me by force. I then cast myself on my back upon the ground. But they seized me by the hands and feet, and dragged me away, whilst those who were witnesses of all these things, Caius, Faustus, Peter, and Paul, followed on. These also, taking me up, bore me away from the town, and carried me off on an unsaddled ass." Such is the account of Dionysius respecting himself.

CHAPTER XLI.

Of those who suffered martyrdom at Alexandria.

BUT the same writer in the epistle which he addressed to Fabius bishop of Antioch, relates the conflicts of those who suffered martyrdom at Alexandria in the following manner: " The persecution with us did not begin with the imperial edict, but preceded it a whole year. And a certain prophet and poet, inauspicious to the city, whoever he was, excited the mass of the heathen against us, stirring them up to their native superstition. Stimulated by him, and taking full liberty to exercise any kind of wickedness, they considered this the only piety, and the worship of their dæmons, viz., to slay us. First then, seizing a certain aged man named Metra, they called upon him to utter impious expressions, and as he did not obey, they beat his body with clubs, and pricked his face and eyes; after which they led him away to the suburbs, where they stoned him. Next they led a woman called Quinta, who was a believer, to the temple of an idol, and attempted to force her to worship; but when she turned away in disgust, they tied her by the feet, and dragged her through the whole city, over the rough stones of the paved streets, dashing her against the millstones, and scourging her at the same time, until they brought her to the same place, where they stoned her. Then, with one accord, all rushed upon the houses of the pious, and whomsoever of their neighbours they knew, they drove thither in all haste, and despoiled and plundered them, setting apart the more valuable of the articles for themselves; but the more common and wooden furniture they threw about and burnt in the roads, presenting a sight like a city taken by the enemy.

But the brethren retired, and gave way, and like those to whom Paul bears witness, they also regarded the plunder of their goods with joy. And I know not whether any besides one, who fell into their hands, has thus far denied the Lord. But they also seized that admirable virgin, Apollonia, then in advanced age, and beating her jaws, they broke out all her teeth, and kindling a fire before the city, threatened to burn her alive, unless she would repeat their impious expressions. She appeared at first to shrink a little, but when suffered to go, she suddenly sprang into the fire and was consumed. They also seized a certain Serapion in his own house, and after torturing him with the severest cruelties, and breaking all his limbs, threw him headlong from an upper story. But there was no way, no public road, no lane, where we could walk, whether by day or night; as they all, at all times and places, cried out, whoever would refuse to repeat those impious expressions, that he should be immediately dragged forth and burnt.

These things continued to prevail for the most part after this manner. But as the sedition and a civil war overtook the wretches, their cruelty was diverted from us to one another. We then drew a little breath, whilst their rage against us was a little abated. But, presently, that change from a milder reign was announced to us, and much terror was now threatening us. The decree had arrived, very much like that which was foretold by our Lord, exhibiting the most dreadful aspect; so that, if it were possible, the very elect would stumble. All, indeed, were greatly alarmed, and many of the more eminent immediately gave way to them; others, who were in public offices, were led forth by their very acts; others were brought by their acquaintance, and when called by name, they approached the impure and unholy sacrifices. But, pale and trembling, as if they were not to sacrifice, but themselves to be the victims and the sacrifices to the idols, they were jeered by many of the surrounding multitude, and were obviously equally afraid to die and to offer the sacrifice. But some advanced with greater readiness to the altars, and boldly asserted that they had never before been Christians. Concerning whom the declaration of our Lord is most true, that they will scarcely be saved. Of the rest, some followed the one or the other of the preceding; some fled, others were taken, and of these some held out as far as the prison and bonds, and some after a few days imprisonment abjured (Christianity) before they entered the tribunal. But some, also, after enduring the torture for a time, at last renounced. Others, however, firm and blessed pillars of the Lord, confirmed by the Lord himself, and receiving in themselves strength and power, suited and proportioned to their faith, became admirable witnesses of his kingdom.

The first of these was Julian, a man afflicted with the gout, neither able to walk nor stand, who, with two others that carried him, was arraigned. Of these, the one immediately denied, but the other, named Cronion, surnamed Eunus, and the aged Julian himself, having confessed the Lord, was carried on camels throughout the whole city, a very large one as you know, and in this elevation were scourged, and finally consumed in an immense fire, surrounded by the thronging crowds of spectators. But a soldier, whose name was Besas, standing near them, who had opposed the insolence of the multitude, whilst they were led away to execution, was himself assailed with their loud vociferations, and thus this brave soldier of God, after he had excelled in the great conflict of piety, was beheaded. Another, who was a Lybian by birth, but both in name and blessedness a Macar (blessed), after much solicitation from the judge to have him renounce, still remaining inflexible, was burnt alive. After these, Epimachus and Alexander, who had continued for a long time in prison, enduring innumerable suffering from the scourges and scrapers,* were also destroyed in an immense fire.† With these there were also

---

* The instrument of torture here mentioned was an iron scraper, calculated to wound and tear the flesh as it passed over it.

† The same expression, πυρι ασβεστω, occurs here as above. We have rendered it, therefore, as above, by the word *fire*. Valesius, who is followed by Shorting, translates *unslacked lime*. But why he should understand it differently here from what he does above, does not appear. The martyrs here were destroyed by the same kind of death as the preceding. If the word πυρ did not determine the sig-

four women; Ammonarium, a holy virgin, who was ingeniously tortured for a very long time by the judge, because she had plainly declared she would utter none of those expressions which he dictated; and having made good her promise, she was led away. The others were the venerable and aged Mercuria; Dionysia, also, who was the mother of many children, but did not love them more than the Lord. These, after the governor became ashamed to torture them to no purpose, and thus to be defeated by women, all died by the sword, without the trial by tortures. But as to Ammonarium, she, like a chief combatant, received the greatest tortures of all. Heron and Ater and Isidorus, who were Egyptians, and with them a youth named Dioscorus, about the age of fifteen, were delivered up. At first he attempted to deceive the youth with fair words, as if he could be easily brought over, and to force him by tortures, as if he would readily yield. Dioscorus, however, was neither persuaded by words nor constrained by tortures.

After scourging the rest in a most savage manner, and seeing them persevere, he also delivered these to the fire. But Dioscorus was dismissed by the judge, who admired the great wisdom of his answers to the questions proposed to him, and was also illustrious in the eyes of the people, with the view, as he said, to give him further time for repentance on account of his age. And now this most godly Dioscorus is among us, expecting a longer and a more severe conflict. A certain Nemesion, also an Egyptian, was first indeed accused as a companion of thieves; but when he had repelled this charge before the centurion, as a slander against him, in which there was no truth, being reported as a Christian, he was brought as a prisoner before the governor. He, a most unrighteous judge, inflicted a punishment more than double that of robbers, both scourges and tortures, and then committed him to the flames between thieves; thus honouring

---

nification, there might be some reason, perhaps, for this version, the word αποβιστος; having τιτανος understood. But it is surely going far out of our way to look for this meaning, when the meaning is so obviously determined by the many circumstances which here combine. It may be remarked, by the way, that the expression is literally *inextinguishable fire*, a strong hyperbole for *immense fire*.

the blessed martyr after the example of Christ. But there was a band of soldiers, standing in a dense body before the tribunal, who were Ammon, and Zeno, and Ptolemy, and Ingenuus, together with the aged Theophilus. A certain one being brought and tried as a Christian, and already inclining to deny, they stood near, gnashed with their teeth, and beckoned to them with their faces, and stretched out their hands, and made gestures with their bodies. And whilst all were directing their eyes upon them, before they were seized by any one else, they ran up to the tribunal and declared that they were Christians; so that the governor and his associates themselves were greatly intimidated, whilst those who were condemned were most cheerful at the prospect of what they were to suffer; but their judges trembled. And these, therefore, retired from the tribunals, and rejoiced in their testimony, in which God had enabled them to triumph gloriously.

CHAPTER XLII.

Other accounts given by Dionysius.

But many others were also torn asunder in cities and villages, of which I shall mention one as an example. Ischyrion was hired by one of the rulers in the capacity of a steward. This man was ordered by his employer to sacrifice, but as he did not obey, he was abused by him. Persevering in his purpose, he was treated with contumely, and as he still continued to bear with all, his employer seized a long pole and slew him, by thrusting it through his bowels. Why should I mention the multitudes that wandered about in deserts and mountains, that perished by hunger and thirst, and frost and diseases, and robbers and wild beasts? The survivors of whom are the witnesses both of their election and victory. But I will add one fact to illustrate this: "Chæremon was a very aged bishop of the city called Nile. He fleeing into the Arabian* mountain, with his partner, did not re-

* Valesius thinks that the mountain here mentioned, was not, as the name seems to imply, in Arabia, but translates in both places where it occurs, Arabicus mons,

turn again, nor could the brethren learn any thing of him any
more, though frequent search was made for him. They neither
found them nor their bodies, but many were carried off as slaves
by the barbarous Saracens, to the same mountains. Some of
these were ransomed with difficulty, others not even to the present day. And these facts, I have stated brethren, not without
an object, but that thou mayest see how great and terrible distresses have befallen us. Of which, indeed, they who have been
most tried, also understand the most." Then, after a few remarks, he observes: " But these same martyrs, who are now sitting with Christ, and are the sharers in his kingdom, and the
partners in his judgment, and who are now judging with him, received those of the brethren that fell away, and had been convicted of sacrificing, (to idols,) and when they saw their conversion and repentance, and that it might be acceptable to him who
doth not by any means wish the death of the sinner so much as
their repentance, and having proved them (as sincere) they received and assembled with them. They also communicated
with them in prayer and at their feasts. What then, brethren,
do ye advise concerning these? What should we do? Let us
join in our sentiments with them, and let us observe their judgment and their charity; and let us kindly receive those who were
treated with such compassion by them. Or should we rather
pronounce their judgment unjust, and set ourselves up as the
judges of their opinion? And thus grieve the spirit of mildness,
and overturn established order?" These remarks were probably
added by Dionysius when he spoke of those that had fallen away
through weakness, during the persecution.

Arabian mountain. He thinks that it was so called merely from its vicinity or
contiguity to Arabia.

CHAPTER XLIII.

Of Novatus, his manners and habits, and his heresy.

ABOUT this time appeared Novatus, a presbyter of the church of Rome, and a man elevated with haughtiness against these (that had fallen), as if there was no room for them to hope salvation, not even, if they performed every thing for a genuine and pure confession. He thus became the leader of the peculiar heresy of those who, in the pomp of their imaginations, called themselves Cathari. A very large council being held on account of this, at which sixty indeed of the bishops, but a still greater number of presbyters and deacons were present; the pastors of the remaining provinces, according to their places, deliberated separately what should be done: this decree was passed by all; "That Novatus, indeed, and those who so arrogantly united with him, and those that had determined to adopt the uncharitable and most inhuman opinion of the man, these they considered among those that were alienated from the church; but that brethren who had incurred any calamity should be treated and healed with the remedies of repentance."

There are also epistles of Cornelius, bishop of Rome, addressed to Fabius, bishop of Antioch, which show the transactions of the council of Rome, as also, the opinions of all those in Italy and Africa, and the regions there. Others there are also written in the Roman tongue, from Cyprian, and the bishops with him in Africa. In these, it is shown that they also agree in the necessity of relieving those who had fallen under severe temptations, and also in the propriety of excommunicating the author of the heresy, and all that were of his party. To these is attached also an epistle from Cornelius on the decrees of the council, besides others on the deeds of Novatus, from which we may add extracts, that those who read the present work may know the circumstances respecting him. What kind of a character Novatus was, Cornelius informs Fabius, writing as follows : "But that you may know, says he, how this singular man, who formerly

aspired to the episcopate, and secretly concealed within himself
this precipitate ambition, making use of those confessors that
adhered to him from the beginning, as a cloak for his own folly
I will proceed to relate: Maximus, a presbyter of our church,
and Urbanus, twice obtained the highest reputation for their confessions.   Sidonius also, and Celerinus, a man who, by the mercy
of God, bore every kind of torture in the most heroic manner, and
by the firmness of his own faith strengthened the weakness of the
flesh, completely worsted the adversary.   These men, therefore,
as they knew him, and had well sounded his artifice and duplicity, as also his perjuries and falsehoods, his dissocial and savage
character, returned to the holy church, and announced all his
devices and wickedness, which he had for a long time dissembled
within himself, and this too in the presence of many bishops ; and
the same also, in the presence of many presbyters, and a great
number of laymen, at the same time lamenting and sorrowing
that they had been seduced, and had abandoned the church for a
short time, through the agency of that artful and malicious
beast."   After a little, he further says : " We have seen, beloved
brother, within a short time, an extraordinary conversion and
change in him.   For this most illustrious man, and he who affirmed with the most dreadful oaths, that he never aspired to the
episcopate, has suddenly appeared a bishop, as thrown among us
by some machine.   For this dogmatist, this (pretended) champion of ecclesiastical discipline, when he attempted to seize and
usurp the episcopate not given him from above, selected two
desperate characters as his associates, to send them to some small,
and that the smallest, part of Italy, and from thence, by some fictitious plea, to impose upon three bishops there, men altogether ignorant and simple, affirming and declaring, that it was necessary
for them to come to Rome in all haste, that all the dissension
which had there arisen might be removed through their mediation, in conjunction with the other bishops.   When these men
had come, being, as before observed, but simple and plain in discerning the artifices and villany of the wicked, and when shut up
with men of the same stamp with himself, at the tenth hour, when
heated with wine and surfeiting, they forced them by a kind of

shadowy and empty imposition of hands, to confer the episcopate upon him, and which, though by no means suited to him, he claims by fraud and treachery. One of these, not long after, returned to his church, mourning and confessing his error, with whom also we communed as a layman, as all the people present interceded for him, and we sent successors to the other bishops ordaining them in the place where they were. This assertor of the gospel then did not know that there should be but one bishop in a catholic church.* (εν καθολικη εκκλησια.) In which, however, he well knew, (for how could he be ignorant?) that there were forty-six presbyters, seven deacons, seven sub-deacons, forty-two acoluthi (clerks,) exorcists, readers, and janitors, in all fifty-two: widows, with the afflicted and needy, more than fifteen hundred; all which the goodness and love of God doth support and nourish. But neither this great number, so necessary in the church, nor those that by the providence of God were wealthy and opulent, together with the innumerable multitude of the people, were able to recall him and turn him from such a desperate and presumptuous course."

And, again, after these, he subjoins the following: " Now let us also tell by what means and conduct he had the assurance to claim the episcopate. Whether, indeed, it was because he was engaged in the church from the beginning, and endured many conflicts for her, and encountered many and great dangers in the

* The word catholic, in its Greek etymology, means universal, as we have sometimes explained it in this translation. It is applied to the Christian, as a universal church, partly to distinguish it from the ancient church of the Jews, which was limited, partial, and particular in its duration, subjects, and country. The Christian is also called a universal or catholic church, because it must in regard to doctrine hold *quod semper, quod ubique, quod ab omnibus*. In this latter view, which it should be well observed is the original application, it is synonymous with *orthodox*. This is evident, from the fact that our author applies it to different churches in other parts of his history. And in the present instance the expression is general, *a catholic church*. It is in a sense allied to this also, that we are, no doubt, to understand the title of our general (*catholic*) epistles, in the New Testament. They are *catholic*, because as consonant to the doctrines of the church *in* all respects, they have been also universally received. In this sense, the term is also synonymous with *canonical*.

cause of true religion? None of all this. To him, indeed, the author and instigator of his faith was Satan, who entered into and dwelt in him a long time. Who aided by the exorcists, when attacked with an obstinate disease, and being supposed at the point of death, was baptised by aspersion, in the bed on which he lay; if, indeed, it be proper to say that one like him did receive baptism. But neither when he recovered from disease, did he partake of other things, which the rules of the church prescribe as duty, nor was he sealed (in confirmation) by the bishop. But as he did not obtain this, how could he obtain the holy spirit?" And, again, soon after, he says: " He denied he was a presbyter, through cowardice and the love of life, in the time of persecution. For when requested and exhorted by the deacons, that he should go forth from his retreat, in which he had imprisoned himself, and should come to the relief of the brethren, as far as was proper and in the power of a presbyter to assist brethren requiring relief, he was so far from yielding to any exhortation of the deacons, that he went away offended and left them. For he said that he wished to be a presbyter no longer, for he was an admirer of a different philosophy."

Passing over some other matters, our author again adds:— " This illustrious character abandoning the church of God, in which, when he was converted he was honoured with the presbytery, and that by the favour of the bishop placing his hands upon him (ordaining him), to the order of bishops, and as all the clergy and many of the laity resisted it, since it was not lawful that one baptized in his sick bed by aspersion, as he was, should be promoted to any order of the clergy, the bishop requested that it should be granted him to ordain only this one." After this, he adds another deed, the worst of all the man's absurdities, thus ; " For having made the oblation, and distributed a part to each one, whilst giving this, he compels the unhappy men to swear instead of blessing; holding the hands of the one receiving, with both of his own, and not letting them go until he had sworn in these words, for I shall repeat the very words: ' Swear to me, by the body and blood of our Saviour, Jesus Christ, that you will never desert me, nor turn to Cornelius.' And the unhappy man is then not suffered to taste until he has first cursed himself; and instead of saying Amen after he had taken the bread, he says, ' I will no longer return to Cornelius.' " And, after other matters, he again proceeds, as follows: " Now, you must know, that he is stripped and abandoned, the brethren leaving him every day and returning to the church. He was also excommunicated by Moses, that blessed witness, who but lately endured a glorious and wonderful martyrdom, and who, whilst yet among the living, seeing the audacity and the folly of the man, excluded him from the communion, together with the five presbyters that had cut themselves off from the church."

At the close of the epistle, he gives a list of the bishops who had come to Rome, and had discarded the incorrigible disposition of Novatus; at the same time adding the names, together with the churches governed by each. He also mentions those that were not present at Rome, but who, by letter, assented to the decision of the former, adding also the names and the particular cities whence each one had written. Such is the account written by Cornelius to Fabius bishop of Antioch.

CHAPTER XLIV.

Dionysius's account of Serapion.

In a letter to this same Fabius, who in some measure seemed to incline to this schism, Dionysius of Alexandria, amongst many other matters that he wrote to him on repentance, and in which he describes the conflicts which the martyrs had recently endured at Alexandria, with other accounts, relates one fact wonderful indeed. This we deem belonging to our history, and is as follows. " But I will give you one example that occurred with us. There was a certain Serapion, an aged believer, who had passed his long life irreproachably, but as he had sacrificed during the persecution, though he frequently begged, no one would listen to him. He was taken sick, and continued three days in succession speechless and senseless. On the fourth day, recovering a little, he called his grandchild to him, and said, " O son, how long do you detain me? I beseech you hasten, and quickly absolve me. Call one of the presbyters to me. Saying this, he again became speechless. The boy ran to the presbyter. But it was night, and the presbyter was sick. As I had, however, before issued an injunction, that those at the point of death, if they desired it, and especially if they entreated for it before, should receive absolution, that they might depart from life in comfortable hope, I gave the boy a small portion of the eucharist, telling him to dip it in water, and to drop it into the mouth of the old man. The boy returned with the morsel. When he came near, before he entered, Serapion having again recovered himself, said, ' Thou hast come, my son, but the presbyter could not come. But do thou quickly perform what thou art commanded, and dismiss me.' The boy moistened it, and at the same time dropped it into the old man's mouth. And he, having swallowed a little, immediately expired. Was he not, then, evidently preserved, and did he not continue living until he was absolved; and his sins being wiped away, he could be acknowledged as a believer for the many good acts that he had done?" Thus far Dionysius.

CHAPTER XLV.

The epistle of Dionysius to Novatus.

LET us also see what kind of epistle the same writer addressed to Novatus, who was then disturbing the brethren at Rome; since he pretended that certain brethren were the cause of his apostacy and schism, because he had been forced by them to proceed thus far. Observe the manner in which he writes to him: " Dionysius sends greeting to his brother Novatus. If, as you say, you were forced against your will, you will show it by retiring voluntarily. For it was a duty to suffer any thing at all, so as not to afflict the church of God; and, indeed, it would not be more inglorious to suffer even martyrdom for its sake, than to sacrifice; and in my opinion it would have been a greater glory For there, in the one case, the individual gives a testimony for his own soul, but in the other he bears witness for the whole church. And now, if thou persuade or constrain the brethren to return to unanimity, thy uprightness will be greater than thy delusion, and the latter will not be laid to thy charge, but the other will be applauded; but if thou art unable to prevail with thy friends, save thy own soul. With the hope that thou art desirous of peace in the Lord, I bid thee farewell." Such was the epistle of Dionysius to Novatus.

CHAPTER XLVI.

Other epistles of Dionysius.

He wrote, also, an epistle to the brethren in Egypt, On Repentance, in which he gives his opinion respecting those who had fallen, and in which he also gives the degrees of faults. There is also a separate work of his extant, On Repentance, addressed to Conon bishop of Hermopolis; and also another epistle of reproof to his flock at Alexandria. Among these, is also the work addressed to Origen, On Martyrdom; also, an epistle to the brethren of Laodicea, where Thelymidres was bishop. He wrote in like manner to the Armenians, On Repentance, where Meruzanes was bishop. Besides all these, he wrote to Cornelius at Rome, in answer to an epistle from him, against Novatus; in which answer he shows that he had been invited by Helenus, bishop of Tarsus in Cilicia, and the rest that were collected with him, viz. Firmilianus, bishop in Cappadocia, and Theoctistus of Palestine, that he should meet them at the council of Antioch, where certain persons were trying to establish the schism of Novatus. Besides this, he wrote that he had been informed Fabius was dead but that Demetrianus was appointed his successor in the episcopate of the church at Antioch. He also writes respecting the bishop of Jerusalem, in these words: " As to the blessed

Alexander, he was cast into prison, and departed happily." Next to this, there is also another epistle of Dionysius to the Romans, On the Office of Deacons, sent by Hippolytus. To the same people he also wrote another epistle, On Peace; also, On Repentance; and another, again, to the confessors there, who were yet affected with the opinion of Novatus. To these same he wrote two others, after they had returned to the church. To many others, also, he addressed letters of admonition and exhortation, calculated to afford various advantage, even now, to those who wish to study his writings.

BOOK VII.

Тнат great bishop of Alexandria, Dionysius, shall aid us also in the composition of the seventh book of our history, by extracting from his works whatsoever particulars of his day he has separately detailed in the epistles that he has left us. With these, at least, we shall commence our account.

CHAPTER I.

The great wickedness of Decius and Gallus.

Decius had scarcely reigned two years, when he, with his children, was slain. Gallus was his successor. Origen died at this time, in the seventieth year of his age. Dionysius, in an epistle to Hermamon, makes the following remarks on Gallus: " But neither did Gallus understand the wickedness of Decius, nor did he foresee what it was that had destroyed him, but he stumbled at the same stone lying before his eyes. For when his reign was advancing prosperously, and his affairs succeeding according to his wishes, he persecuted those holy men, who interceded with God both for his peace and safety. Hence, together with them, he also persecuted the very prayers that were offered up in his behalf." Thus much he has said respecting him.

CHAPTER II.

The bishops of Rome at this time.

After Cornelius had held the episcopal office at Rome about three years, he was succeeded by Lucius, but the latter did not hold the office quite eight months, when dying he transferred it to Stephen. To this Stephen, Dionysius wrote the first of his epistles on baptism, as there was no little controversy, whether those turning from any heresy whatever, should be purified by baptism; as the ancient practice prevailed with regard to such, that they should only have imposition of hands with prayer.

CHAPTER III.

Cyprian, and the bishops connected with him, maintained, that those who had turned from heretical error, should be baptized again.

CYPRIAN, who was bishop $(\pi o \iota \mu \eta \nu)$ of the church of Carthage, was of opinion, that they should be admitted on no conditions, before they were first purified from their error by baptism. But Stephen, who thought that no innovations should be made contrary to traditions that had prevailed from ancient times, was greatly offended at this.

CHAPTER IV.

The epistles that Dionysius wrote on this subject.

DIONYSIUS, therefore, after addressing to him many arguments by letter, on this subject, finally showed, that as the persecution had abated, the churches, every where averse to the innovations of Novatus, had peace among themselves. But he writes as follows.

CHAPTER V.

The peace after the persecution.

" Now I wish you to understand, my brother, that all the churches throughout the east, and farther, that were formerly divided, have been united again. All the bishops, also, are every where in harmony, rejoicing exceedingly at the peace which has been established beyond all expectation. These are, Demetrianus of Antioch, Theoctistus of Cesarea, Mazabanes of Ælia after the death of Alexander, Marinus of Tyre, Heliodorus of Laodicea after the decease of Thelymidres, Helenus of Tarsus, and all the churches of Cilicia, Firmilianus, and all Cappadoc`a; for I have mentioned only the more distinguished of the bishops by name, that neither the length of my letter, nor the burden of my words, may offend you. All the provinces of Syria and Arabia, which at different times you supplied with necessaries, and to whom you have now written, Mesopotamia, Pontus, and Bithynia, and to comprehend all in a word, all are rejoicing every where at the unanimity and brotherly love now prevailing, and are glorifying God for the same." Such are the words of Dionysius.

But after Stephen had held the episcopal office two years, he was succeeded by Xystus, and Dionysius having addressed a second letter to him on baptism, at the same time showing the opinion and decision passed by Stephen and the rest of the bishops, makes the following remarks on Stephen : " He had written before respecting Helenus and Firmilianus, and all those from Cilicia, and Cappadocia, and Galatia, and all the nations adjoining, that he would not have communion with them on this account, because they, said he, rebaptized the heretics. And behold, I pray you, the importance of the matter. For in reality, as I have ascertained, decrees have been passed in the greatest councils of the bishops, that those who come from the heretics, are first to be instructed, and then are to be washed and purified from the filth of their old and impure leaven. And respecting all these things, I have sent letters entreating them. After stating other matters, he proceeds: " But I have also written to our beloved and fellow-presbyters Dionysius and Philemon, who agreed before with Stephen in sentiment, and wrote to me on these matters; before, indeed, I wrote briefly, but now more fully." Such were the accounts respecting the controversy mentioned.

CHAPTER VI.

The heresy of Sabellius.

SPEAKING of the heresy of Sabellius, that arose about this time, and that was then .increasing, he writes as follows: " But as to the opinion which is now agitated at Ptolemais of Pentapolis, it is impious, and replete with blasphemy towards Almighty God and the Father of our Lord Jesus Christ, and abounds also in much infidelity in regard to his only begotten Son, and the first born of all creation, the incarnate word; it abounds also in irreverence to the Holy Spirit. But as the brethren came to me from both sides, both before the letters were received and the question was discussed, I drew up a more regular treatise on the subject, as far as I was enabled under God; copies of which I have sent to thee.

CHAPTER VII.

The execrable error of the heretics, the divine vision of Dionysius, and the ecclesiastical canon given to him.

BUT in the third epistle on baptism, which Dionysius wrote to Philemon a presbyter of Rome, he relates the following circumstances: " I perused," says he, " the works and traditions of the heretics, defiling my mind for a little with their execrable sentiments; but I have also derived this benefit from them, viz., to refute them in my own mind, and to feel the greater disgust at 'hem. And when a certain brother of the presbyters attempted to restrain me, and was much in dread lest I should be carried away by this sink of iniquity, saying that my mind would be corrupted, in which he spoke the truth, as I thought, I was confirmed in my purpose by a vision sent me from heaven, when a voice came to me and commanded me in words as follows : ' Read all that thou takest in hand, for thou art qualified to correct and prove all, and this very thing has been the cause of thy faith in Christ from the beginning.' I received the vision, as coinciding with the apostolic declaration, which says to the more competent, ' Be ye skilful moneychangers.' "

Then after some remarks on all the heresies, he adds: " This rule and form I have received from our father* (παπα) the blessed Heraclas, that those who come from the heretics, although they had apostatized from the church, or rather that had not apostatized, but seemed to have communion with the brethren, but were reported as frequenting some one of those who taught strange doctrines, after they had been expelled from the church were not admitted again by him, though they entreated much, until they had publicly declared all that they had heard from their adversaries ; and then indeed he admitted them to commune, without deeming another baptism necessary for them. For they had already before received the Holy Spirit† from him." But after agitating the question again considerably, he adds : " I have also understood that this practice was introduced not only by those of Africa, but also long since, during the times of those bishops before us, in the most populous churches, the same thing was decreed by the councils of the brethren at Iconium and Synada." To overturn their determinations, and to drive them into contention and strife, I cannot endure. For thou shalt not remove, as it is

---

* The word παπας here used, and applied by Dionysius to his predecessor at Alexandria was, as we see in this instance, applied to the more aged and venerable prelates. We thus see the origin of the word *pope*, Latin *papa*, German *pabst*. This word is no doubt to be traced to the language of nature, as forming the first syllables that the infant lisps. It is explained by a scholiast on Juvenal, Senex veneratione dignus, pater. See Juv. Sat. vi. 632.

† This phrase was applied where the bishop admitted the heretics by the imposition of hands

said, the landmarks of thy neighbour, which thy fathers nave placed. His fourth epistle On Baptism was written to Dyonisius at Rome, who was then a presbyter, but ere long was ordained bishop of that church. From this it is evident, that this same Dionysius of Rome was a learned and excellent man. as is proved by the Dionysius of Alexandria. But he wrote to him, among other matters, respecting the affairs of Novatus, as follows.

CHAPTER VIII.

The heterodoxy of Novatus.

We justly cherish an aversion to the Novatian, says he, by whom the church is split asunder, and some of the brethren have been drawn into impiety and blasphemy, and most nefarious doctrine has been introduced respecting God, and our most gracious Lord and Saviour Christ has been calumniated as devoid of compassion; which also, beside all this, sets aside the holy baptism, and overturns the faith and confession that precede it, and totally drives away the Holy Spirit from themselves, should there happen to be any hope yet, that he would remain or return to them.

CHAPTER IX.

The ungodly baptism of heretics.

But there was also a fifth epistle written by him to Xystus, bishop of Rome, in which, stating many things against the heretics, he relates that some occurrence like the following took place in his times. " Really brother," says he, " I need your counsel, and I beg your opinion, on an affair that has presented itself to me, and in which, indeed, I am afraid I may be deceived. One of the brethren that collected with us, who was considered a believer long since, even before my ordination, and who I think assem-

bled with us before the appointment, (consecration) of the blessed
Heraclas; this man happening to be present with those that were
immediately baptized, and listening to the questions and answers,
came to me weeping and bewailing himself, casting himself also
at my feet; he began to acknowledge and abjure his baptism by
the heretics, because their baptism was nothing like this, nor in
deed, had any thing in common with it, for it was filled with impiety and blasphemies. He said also, that his soul now was
wholly pierced, and he had not confidence enough to raise
his eyes to God, coming from those execrable words and deeds.
Hence he prayed that he might have the benefit of this most perfect cleansing, reception and grace, which indeed I did not dare
to do, saying, that his long communion was sufficient for this.
For one who had been in the habit of hearing thanksgiving, and
repeating the amen, and standing at the table, and extending his
hand to receive the sacred elements, and after receiving and becoming a partaker of the body and blood of our Lord and Saviour Christ for a long time, I would not dare to renew again any
further. I exhorted him, therefore, to take courage, and with a
firm faith and good conscience to approach and take part with
the saints in the solemnity of the holy supper. But he did not
cease lamenting. He shuddered to approach the table, ana
scarcely could endure it, even when exhorted to be present at
prayers."

There is beside the above epistles, also, one and another of
the same on baptism, from him and his church, addressed to
Xystus and the church of Rome. In this he protracts his discourse to a great length of argument on the question there discussed. There is also a certain other epistle of his besides these,
addressed to Dionysius of Rome, that concerning Lucianus. But
thus much respecting these.

CHAPTER X.

Valerian, and the persecution raised by him.

GALLUS had not held the government quite two years when he was removed, and Valerian, with his son Gallienus, succeeded in his place. What Dionysius has also said respecting him, may be learned from his epistle to Hermammon, in which he gives the following account: "In like manner it was revealed to John, and there was," says he, "a mouth given him, speaking great things, and blasphemy. And there was given him power, and forty-two months, but it is wonderful that both took place in Valerian, and especially when we consider the condition of the man before this, how kind and friendly he was towards the pious. For never was there any of the emperors before him so favourably and benevolently disposed toward them, not even those who were openly said to be Christians, so plainly received them, with such excessive civility and friendship in the commencement of his reign. All his house was likewise filled with pious persons, and was, indeed, a congregation (εκκλησια) of the Lord. But the master and chief ruler of the Egyptian magi (Macrianus,) persuaded him to abandon this course, exhorting him to persecute and slay these pure and holy men, as enemies and obstacles to their wicked and detestable incantations. For there were, and still are, men who, by their very presence, or when seen, and only breathing and speaking, are able to dissipate the artifices of wicked dæmons. But he suggested to him to study rites of initiation, and abominable arts of sorcery, to perform execrable sacrifices, to slay unhappy infants, and to sacrifice the children of wretched fathers, and to search the bowels of new-born babes, and to mutilate and dismember the creatures of God, as if by doing this they should obtain great felicity." To this account he also subjoins the following: "Macrianus, therefore, returned them handsome rewards for his desired accession to the government, who before was generally called, from his character, the emperor's steward and receiver-general, now did nothing that could be pronounced for the public good, or even reasonable;* but that prophetic malediction which says, 'Wo to those that prophesy according to their own hearts, and do not see to the public good;' for neither did he perceive that Providence that regulates the whole; and neither did he expect that judgment of him that is before all, and through all, and over all.   Hence, he became an enemy to his universal church.   But he also estranged and stripped himself of the mercy of God, and thus fled as far as possible from his salvation.   In this, indeed, he really expressed the peculiarity of his name."† Again, he says: "Valerian, indeed, was thus urged by this man to these measures, whilst he exposed himself to insults and reproaches, according to what Isaias has said: 'And these have chosen their own ways, and their own abominations, which their soul hath desired.   And I will choose their derisions, and will repay them their sins.'   But the latter (viz. Macrianus,) anxious without any merit to have the government. and yet unable to assume the imperial garb, with his feeble body, appointed his two sons to take upon them, as it were, their father's crimes.   For the declaration of God respecting such, proved its truth, when he said, 'visiting the sins of the fathers upon the children, to the third and fourth generations of them that hate me.'   For heaping his own wicked passions, in the gratification of which he did not succeed, upon the heads of his children, he swept off upon them his own wickedness and hatred of God."   And such is the account which Dionysius has given of Valerian.

* Dionysius here puns upon the honourable title and office that Macrianus had borne, as the emperor's faithful minister, επι καδολουλογων, but to which his subsequent conduct did not correspond. The pun is lost in a translation.

† Macrianus, derived from the Greek μαχρος *long*, or μαχραν *at a distance;* another witty allusion.

CHAPTER XI.

The sufferings of Dionysius, and those in Egypt.

But as to the persecutions that raged so violently under him, and what sufferings he with others endured for their piety towards the Supreme God, his own words shall declare, which he addressed to Germanus, one of the contemporary bishops that attempted to slander him. His words are as follows: "But," says he, "I apprehend that as I am forced to relate the wonderful providence of God respecting us, I shall be liable to much folly and insensibility. But, as it is said, it is honourable to conceal the secrets of the king, and glorious to make manifest the works of God, I will face the violence of Germanus. I came to Æmilianus not alone, but in company with my fellow-presbyter Maximus, and the deacons Faustus, Eusebius, and Chæremon, together with a certain one of the brethren who had come from Rome. Æmilianus, however, did not at first say to me, hold no assemblies, as this was superfluous, and was the last to one who was aiming at what was the first in importance;* for he was not concerned about my collecting others, but that we should not be Christians, and from this he commanded me to desist, thinking, no doubt, that if I changed, others would follow my example. But I answered him not without good reason, and without many words, 'We must obey God rather than man.' But I directly bore witness, that I could neither change worshipping the only true God and none other, nor ever cease to be a Christian. Upon this he commanded us to go away to a neighbouring village of the desert, called Cephro.

"But hear the words that were uttered by both of us, as they were recorded. Dionysius and Faustus, Maximus, Marcellus,

---

* The great question with the judge was, not whether those arraigned held meetings, but whether they were Christians. To have commenced with the former, when the latter was the great object, would have been a kind of υστερον πρωτερον, that abandoned the primary for the secondary. Hostility to Christianity as a religion, was the great incentive here, to which all other acts were referred, as their head and fountain.

and Chæremon, being arraigned, Æmilianus, the prefect, said:
' I have even personally reasoned with you on the clemency of
our sovereigns, which you have also experienced. For they
have given you the chance of saving yourselves, if you are disposed to turn to the course of nature, and worship the gods that
have preserved them in their government, and to forget those
practices which are so unnatural (των παρα φυσιν). What,
then, say ye to these things ? For neither do I expect that you
will be ungrateful for their kindness, since they would dispose
you to a better cause.' Dionysius answered, ' All the gods are
not worshipped by all, but each party worships those whom they
think to be gods. We, therefore, worship the one God and Creator of all things, and the very same that has committed the
government to their most excellent and sacred majesties, Valerian and Gallienus. Him we worship and adore, and to him we
incessantly pray that their reign may continue firm and unshaken.' Æmilianus, the prefect, again replied : ' But who
prevents you from worshipping this one God, if he is a god, together with those that are the natural gods ? For you are commanded to worship the gods, and those gods which all know to
be such.' Dionysius answered : ' We worship no other one.'
Æmilianus, the prefect, said, ' I perceive that you are at the
same time ungrateful, and insensible to the clemency of our Cesars. Therefore you shall not remain in this city, but you shall
be sent to the parts of Lybia, to a place called Cephro. For
this place I have selected according to the orders of our Cesars.
But neither you, nor any others, shall in any wise be permitted,
either to hold conventions, or to enter what you call your cemeteries.* But if any one appear not to have gone to the place

* The Christians called their burial places cemeteries, κοιμητηρια, *dormitories*, because death, in the light of the gospel, is a sleep. These dormitories, as we here
see, were frequented by the Christians, as peculiarly calculated to cherish religious
sentiments, particularly if these places had been the depositories of martyred confessors. It was here, too, where, in the firm faith that death is but a sleep, they
could hold a kind of communion with departed virtue, and find their own strengthened by it. Well may Christianity be pronounced the only true philosophy, when
she arrays our greatest terrors in such a light.

which I have commanded, or if he shall be found in any assembly, he will do it at his peril. For the necessary punishment will not fail. Remove, therefore, whither ye are commanded.' Thus he compelled me, sick as I was, nor did he grant me a day's respite. What leisure, then, had I to hold assemblies, or not to hold them?"

After other matters, he says again, " But neither did we keep aloof from assembling ourselves by divine assistance; but so much the more diligently did I gather those that were in the city, as if I were in their midst: absent, indeed, in the body, as I said, but present in spirit. But in Cephro a large congregation collected with us, partly of the brethren that accompanied us from the city, partly of those that joined us from Egypt; and thus God opened a door for the word likewise there. And at first, indeed, we were persecuted, we were stoned; but, at last, not a few of the heathen, abandoning the idols, turned to God, for the word was then first sown among them, as they had never before heard it. And thus, as if God had conducted us for this cause to them, after we had fulfilled this ministry, we were again transferred to another part. For Æmilianus designed to transport us, as it seemed, to places more rough, and more replete with Libyan horrors (more Libyan-like), and he commanded those in the Mareotic district every where to collect, appointing them separate villages throughout the country. But our party, together with those that should be first taken, he commanded to be left on the way. For, no doubt, it was among his plans and preparations, that whenever he wished to seize us he might easily take us captive. But when I was first ordered to go away to Cephro, though I knew not the place where it was, having scarcely even heard the name before, yet I nevertheless went away cheerfully and calmly. But when it was told me to remove to the parts of Colluthion, those present know how I was affected. For here I shall accuse myself. At first, indeed, I was afflicted, and bore it hard. For though these places happened to be more known and familiar to me, yet they said that it was a region destitute of brethren and good men, and exposed to the insolence of travellers, and the incursions of robbers. But I received comfort from the brethren, who reminded me that it was nearer to the city. Cephro, indeed, brought us a great number of brethren promiscuously from Egypt, so that we were able to spread the church farther; but as the city was nearer there, we should more frequently enjoy the sight of those that were really beloved and most dear to us. For they would come, and would tarry, and as if in the more remote suburbs, there would be still meetings in part. And so it was."

After these, and other remarks, he proceeds to tell what happened to him again : " Germanus, indeed, may pride himself for many confessions; he may have much to say of what happened to him : he may, as well as we, speak of the great number of sentences of condemnation, confiscations, proscriptions, spoliations of goods; loss of dignities ; contempt of worldly honour; contempt of praise from the prefects or from counsellors, and the endurance of the opposite threats of outcries ; of dangers of persecutions; of exile ; of great trouble and various kinds of affliction, such as happened to me under Decius and Sabinus, such as I have suffered until the present persecution of Æmilianus. But where in the world was Germanus ? What is said of him ? But I will abstain from the great folly into which I have fallen on account of Germanus. And hence, also, I shall dismiss giving a particular account of what happened to the brethren, who already know the facts."

The same writer, also, in the epistle to Domitius and Didymus, again makes mention of some particulars, in reference to the persecution, as follows : " But it is superfluous for me to recount to you our brethren by name, as they are both numerous and unknown to you. But you must know that they are men and women, young and old, young virgins and aged matrons, soldiers and private men, every class and every age, some that obtained the crown of victory under stripes and in the flames, some by the edge of the sword. For many, however, the lapse of a very long time was not sufficient to appear acceptable to God, as indeed it has not appeared to me to the present time. Therefore, I have been reserved for a time which he knows most suitable, who has said, ' In the accepted time I have heard thee, and in the day of salvation I have assisted thee.' But since you have inquired, and wish to be informed of all concerning us, you have fully heard how we fare: how we were led away as prisoners by the centurion and magistrates, and the soldiers and officers with them, myself and Caius, Faustus, Peter, Paul, when a certain party came from Mareotis and forcibly dragged us away, we following them not of our own accord, but forced. But now Caius and Peter, with myself, solitary and deprived of the rest of our brethren, are shut up in a wild and desert place of Libya, three days' journey distant from Paraetonium."

After some further remarks, he proceeds: " But in the city some concealed themselves, secretly visiting the brethren; presbyters Maximinus, Dioscorus, Demetrius, and Lucius. For Faustinus and Aquila, who are more prominent in the world, are wandering about in Egypt. But of those that died of the sickness, the surviving deacons are Faustus, Eusebius, Chæremon. Eusebius, who was strengthened by the Lord from the beginning, and who was well qualified to fulfil the arduous and necessary duties to those confessors that were in prison, and to perform the dangerous office of burying those perfected and blessed men who suffered martyrdom. For, to the present day, the governor does not cease killing some, as I before said, in a most cruel manner, whenever they are arraigned, torturing others with scourging, wasting others with imprisonment and bonds, and commanding that no one shall go nigh them, and examining whether any, perhaps, is seen to do so. And yet God, by the alacrity and kindness of the brethren, has afforded some relief to the afflicted.' Such is the statement of Dionysius in this epistle.

But it should be observed, that this Eusebius, whom he called a deacon, was not long after appointed bishop of Laodicea, in Syria. But Maximus, whom he called a presbyter, at that time succeeded Dionysius as bishop of the church at Alexandria. But Faustus, who was at that time greatly distinguished for his confession, being reserved until the persecution of our times, in a very advanced age, and full of days, was made perfect as a martyr, and was beheaded. Such, however, were the events that happened to Dionysius at this time.

CHAPTER XII.

The martyrs at Cesarea of Palestine.

In the persecution of Valerian, mentioned above, three men of Cesarea in Palestine, who shone gloriously in their confession of Christ, were honoured with divine martyrdom by becoming the food of wild beasts. Of these, one was called Priscus, another Malchus, the third was named Alexander. These, it is said, lived at first in the country, pretending to be careless and indifferent; but when occasion presented itself from heaven to them, already burning with desire to obtain the prize, they would then cease, with the view that they might not be too forward in seizing the martyr's crown. With these purposes, therefore, they hasted to Cesarea, and advanced to the judge, and obtained the sentence mentioned. It is also said, that a certain female endured a similar conflict in the same persecution and city, but who is also said to have been of the sect of Marcion.

CHAPTER XIII.

The peace after Gallienus.

But as it was not long before Valerian was taken captive, and reduced to slavery by the barbarians, his son Gallienus, obtaining the sole command, was disposed to use more clemency in the exercise of his power. He, therefore, immediately restrained the persecution against us, by sending edicts, in which he commanded that the ministers of the word might perform the customary duties of their office with freedom, the copy of which was as follows: " The emperor Cesar, Publius, Licinius, Gallienus, Pius, Felix, Augustus, to Dionysius, Pinna, Demetrius and the other bishops. The benefit of the privilege granted by me, I have ordered to be issued throughout the whole world, that all may depart from their religious retreats; and therefore you also may make use of this copy of my edict, that no one may molest you. And this liberty indeed, which you are now permitted to have, has been long since granted by me. Aurelius Cyrenius, therefore, who has the chief administration of affairs, will observe the copy here given by me." This, that it may be the better understood, we have here presented to our readers, in a translation from the Latin tongue. There is also another ordinance from him, which he addressed to other bishops, in which he grants permission to recover what are called the cemeteries.

CHAPTER XIV.

The bishops that flourished at this time.

At this time the episcopate in the Roman church was yet held by Xystus; but in the church of Antioch, after Fabius, by Demetrianus; of Cesarea in Cappadocia by Firmilianus; of the churches in Pontus, by Gregory, and his brother Athenodorus, both of them familiar friends of Origen. At Cesarea, however, of Palestine, after the death of Theoctistus, the episcopal office was conferred on Domnus, and he not surviving long, was succeeded by Theotecnus our contemporary. He was also of the school of Origen, but in Jerusalam, after the decease of Mazabanus, Hymenæus followed as his successor in the episcopal seat, the same that has obtained much celebrity in our times for many years.

CHAPTER XV.

The martyrdom of Marinus at Cesarea.

About this time, as peace was every where restored to the churches, Marinus of Cesarea in Palestine, who was one of the army, distinguished for his military honours, and illustrious for his family and wealth, was beheaded for his confession of Christ, on the following account: " There is a certain honour among the Romans, called the vine, which they who obtain are said to be centurions. A place becoming vacant, Marinus, by the order of succession, was called to this promotion; but when he was on the point of obtaining this, however, another one advancing to the tribunal began to make opposition, by saying that according to the ancient institutions it was not lawful for him to share in the Roman honours, as he was a Christian, and refused to sacrifice to the emperors; but that the office devolved on him. The judge, whose name was Achæus, roused at this, first began to ask what the opinions of Marinus were; and when he saw him constantly affirming that he was a Christian, he granted him three hours for reflection. But as soon as he came out of the prætorium, or judgment hall, Theotecnus, the bishop of the place, coming to him, drew him aside in conversation, and taking him by the hand, conducted him to the church; and having placed him within by the altar, he raised his cloak a little, and pointing to the sword that was attached to his side, at the same time presenting before him the book of the holy gospels, told him to choose either of the two according to his wish. Without hesitation he extended his hand and took the book. " Hold fast, then, hold fast to God," said Theotecnus, " and strengthened by him, mayest thou obtain what thou hast chosen—go in peace." Immediately upon his return from thence, a crier began to proclaim before the prætorium, for the appointed time had already passed away; and being thus arraigned, after exhibiting a still greater ardour in his faith, he was forthwith led away as he was, and made perfect by martyrdom.

CHAPTER XVI.

Some account of Astyrius.

MENTION is also made in these times of the pious confidence of Astyrius, a man who was a Roman of senatorial rank, in great favour with the emperors, and well known to all for his noble birth and his wealth. As he was present at the death of the abovementioned martyr; taking up the corpse, he bore him on his shoulder in a splendid and costly dress, and covering it in a magnificent manner, committed it to a decent burial. Many other facts are stated of the man by his friends, who have lived to the present times.

CHAPTER XVII.

The miracles of our Saviour at Paneas.

AMONG these there was the following remarkable occurrence. At Cesarea Philippi, which is called Paneas by the Phœnicians, they say there are springs that are shown there, at the foot of the mountain called Panius, from which the Jordan rises; and that on a certain festival day there was usually a victim thrown into these, and that this, by the power of the dæmon, in some wonderful manner entirely disappeared. The thing was a famous wonder to all that were there to see it. Astyrius happening to be once present at these rites, and seeing the multitude astonished at the affair, pitied their delusion. Then raising his eyes to heaven, he implored the God over all through Christ, to refute this seducing dæmon, and to restrain the delusion of the people. As soon as he prayed, it is said that the victim floated on the stream, and that thus this miracle vanished, no wonder ever more occurring in this place.

CHAPTER XVIII.

The statue erected by the woman having an hemorrhage.

BUT as we have mentioned this city, I do not think it right to pass by a narrative that also deserves to be recorded for posterity. They say that the woman who had an issue of blood, mentioned

by the evangelists, and who obtained deliverance from her affliction by our Saviour, was a native of this place, and that her
house is shown in the city, and the wonderful monuments of our
Saviour's benefit to her are still remaining. At the gates of her
house, on an elevated stone, stands a brazen image of a woman
on her bended knee, with her hands stretched out before her
like one entreating. Opposite to this there is another image of a
man, erect, of the same materials, decently clad in a mantle (di-
plois,) and stretching out his hand to the woman. Before her
feet, and on the same pedestal, there is a certain strange plant
growing, which rising as high as the hem of the brazen garment,
is a kind of antidote to all kinds of diseases. This statue, they
say, is a statue of Jesus Christ, and it has remained even until
our times; so that we ourselves saw it whilst tarrying in that
city. Nor is it to be wondered at, that those of the Gentiles who
were anciently benefited by our Saviour, should have done these
things. Since we have also seen representations of the apostles
Peter and Paul, and of Christ himself, still preserved in paintings;
as it is probable that, according to a practice among the Gentiles,
the ancients were accustomed to pay this kind of honour indiscriminately to those who were as saviours or deliverers to them.

CHAPTER XIX.

The episcopal seat of James.

JAMES being the first that received the dignity of the episcopate
at Jerusalem, from our Saviour himself, as the sacred Scriptures
show that he was generally called the brother of Christ; this see,
which has been preserved until the present times, has ever been
held in veneration by the brethren that have followed in the succession there, in which they have sufficiently shown what reverence both the ancients and those of our own times exhibited, and
still exhibit, towards holy men on account of their piety. But
enough of this.

CHAPTER XX.

The epistles of Dionysius, on festivals, in which he gives the canon on the Passover.

Besides these epistles, the same Dionysius, about this time also composed others, called his Festival Epistles, in which he discourses much in praise of the festival of the Passover. One of these he addressed to Flavius, another to Domitius and Didymus, in which also he gives the canon for eight years, showing that it is not proper to observe the paschal festival before the vernal equinox was past. Beside these, he composed another epistle, addressed to his compresbyters at Alexandria. Also, to several others, and these during the prevalence of the persecution.

CHAPTER XXI.

The events that occurred at Alexandria.

Peace having been scarcely established, he returned, indeed, to Alexandria ; but as sedition and war again broke out, so that it was impossible for him to superintend all the brethren then divided into different parties, he again addresses them by letter at the passover, as if he were still an exile from Alexandria. He also wrote, after this, another paschal letter to Hierax, a bishop of Egypt, in which he makes mention of the sedition then existing at Alexandria, as follows : " But what cause of wonder is there, if it be difficult for me also to address epistles to those that are so very remote, when I am at a loss to consult for my own life, or to reason with myself. For, indeed, I have great need to send epistolary addresses to those who are as my own bowels, my associates and dearest brethren and members of the same church. But how I shall send these I cannot devise. For it would be more easy for any one, I would not say to go beyond the limits of the province, but even to travel from east to west, than to go from Alexandria to Alexandria itself. For the very heart of the city is more desolate and impassable than that vast and trackless desert which the Israelites traversed in two generations, and our smooth and tranquil harbours have become like that sea which opened and arose like walls on both sides, enabled them to drive through, and in whose highway the Egyptians were overwhelmed. For often they appear like the Red Sea, from the frequent slaughters committed in them; but the river which washes the city, has sometimes appeared more dry than the parched desert, and more exhausting than that in which Israel was so overcome with thirst on their journey that they exclaimed against Moses, and the water flowed for them from the broken rock, by the power of Him who alone doeth wondrous works. Sometimes, also, it has so overflowed, that it has inundated all the country round; the roads and the fields seeming to threaten that flood of waters which happened in the days of Noah. It also flows always polluted with blood and slaughter, and the constant drowning of men, such as it formerly was, when, before Pharaoh, it was changed by Moses into blood and putrid matter. And what other purification could be applied to water which itself purifies all? Could that vast and impassable ocean ever wash away this bitter sea? or could that great river, itself, which flowed from Eden, though it poured the four heads into which it was divided, into one Gihon, wash away this filth? When will this air, corrupted as it is by the noxious exhalations every where rising, become pure and serene? For there are such vapours from the earth, and such storms from the sea-breezes, from the rivers and mists coming from the harbours, that make it appear as if we should have for dew, the gore of these dead bodies that are putrifying in all the elements around us.

" Then, and notwithstanding all this, men wonder, and are at a loss to know whence come the constant plagues; whence these malignant diseases; whence those variegated infections; whence all that various and immense destruction of human lives. Wherefore it is, that this mighty city no longer cherishes within it such a number of inhabitants, from speechless children to the aged and decrepid, as it formerly had of those whom it could pronounce firm and vigorous in years. But those of forty years and up to seventy, were so much the more numerous then, that their number cannot now be made up, if even those from fourteen to eighty were inserted and enrolled among the receivers of the public grain. And those who in appearance are but the youngest, are now as of an age with those formerly the oldest. And yet, though they constantly see the human race diminishing, and constantly wasting away, in the very midst of this increasing destruction, and this annihilation, they are not alarmed."

CHAPTER XXII.

The pestilence which then prevailed.

THE pestilence, after these things, succeeding the war, and the festival being at hand, he again addresses the brethren in epistles; in which he shows the great calamities attending this affliction, as follows: " To other men, indeed, the present would not appear a fit season for a festival, and neither is this, nor any other time a festival for them, not to speak of sorrowful times, but not even that which a cheerful person might especially deem such. But now all things are filled with tears, all are mourning, and by reason of the multitudes already dead, and still dying, groans are daily resounding throughout the city. For as it is written respecting the first born of Egypt, thus now, also, a great lamentation has arisen, for there is not a house in which there is not one dead. And I wish, indeed, this were all. Many, indeed, and horrible calamities have preceded this. First, indeed, they drive us away, and solitary and in exile, and persecuted and put to death by all, we still celebrated the festival; and every place, marked by some particular affliction, was still a spot distinguished by our solemnities; the open field, the desert, the ship, the inn, the prison. But the most joyous festival of all was celebrated by those perfect martyrs who are now feasting in the heavens.

" After this, war and famine succeeded, which indeed we endured with the heathen, but bore alone those miseries with which they afflicted us, whilst we also experienced the effects of those which they inflicted, and suffered from one another. And again we rejoiced in the peace of Christ, which he gave to us alone, and when both we and they obtained a very short respite, then we were assailed by this pestilence. A calamity more dreadful to them than any dread, and more afflictive that any affliction, and which as one of their own historians has said, was of itself alone beyond all hope. To us, however, it did not wear this character, but no less than other events it was a school for exercise and probation. For neither did it keep aloof from us, although it assailed the heathen most." To this he afterwards adds: "Indeed, the most of our brethren, by their exceeding great love and brotherly affection, not sparing themselves, and adhering to one another, were constantly superintending the sick, ministering to their wants without fear and without cessation, and healing them in Christ, have departed most sweetly with them." Though filled with the disease from others, and taking it from their neighbours, they voluntarily, by exsuction, extracted their pains. Many also, who had healed and strengthened others, themselves died, transferring their death upon themselves, and exemplifying in fact, that trite expression which seemed before only a form of politeness, or an empty compliment; they were in fact, in their death, the offscouring of all. ($\pi\varepsilon\rho\iota\psi\eta\mu\alpha$ $\pi\alpha\nu\tau\omega\nu$.) The best of our brethren, indeed, have departed this life in this way, some indeed presbyters, some deacons, and of the people those that were exceedingly commended. So that this very form of death, with the piety and ardent faith which attended it, appeared to be but little inferior to martyrdom itself. They took up the bodies of the saints with their open hands and on their bosoms, cleaned their eyes and closed their mouths, carried them on their shoulders, and composed their limbs, embraced, clung to them, and prepared them decently with washing and garments, and ere long they themselves shared in receiving the same offices. Those that survived always following those before them. Among the heathen it was the direct reverse. They both repelled those who began to be sick, and avoided their dearest friends. They would cast them out into the roads half dead, or throw them when dead without burial, shunning any communication and participation in death, which it was impossible to avoid by every precaution and care." After this epistle, when the city was at peace, he addressed another paschal epistle to the brethren in Egypt, and wrote many others besides. There is one of his extant, On the Sabbath, another On Exercise. He also addressed one to Hermammon, and to the brethren in Egypt. Many other facts, after describing the wickedness of Decius and his successors, he states, and also mentions the peace of Gallienus.

CHAPTER XXIII.

The reign of Gallienus.

But it is best to hear his own words, as follows: "He indeed. viz., Macrianus, having betrayed the one, and waged war with the other emperor, suddenly perished with his whole family. But Gallienus was proclaimed and universally acknowledged emperor, an emperor at once new and old, having been before them, and now surviving them. For as it is said by the prophet Isaiah, Those things that were from the first, lo they have come, and those are new which shall now arise. As the cloud which enters the sun's rays, and for a little obscures it by its shadow and appears in its place, when the cloud has passed by, or is dissipated, the sun which had arisen before seems to rise again. Thus Macrianus, who had established himself, and aspired higher, to the very power of Gallienus, himself is now no more, because he never was; but the latter is just as he was, and his government as if it had lost the feebleness of age, and had become purified of its former filth, now arose and assumed a more flourishing aspect. And it is now seen and heard at a greater distance, and expanded to every part." After this he also indicates the time when he wrote this. " And it occurs to me again, to survey the days of our emperor's reign. For I see, indeed, that those most impious men, once honoured, and famous, ere long became without a name. But the more holy and pious emperor, surviving the seventh year, is now in'the ninth, in which we are about to celebrate the festival."

CHAPTER XXIV.

Of Nepos, and his schism.

BESIDES these, there are two works of his on the Promises; the occasion of which was Nepos a bishop in Egypt. He taught, that the promises given to holy men in the Scriptures, should be understood more as the Jews understood them, and supposed that there would be a certain millennium of sensual luxury on this earth. Thinking, therefore, that he could establish his own opinion by the Revelation of John, he composed a book on this subject, with the title, Refutation of the Allegorists. This, therefore, was warmly opposed by Dionysius, in his work on the Promises. In the former, indeed, he gives his own opinion on the subject; in the other he enters into a discussion on the Revelation of John, where, in the introduction, he makes mention of Nepos, as follows: " But they produce a certain work of Nepos, upon which they lay great stress, as if he advanced things that are irrefragable, when he asserts that there will be an earthly reign of Christ. In many other respects I accord with and greatly love Nepos, both on account of his faith and industry, and his great study in the Scriptures; as also for his great attention to psalmody, by which many are still delighted. I greatly reverence the man also, for the manner in which he has departed this life. But the truth is to be loved and honoured before all. It is just, indeed, that we should applaud and approve whatever is said aright, but it is also a duty to examine and correct whatever may not appear to be written with sufficient soundness. If, indeed, he were present, and were advancing his sentiments orally, it would be sufficient to discuss the subject without writing, and to commence and confirm the opponents by question and answer. But as the work is published, and as it appears to some, is calculated to convince, and there are some teachers who say that the law and prophets are of no value, and who give up following the gospels, and who depreciate the epistles of the apostles, and who at the same time announced the doctrine of this work as a great and hidden mystery, and who also do not allow that our brethren have any sublime and great conception, either of the glorious and truly divine appearance of our Lord, nor of our own resurrection, and our being gathered, and assimilated to him; but persuade them to expect what is little and perishable, and such a state of things as now exists in the kingdom of God. It becomes, therefore, necessary for us also, to reason with our brother Nepos as if he were present." To these he adds, after other remarks: "When I was at Arsinoe, where, as you know long since, this doctrine was afloat, so that schisms and apostacies of whole churches followed, after I had called the presbyters and teachers of the brethren in the villages, when those brethren had come who wished to be present, I exhorted them to examine the doctrine publicly. When they had produced this book as a kind of armour and impregnable fortress, I sat with them for three days, from morning till evening, attempting to refute what it contained. Then, also, I was greatly pleased to observe the constancy, the sincerity, the docility, and intelligence of the brethren, as we proceeded to advance in order, and the moderation of our questions and doubts and mutual concessions. For we carefully and studiously avoided, in every possible way, insisting upon those opinions which were once adopted by us, though they might appear to be correct. Nor did we attempt to evade objections, but endeavoured as far as possible to keep to our subject, and to confirm these. Nor ashamed if reason prevailed, to change opinions, and to acknowledge the truth; but rather received with a good conscience and sincerity, and with single hearts, before God, whatever was established by the proofs and doctrines of the holy Scriptures. At length Coracio, who was the founder and leader of this doctrine, in the hearing of all the brethren present, confessed and avowed to us, that he would no longer adhere to it, nor discuss it, that he would neither mention nor teach it, as he had been fully convinced by the opposite arguments. The other brethren present rejoiced also at this conference, and at the conciliatory spirit and unani mity exhibited by all."

CHAPTER XXV.

The apocalypse of John.

AFTER this, he proceeds further to speak of the Revelation of John, as follows: "Some, indeed, before us, have set aside, and have attempted to refute the whoie book, criticising every chapter, and pronouncing it without sense and without reason. They say that it has a false title, for it is not of John. Nay, that it is not even a revelation, as it is covered with such a dense and thick veil of ignorance, that not one of the apostles, and not one of the holy men, or those of the church could be its author. But that Cerinthus, the founder of the sect of Cerinthians, so called from him, wishing to have reputable authority for his own fiction, prefixed the title. For this is the doctrine of Cerinthus, that there will be an earthly reign of Christ; and as he was a lover of the body, and altogether sensual in those things which he so eagerly craved, he dreamed that he would revel in the gratification of the sensual appetite, *i. e.* in eating and drinking, and marrying; and to give the things a milder aspect and expression, in festivals and sacrifices, and the slaying of victims. For my part I would not venture to set this book aside, as there are many brethren that value it much; but having formed a conception of its subject as exceeding my capacity, I consider it also containing a certain concealed and wonderful intimation in each particular. For, though I do not understand, yet I suspect that some deeper sense is enveloped in the words, and these I do not measure and judge by my private reason; but allowing more to faith, I have regarded them as too lofty to be comprehended by me, and those things which I do not understand, I do not reject, but I wonder the more that I cannot comprehend."

After this, he examines the whole book of the Revelation, and after proving that it is impossible that it should be understood according to the obvious and literal sense, he proceeds : " The prophet, as I said, having completed the whole prophecy, he pronounces those blessed that should observe it as also himself. ' For blessed,' says he, ' is he that keepeth the words of the prophecy of this book, and I, John,* who have seen and heard these things.' I do not, therefore, deny that he was called John, and that this was the writing of one John. And I agree that it was the work, also, of some holy and inspired man. But I would not easily agree that this was the apostle, the son of Zebedee, the brother of James, who is the author of the gospel, and the general (catholic) epistle that bears his name. But I conjecture, both from the general tenor of both, and the form and complexion of the composition, and the execution of the whole book, that it is not from him. For the evangelist never prefixes his name, never proclaims himself, either in the gospel or in his epistle."

'A little farther, he adds: " But John never speaks as of himself (in the first person), nor as of another (in the third), but he that wrote the apocalypse, declares himself immediately in the beginning: ' The Revelation of Jesus Christ, which he gave to him to show to his servants quickly. And he sent and signified it by his angel, to his servant John, who bare record of the word of God, and of his testimony (of Jesus Christ) and of all things that he saw.'

" Besides this, he wrote an epistle : ' John to the seven churches of Asia, grace and peace to you.' But the evangelist does not prefix his name even to his general epistle ; but, without any introduction or circumlocution, begins from the very mystery of the divine revelation: ' That which was from the beginning, which we have heard, which we have seen with our eyes ;' for upon such a revelation as this Peter was blessed by our Lord: ' Blessed art thou, Simon Bar-jona, because flesh and blood hath not revealed it to thee, but my Father in heaven.' But neither in

---

* Dionysius here understands the author of the Apocalypse, introducing himself as a subject of the same blessedness of which he speaks. This connexion, though not usually regarded, is obvious on an inspection of the original.

the second nor third epistle ascribed to John (the apostle), though they are very brief, is the name of John presented. But anonymously it is written, *the presbyter.* But the other did not consider it sufficient to name himself but once, and then to proceed in his narration, but afterwards again resumes, ' I, John, your brother and partner in tribulation, and the kingdom and patience of Jesus, was on the island called Patmos, on account of the word of God, and the testimony of Jesus.' And, likewise, at the end (of the book) he says; ' Blessed is he that keepeth the words of the prophecy of this book, and I am John that saw and heard these things.'

" That it is a John that wrote these things we must believe him, as he says it; but what John it is, is uncertain. For he has not said that he was, as he often does in the gospel, the beloved disciple of the Lord, neither the one leaning on his bosom, nor the brother of James, nor he that himself saw and heard what the Lord did and said. For he certainly would have said one of these particulars, if he wished to make himself clearly known. But of all this there is nothing, he only calls himself our brother and companion, and the witness of Jesus, and blessed on account of seeing and hearing these revelations. I am of opinion there were many of the same name with John the apostle, who, for their love and admiration and emulation of him, and their desire at the same time, like him, to be beloved of the Lord, adopted the same epithet, just as we find the name of Paul and of Peter to be adopted by many among the faithful.

" There is also another John, surnamed Mark, mentioned in the Acts of the Apostles, whom Paul and Barnabas took in company with them. Of whom it is again said : ' But they had John as their minister.' (Acts xiii. 5.) But whether this is the one that wrote the Apocalypse, I could not say. For it is not written that he came with them to Asia. But he says ; 'When Paul and his company loosed from Paphos, they came to Perga in Pamphylia, but John, departing from them, returned to Jerusalem.' I think, therefore, that it was another one of those in Asia. For they say that there are two monuments at Ephesus, and that each bears the name of John, and from the sentiments and the expres-

sions, as also their composition, it might be very reasonably conjectured that this one is different from that.   For the gospel and
epistle mutually agree.   They commence in the same way ; for
the one says, ' In the beginning was the word ;' the other, ' That
which was from the beginning.'   The one says, ' and the word
was made flesh, and dwelt (tabernacled) among us, and we saw
his glory, the glory as of the only begotten of the Father.'   The
other says the same things, a little altered : ' That which we
have heard, which we have seen with our eyes, that which we
have seen and our hands have handled of the word of life, and
the life was manifested.'   These things, therefore, are premised,
alluding, as he has shown in the subsequent parts, to those who
say that the Lord did not come into the flesh.   Wherefore, also,
he has designedly subjoined : ' What we have seen we testify,
and we declare to you that eternal life, which was with the
Father, and was made manifest to us ; what we have seen and
heard we declare to you.'   He keeps to the point, and does not
depart from his subjects, but goes through all in the same chapters and names, some of which we shall briefly notice.

   " But the attentive reader will find the expressions, *the life,
the light,* frequently occurring in both ; in both he will find the
expressions, *fleeing from darkness, the truth, grace, joy, the flesh
and blood of the Lord, the judgment, forgiveness of sins, the love
of God to us, the commandment given us of love to one another,
that we ought to keep all the commandments, the conviction of the
world, the devil, of anti-christ, the promise of the holy spirit, the
adoption of God* (*i. e.* the adoption made by God), *the faith to be
exhibited by us in all matters, the Father and the Son,* every where
occurring in both.   And altogether throughout, to attentive ob-
servers, it will be obvious that there is one and the same complexion and character in the gospel and epistle.   Very different
and remote from all this, is the apocalypse ; not even touching, or
even bordering upon them in the least, I might say.   Not even
containing a syllable in common with them ; but the epistle, to
say nothing of the gospel, has not made any mention, or given
any intimation of the apocalypse, nor does the apocalypse mention the epistle.   Whereas, Paul indicates something of his reve

lations in his epistles; which, however, he never recorded in writing.

" We may, also, notice how the phraseology of the gospel and the epistle differs from the apocalypse. For the former are written not only irreprehensibly, as it regards the Greek language, but are most elegant in diction in the arguments and the whole structure of the style. It would require much to discover any barbarism or solecism, or any odd peculiarity of expression* at all in them. For, as is to be presumed, he was endued with all the requisites for his discourse; the Lord having granted him both that of knowledge and that of expression and style. That the latter, however, saw a revelation, and received knowledge and prophecy, I do not deny. But I perceive that his dialect and language is not very accurate Greek; but that he uses barbarous idioms, and in some places solecisms, which it is now unnecessary to select; for neither would I have any one suppose that I am saying these things by way of derision, but only with the view to point out the great difference between the writings of these men."

CHAPTER XXVI.

The epistles of Dionysius.

BESIDES these, there are many other epistles of Dionysius extant, as those to Ammon, bishop of the church at Bernice, against Sabellius; another to Telesphorus, and one to Euphranor; another to Ammon and Euporus. He wrote also four books on the same subject, which he addressed to his namesake Dionysius at Rome. There are also many other epistles beside these written by him, together with longer treatises in the form of epistles, as those addressed to the youth Timothy, and that On Temptations, which he also dedicated to Euphranor. He also says, in a letter to Basilides, bishop (of the churches) of Pentapolis, that he

---

* We have here paraphrased the word ιδιοτισμος.

had written a commentary on the beginning of Ecclesiastes. But he has also left us several epistles addressed to the same Basilides. These are the works of Dionysius. Having given this account, let us now proceed to inform posterity of the nature and character of our own age.

CHAPTER XXVII.

Paul of Samosata, and the heresy introduced by him at Antioch.

XYSTUS had been bishop of Rome eleven years, when he was succeeded by Dionysius, the namesake of the bishop of Alexandria. At this time also, Demetrianus dying at Antioch, the episcopate was conferred on Paul of Samosata. As he entertained low and degrading notions of Christ, contrary to the doctrine of the church, and taught that he was in nature but a common man, the Dionysius of Alexandria being invited to attend the council, urged his age and the infirmity of his body, as his reason for deferring his attendance, but gave his sentiments of the subject before them in an epistle. But the other heads of churches, assembled in all haste from different parts, at Antioch, as against one who was committing depredations on the flock of Christ.

CHAPTER XXVIII.

The different bishops then distinguished.

AMONG these, the most eminent were Firmilianus, bishop of Cesarea in Cappadocia, Gregory and Athenodorus, brothers and pastors of the churches in Pontus; also Helenus, bishop of the church at Tarsus, and Nicomas, of Iconium ; besides Hymenæus of the church at Jerusalem, and Theotecnus, of the adjacent church at Cesarea : moreover, Maximinus, who governed the brethren at Bostra with great celebrity. The vast number of others, both presbyters and deacons, that assembled in the said city, for the same cause, one could hardly number, but these were the most distinguished ; all, therefore, having convened at different times and frequently, various subjects and questions were agitated at every meeting : the adherents of the Samosatians, attempting to conceal and cover over their heterodoxy, but at the same time those on the other side used every effort to unmask and bring to light the heresy, and the blasphemy, of the men against Christ. In the mean time Dionysius died, in the twelfth year of the reign of Gallienus, having presided over the church of Alexandria seventeen years. He was succeeded by Maximinus. But Gallienus reigned fifteen years in all, when he was succeeded by Claudius, who, after the lapse of two years, transferred the government to Aurelian.

CHAPTER XXIX.

Paul refuted by a certain Malchion, one of the presbyters who had been a sophist, was deposed.

It was in the reign of this emperor, when a final council was convened, in which a great number of bishops was present, and this arch heretic at Antioch being detected, and now evidently discarded by all, was now excommunicated from the whole catholic church under heaven. He was refuted, however, and argued out of his lurking place, chiefly by Malchion ; a man well versed in other departments of learning, and who had been at the head of the sophist's Greek school of sciences at Antioch ; but who also, on account of his great and sincere faith in Christ, was honoured with the office of presbyter in that church. This man indeed, was the only one who, after commencing the discussion with him, which, as there were ready writers that took down the whole, we know to be now extant, was able to ferret out the sly and deceitful sentiments of the man.

CHAPTER XXX.

The epistle of the council against Paul.

THE pastors, therefore, who had been convened, having drawn up an epistle, by common consent addressed it to Dionysius bishop of Rome, and to Maximus of Alexandria, and sent it to all the provinces. In this, they set forth their own zeal to all, and the perverse doctrine of Paul, together with the arguments and discussions which they had had with him; stating at the same time, the whole life and conduct of the man, from whose statement it may be well perhaps to give the following extracts for the present. The epistle: " To Dionysius and Maximus, and to all our fellow-ministers throughout the world, the bishops and presbyters and deacons, and to the whole catholic church throughout the world under heaven: Helenus, Hymenæus, and Theophilus, and Theotecnus, and Maximus, Proculus, Nicomas and Ælianus, Paul and Bolanus and Protogenes, Hierax, and Eutychius and Theodorus, and Malchion and Lucius, and all the rest, who are bishops, presbyters, or deacons, dwelling with us, in the neighbouring cities, and nations, together with the churches of God, wish joy to the beloved brethren in the Lord." After a short preliminary, the following is subjoined: " We have addressed epistles, and at the same time have exhorted many of the bishops at a distance, to come to our relief from this destructive doctrine: among these, to Dionysius the bishop of Alexandria, and Firmilianus of Cappadocia, those holy men, of whom the one wrote to Antioch, not even deigning to honour the leader in this delusion with an address, nor writing to him in his name, but to the whole church, of which epistle we have also added a copy. But Firmilianus who came twice to Antioch, despised his new fangled doctrines, as we who were present, and many others besides, well know, and can attest. But as he promised to change his mind, he believed him, and hoped that, without any reproach upon the word, the matter would be settled in a proper manner. He deferred it therefore; in which, however, he was deceived by this denier of his God and Lord, and this deserter of his former faith. Firmilianus was now, also, on his way to Antioch, and had come as far as Tarsus, because he had before made trial of his infidel wickedness: but whilst we were thus collecting and requesting him to come, and awaiting his arrival, he departed this life."

After these, and other matters, they also describe what kind of a life the man led, as follows: " But in those instances where he abandoned the rule of faith, and went over to spurious and corrupt doctrines before, there is no necessity of judging his conduct, when he was yet in no connexion with the church; nor that he was in poverty and beggary; and that he who had received neither wealth from his fathers, nor obtained possessions by any art, or any trade or business, has now arrived at excessive wealth, by his iniquities and sacrileges, and by those various means which he employed to exact and extort from the brethren, depressing the injured, and promising to aid them for a reward; and yet how he deceived them, and without doing them any good, took advantage of the readiness of those who were in difficulties, to make them give any thing in order to be freed from their oppressors. We shall say nothing of his making merchandise of piety; (1 Tim. 6.) nor how he affected lofty things, and assumed with great haughtiness worldly dignities, wishing rather to be called a magistrate (ducenarius) than a bishop, strutting through the forum, and reading letters, and repeating them as he walked in public, and how he was escorted by multitudes going before and following after him: how he, also, brought envy and odium upon the faith, by his pomp, and the haughtiness of his heart. We shall say nothing of the vanity and pretensions with which he contrived, in our ecclesiastical assemblies, to catch at glory and empty shadows, and to confound the minds of the more simple, with such things as these; nothing of his preparing himself a tribunal and throne, not as a disciple of Christ, but having, like the rulers of this world, a secretum,* and

* The *secretum*, was the exclusive seat or place where the magistrate sat to decide cases. It was elevated and enclosed with railings and curtains, so as the more

calling it by this name; nothing of his striking his thigh and his stamping on the tribunal with his feet, and his reproving and insulting those that did not applaud nor clap* as in the theatres, nor exclaim and leap about at these things with his partisans, men and women around him, who were the indecent listeners to these things; but I say, reproving those that were modestly and orderly hearing as in the house of God: nothing of his harsh invectives in the congregation, against the expounders of the word, who had departed this life, and of his magnifying himself, not as a bishop, but as a sophist and juggler. Besides this, he stopped the psalms that were sung in honour of our Lord Jesus Christ, as the late compositions of modern men, but in honour of himself he had prepared women to sing at the great festival in the midst of the church, which one might shudder to hear. He suborned, also, those bishops and presbyters of the neighbouring districts and cities of his party, to advance the same things in their addresses to the people. For if we may here anticipate something of what we intend to write below, he does not wish to confess with us that the Son of God descended from heaven. And this we do not intend merely to assert in words, but it is proved abundantly from those records that we have sent you, and that too not the least, where he says that Jesus is from below. Whilst they who sing to his praise, and extol him among the people, say that he has descended as an angel from heaven. And these things he by no means prohibits, but the haughty mortal is even present when they are said. And as to these women, these adopted sisters,† as the inhabitants of Antioch call them, which belong to him, and the presbyters and deacons about him, whose incurable sins, in this and other respects, he conceals with them,

effectually to keep the magistrate separate from those present. Hence its name from the Latin *secerno*, to separate. The Latin word is used in the Greek text here.

* The practice here referred to, was that of shaking and striking the *oraria*, or linen handkerchiefs, in token of applause. It was accompanied with other expressions of popular approbation.

† The words literally mean, *sub-introduced sisters*, a sort of female companions, on such terms of familiarity as gave occasion to scandal.

though he is conscious of the facts, and has convicted them, he dissembles, in order to have them subservient to his purposes; so that fearing for themselves, they dare not venture to accuse him in regard to his impious conduct and doctrine. Besides this, he has made them rich, for which he is both beloved and admired by those who covet these things. But why should we write these things? For beloved, we know that the bishop and all the clergy ought to be an example to the people of all good works. Nor are we ignorant how many, by the introduction of such females, have fallen, or have incurred suspicion. So that should any one even grant, that nothing disgraceful has been done by him, yet it was a duty to avoid, at least, the suspicion growing out of the matter; so that no one might take offence, nor any be induced to imitate him. For how could any one reprove or admonish another to beware of yielding too much to this familiarity with a woman, lest perchance, he should slip, as it is written; especially when, after having already dismissed one, he retains two others with him, blooming in age and eminent for beauty, and takes them with him wherever he goes; and all this, too, indulging in luxury and surfeiting, on account of which things all around them are groaning and lamenting. But they are so much afraid of his tyranny and power, that they do not venture to accuse him. And these matters, indeed, one might perhaps correct, in a man who was of the catholic faith, and associated with us; but as to one who has trifled away the sacred mystery (of religion,) and who parades with the execrable heresy of Artemas, (for why should we not mention his father,) we deem it unnecessary to exact of him a reason for all these things."

After this, at the close of the epistle, they add the following. " We have been compelled, therefore, to excommunicate this man who sets himself up in opposition to God, and is unwilling to yield, and to appoint another bishop in his place over the catholic church; and this we trust, with the providence of God, viz., Domnus the son of Demetrianus, of blessed memory, and who before this presided with much honour over the same church, a man we believe fully endowed with all the excellent qualities of a bishop. We have also communicated this to you, that you may write, and receive letters of communion from him. But the other may write to Artemas if he pleases, and those that think with Artemas may have communion with him." And this may suffice in this place. Paul, therefore, having thus fallen from the episcopate, together with the true faith, as already said, Domnus succeeded in the administration of the church at Antioch. But Paul being unwilling to leave the building of the church, an appeal was made to the emperor Aurelian, who decided most equitably on the business, ordering the building to be given up to those whom the Christian bishops of Italy and Rome should write. Thus, then, this man was driven out of the church with extreme disgrace, by the temporal power itself. And such was the disposition of Aurelian at this time; but in the progress of his reign, he began to cherish different sentiments with regard to us, and then proceeded, influenced by certain advisers, to raise a persecution against us. And the rumor of this was now every where abroad. But whilst he was already on the point, and so to say, in the very act of subscribing the decrees, the divine vengeance overtook him, all but, as we might say, restraining him from his design at the very elbow, and illustriously proving to all, that there can be no privilege granted the rulers of the world against the churches of Christ, unless by the sovereign hand of God, and the decree of heaven permitting it to be done for our correction and amendment, and in those times and seasons that he may approve. Aurelian, therefore, after a reign of six years, was succeeded by Probus, and he held the government the same number of years, when he was succeeded by Carus, together with Carianus and Numerianus. These again did not continue three full years, when the government devolved on Diocletian, and those subsequently associated with him. In their times the persecution of our own day was begun, and the destruction of the churches at the same time; but a little before this, Dionysius, who had been bishop of Rome for nine years, was succeeded by Felix.

CHAPTER XXXI.

The error of the Manichees, which commenced at this time.

In the mean time, also, that madman (*μανεις τας φρενας*) Manes, * as he was called, well agreeing with his name, for his dæmoniacal heresy, armed himself by the perversion of his reason, and at the instigation of Satan, to the destruction of many. He was a barbarian in his life, both in speech and conduct, but in his nature as one possessed and insane. Accordingly, he attempted to form himself into a Christ, and then also proclaimed himself to be the very paraclete† and the Holy Spirit, and with all this was greatly puffed up with his madness. Then, as if he were Christ, he selected twelve disciples, the partners of his new religion, and after patching together false and ungodly doctrines, collected from a thousand heresies long since extinct, he swept them off like a deadly poison, from Persia, upon this part of the world. Hence the impious name of the Manichees spreading among many, even to the present day. Such then was the occasion of this knowledge, as it was falsely called, that sprouted up in these times.

---

* Our author here uses an epithet, *μανεις*, instead of the proper name of this heretic. Eusebius here taking occasion to rail at the folly of Manes, by an allusion to his name, finds a word in his own language which seems to characterise, whilst it gives his name nearly. We cannot, however, infer from this, that Eusebius considered the name Greek. He doubtless knew as well as we, that Manes was a Persian name, or at least that it was not Greek. But he wanted nothing more than similarity of sound for his purpose.

Shorting is mistaken in supposing our author here to intimate the word was Greek. The truth is, the orientals call the name Mani, whence the Greek and Latin *Manes*. The resemblance of this name to the Greek *μανεις*, madman, gave our author an opportunity to exercise his wit, by the application of the epithet without the name.

† *Paraclete.*] See note, Book V. ch. 16. The names of three prominent leaders in delusion, to whom the holy epithet paraclete was either applied, or by whom it was claimed, however different their errors, seem almost to coalesce by alliteration; Montanus, Manes, Mahomet; the first a deluded and ignorant fanatic, the second a crazed philosopher, and the third an ambitious, artful voluptuary, presenting a singular *concordia discors*, all at antipodes in doctrine, yet all aspiring to the exalted attributes of the Paraclete.

CHAPTER XXXII.

Of those distinguished ecclesiastical writers of our own day, and which of them survived until the destruction of the churches.

AT this time Felix, having held the episcopate at Rome five years, was succeeded by Eutychianus, and he did not hold the office quite ten months, when he left his place to be occupied by Caius of our own day. Caius, also, presided about fifteen years, when he was succeeded by Marcellinus. He was overtaken by the persecution, and in these times, also, Timæus, after Domnus, governed the church of Antioch, who was succeeded by our contemporary Cyrillus, under whom we have known Dorotheus, a learned man, who was honoured with the rank of presbyter of Antioch at that time. He was a man of fine taste in sacred literature, and was much devoted to the study of the Hebrew language, so that he read the Hebrew Scriptures with great facility. He, also, was of a very liberal mind, and not unacquainted with the preparatory studies pursued among the Greeks, but in other respects a eunuch by nature, having been such from his birth; so that the emperor, on this account, as if it were a great miracle, received him into his house and family, and honoured him with an appointment over the purple dye establishment of Tyre. Him we have heard in the church expounding the Scriptures with great judgment; after Cyrillus, the duties of the episcopal office in the church of Antioch were administered by his successor Tyrannus, under whom the destruction of the churches took place. At Laodicea, the church was governed by Eusebius, the successor of Socrates, who was sprung from an Alexandrian family. The occasion of his removal was the affair respecting Paul of Samosat, on which account having come to Syria, he was prevented from returning home by those who took great interest in the Scriptures there. He was also an amiable instance of religion among our contemporaries, as may be readily seen in those extracts from Dionysius, which we have inserted above. Anatolius was appointed his successor, a good man, as they say, in the place of the good. He, too, was an Alexandrian. But for his learning and skill in the Greek philosophy, he was superior to any of the most distinguished men of our day, as he had attained unto the highest eminence in arithmetic, geometry, and astronomy, besides his proficiency in dialectics, and physics, and rhetoric. On this account it is said, that he was also requested by the Alexandrians to establish a school there of the succession (or order) of Aristotle. They relate innumerable achievements of his at the siege of the Bruchium,* at Alexandria, as he was honoured by all in office, with extraordinary distinction; but as a specimen, we shall only mention this.—When the bread, as they say, failed in the siege, so that they were better able to sustain their enemies from without than the famine within, Anatolius being present, devised a project like the following. As the other part of the city was in alliance with the Roman army, and therefore happened not to be besieged, he sent to inform Eusebius, who was among those not besieged, for he was yet there before his removal to Syria, and was very celebrated, and in high repute even with the Roman general, to inform him of the siege and those perishing with famine. On learning this, he begs of the Roman general to grant safety to those who would desert from the enemy, as the greatest favour he could grant him. Obtaining his request, he immediately communicates it to Anatolius. The latter receiving the promise, collected the senate of Alexandria, and at first began to propose that they should come to a reconciliation with the Romans. But as he perceived that they were incensed at the suggestion, he said, But I do not think you will oppose me, if I should advise you to send forth the superfluous number, and those that are of no use to us, the old women and children, and old men, and let them go where they wish. For why should we keep those with us, who will ere long at any rate die to no purpose? and why should we destroy with famine those that are already bereft of sight and mutilated in body? We ought to feed only men and youth, and furnish the

---

* The Bruchium here mentioned, was a part of Alexandria; it seems derived from πυρουχος, *annonæ præfectus*, and was a kind of corn-market.

necessary provisions to those that are necessary for the defence of the city. With such reasoning, having persuaded the senate, he was the first that rose and proposed the resolution, that the whole multitude whether of men or women, that were not needed for the army, should be dismissed from the city, because there would be no hope of safety at all for them, who, at any rate were about to perish with the famine, if they continued and lingered in the city until the state of affairs was desperate. All the rest of the senate agreeing to this decree, he nearly saved the whole of the besieged; among the first providing, that those of the church, then those of every age in the town, should make their escape, and among these not only those that were included in the decree, but taking the opportunity, many others, secretly clad in women's clothes, went out of the city by his management at night, and proceeded to the Roman camp. There Eusebius receiving them all, like a father and physician, recovered them, wasted away by a protracted siege, with every kind of attention to their wants. With two such pastors in succession, was the church of Laodicea honoured by the divine interposition, who after the termination of the war mentioned, had left the city of Alexandria, and came to these parts. But in other respects not many books were written by Anatolius; so many, however, have come down to us, by which we may both learn his eloquence and erudition. In these he sets forth his opinions on the Passover, from which it might be proper to extract the following :— Extracts from the Canons of Anatolius on the Paschal Festival. " You have, therefore, in the first year, the new moon of the first month, which is the beginning of every cycle of nineteen years, on the twenty-sixth of the Egyptian month Phamenoth. But according to the months of the Macedonians the twenty-second of Dystrus. But as the Romans would say, before the eleventh of the calends of April. But the sun is found on the said twenty-sixth of the month Phamenoth, not only as entering the first segment (of the zodiac), but on the fourth day is already found passing through it. But this segment they generally call the first dodecatomorium, and the equinox, and the beginning of the months, and the head of the cycle, and the head of the planetary course. But that (segment) before this, they call the last of the months, the twelfth segment, and the last dodecatemorium, and the end of the planetary revolution. Hence, also, those that place the first month in it, and that fix the fourteenth of the month by it, commit, as we think, no little and no common blunder. But neither is this our opinion only, but it was also known to the Jews anciently, and before Christ, and was chiefly observed by them, as we may learn from Philo, Josephus, and Musæus; and not only from these, but also from those still more ancient, *i. e.* the two Agathobuli, commonly called the masters, and of Aristobulus, that most distinguished scholar, who was one of the seventy that translated the holy Scriptures from the Hebrew for Ptolemy Philadelphus, and his father, and dedicated his exposition of the law of Moses to the same kings. These, when they resolve inquiries on Exodus, say that all ought to sacrifice the passover alike after the vernal equinox, in the middle of the first month. But this is found to be when the sun passes through the first segment of the solar, or, as some call it, the zodiacal circle. But this Aristobulus also adds, it was requisite that not only the sun should have passed the equinoctial segment for the feast of the passover, but the moon also. For as there are two equinoctial segments, the vernal and the autumnal, and diametrically opposite to each other, and since the day of the passover is given on the fourteenth of the month at the evening, the moon will stand diametrically opposite to the sun, as may be seen in full moons. Thus the sun will be at the vernal equinox, the moon, on the contrary, at the autumnal equinox.

" Many other matters, I know, have been discussed by him; some of them with great probability, others established with the most certain demonstrations, in which he attempts to show that the festival of the passover, and of unleavened bread, ought to be observed altogether after the equinox; but I shall omit demanding such full demonstrations of matters from which the veil of the Mosaic law has been removed; and it now remains for us, in this uncovered surface, to contemplate, as in a mirror, the reflected doctrines and sufferings of Christ. But that the first month of the Hebrews is about the equinox, may be gathered from the book of Enoch."

The same author has also left an elementary work, On Calculation, ten books in all; and other proofs of his great study and proficiency in sacred literature. Theotecnus, bishop of Cesarea in Palestine, was the first that laid his hands upon him in his ordination to the episcopate, designing to constitute him his successor in his own church after his death; and, indeed, both of them presided for a short time over the same church. But when the synod at Antioch called him to Antioch against Paul, as he passed through the city of Laodicea, Eusebius, the bishop of that place being dead, he was constrained by the brethren to remain. And Anatolius also dying, Stephen was made bishop of that church, the last bishop before the persecution; a man greatly admired for his knowledge of philosophy, and other branches of Greek learning. But he was not equally disposed towards the divine faith, as the progress of the persecution evinced; in which he was proved to be timid and cowardly, rather than a sound philosopher. The affairs of the church, however, were not likely to be ruined by this, for these were corrected and restored by Theodotus, who, under a special providence of God, the saviour of all, was ordained bishop of the church there; and by his deeds proved the reality of his name (given of God), and of his office as bishop. For he excelled in his knowledge of the medical art, as applied to the body, and was skilled in that healing art which is applied to the soul. No one was ever his equal in kindness, sincerity, sympathy, and a zeal to benefit those that needed his aid. He was, also, much exercised in the study of divine things. Such was he.

But at Cesarea in Palestine, Theotecnus, after a most diligent and active episcopate, was succeeded at his death by Agapius. Him we know to have laboured much, and to have kept a most thorough oversight in superintending the people, and with his liberal hand to have paid regard especially to the poor. In his time, we were acquainted with that most eloquent man, and truly practical philosopher, who was honoured with the rank of presbyter in that church; I mean Pamphilus, whose character and greatness would be no trifling subject to elucidate. But we have dwelt in a separate work on the particulars of his life, and the school which he established, as also the trials which he endured amid the persecution in the different confessions, and besides this, the death of martyrdom with which he was crowned. He, indeed, was the most admirable of all here. Among the very eminent men that have flourished near our own times, of presbyters we have known Pierius of Alexandria, Melchius also bishop of the churches in Pontus. The former indeed was greatly celebrated for his voluntary poverty, and his philosophical knowledge, and was abundantly exercised in expositions of the Scriptures, and the discourses in the public assemblies of the church. But Miletius was called by the learned, the honey (μελι) of Attica, and was the most perfect original of learned men that could be described. It is impossible also to admire sufficiently the superiority of his eloquence: it might be said perhaps that he derived this from nature, but who is there that could excel him in the excellence of his other skill and erudition. For in all the sciences that require the exercise of argumentation, if you were to make trial, you would readily say that he was a most subtle and acute reasoner. The virtues of his life were also a parallel to these. We have had the opportunity of observing him during the persecution, escaping its fury for seven years, in the regions of Palestine. But the church of Jerusalem, after Hymenæus, was under the episcopal care of Zambdas, and he not long after dying, Hermon was the last before the persecution of our day; the same that now holds the apostolic chair preserved there to this day. At Alexandria, however, Maximus, who held the episcopal office eighteen years after the death of Dionysius, was succeeded by Theonas. In his time Achillas, who had been honoured with the order of presbyter, was noted at Alexandria, having entrusted to him the school for religious instruction. In his life and actions he exhibited a most rare instance of sound wisdom, and a genuine specimen of evangelical deportment. But after Theonas had discharged the duties of the office nineteen years, he was succeeded in the episcopate of Alexandria by Peter, who was also very eminent, and held the office twelve years;

nearly three of which he governed the church, before the persecution; but the rest of his life he subjected himself to a more rigid course of discipline, but still continued to manifest great interest in advancing the welfare of the church. Hence, in the ninth year of the persecution he was beheaded, and thus obtained the crown of martyrdom. But after giving in our history an account of the successors, since the birth of our Saviour until the demolition of the churches, embracing a period of three hundred and five years, now let us here attempt to give the conflicts which have been endured in the cause of religion, in our own times, in all their extent and magnitude, that it may be on record also for the benefit of posterity.

BOOK VIII.

HAVING already related the successions of the apostles in seven books, in this eighth we consider it necessary to record, for the benefit of posterity, the events of our own times that deserve a more than superficial narration. And our account, therefore, shall begin with these.

CHAPTER I.

The events that preceded the persecution in our times.

To give a satisfactory account of the extent, and the nature of that glory and liberty, with which the doctrine of piety towards the supreme God, as announced to the world through Christ, was honoured among all, both Greeks and barbarians, before the persecution in our day, this, we say, were an undertaking beyond our power. As a proof, we might refer to the clemency of the emperors toward our brethren, to whom they even entrusted the government of provinces, exonerating them from all anxiety as it regarded sacrificing, on account of that singular good will that they entertained toward the doctrine. Why should we speak of those in the imperial palaces, and the sovereigns themselves, who granted their domestics the liberty of declaring themselves freely, in word and deed, on religion, and I would say almost the liberty of boasting of their freedom in the practice of the faith ? These, indeed, they eminently valued, and considered them as more acceptable than their associates in the imperial service.

Such was that Dorotheus, the most devoted and most faithful of all to them, and, on this account, exceedingly honoured beyond all those that had the charge of government, and the most honourable stations in the provinces. We may also add Gorgonius, equally celebrated with him; and so many others that were honoured with the same distinction as these on account of the divine word. The same privileges one could observe conferred on the rulers in every church, who were courted and honoured with the greatest subserviency by all the rulers and governors. Who could describe those vast collections of men that flocked to the religion of Christ, and those multitudes crowding in from every city, and the illustrious concourse in the houses of worship? On whose account, not content with the ancient buildings, they erected spacious churches from the foundation in all the cities These, advancing in the lapse of time, and daily increasing in magnitude and improvement, were not restrained by any odium or hostility. Nor was any malignant dæmon able to infatuate, nor human machinations prevent them, as long as the providential hand of God superintended and guarded his people as the worthy objects of his care. But when, by reason of excessive liberty, we sunk into negligence and sloth, one envying and reviling another in different ways, and we were almost, as it were, on the point of taking up arms against each other, and were assailing each other with words as with darts and spears, prelates inveighing against prelates, and people rising up against people, and hypocrisy and dissimulation had arisen to the greatest height of malignity, then the divine judgment, which usually proceeds with a lenient hand, whilst the multitudes were yet crowding into the church, with gentle and mild visitations began to afflict its episcopacy; the persecution having begun with those brethren that were in the army. But, as if destitute of all sensibility, we were not prompt in measures to appease and propitiate the Deity; some, indeed, like atheists, regarding our situation as unheeded and unobserved by a providence, we added one wickedness and misery to another. But some that appeared to be our pastors, deserting the law of piety, were inflamed against each other with mutual strifes, only accumulating quarrels and threats, rivalship, hostility and hatred to each other, only anxious to assert the government as a kind of sovereignty for themselves. Then, as Jeremiah says, " the Lord in his anger darkened the daughter of Sion, and hurled from heaven to earth the glory of Israel. Neither did he remember his footstool in the day of his wrath. But the Lord, also, overwhelmed all the beauty of Israel, and tore down all his walls." And, as it is predicted in the Psalms, " He overturned the covenant of his servant, and he prostrated his sanctuary to the earth," by the demolition of the churches. " He has destroyed all his walls, and has made all his bulwarks fear. All the multitudes that pass through have ravaged him, and hence he has become a reproach to his neighbours. For he has exalted the right arm of his enemies, and has turned away the help of his sword, nor aided him in war. But he has also deprived him of his purification, and his throne he has cast to the ground. He has shortened the days of his time, and has poured upon him all his disgrace."

CHAPTER II.

The demolition of the churches.

ALL this has been fulfilled in our day, when we saw, with our own eyes, our houses of worship thrown down from their elevation, the sacred Scriptures of inspiration committed to the flames in the midst of the markets, the shepherds of the people basely concealed here and there, some of them ignominiously captured, and the sport of their enemies ; when, also, according to another prophetic declaration, " contempt was poured out upon their rulers, and he has made them to err in a trackless by-path, and where there is no road."

But it is not for me to describe fully the sorrowful calamities which they endured, since neither does it belong to me to record the dissensions and follies which they exercised against each other before the persecution. Hence, also, we have purposed not to extend our narration beyond the events in which we perceive the just judgment of God. Hence, also, we shall not make mention of those that were shaken by the persecution, nor of those that suffered shipwreck in their salvation, and of their own accord were sunk into the depths of the watery gulph. But we shall only, upon the whole, introduce those events in our history that may be profitable first to us of the present day, and hereafter to posterity. Now let us proceed to describe, in a condensed account, the holy conflicts of the witnesses of divine truth.

It was the nineteenth year of the reign of Diocletian, and the month of Dystrus, called by the Romans March, in which the festival of our Saviour's passion was at hand, when the imperial edicts were every wnere published, to tear down the churches to the foundation, and to destroy the sacred Scriptures by fire, and which commanaed, also, that those who were in honourable stations, should be degraded, but those who were freedmen should be deprived of their liberty, if they persevered in their adherence to Christianity. The first edict against us was of this nature; but it was not long before other edicts were also issued, in which it was ordered that all the prelates in every place, should first be committed to prison, and then, by every artifice constrained to offer sacrifice to the gods.

CHAPTER III.

The nature of the conflicts endured by the manly s, in the per secution.

THEN, indeed, vast numbers of the prelates of the church en dured with a noble resolution the most appalling trials, and exhibited instances of illustrious conflicts for the faith. Vast numbers, however, of others, broken and relaxed in spirit, by timidity before the contest, voluntarily yielded at the first onset. But of the rest, each encountered various kinds of torments. Here was one that was scourged with rods, there another tormented with the rack and excruciating scrapings, in which some at the time endured the most terrible death; others again passed through other torments in the struggle. Here one, whilst some forced him to the impure and detestable sacrifices, was again dismissed, as if he had sacrificed, although this was not the case. There another, though he had not in the least approached the altar, not even touched the unholy thing, yet when others said that he had sacrificed, went away, bearing the calumny in silence. Here one, again taken up when half dead, was thrown out as if he were already dead; there another, again lying upon the ground was dragged a long distance by the feet, and numbered among those that had sacrificed. One, however, would cry out, and with a loud voice declared his abhorrence of the sacrifice. Another exclaimed that he was a Christian, furnishing, by confession, an illustrious example of this salutary name. Another asserted that he neither had sacrificed nor intended to sacrifice; but these were forced to silence by numerous bands of soldiers, prepared for this purpose, by whom they were struck on the face and cheeks, and violently driven away. Thus the enemies of religion, upon the whole, deemed it a great matter even to appear to have gained some advantage. But these things did not avail them much against the saints, to give an exact account of whom no description could suffice.

CHAPTER IV.

The illustrious martyrs of God, who filled every place with the celebrity of their name, and obtained various crowns of martyrdom for their piety.

MANY instances might be related of those who exhibited noble alacrity in the cause of that religion which acknowledges only the one Supreme God, and that not only from the time that the general persecution was raised, but also long before, when al was yet in a state of peace. Already then, when he who ha, received such power, was first roused as from a deep slumber, he had secretly and unobserved, been plotting after the times of Decius and Valerian, how to assault the churches; but he did not all at once, nor in a mass, wage an open war against us, but as yet only made trial of those that were in the armies. For in this way he supposed that the rest could easily be taken, if he could first succeed in subduing these. Then one could see great numbers of the military, most cheerfully embracing a private life, so as not to renounce their reverence for the Supreme Creator of the universe. For when the general, whoever he was, first undertook the persecution against the soldiers, he began by a review and lustration of those that were enrolled in the army, and gave them their choice, either to enjoy the honour conferred upon them if they obeyed, or on the contrary to be deprived of this, if they disobeyed the command. Very many who were soldiers in the kingdom of Christ, without hesitating, preferred the confession of his name to that apparent glory and comfort which they enjoyed, and of these a few here and there exchanged their honours, not only for degradation but even for death, for their perseverance in religion. These last, however, were not yet many, as the great instigator of these violent measures had, as yet, but moderately proceeded, and ventured only so far as to shed the blood of some only. The great number of the believers, probably deterred and caused him to shrink from a general attack upon all; but when he began to arm more openly, it is impossible to tell how many and how eminent those were that presented themselves in every place and city and country, as martyrs in the cause of Christ.

CHAPTER V.

The affairs of Nicomedia.

IMMEDIATELY on the first promulgation of the edict, a certain man of no mean origin, but highly esteemed for his temporal dignities, as soon as the decree was published against the churches in Nicomedia, stimulated by a divine zeal, and exerted by an ardent faith, took it as it was openly placed and posted up for public inspection, and tore it to pieces as a most profane and wicked act. This, too, was done when two of the Cesar's were in the city, the first of whom was the eldest and chief of all, and the other held the fourth grade of the imperial dignity after him. But this man, as the first that was distinguished there in this manner, after enduring what was likely to follow an act so daring, preserved his mind calm and serene until the moment when his spirit fled.

CHAPTER VI.

Those that were in the palace.

But of all those that were celebrated, or admired for their courage, whether among Greeks or barbarians, these times produced noble and illustrious martyrs, in the case of Dorotheus and his associates, domestics, in the imperial palace. These though honoured with the highest dignity by their masters, and treated by them with not less affection than their own children, esteemed the reproaches and trials in the cause of religion, as of much more real value than the glory and luxuries of life; and even the various kinds of death that were invented against them were preferred to these, when they came into competition with religion. We shall give an account of the end of one, leaving it for our readers to conjecture what must have been the character of the sufferings inflicted on the others. He was led into the middle of the aforesaid city, before those emperors already mentioned. He was then commanded to sacrifice, but as he refused, he was ordered to be stripped and lifted on high, and to be scourged with rods over his whole body, until he should be subdued in his resolution, and forced to do what he was commanded. But as he was unmoveable amid all these sufferings, his bones already appearing bared of the flesh, they mixed vinegar with salt, and poured it upon the mangled parts of the body. But as he bore these tortures, a gridiron and fire was produced, and the remnants of his body, like pieces of meat for roasting and eating, were placed in the fire, not at once, so that he might not expire soon,

but taken by little and little, whilst his torturers were not permitted to let him alone, unless after these sufferings he breathed
his last before they had completed their task. He, however, persevered in his purpose, and gave up his life victorious in the
midst of his tortures. Such was the martyrdom of one of the
imperial domestics, worthy in reality of his name, for he was
called Peter. But we shall perceive in the course of our narration, in which we shall study brevity, that the martyrdoms of the
rest were in no respect inferior to this. We shall only state of
Dorotheus, and Gorgonius, with many others of the imperial
freedmen, that after various sufferings, they were destroyed by
the halter, and bore away the prize of a heavenly victory. At
this time also, Anthimus, then bishop of the church of Nicomedia, was beheaded for his confession of Christ, and to him were
added a multitude of believers that thronged around him.

I know not how it happened, but there was a fire that broke
out in the imperial palace at Nicomedia, in these days, which, by
a false suspicion reported abroad, was attributed to our brethren
as the authors; in consequence of which, whole families of the
pious here were slain in masses at the imperial command, some
with the sword, some also with fire. Then it is said that men
and women, with a certain divine and inexpressible alacrity,
rushed into the fire. But the populace binding another number
upon planks, threw them into the depths of the sea. But the imperial domestics, also, who after death had been committed to
the earth with proper burial, their legal masters thought necessary to have dug up again from their sepulchres, and likewise
cast into the sea, lest any, reasoning like themselves, should worship them in their graves, as if they were gods. And such, then,
was the complexion of things in the commencement of the persecution at Nicomedia.

But, ere long, as there were some in the region called Melitina,
and others, again, in Syria, that attempted to usurp the government, it was commanded, by an imperial edict, that the heads of
the churches every where should be thrust into prison and bonds.
And the spectacle of affairs after these events exceeds all description. Innumerable multitudes were imprisoned in every

place, and the dungeons, formerly destined for murderers and the vilest criminals, were then filled with bishops, and presbyters, and deacons, readers and exorcists, so that there was no room left for those condemned for crime. But when the former edict was followed by another, in which it was ordered that the prisoners should be permitted to have their liberty if they sacrificed, but persisting they should be punished with the most excruciating tortures, who could tell the number of those martyrs in every province, and particularly in Mauritania, Thebais, and Egypt, that suffered death for their religion? From the last place, especially, many went to other cities and provinces, and became illustrious for their martyrdom.

CHAPTER VII.

The Egyptians that suffered in Phœnice.

WE are already acquainted with those of them that shone conspicuous in Palestine, and know also those in Tyre and Phœnice ; and at the sight of whom, who would not himself be struck with astonishment at the numberless blows inflicted, and the perseverance of those truly admirable wrestlers for the true religion? Who can behold, without amazement, all this: their conflicts, after scourging, with bloody beasts of prey, when they were cast as food to leopards and bears, wild boars and bulls, goaded with fire, and branded with glowing iron against them? And in each of these, who can fail to admire the wonderful patience of these noble martyrs? At these scenes we have been present ourselves, when we also observed the divine power of our Lord and Saviour Jesus Christ himself present, and effectually displayed in them ; when, for a long time, the devouring wild beasts would not dare either to touch or to approach the bodies of these pious men, but directed their violence against others that were any where stimulating them from without.* But they would not even touch the holy wrestlers standing naked and striking at them with their hands, as they were commanded, in order to irritate the beasts against them. Sometimes, indeed, they would also rush upon them, but, as if repulsed by some divine power, they again retreated.

This continuing, also, for a long time, created no little wonder to the spectators ; so that now again on account of the failure in the first instance, they were obliged to let loose the beast a second and a third time upon one and the same martyr. One could not help being astonished at the intrepid perseverance of these holy men, and the firm and invincible mind of those, also, whose bodies were but young and tender. For you could have seen a youth of scarcely twenty years, standing unbound, with his arms extended, like a cross, but with an intrepid and fearless earnestness, intensely engaged in prayer to God, neither removing nor declining from the spot where he stood, whilst bears and leopards breathed rage and death, and almost touched his very flesh, and yet I know not how, by a divine and inscrutable power, they had their mouths in a manner bridled, and again retreated in haste. And such was he of whom we now speak.

Again, you might have seen others, for they were five in all, cast before a wild bull, who indeed seized others, that approached from without, with his horns, and tossed them in the air, leaving them to be taken up half dead, but only rushing upon the saints with rage and menaces ; for the beast was not able even to approach them, but beating the earth with his feet, and pushing with his horns hither and thither, and from the irritation excited by the brands of glowing iron, he breathed madness and death, yet was drawn back again by a divine interposition. So that as

---

* Valesius and others understand this expression figuratively, as in the passage, " What have we to do with those without ?" meaning the heathen. But the litera. meaning seems to be natural and obvious, and refers to those who, standing without the arena, in the amphitheatre, were urging and stimulating the beasts. Our author uses the same expression below, evidently with the same intention as here, to designate particular persons. The figurative sense seems to be too general in account like this.

he did not even injure them in the least, they let loose other beasts upon them. At length, however, after these various and terrible assaults, all of them were despatched with the sword, and instead of an interment and sepulchre, they were committed to the waves of the sea.

CHAPTER VIII.

Those who suffered in Egypt.

AND such, too, was the severity of the struggle which was endured by the Egyptians, who wrestled gloriously for the faith at Tyre. But one cannot but admire those that suffered also in their native land, where thousands, both men, and women, and children, despising the present life for the sake of our Saviour's doctrine, submitted to death in various shapes. Some, after being tortured with scrapings and the rack, and the most dreadful scourgings, and other innumerable agonies, which one might shudder to hear, were finally committed to the flames; some plunged and drowned in the sea, others voluntarily offering their own heads to the executioners, others dying in the midst of their torments, some wasted away by famine, and others again fixed to the cross. Some, indeed, were executed as malefactors usually were; others more cruelly, were nailed with the head downwards, and kept alive until they were destroyed by starving on the cross itself.

CHAPTER IX.

Of those in Thebais.

BUT it would exceed all power of detail to give an idea of the sufferings and tortures which the martyrs of Thebais endured. These, instead of hooks, had their bodies scraped with shells, and were mangled in this way until they died. Women tied by one foot, and then raised on high in the air by certain machines, with their naked bodies and wholly uncovered, presented this most foul, cruel, and inhuman spectacle to all beholders ; others again perished, bound to trees and branches.　For, drawing the stoutest of the branches together by machines for this purpose, and binding the limbs of the martyrs to each of these, they then let loose the boughs to resume their natural position, designing thus to produce a violent action, to tear asunder the limbs of those whom they thus treated.　And all these things were doing not only for a few days or some time, but for a series of whole years. At one time, ten or more, at another, more than twenty, at another time not less than thirty, and even sixty, and again at another time, a hundred men with their wives and little children were slain in one day, whilst they were condemned to various and varied punishments.　We ourselves have observed, when on the spot, many crowded together in one day, some suffering decapitation, some the torments of flames ; so that the murderous weapon was completely blunted, and having lost its edge, broke to pieces ; and the executioners themselves, wearied with slaughter, were obliged to relieve one another.　Then, also, we were witnesses to the most admirable ardour of mind, and the truly divine energy and alacrity of those that believed in the Christ of God.　For as soon as the sentence was pronounced against the first, others rushed forward from other parts to the tribunal before the judge, confessing they were Christians, most indifferent to the dreadful and multiform tortures that awaited them, but declaring themselves fully and in the most undaunted manner on the religion which acknowledges only one Supreme God.　They received, indeed, the final sentence of death with gladness and exultation, so far as even to sing and send up hymns of praise and thanksgiving, until they breathed their last.　Admirable, indeed, were these, but eminently wonderful were also those who, though they were distinguished for wealth and noble birth and great reputation, and excelled in philosophy and learning, still regarded all as but secondary to the true religion and faith in our Lord and Saviour Jesus Christ.　Such was Philoromus, who held no mean office in the imperial district of Alexandria, and who, according to his rank and Roman dignity, was attended by a military guard, when administering justice every day. Phileas, also, bishop of the churches of Thmuis, a man eminent for his conduct and the services rendered to his country, as well as in the different branches of philosophy. These, although urged by innumerable relatives and other friends, and though many eminent persons and the judge himself entreated them, that they should take compassion on themselves and have mercy upon their children and wives, were nevertheless not in the least induced by these things to prefer life, when it stood in competition with the command that regarded the confession or the denial of our Saviour. And thus, with a manly and philosophical mind, rather let me say with a mind devoted to God and his religion, persevering in opposition to *all* the threats and the insults of the judge, both of them were condemned to lose their heads.

CHAPTER X.

The writings of Phileas, which give an account of the martyrs of Alexandria.

But since we have mentioned Phileas, as highly estimable for his great proficiency also in foreign literature and science, we will let him bear witness for himself, whilst he may also show us who he was, and also what martyrdoms happened at Alexandria, all which he can state more accurately than ourselves, in the extract we here present.

From the epistle of Phileas to the inhabitants of Thmuis. "As all these signs, examples, and noble precepts are presented to us in the Holy Scriptures, those holy martyrs with us did not hesitate, whilst they sincerely directed their mental eye to that God who rules over all, and in their minds preferred death for their religion, and firmly adhered to their vocation. They had well understood that our Lord Jesus Christ became man for us, that he might remove all sin, and furnish us with the means of entering into eternal life. For he thought it not robbery to be equal with God, but humbled himself, taking upon him the form of a servant, and being found in the fashion of man, he humbled himself unto death, even the death of the cross." Hence, also, these Christ-bearing * martyrs, zealously strove to attain unto better gifts, and endured every kind of trial, every series of tortures not merely once, but once and again, the second time; and though the guards assailed them with every kind of threat, not merely in words, but vied with one another in violent acts, they did not surrender their faith, because " perfect love casteth out fear." And what language would suffice to recount their virtues, and their fortitude under every trial? For as every one had the liberty to abuse them, some beat them with clubs, some with rods, some with scourges, others again with thongs, others with ropes. And the sight of these torments was varied and multi-plied, exhibiting excessive malignity. For some had their hands tied behind them, and were suspended on the rack,† and every limb was stretched with machines. Then the torturers, accord-ing to their orders, applied the pincers to the whole body, not merely as in the case of murderers, to the sides, but also to the stomach and knees and cheeks. Some, indeed, were suspended on high by one hand, from the portico, whose sufferings by rea-son of the distention of their joints and limbs, were more dreadful than any. Others were bound face to face to pillars, not resting

---

* The original here is the expressive epithet χριστοφοροι, Christ-bearing, Christo-phori; as they bore all for the sake of Christ, by a strong synecdoche, they were said to bear Christ himself, the voluntary object of their love; and thus the indirect cause of these sufferings in which they rejoiced. We must indulge such anoma-lous compounds, as this, in our language, when a novel idea seems to require it. The composition itself is not more singular than the idea which it expresses. Va-lesius, though he does not follow the idea in his version, explains the word as meaning *full of Christ*, and refers to the epithet Theophorus given to Ignatius. Shorting has rendered it, therefore, *full of Christ*. But by such a version and ety-mology, the allusion in the context is entirely lost. The martyrs were called by a strong figure, Christophori, because they *bore*, and Ignatius was called Theophorus for the same reason.

† The instrument of torture here mentioned, appears to have been the Roman *eculeus*. It was so constructed, that the person was suspended on it, and his limbs stretched by screws. It was applied at first only to slaves.

upon their feet, but forced down by the weight of the body, whilst the pressure of their weight also increased the tension of their cords. And this they endured, not merely as long as the governor spoke to them, or as long merely as he had leisure to hear, but nearly the whole day. For when he passed on to others, he left some of his subordinate officers to attend to the former, to observe whether any of them seemed overcome by the torments, to surrender. But he gave orders to proceed without sparing, to bind with bonds, and afterwards, when they had breathed out their life, to drag them on the ground. For they said that there should not the least regard be paid to us, but that they should think and act with us as if we were nothing at all.

Our enemies, therefore, had devised this second torture beside the scourging. But there were some, also, after the tortures, placed in the stocks, stretched by both feet to the fourth hole. So that they were of necessity obliged to keep in a lying posture on their back, not being able to have any command of their mangled bodies, in consequence of the blows and scourges they had received. Others, again, being cast on the ground, lay prostrated by the accumulated tortures which they had endured, exhibiting a still more dreadful spectacle in that condition than when under the actual infliction of the torture, and bearing on their bodies the various and multiplied proofs of the ingenuity of their torturers.

Whilst these things were doing, some indeed died under their torments, covering their enemies with shame by their perseverance. Others, again, almost dead, were thrust into prison, and before many days ended their life through incessant pain. The rest, however, somewhat recovering by the application of remedies, by time and their long detention in prison, became more confident. Thus, then, when ordered to take their choice, either by touching the unholy sacrifice, to remain without further molestation, and to obtain the execrable sentence of liberation from them, or else, without sacrificing, to expect the sentence of death they without delay cheerfully embraced death. They well knew what had been anciently prescribed in the sacred Scriptures " For he that offereth sacrifice to other gods," saith the Scrip tures, " shall be destroyed." And, again, " thou shalt have none other gods but me." These are the expressions of a martyr, who was at once a sound philosopher and one devoted to God. These he addressed before the final sentence, whilst yet in prison, to the brethren of his church, at the same time representing his own condition, and exhorting them to adhere firmly, even after his death, which was close at hand, to the Christian religion. But why should we say much, and add one new species of struggle after another, as they were endured by these pious martyrs throughout the world ; especially when they were no longer assailed in a common way, but regularly invaded as in war ?

CHAPTER XI.

The events in Phrygia.

INDEED the armed soldiery surrounded a certain Christian town in Phrygia, together with the garrison, and hurling fire into it, burnt them, together with women and children, calling upon Christ the God of all. And this, because all the inhabitants of this town, even the very governor and magistrate, with all the men of rank, and the whole people, confessed themselves Christians, and would not obey, in any degree, those that commanded them to offer sacrifices.

Another one, also, of Roman dignity, Adauctus by name. of a noble Italian family, a man that had been advanced through every grade of dignity by the emperors, and had reputably filled the offices of general administrator, called by them the master of the revenue, and prime minister. And yet with all this he was pre-eminent, also, for his pious acts, and his profession of Christ, and was nobly crowned with martyrdom ; nobly enduring the conflict in the cause of piety whilst he was yet clad with the office of prime minister.

CHAPTER XII.

*Of many others, both men and women, who suffered in different
ways.*

WHY should I now mention the names of others, or number the
multitude of men, or picture the various torments of the admirable martyrs of Christ; some of whom were slain with the axe,
as in Arabia; some had their limbs fractured, as in Cappadocia;
and some were suspended by the feet, and a little raised from the
ground, with their heads downward, were suffocated with the
ascending smoke of a gentle fire kindled below, as was done to
those in Mesopotamia; some were mutilated by having their
noses, ears, and hands cut off, and the rest of their limbs, and
parts of their body cut to pieces, as was the case at Alexandria?
Why should we revive the recollection of those at Antioch, who
were roasted on grates of fire, not to kill immediately, but torture
them with a lingering punishment? Others, again, rather resolved
to thrust their arm into the fire, than touch the unholy sacrifice;
some shrinking from the trial, sooner than be taken and fall into
the hands of their enemies, cast themselves headlong from the
lofty houses, considering death an advantage compared with the
malignity of these impious persecutors. A certain holy and admirable female, admirable for her virtue, and illustrious above all
at Antioch for her wealth, family, and reputation, had educated
her two daughters, who were now in the bloom of life, noted for
their beauty, in the principles of piety. As they had excited
great envy among many, every measure was tried to trace them
in their concealment; but when it was discovered that they were
abroad, they were, with a deep-laid scheme, called to Antioch.
They were now caught in the toils of the soldiery. The mother,
therefore, being at a loss for herself and daughters, knowing what
dreadful outrages they would suffer from the men, represented
their situation to them, and, above all, the threatened violation
of their chastity, an evil more to be dreaded than any other, to
which neither she nor they should even listen for a moment. At

the same time declaring, that to surrender their souls to the slavery of dæmons was worse than death and destruction.   From all
these, she suggested there was only one way to be delivered, to
betake themselves to the aid of Christ.   After this, all agreeing
to the same thing, and having requested the guards a litt.e tim?
to retire on the way, they decently adjusted their garments, and
cast themselves into the flowing river.   These, then, destroyed
themselves.

Another pair of virgins at this same Antioch, distinguished for
piety, and truly sisters in all respects, illustrious in family, wealth,
youth, and beauty, but no less so for their serious minds, their
pious deportment, and their admirable zeal, as if the earth could
not bear such excellence, were ordered by the worshippers of
dæmons to be thrown into the sea.   Such were the facts that
occurred at Antioch.   Others at Pontus, endured torments that
are too horrible to relate.   Some had their fingers pierced with
sharp reeds thrust under their nails.   Others, having masses of
melted lead, bubbling and boiling with heat, poured down their
backs, and roasted, especially in the most sensitive* parts of the
body.   Others, also, endured insufferable torments on their bowels
and other parts, such as decency forbids to describe, which those
generous and equitable judges, with a view to display their own
cruelty, devised as some pre-eminence in wisdom, worthy their
ambition.   Thus constantly inventing new tortures, they vied
with one another, as if there were prizes proposed in the contest,
who should invent the greatest cruelties.   But as to the last of these
calamities, when the judges now had despaired of inventing any
thing more effectual, and were weary with slaughter, and had
surfeited themselves with shedding of blood, they then applied
themselves to. what they considered kindness and humanity, so
that they seemed disposed to exercise no further cruelty against
us.   For said they, the cities should not be polluted with blood
any more, and the government of the sovereigns which was so
kind and merciful toward all, should not be defamed for exces-

---

* Rufimus translates, or rather paraphrases, with much elegance, Usque ad ,loca
pudenda quibus naturalis egestio procurari solet.

sive cruelty: it was more proper that the benefits afforded by their humane and imperial majesties, should be extended to all, and that we should no longer be punished with death. For we were liberated from this punishment by the great clemency of the emperors. After this, therefore, they were ordered only to tear out our eyes, to deprive us of one of our legs. Such was their kindness, and such the lightest kind of punishment against us; so that in consequence of this humanity of theirs it was impossible to tell the great and incalculable number of those that had their right eye dug out with the sword first, and after this seared with a red hot iron; those too, whose left foot was maimed with a searing iron; after these, those who in different provinces were condemned to the copper mines, not so much for the service as for the contumely and misery they should endure. Many, also, endured conflicts of other kinds, which it would be impossible to detail; for their noble fortitude surpasses all power of description. In this the magnanimous confessors of Christ that shone conspicuous throughout the whole world, every where struck the beholders with astonishment, and presented the obvious proofs of our Saviour's divine interposition in their own persons. And hence, to mention each by name, would be at least a long and tedious work, not to say impossible.

CHAPTER XIII.

*Those prelates that evinced the reality of the religion they pro-
claimed with their blood.*

OF those prelates of the church, however, who suffered martyrdom in the most celebrated cities, the first of which we shall mention, recorded by the pious as a witness of the kingdom of Christ, is Anthimus, bishop of Nicomedia, who was beheaded. Of the martyrs at Antioch, we also name Lucian, that presbyter of this church, who during all his life was pre-eminent for his excellent character and piety. He had before, at Nicomedia, and in the presence of the emperor, proclaimed the heavenly kingdom of Christ, in the defence that he delivered, and afterwards bore testimony to its truth in his actions. Among the martyrs at Phœnice, the most noted of all, were those pious and devoted pastors of the spiritual flocks of Christ, Tyrannio, bishop of the church of Tyre, Zenobius of Sidon, and Silvanus bishop of Emisa. The last of these was cast as food to wild beasts at Emisa, and thus ranked in the number of martyrs, but each of the former glorified the doctrine of God, by suffering with patience until death. The one, the bishop, was committed to the depths of the sea; but Zenobius, the other, a most excellent physician, died with great fortitude under the tortures applied to his sides. But among the martyrs at Palestine, Silvanus, bishop of the churches about Gaza, was beheaded with thirty-nine others at the copper mines of Phœno. Also, those of Egypt there, Peleus and Nilus, who were bishops, suffered death by the flames. Among these must be mentioned the presbyter Pamphilus, a most admirable man of our times, and the glory of the church at Cesarea whose illustrious deeds we have set forth in its proper place. But of those that were prominent as martyrs at Alexandria, all Egypt and Thebais, the first whom we shall mention is Peter, bishop of Alexandria, a man wonderful as a teacher of the Christian faith, and the presbyters with him, Faustus, and Dius, and Ammonius, perfect witnesses* of Christ. Phileas, Pochumius, Hesychius and Theodorus, bishops of churches in Egypt, with many others, are also mentioned as distinguished martyrs, by the

---

* We have translated the word martyrs here, or rather presented its original meaning, as the evident intention of our author. The word in the Greek, from signifying a witness, was applied to those by way of eminence, who by their death gave the most striking evidence of their faith that mortals can give. Such, therefore, were called witnesses emphatically, both in reference to the *truth* to which they witnessed, and the *manner* in which they thus gave their testimony. In this sense our Lord himself is called the "true and faithful witness," (martyr.) Our author here, by attaching the attribute *perfect*, evidently intimates that he means to lay some stress on the meaning of the word martyrs, as witnesses made perfect by their death. The death of these witnesses is, indeed, according to the ecclesiastical phraseology implied in the word *perfect*. It was by death that they were constituted perfect confessors; before that they were regarded only as confessors. This may suffice to explain why we here differ from Valesius and others. See note, Book VI. ch. x.

churches in those places and regions. To give a minute description of the conflict which they endured in the cause of piety, throughout the whole world, and to give a full account of the circumstances respecting each, could not be expected in the present work. This would rather belong to those who were eye-witnesses of the facts. Those, indeed, at which I myself was present, I shall publish for the benefit of posterity in another work.

In the present work, however, I shall, to the abovementioned facts, add the revocation issued by our persecutors, as also those events that occurred at the beginning of the persecution, believing that they will be read not without profit. To tell the state of the Roman empire before the war was waged against us, how long the emperors continued friendly and peaceable towards us, and how great was the abundance and prosperity of the empire, what description would suffice? Then, indeed, those who held the supreme command, who had been at the head of government ten and twenty years, passed their time in festivities and shows, and joyous feasts and entertainments in peace and tranquillity. And in this state of uninterrupted and increasing prosperity and power, they suddenly changed our peaceful condition, and excited against us a most unjust and nefarious war. For scarcely had the second year of this war been passed, when a revolution taking place in the whole government, it was completely overturned. A disease of a most obstinate nature attacked the chief of the abovementioned emperors, by which he was reduced to a state of insanity, together with him that was honoured with the second rank, and thus betook himself to a private life. But these things had been scarcely thus done when the whole empire was divided, a circumstance which, in the annals of history, never happened before, any where. But, it was not long before the emperor Constantius, who was all his life most kindly and favourably disposed towards his subjects, and also most favourably disposed toward the divine word, departed this life, leaving his son Constantine a true copy of himself, as emperor and Augustus, his successor. He was the first of these emperors that was ranked among the gods * by them, having every honour conferred upon him, after death, that was due to an emperor. He was the kindest and mildest of the emperors, and indeed the only one of them in our times, that passed his life consistently with the imperial dignity, and who likewise in all other respects exhibited the greatest condescension and benevolence to all, and had no share in the hostility raised against us, but even preserved and protected those pious persons under him free from harm and calumny. Neither did he demolish the churches, nor devise any other mischief against us, and at length enjoyed a most happy and blessed death, being the only one who, at his death, did peaceably and gloriously leave the government to his own son, as his successor; a prince who in all respects was endowed with the greatest moderation and piety. His son Constantine, therefore, in the very commencement, being proclaimed supreme emperor and Augustus by the soldiers, and much longer before this, by the universal sovereign God, resolved to tread in the footsteps of his father, with respect to our faith. And such, indeed, was he. But Licinius after this was appointed emperor and Augustus, by a common vote of the emperors. Maximinus was greatly offended at this, since he had yet received only the title of Cesar from all. He, therefore, being particularly of a tyrannical temper, arrogating to himself the dignity, was created Augustus by himself. In the mean time, being detected in a conspiracy against the life of Constantine, the same (Maximian) that we have mentioned as having resumed the imperial dignity after his resignation was carried off by a most disgraceful death. And

* This is to be understood of the four emperors then reigning; Diocletian, Maximian, Constantius, and Galerius. It was the custom of the Roman senate to deify the emperors at their death. Our author, without intending to commend the practice, simply states the fact as a proof of the popularity of Constantius; as the honour was not indiscriminately conferred. Otherwise, in regard to this deification, our author, in the midst of his commendations, almost appears a little ironical, upon the practice, how much soever he honoured the memory of Constantius. We are here forcibly reminded of the humorous strife between Æsculapius and Hercules, in Lucian's dialogues, where Jupiter at last decides the dispute about priority, by assigning it to Æsculapius, *because he died first.*

ne was the first of these emperors whose statues and public monuments were demolished as commemorative of an impious and execrable man.

CHAPTER XIV.

The morals of the persecutors.

MAXENTIUS, the son of Maximian, who had established his government at Rome, in the commencement, pretended indeed, by a species of accommodation and flattery towards the Romans, that he was of our faith. He, therefore, commanded his subjects to desist from persecuting the Christians, pretending to piety with a view to appear much more mild and merciful than the former rulers. But he by no means proved to be in his actions such as he was expected. He sunk into every kind of wickedness, leaving no impurity or licentiousness untouched; committing every species of adultery and fornication, separating wives from their lawful husbands, and after abusing these, sending them thus most shamefully violated back again to their husbands. And these things he perpetrated not upon mean and obscure individuals, but insulting more particularly the most prominent of those that were most distinguished in the senate. Whilst he was thus dreaded by all, both people and magistrates, high and low were galled with a most grievous oppression ; and though they bore this severe tyranny quietly, and without rebellion, it produced no relief from his murderous cruelty. On a certain very slight occasion, therefore, he gave up the people to be slaughtered by the prætorian guards, and thus multitudes of the Roman people were slain in the very heart of the city, not with the arrows and spears of Scythians or barbarians, but of their own fellow-citizens. It would be impossible to tell what slaughter was made of the senators merely for the sake of their wealth, thousands being destroyed on a variety of pretexts and fictitious crimes. But when these evils had reached their greatest height, the tyrant was induced to resort to the mummery of magic. At

one time he would cut open pregnant females, at another examin
ing the bowels of new born babes ; sometimes also slaughtering
lions and performing any kind of execrable acts, to invoke the
dæmons, and to avert the impending war. For all his hope now
was that victory would be secured to him by these means. It is
impossible then to say, in what different ways this cruel tyrant
oppressed his subjects, so that they were already reduced to
such extreme want and scarcity, such as they say has never
happened at Rome, or elsewhere in our time. But Maximinus,
who was sovereign of the east, as he had secretly formed an alliance with Maxentius, his true brother in wickedness at Rome,
designed to conceal his designs as long as possible. But being
at length detected, he suffered the deserved punishment. It was
wonderful how nearly allied, and similar, rather how vastly beyond the tyranny of the Roman, were the cruelties and crimes of
this tyrant. The first of impostors and jugglers, were honoured
by him with the highest rank. He became so extremely timo-
rous and superstitious, and valued the delusion and supposed influence of dæmons above all, so that he was hardly able to move
his finger, one might say, or undertake any thing without sooth-
sayers and oracles. Hence, also, he assailed us with a more violent and incessant persecution than those before him. He ordered
temples to be erected in every city, and those that had been demolished by time, he commanded in his zeal to be renewed.
Priests of the idols he established in every place and city ; and
over these a high priest in every province, some one of those
who had been particularly distinguished for his skill in the management of political affairs, adding a military guard. He
granted to all his jugglers the same reverence as if they were
the most pious and acceptable to the gods, freely bestowing on
them governments, and the greatest privileges.

And from this time forth he began to vex, not merely a single
city or region, but harassed all the provinces under him, by ex-
actions of silver and gold and money, by the most oppressive
seizures and confiscations of property, in different ways and on
various pretexts. Despoiling the wealthy of the substance in-
herited from their fathers, he bestowed vast wealth, and heaps

of money upon the flatterers around him. And he had now advanced to such a pitch of rashness, and was so addicted to intoxication, that, in his drunken frolics he was frequently deranged and deprived of his reason, like a madman; so that what he commanded when he was intoxicated, he afterwards regretted when he became sober. But determined to leave no one his superior in surfeiting and gluttony, he presented himself a fit master of iniquity to the rulers and subjects around him. Initiating the soldiers, by luxury and intemperance, into every species of dissipation and revelling, encouraging the governors and generals, by rapacity and avarice, to proceed with their oppressions against their subjects, with almost the power of associate tyrants. Why should I mention the degrading and foul lust of the man? Or why mention his innumerable adulteries? There was not a city that he passed through in which he did not commit violence upon females. And in these he succeeded against all but the Christians. For they, despising death, valued his power but little.

The men bore fire, sword, and crucifixions, savage beasts, and the depths of the sea, the maiming of limbs, and searing with red hot iron, pricking and digging out the eyes, and the mutilations of the whole body. Also hunger, and mines, and prisons; and after all, they chose these sufferings for the sake of religion, rather than transfer that veneration and worship to idols which is due to God only. The females, also, no less than the men, were strengthened by the doctrine of the divine word; so that some endured the same trials as the men, and bore away the same prizes of excellence. Some, when forced away, yielded up their lives rather than submit to the violation of their bodies.

The tyrant having fully gratified his lust on others at Alexandria, his unbridled passion was defeated by the heroic firmness of one female only, who was one of the most distinguished and illustrious at Alexandria, and she was a Christian. She was in other respects distinguished both for her wealth, and family, and condition, but esteemed all inferior to modesty. Having frequently made attempts to bring her over to his purposes, though she was prepared to die, he could not destroy her, as his passion was stronger than his anger; but, punishing her with exile, he took away all her wealth. Many others, also, unable to bear even the threats of violation from the rulers of the heathen, sub mitted to every kind of torture, the rack and deadly punishment. Admirable, indeed, were all these; but far above all most admir- able, was that lady who was one of the most noble and modest of those whom Maxentius, in all respects like Maximinus, at- tempted to violate. For when she understood that the minions of the tyrant in such matters, had burst into the house (for she was also a Christian), and that her husband, who was the prefect of Rome, had suffered them to carry her off, she requested but a little time, as if now for the purpose of adorning her body : she then entered her chamber, and when alone thrust a sword into her breast. Thus, dying immediately, she indeed left her body to the conductors; but in her deeds, more effectually than any language, proclaims, to all who are now and will be hereafter, that virtue, which prevails among Christians, is the only invinci- ble and imperishable possession. Such, then, was the flood of iniquity which rushed on at one and the same time, and which was wrought by the two tyrants that swayed the east and the west. And who is there that examines the cause of these evils, that would be in doubt whether he should pronounce the persecution raised against us, proceeding from these as their cause? Espe- cially as the confusion of the empire, which prevailed to a great extent, did not cease before the Christians received full liberty of conscience to profess their religion?

CHAPTER XV.

The events that happened to the heathen.

During the whole ten years of the persecution, there was no cessation of plots and civil wars among the persecutors them- selves. For the sea indeed was impassable to the mariner, nor could any set sail from any part, without being exposed to every kind of torment, either scourged, or racked in their limbs, or lacerated and galled with torturing instruments in their sides, to ascertain whether they had come from the enemy of the opposite party, and at last were subjected either to the punishment of the cross or of fire. Besides these things, one saw every where shields and coats of mail preparing, darts and javelins and other implements of war; and in every place, also, were collections of galleys and naval armour. Neither was there any thing expected any where but the attacks of enemies from day to day. Besides this, famine and pestilence were superadded, of which we shall relate what is most important in its proper place.

CHAPTER XVI.

The change of affairs for the better.

Such was the state of things throughout the whole period of the persecution. This, by the goodness of God, had entirely ceased in the tenth year, although it had already begun to relax after the eighth. For when the kindness of God's providence regarded us again with a gracious and merciful eye, then indeed our rulers, and those very persons who were formerly the principal agents of the persecutions, most remarkably changed in their sentiments, began to recant, and attempted to extinguish the blaze of persecution kindled against us by mild proclamations and ordinances. But this was not done by any mere human agency, nor was it, as might perhaps be supposed, by the compassion or the humanity of our rulers. For, so far from this, they were daily devising more and severer measures against us from the beginning of the persecution until then, constantly inventing new tortures from time to time by an increasing variety of machinery and instruments for this purpose. But the evident superintendence of divine Providence, on the one hand, being reconciled to his people, and on the other assailing the author of these miseries, exhibited his anger against him as the ringleader in the horrors of the whole persecution. Though it had been necessary that these things should occur by some divine judgment, yet it is

declared, " Wo to him through whom the offence cometh.'
Hence he was visited by a judgment sent from God, which beginning in his flesh proceeded to his very soul. For a sudden
tumor appeared about the middle of the body, then a spongy
fistula in these parts,* which continued to extend and penetrate
with its ulcerations to the inmost parts of the bowels. Hence
sprung an immense multitude of worms, hence also an insufferable death-like effluvia exhaled, as his whole body before his disease, by reason of his gluttony, had been changed into an excessive mass of fat, which then becoming putrid, exhibited a dreadful and intolerable spectacle to those that drew near. Some,
indeed, of the physicians, totally unable to endure the excessively
offensive smell, were slain ; others again, as the swelling had penetrated every where, and they unable to give any relief, despaired of safety, and were put to death without mercy.

CHAPTER XVII.

The revocation of the emperors.

THUS struggling with so many miseries, he had some com
punctions for the crimes that he had committed against the
pious. Turning, therefore, his reflections upon himself, first of all
he confessed his sin to the supreme God, then summoning his
officers, he immediately orders that, without delay, they should
stop the persecution against the Christians, and by an imperial
ordinance and decree, commanded that they should hasten to rebuild the churches, that they might perform their accustomed
devotions, and offer up prayers for the emperor's safety. This
decree was immediately followed by its effects ; the imperial decrees were published in the cities, embracing the following revocation with regard to us.

---

* Valesius renders, Repente enim circa media occultiorum corporis partium loca
ibscessus ei nascitur : ulcus deinde in imo fistulosum.

The Emperor Cesar Galerius Valerius Maximianus, Invictus, Augustus, Pontifex Maximus, Germanicus Maximus, Ægyptiacus Maximus, Thebaicus Maximus, Sarmaticus Maximus, the fifth time Persicus Maximus, second time Carpicus Maximus, sixth time Armeniacus Maximus, Medicus Maximus, Adiabenicus Maximus, Tribune of the People XX. Emperor XIX. Consul VIII. Father of his country, Proconsul : and the Emperor Cesar Flavius, Valerius Constantinus, Pius, Felix, Invictus, Augustus, Pontifex Maximus, Tribune of the People, and Emperor V. Consul, Father of his country, Proconsul : also, the Emperor Cesar Valerius Licinianus, Pius, Felix, Invictus, Augustus; Pontifex, Maximus, Tribune of the People IV. Emperor III. Consul, Pater Patriæ, Proconsul ; to their subjects in the provinces, send greeting :

Among* other matters which we have devised for the benefit and common advantage of our people, we have first determined to restore all things according to the ancient laws and the public institutions,† of the Romans. And to make provision for this, that also the Christians, who have left the religion of their fathers, should return again to a good purpose and resolution. For by some means,‡ such arrogance had overtaken and such stupidity had beset them, that they would not follow the principles an-

---

* This edict, as Eusebius tells us below, he translated from the Latin, and had ne not mentioned it, it could be inferred from the style and phraseology ; as the Latin idiom appears more than once. The very beginning is calculated to make this impression.

† The word ιπιϛτημην, here occurring, is very ambiguous. We suspected at first, our author had before him *ex sententia Romani populi*, or perhaps *plebiscitum*, of which δημοσια επιϛτημην, might serve as a literal translation, though not very intelli gible. After writing this conjecture, however, we examined the Latin edict preserved by Lanctantius, and find the original was *disciplinam*.

‡ We suspect the Latin here was *quadam ratione*, which our author has translated τινι λογισμω, by *a certain mode of reasoning*. Valesius seems to have overlooked the Latin idiom as well as the Greek, and rendered *quodam consensu*. But Eusebius appears to have mistaken *quadam ratione*, and translated into the Greek accordingly. What confirms our conjecture is, that the edict does not ascribe any thing like reason to the Christians, but imputes their conduct to some stupid infatuation.

This note was written before we examined the Latin copy of the edict in Lanctantius.

ciently prescribed to them, which in all probability their ancestors had established, but they began to make and follow laws, each one according to his own purpose and his own will, and thus different multitudes assembled with different opinions and of different sects.   Hence, when a decree of this kind was issued by us, that they should return again to the established usages of their forefathers, vast numbers were subjected to danger, many, when threatened, endured various kinds of death.   But though we saw the great mass still persevering in their folly, and that they neither gave the honour that was due to the immortal gods, nor heeded that of the Christians, still having a regard to our clemency and our invariable practice, according to which we are wont to grant pardon to all, we most cheerfully have resolved to extend our indulgence in this matter also: that there may oe Christians again, and that they may restore their houses in which they were accustomed to assemble, so that nothing be done by them contrary to their profession.   In another epistle we shall point out to the judges, what they will be required to observe; whence, according to this condescension of ours, they are obligated to implore their God for our safety, as well as that of the people and their own.   That in every place the public welfare may be preserved, and they may live unmolested in their respective homes and fire-hearths.

Such was the purport of this ordinance, which, according to our ability, we have translated from the Latin into the Greek.*   But the affairs after this we are now farther to consider.

---

* Since writing the above notes, we have compared the original Latin edict, which is still preserved in Lanctantius, " *de mortibus persecutorum.*"   Our conjectures, as it regards style and phraseology, we have found considerably confirmed by this comparison.   The Latinity, however, of the edict itself, savours of the degeneracy of the day.   It is surprising, that neither Valesius nor his translator Shorting, has noticed the edict as preserved by Lanctantius.   And yet the former has struck upon the signification of ἐπιστημη, occurring twice in this edict.

[*In some copies, this is appended to the eighth Book.**]

BUT the author of this edict after this acknowledgment, soon
after was liberated from his pains, and terminated his life. It is
agreed he was the original cause of the miseries of the persecution, as he had long before the movements of the other emperors,
attempted to seduce the Christian soldiers of his own house from
their faith, degrading some from their military rank, and insulting
others in the most abusive manner, even punishing some with death,
and at last exciting his associate emperors to a general persecution
against all. Nor have I thought proper, that the death of these
emperors should be passed over in silence. As there were four,
therefore, that held the sovereignty divided among them, those
that were advanced in years and honours, after nearly two years
from the persecution, abdicated the government, as we have
already shown; and thus passing their days in common and retired life, ended their life in the following manner.—The one,
indeed, who preceded the others in honour and age, was at
length overpowered by a long and distressing disease, but the
next to him in dignity destroyed himself by strangling, suffering thus according to certain dæmoniacal prognostics, on account of the innumerable crimes that he had committed. But
of the two after these, the last, whom we have mentioned as the
leader of the whole persecution, suffered such things as we have
already stated. But he that surpassed them all in kindness and
condescension, the emperor Constantius, who had conducted his
government the whole time consistently with the imperial dignity, and who exhibited himself a most gracious and benevolent
prince in other respects, also, had no hand in raising the perse
cution against us, but even protected and patronised those pious
persons that were under him. He neither demolished the buildings of the churches, nor devised any thing in opposition to us;

* The two sections that here follow, are regarded as supplementary to the work.
The first being an Appendix to the eighth Book, and the following one a preliminary
to the Book of Martyrs. The statements at the head of each are from some of
the copyists, as they are found in the most appro d manuscripts.

and finally enjoyed a death really happy and blessed, being the only one of the four that in the midst of a tranquil and glorious reign, at his death, transmitted the government to his own son as his successor, a prince most eminent in all respects for his wisdom and piety.   He, at the very beginning, was proclaimed supreme emperor and Augustus, by the armies, and exhibited himself a generous rival of his father's piety, with regard to us. Such then, was the issue of the life of the four emperors, at different times.   Of these the only one that yet left the abovementined confession, was he whom we mentioned above, together with those whom he had afterwards associated with him in the government, which confession also, he sent abroad in his proclamation to all.

The following we also found appended to the eighth Book.

THIS was the eighth year of the reign of Diocletian, in the month of Xanthicus, which one would call April according to the Romans, about the time when the paschal festival of our Saviour took place, when Flavianus was governor of Palestine. Suddenly edicts were published every where to raze the churches to the ground, and to destroy the sacred Scriptures in the flames, to strip those that were in honour of their dignities, and to deprive the freedmen of their liberty if any persisted in the Christian profession.   Such was the first violence of this edict against us; but it was not long before other mandates were issued, in which it was ordered that the prelates of the churches should first be cast into prison everywhere, and then compelled by every artifice to offer the sacrifice.

THE BOOK OF MARTYRS.

CHAPTER I.

Procopius, Alpheus, and Zaccheus.

THE first, therefore, of the martyrs of Palestine, was Procopius, who, before he was tried by imprisonment, was immediately at the beginning arraigned before the tribunal of the governor. When commanded to sacrifice to those called gods, he declared that he knew but one, to whom it was proper to sacrifice, as He himself had commanded ; but when he was ordered to make libations to the four emperors, he uttered a sentence which did not please them, and was immediately beheaded. The sentence was from the poet: "A plurality of sovereigns is not good, let there be but one prince and one sovereign Lord."* This happened on the eighth of the month Desius, or as one would say with the Romans, the seventh before the Ides† of June, the fourth day of the week. This was the first signal that was given at Cesarea in Palestine. After him many bishops in the same city, of the provincial churches, cheerfully struggled with dreadful tortures, and exhibited noble specimens of mighty conflicts. Some indeed, from excessive dread, broken down and overpowered by their terrors, sunk and gave way immediately at the first onset. but each of the rest experienced various kinds of torture. Some were scourged with innumerable strokes of the lash, others racked in their limbs and galled in their sides with torturing instruments, some with intolerable fetters, by which the joints of their

---

* The words of Ulysses, in the Iliad, book ii. line 208. Ουκ αγαθον πολυκοιρανιη. Sentences from Homer were among the proverbs of the day. The same passage was on a certain occasion repeated by Domitian. See his Life by Suetonius, ch. 13.

† The Romans had three divisions of the month, Calends, Nones, and Ides, and in marking the days they counted backwards. For the days given here, see any tabular view of the Roman calendar.

hands were dislocated. Nevertheless they bore the event, as regulated by the secret determinations of God. One was seized by the hands, and led to the altar by others who were thrusting the polluted and unhallowed victim into his right hand, and then suffered to go again as if he had sacrificed. Another, though he had not even touched, when others said that he had sacrificed, went away in silence. Another was taken up half dead, and cast out as already dead, and was released from his bonds, and ranked among the sacrificers. Another crying out, and asserting that he did not assent to these things, was struck on the mouth; and thus silenced by the many blows of those that were suborned for this purpose, was thrust away by violence, although he had never sacrificed. So much was it valued by them, for one upon the whole only to appear to have performed their desire. Of these therefore, so many in number, only Alpheus* and Zaccheus were honoured with the crown of the holy martyrs, who after scourging and scraping with iron hooks, and severe bonds, and the tortures consequent on these, and other different tortures on the rack, having their feet stretched a night and day, to the fourth hole of the stocks, were at length beheaded on the seventeenth day of the month Dius, the same that is called the fifteenth of the Calends of December. Thus for confessing the only God and Jesus Christ the only king, they suffered martyrdom with the former martyr, just as if they had uttered some dreadful blasphemy.

CHAPTER II.

The martyr Romanus.

WORTHY of record, also, are the circumstances respecting Romanus, which occurred on the same day at Antioch. He was a

* The names of some of these martyrs are to be found in some of the old calendars. Thus Alpheus is found on the 17th of November, corresponding to the date here given. Others may be found in the same way. The names of some have in the lapse of time given way to others.

native of Palestine, a deacon and exorcist, of the church at Ce
sarea, and was present at the demolition of the churches there,
and as he saw many men with women and children approaching
the idols in masses, and sacrificing, considering the sight intolerable, and stimulated by a zeal for religion, he cried out with a
loud voice, and reproved them. But he was immediately seized
for his boldness, and proved, if any, to be a most noble witness of
the truth. When the judge had informed him that he was to die
by the flames, with a cheerful countenance and a most ardent
mind, he received the sentence, and was led away. He was then
tied to the stake, and when the wood was heaped up around him,
and they were about kindling the pile, only awaiting the word from
the expected emperor, he exclaimed, " where then is the fire ?"
Saying this, he was summoned again before the emperor, to be subjected to new tortures, and therefore had his tongue cut out, which
he bore with the greatest fortitude, as he proved in his actions to
all, showing also that the power of God is always present to the
aid of those who are obliged to bear any hardship for the sake
of religion, to lighten their labours, and to strengthen their ardour. When, therefore, he learned the novel mode of punishment,
the heroic man by no means alarmed, readily thrust out his
tongue and offered it with the greatest alacrity to those who cut
out. After this he was cast into bonds, and having suffered there
a very long time, at length when the twentieth anniversary of the
emperor was at hand, according to an established usage of
granting liberty every where to those that were kept in prison, he
alone had his feet stretched to the fifth hole in the stocks, lying
upon the very wood with a halter round his neck, was adorned
with martyrdom, according to his earnest desire. This one,
though he suffered beyond his country, yet as a native of Palestine deserved to be ranked among the martyrs of Palestine.
These were the events that occurred of this description in the
first year of the persecution, as it was then excited only against
the prelates of the church.

CHAPTER III.

Timotheus, Agapius, Thecla, and eight others.

In the course of the second year, when the war was blazing
more violently against us, when Urbanus had the government of
the province, imperial edicts were first issued to him, in which it
was ordered by a general command, that all persons of every
people and city should sacrifice and make libations to the idols.
Timotheus, at Gaza, a city of Palestine, endured a multitude of
tortures, and after the rest was condemned to be consumed by a
slow and gentle fire, exhibiting in all his sufferings a most indubit-
able proof of his sincere devotedness to God, and thus bore away
the crown of those holy wrestlers who triumphed in the cause
of piety. At the same time with him were condemned to be
cast to the wild beasts, Agapius, who displayed the noblest
firmness in his confession, and Thecla, our contemporary.* But
who could help being struck with admiration and astonishment
at the sight, or even at the very recital of those things that then
occurred ? For, as the heathen in every place were on the point
of celebrating their accustomed games and festivals, it was much
noised abroad, that besides the other exhibitions with which they
were so greatly captivated, those that were just condemned to
the wild beasts would exhibit a combat. This report being increased, and spreading among all, there were six young men,
who, first binding their hands, hastened with all speed to Urbanus, to prove their great alacrity to endure martyrdom, who was
then going to the amphitheatre, and declared themselves Christians. The names of these were Timolaus, a native of Pontus,
Dionysius of Tripolis in Phœnice, Romulus a subdeacon of the
church at Diospolis, Paesis and Alexander, both Egyptians;
another Alexander from Gaza. These, by their great promptness in the face of all terrors, proved that they gloried in the

---

* Eusebius seems to add " our contemporary," to distinguish this Thecla from
the companion of St. Paul, mentioned by the Greek and Latin fathers

worship of the true God, and were not alarmed at the assaults of beasts of prey; and, indeed, both the governor and those around him were amazed. They were, however, immediately committed to prison. Not many days after, two others were added to their number, of whom one had already before sustained the conflict of confession several times, under a variety of dreadful torments; he was, also, called Agapius, but the other who supplied them with the necessaries of life, was named Dionysius. All these, eight in number, were beheaded in one day at Cesarea, on the twenty-third day of the month Dystrus, that is, the ninth of the calends of April. In the mean time, a certain change took place with the emperors, the first and the second in the imperial dignity retiring to private life, and public affairs began to wear a troubled aspect. Shortly after, the Roman empire was divided, and a dreadful civil war arose among the Romans themselves; nor did the schism cease, nor the consequent commotions become finally settled, before peace was proclaimed toward us throughout the whole Roman world. For as soon as this arose like a light upon all, springing up from the densest and most gloomy night, the government was again restored to firmness, tranquillity, and peace, and they resumed that benevolent disposition towards one another, which they had derived from their ancestors. But of these matters we shall give a more full account in its proper place. Now let us pursue the thread of our narrative in due order.

CHAPTER IV.

Apphianus.

Maximinus Cesar, who was afterwards raised to the government, as if to exhibit the evidences of his innate hatred to God and his aversion to piety, armed himself to persecute with greater violence than those before him. Hence, as there was no little confusion raised among all, some scattered here and others there, and endeavouring by all means to escape the danger; and as there was the greatest tumult throughout the empire, what description would suffice to give a faithful account of that divine love and that freedom of confession, that distinguished the martyr Apphianus, that blessed and truly innocent lamb? He was scarcely twenty years old, when he presented a wonderful instance of solid piety toward the one only God, as a kind of spectacle to all before the gates of Cesarea. And first when for the purpose of pursuing Greek literature, as he was of a very wealthy family, he passed the most of his time at Berytus, it is wonderful to tell how in the midst of such a city, notwithstanding the enticements of youthful passions, he was superior to all, and was neither corrupted in his morals by the vigour of his body, nor his association with young men, but embraced a modest and sober life, walking honestly and piously, and regulating his conversation as one who had embraced the Christian faith. Were it necessary to mention his country, and thus to celebrate the place that gave birth to so noble a wrestler in the cause of religion, we shall cheerfully do also this. Pagas, a city of Lycia, of no mean account, and which may be known to some of my readers, was the place whence this youth derived his origin. After his return from his studies at Berytus, though his father held the first rank in his country, being unable to bear dwelling with his father and the rest of his kindred, because they did not approve of living according to the laws of piety, as if impelled by the divine Spirit and by a kind of natural, rather say an inspired and genuine, philosophy, deeming it better than what is considered glory in life, and despising the soft pleasures of the body, he secretly fled from his friends. And without any concern for his daily expenses, in his trust and faith in God, he was conducted as if led by the Holy Spirit, to the city of Cesarea, where was prepared for him the crown of martyrdom, for his piety. Having associated with us there, and having studied the holy Scriptures as much as could be for a short time, and having prepared himself most cheerfully by the proper exercises and discipline, he finally made so illustrious an end, as could not be witnessed again without amazement.

Who could listen without wonder to the freedom with which

he spoke, behold his firmness, and before this, the courage and the energy of this youth, who gave evidence of a zeal for piety and a spirit more than human? For when a second excite ment was raised against us by Maximinus, in the third year of the persecution, and the edicts of the tyrant, to this effect were first issued, that all persons every where should publicly offer sacrifices, and that the rulers of the cities should see to this with all care and diligence, when the heralds also were proclaiming throughout all Cesarea, that men women and children should come to the temples of the idols, at the command of the gover nor; and moreover, the military tribunes were calling upon each one by name, from a list, and the heathen were rushing in an immense crowd from every quarter, this youth fearlessly and with out imparting his purpose to any, stealing away from us who dwelt in the same house, and unobserved by the military band around the governor, approached Urbanus who happened then to be making libations. Fearlessly seizing his right hand, he sud denly interrupted him in the act of sacrificing. Then he coun selled and exhorted him in a solemn and serious tone to abandon his error, saying it was not right that we should desert the one only and true God, to sacrifice to idols and dæmons. This was done by the youth, as is very probable, under the impulse of a divine power, which by this deed gave a kind of audible testi mony, that the Christians, those to wit that were really such, were so far from abandoning the religion which they had once embraced, that they were not only superior to all the threatened dangers, and the punishments consequent on these; but over and above this, acted with still greater freedom, and declared them selves with a noble and fearless utterance, and were it possible that their persecutors could be delivered from their ignorance, even exhorted them to acknowledge the one only and true God. After this, he of whom we are now speaking, as might be ex pected in the case of an act so daring, was immediately seized and torn by the soldiers like ravenous beasts, and after suffering most heroically innumerable stripes on his whole body, was cast into prison until further orders. There, being stretched by the ormentor with both feet a night and day, on the rack, he was the next day brought to the judge, and when force was applied to make him sacrifice, he exhibited an invincible fortitude in bearing pain and horrid tortures. His sides were not only once or twice, but often furrowed and scraped to the very bones and bowels, and at the same time he was beaten with so many blows on the face and neck, that by reason of his bruised and swollen face, he was no more recognised by those who had known him well. But as he did not yield even to this, they covered his feet with linen steeped in oil, and at the command of the governor the tormentors applied fire to these. The sufferings which this blessed youth then endured, seems to me to exceed all power of description. The fire, after consuming his flesh, penetrated to the bones, so that the humours of the body, liquefied like wax, fell in drops; but as he did not yield even to this, his antagonists being defeated, and now only at a loss to account for his more than human perseverance, he was again committed to prison. At last he was summoned the third day before the judge again, and still declaring his fixed purpose in the profession of Christ, already half dead, he was thrown into the sea and drowned.

What happened immediately after this, would scarcely be credited by any who had not seen with his own eyes. But notwithstanding this, we cannot but record the events, as we may say, all the inhabitants of Cesarea were witnesses of the fact. There was no age that was not present at this wonderful sight As soon as this really blessed and holy youth was cast into the deepest parts of the sea, suddenly a roaring and uncommon crashing sound, pervaded not only the sea but the whole surrounding heavens. So that the earth and the whole city was shaken by it. And at the same time with this wonderful and sudden shaking, the body of the divine martyr was cast by the sea before the gates of the city, as if unable to bear it. And such was the martyrdom of the excellent Apphianus, on the second day of the month Xanthicus, or, Roman style, the fourth of the nones of April, on the day of the preparation, or Friday.

CHAPTER V.

The martyrs Ulpian and Ædesius.

But about the same time, and in those very days, there was a young man named Ulpianus, at the city of Tyre, who also, after dreadful torments, and the most severe scourgings, was sown in a raw bull's hide, together with a dog and poisonous asp, and thrown into the sea. Hence, also, he appears deservedly to claim a place among the martyrdoms noticed with Apphianus. A short time after, very much the same sufferings were endured by Ædesius, who was the own brother of Apphianus, not only in the flesh but in God, after innumerable confessions, and protracted torments in bonds, after being repeatedly condemned by the judges to the mines in Palestine, and after a life and conversation, in which, amid all these circumstances, his garb and his deportment was that of a philosopher. He had, also, enjoyed an education sti' more finished than his brother, and had studied the different branches of philosophy. When he saw the judge at Alexandria, condemning the Christians there, and rioting beyond all bounds, sometimes insulting grave and decent men in various ways, sometimes consigning females of the greatest modesty, and virgins who had devoted themselves to the duties of religion, to panders, to endure every kind of abuse and obscenity, on seeing this he made an attempt similar to that of his brother. As these things appeared insufferable, he drew near with determined resolution to the judge, and with his words and acts covered him with shame. For this he courageously endured multiplied forms of torment, and was finally honoured with his brother's death, and cast into the sea. But this, as I before said, happened in the way here related, a short time after the death of the former

CHAPTER VI.

The martyr Agapius.

But in the fourth year of the persecution, on the twelltn ᴏɪ ᴜɪe calends of December, which would be on the twentieth of the month of Dius, on the day before the Sabbath, Friday, in the same city of Cesarea, occurred what was eminently worthy of record. This happened in the presence of the tyrant Maximinus, who was gratifying the multitudes with public shows, on the day that was called his birthday. As it was an ancient practice when the emperors were present, to exhibit splendid shows then, if at any time, and for the greater amusement of the spectators, to collect new and strange sights, in place of those customary; either animals from some parts of India, Ethiopia, or elsewhere; sometimes, also, men who, by artificial dexterities of the body, exhibited singular spectacles of adroitness, and to complete the whole, as it was an emperor that exhibited the spectacles at this time, it was necessary to have something more than common and singular, in the preparation of these games; (and what then should this be?) one of our martyrs was led forth into the arena to endure the contest for the one and only true religion. This was Agapius, who we have already said had been thrown, together with Thecla, to the wild beasts. After being paraded with malefactors, from the prison to the stadium, already a third time and often, and after various threats from the judges, whether through compassion, or out of hope of changing his purpose, had been deferred from time to time for other contests; at length, when the emperor was present he was led forth. As if he hac been designedly reserved for that time, and that also the declaration of our Saviour might be fulfilled, which he declared to his disciples in his divine foreknowledge, that they would be led before kings, for the sake of confessing him. He was brought, therefore, into the stadium, with a certain criminal, who they said was charged with killing his master. This latter one then, the murderer, when cast to the beasts, was honoured with cle mercy and mercy, not unlike the manner in which Barnabas was in our Saviour's time. Hence the whole theatre resounded with applauses, that the blood-stained homicide was so humanely saved by the emperor, and was moreover honoured with liberty and dignity. But this wrestler of piety was first summoned by the tyrant, then demanded to renounce his purpose with the promise of liberty. With a loud voice he declared, that he would cheerfully and with pleasure sustain whatever he might inflict on him ; not indeed, for any wickedness, but for his veneration of the God of the universe. Saying this, he combined actions with his words, and rushing against a bear let loose upon him, he most readily offered himself to be devoured by the beast, after which he was taken up yet breathing, and carried to prison. Surviving yet one day, he had stones bound to his feet, and thus was plunged into the midst of the sea. Such then was the martyrdom of Agapius.

CHAPTER VII.

The martyrs Theodosia, Domninus, and Auxentius.

THE persecution had now been extended to the fifth year, when on the second of the month Xanthicus, that is the fourth of the nones of April, on the very day of our Lord's resurrection, again at Cesarea a virgin of Tyre, Theodosia by name, not yet eighteen years old, but distinguished for her faith and virtue, approached some prisoners, confessors of the kingdom of Christ, seated before the judgment seat, with a view to salute them, and as is probable, with a view to entreat them to remember her when they should come before the Lord. Whilst she was doing this, as if it were some impious and atrocious deed, she was seized by the soldiers, and led away to the commander. Presently, merciless and savage as he was, he had her tortured with dreadful and horrific cruelties, furrowing her sides and breasts with instruments even to the very bones, and whilst yet breathing, and with all exhibiting a cheerful and joyous countenance, he orders her to be cast into the sea. Proceeding next from her to the other confessors, he consigned them all to the mines at Phœno in Palestine. After this, on the fifth of the month Dius, on the nones of November, Roman style, in the same city, Silvanus, who was yet a presbyter, became a confessor, and not long after he was both honoured with the episcopate, and finally crowned with martyrdom. The same judge condemned those who exhibited the noblest firmness in the cause of piety, to labour in the same mines, having first ordered their ancles to be disabled by searing with red hot irons. At the same time that this sentence was passed, he ordered one who had rendered himself illustrious on innumerable occasions of confession, to be committed to the flames. This was Domninus, well known to all in Palestine, for his great freedom. After which, this judge, who was a terrible inventor of miseries, and particularly ingenious in new devices against the doctrine of Christ, planned torments against the Christians, such as had never before been heard of. He condemned three to pugilistic combat; but Anxentius, a grave and holy presbyter, he ordered to be cast to the beasts, others who had reached the age of maturity, he made eunuchs, and condemned them to the mines; others again, after dreadful tortures, he cast into prison. Among these was Pamphilus that dearest* of my friends and associates, a man who for every virtue was the most illustrious martyr of our times. Urbanus having first made trial of his skill in the art of rhetoric, and the studies of philosophy, after this attempted to force him to offer sacrifice. When he saw him refusing, and not even regarding his threats, at last becoming transported with rage, he orders him to be tortured with more excruciating pains. Then this monster in cruelty obstinately and incessantly applied the instruments, to furrow and lacerate his sides, all but entering and feeding upon his very flesh, and yet after all, defeated and covered with shame, he committed likewise him to those confessors in prison. But what

---

* This is the Pamphilus from whom Eusebius obtained the surname of Pamphilus. This, however, should not be understood as a surname, but as an appellation indicative of attachment to his friend. It should be written in its original, Ευσεβι Παμφιλου, Eusebius, the friend of Pamphilus; φιλος being understood

kind of return this tormentor will receive at the hands of divine justice, for his cruelties against the saints, and after rioting to such extent against the confessors of Christ, is easy to conjecture from the preludes to these judgments here.   For immediately after his crimes against Pamphilus, whilst he held the government, the divine justice suddenly overtook him, thus.   That man whom we but yesterday saw judging on a lofty seat, and surrounded by a guard of soldiers, and ruling over all Palestine, and the associate, and favourite, and guest of the tyrant, stripped in a single night, and divested of all his honours, and covered with disgrace and ignominy, before those who had courted him as the emperor himself, him we saw timid and cowardly uttering cries and entreaties like a woman before all the people, whom he had ruled.   The same just providence also made that very Maximinus upon whom he so boastingly relied, as if he loved him exceedingly for his dreadful deeds against us ; him I say, in the same city, the justice of God erected into a most relentless and cruel judge, who pronounced sentence of death against him, after the numerous crimes of which he was convicted.   But let this account of him suffice, by the way. Perhaps a suitable occasion may offer, in which we shall also relate the end of those wicked men that were principally concerned in waging war against us, and also of Maximinus himself, together with those of his ministers in this work.

<hr />

CHAPTER VIII.

Other confessors; also Valentina and Paulus.

WHEN the storm had incessantly raged against us into the sixth year, there had been before this a vast number of confessors of true religion in what is called the Porphyry quarry, from the name of the stone which is found in Thebais.   Of these, one hundred, wanting three, men, women, and young infants, were sent to the governor of Palestine, who, for confessing the supreme God and Christ, had the ancles and sinews of their left legs seared off with a red hot iron. Besides this they had their right eyes first cut out, together with the lids and pupils, and then seared with red hot iron, so as to destroy the eye to the very roots. All this was done by the order of Firmilianus, who was sent thither as suc cessor to Urbanus, and acted in obedience to the imperial com mand. After this he committed them to the mines in Palestine, to drag out a miserable existence in constant toil and oppressive labour.

Nor was it enough, that those who endured such miseries were deprived of their eyes, but those natives of Palestine, also, whom we have already mentioned as condemned to pugilistic combats, as they neither would suffer themselves to be supported from the imperial treasury, nor undergo the exercises preparatory to the combat, hence they were now brought, not only before the governors, but before Maximinus himself, where, displaying the noblest firmness in their confessions, by enduriug hunger and stripes, they suffered finally the same that the former did, with the addition of other confessors from the same city. Immediately after these, others were seized, who had assembled in the city of Gaza to hear the holy Scriptures read, some of whom suffered the same mutilations in their eyes and feet; others were obliged to endure still greater sufferings, by having their sides furrowed and scraped in the most dreadful manner. Of these, one who was a female in sex, but a man in reason, not enduring the threat of violation, and having used a certain expression against the tyrant, for committing the government to such cruel judges, she was first scourged, then raised on high on the rack, was lacerated and galled in the sides. But as those who were appointed for this incessantly and vehemently applied the tortures according to the orders of the judge, another woman who, like the former, had contemplated a life of perpetual virginity, though ordinary in bodily form, and common in appearance, yet possessing a mind otherwise firm, and an understanding superior to her sex, was unable to bear the merciless, cruel, and inhuman scene before her, and with a courage exceeding all the far-famed combatants among the Greeks for their liberty, she exclaimed against the judge, from the midst of the crowd, " And how long, then, will you thus cruelly torture my sister ?" He, the more bitterly incensed by this, ordered the woman immediately to be seized. She was then dragged into the midst, and after she had called herself by the august name of our Saviour, attempts were first made to bring her over to sacrifice by persuasion. But when she refused, she was dragged to the altar by force. But her sister remaining the same, and still adhering to her purpose, with a resolute, intrepid step, she kicked the altar, and over-turned all on it, together with the fire. Upon this, the judge, ex-asperated, like a savage beast, applied tortures beyond all that he had done before, all but glutting himself with her very flesh, by the wounds and lacerations of her body. But when his mad-ness was gratified to satiety, he bound her and the former, whom she called sister, together, and condemned them to the flames. The former of these was said to be of Gaza, but the other, Valen-tina by name, was a native of Cesarea, and well known to many. But how could I sufficiently describe the martyrdom that followed this, and with which the most blessed Paulus was crowned ? Who, indeed, was condemned at the same time with these, under one and the same sentence of death. About the time of his ex-ecution, he requested of the executioner, who was on the point of cutting off his head, to allow him a short space of time, which being granted, with a loud and clear voice, he first interceded with God in his prayers, imploring pardon for his fellow-christians, and earnestly entreating that peace and liberty might be soon granted them. Then he prayed for the conversion of the Jews to God through Christ. Then he proceeded, in order, imploring the same things for the Samaritans, and those Gentiles who were in error and ignorance of God, that they might come to his know-ledge, and be led to adopt the true religion, not omitting, or neglecting, to include the mixed multitude that stood around. After all these, oh, the great and inexpressible forbearance ! he prayed for the judge that condemned him to death, for the im-perial rulers themselves, and for him, too, that was about to sever his head from his body, in the hearing of him and all present, supplicating the supreme God, not to impute to them their sin against him.

Praying thus, with a loud voice, and moving almost all to compassion and tears, as one unjustly slain, yet composing himself, and submitting his bare neck to the stroke of the sword, he was crowned with a divine martyrdom on the twenty-fifth of the month Panemus, which would be the eighth of the calends of August. And such was the end of these. But after the lapse of no long time, one hundred and thirty other noble wrestlers of the Christian faith, undergoing the same mutilations of eyes and feet with the former in Egypt; some by the order of Maximinus were condemned and sent away to the mines in Palestine, others to those in Cilicia.

CHAPTER IX.

The renewal of the persecution with greater violence. Antoninus, Zebina, Germanus, and others.

AFTER the flame of persecution had relaxed its violence amid such heroic achievements of the noble martyrs of Christ, and had been almost extinguished with the blood of holy men, and now some relief and liberty had been granted to those condemned to labour in the mines for Christ's sake, and we began to breathe an air somewhat purer, I know not how, he that had received the power to persecute, was again roused by a new impulse against the Christians. Immediately, therefore, edicts were issued against us from Maximinus, every where in the provinces. Governors and the Prætorian Præfect, in proclamations and edicts, and public ordinances, urged the magistrates and generals, and notaries in every city, to execute the imperial mandate, which ordained, that with all speed the decayed temples of the idols should be rebuilt, and that all people, men, women, domestics, and even infants at the breast, should sacrifice and make libations, and that they should be diligently made to taste of the execrable sacrifices, that the things for sale in the markets should be defiled with the libations of victims, and that before the baths guards should be stationed, who should pollute those that had been cleansed in these, with their execrable sacrifices. These things being thus performed, and our brethren, as was natural, being from the beginning most concerned, and the heathen themselves censuring the severity and absurdity of the measure, as superfluous at best, for these measures appeared overbearing and oppressive even to them, and as there was a mighty storm gathering every where upon them, again the divine power of our Saviour infused such courage and confidence into his wrestlers, that without being drawn or even impelled by any one, they voluntarily trampled upon the threats of such opponents. Three, therefore, of the believers joining together, rushed upon the governor, offering sacrifice, and called upon him to desist from his error, for there was no other God but the Supreme Creator and maker of the universe. Then being asked who they were, they boldly confessed they were Christians. On this, Firmilianus, in a rage, and without inflicting tortures, condemns them to capital punishment. Of these, one named Antoninus was a presbyter, another named Zebina was a native of Eleutheropolis, the third was named Germanus. They were executed on the thirteenth of the month Dius, on the ides of November. On the same day Ennathas, a woman of Scythopolis, ennobled also by the virgin's fillet, was added as an associate to them. She had not, indeed, done what the former had, but was dragged by force, and brought before the judge, and after being scourged, and enduring dreadful abuses which were heaped upon her by Maxys, the tribune of the neighbouring district, and that without authority from a higher power, a man who was by no means as good as his name,* a sanguinary character in other respects, exceedingly harsh and inflexible, and in his whole manner so really fierce and violent that he was in bad repute with all that knew him. This man, then, having stripped the blessed virgin of all

---

* Perhaps our author alludes to some such signification as the Hebrew מהסה *refuge*, of which Maxys appears to be a derivative.

her clothes, so as to leave only her body covered from her loins to her feet, but the rest bare, led her about the whole city of Cesarea, considering it a great feat that he caused her to be driven about the markets and beaten with thongs of hide. And after all these cruelties, which she bore with the greatest firmness, she exhibited the same most cheerful alacrity, before the tribunal of the judge himself, when she was there condemned to the flames. Whilst aiming his cruelty and madness against the worshippers of the true God, he also went beyond all the dictates of nature, not even ashamed to deny the lifeless bodies of these holy men a burial. Night and day he ordered the dead bodies to be carefully watched, as they lay exposed in the open air, the food of beasts, and there was no small number of men present several days, of such as attended to this savage and barbarous decree, and some, indeed, were looking out from their posts of observation, as if it were something worthy of their zeal to see that the dead bodies should not be stolen. But wild beasts, and dogs, and carniverous birds of prey, scattered the human limbs here and there in all directions, and the whole city around was spread with the entrails and bones of men, so that nothing ever appeared more dreadful or horrific, even to those who before had been most hostile to us; they did not indeed so much lament the calamity of those against whom these things were done, as the nuisance against themselves, and the abuse heaped upon our common nature.

For at the very gates of the city there was an exhibition presented dreadful beyond all description and tragic recital, human flesh devoured not in one place only but scattered over every place; for it was said that limbs and masses of flesh, and parts of entrails, were to be seen even within the gates. Which things continuing to occur for many days, a strange event, like the following, took place. The air happened to be clear and bright, and the aspect of the whole heavens was most serene. Then, suddenly, from the greater part of the columns that supported the public porticos, issued drops like tears, and the market places and streets, though there was no moisture from the air, I know not whence it came, were sprinkled with water, and became wet: so that it was immediately spread abroad among all, that in an unaccountable manner the earth wept, not being able to endure the extreme impiety of these deeds, and to address a reproof to men of a relentless and callous nature, the very stones and senseless matter could bewail these facts. I well know that this account may, perhaps, appear an idle tale and fable to posterity, but it was not so to those who had its truth confirmed by their presence at the time.*

CHAPTER X.

Petrus Ascetes, Asclepius the Marcionite, and other martyrs.

On the fourteenth of the following month Apellæus, *i. e.* the nineteenth of the calends of January, there were some from Egypt again seized by the spies appointed to observe those going out at the gates. They had been sent for the purpose of ministering to the necessities of the confessors in Cilicia. These experienced the same lot with those they came to serve, and were thus mutilated in their eyes and feet. Three of them, however, exhibited a wonderful fortitude at Ascalon, where they were imprisoned, and bore away different prizes of martyrdom. One of them, named Ares, was committed to the flames, the others, Promus and Elias, were beheaded. But on the eleventh of the month Audynæus, *i. e.* on the third of the ides of January, in the same city of Cesarea, Petrus Ascetes,† also called Apselamus, from the village of Anea, on the borders of Eleutheropolis, like the purest gold, with a noble resolution, gave the proof of his faith in the Christ of God. Disregarding both the judge, and those

---

* Perhaps some might smile at the supposed credulity of our author, but the *miracle* in this account was not greater than the *malignity*, and if man can perform miracles of vice, we can scarcely wonder if Providence should present, at least, miracles of admonition.

† Peter, called the Ascetic, probably from the extraordinary severity of life and self-denial that he exhibited so young.

around him, that besought him in many ways, only to have compassion on himself, and to spare his youth and blooming years, he preferred his hope in the supreme God to all, and even to life itself.

With him, also, was said to be a certain bishop, named Asclepius, a follower of Marcion's error, with a zeal for piety, as he supposed, but not according to knowledge. Yet he departed this life on the same funeral pile.

CHAPTER XI.

Pamphilus and others.

THE time is now come to relate, also, that great and celebrated spectacle exhibited by those who, in martyrdom, were associated with Pamphilus, a name thrice dear to me. These were twelve, who were distinguished by a prophetic and apostolic grace, as well as number. Of these, the leader, and the only one among them, however, with the dignity of presbyter at Cesarea, was Pamphilus; a man who excelled in every virtue through his whole life, whether by a renunciation and contempt of the world, by distributing his substance among the needy, or by a disregard of worldly expectations, and by a philosophic deportment and self-denial. But he was chiefly distinguished above the rest of us, by his sincere devotedness to the sacred Scriptures, and by an indefatigable industry in what he proposed to accomplish, by his great kindness and alacrity to serve all his relatives, and all that approached him. The other features of his excellence, which deserve a more full account, we have already given in a separate work on his life, consisting of three books. Referring, therefore, those that have a taste for these things, and who wish to know them, to this work, let us now prosecute the history of the martyrs in order.

The second after Pamphilus that entered the contest was Valens, deacon of the church of Ælia, a man dignified by his venerable and hoary locks, and most august by the very aspect of his great age; well versed in the sacred Scriptures, in which he had no superior. For he had so much of them treasured up in his memory, that he did not require to read them, if he undertook at any time to repeat any parts of the Scriptures.

The third that was most illustrious among them, was Paul of the city of Jamna, a man most fervent in zeal, and ardent in spirit, who before his martyrdom had already passed through the conflict of a confession for the faith, by enduring the tortures of searing with red hot iron. After these had been two whole years in prison, the occasion of their death was a second arrival of brethren from Egypt, who also suffered martyrdom with them. These had accompanied the confessors in Cilicia to the mines there, and were returning to their homes, and, like the former, at the entrance of the city of Cesarea, being questioned by the guards stationed at the gates, men of barbarous character, as they did not conceal the truth, they were immediately seized as malefactors caught in the very act, and taken in custody. There were five in number. When brought before the tyrant, they declared themselves freely before him, and were immediately committed to prison. On the next day, being the sixteenth of the month Peritisis, and the fourteenth of the calends of March, Roman style, these, according to the decree, together with the associates of Pamphilus, were conducted before the judge. He first made trial of the invincible firmness of the Egyptians by every kind of torture, and by new and various machinery invented for the purpose. And first he asked the chief of them, after he had practised these cruelties upon him, who he was; when, instead of his proper name, he heard him repeat some name of the prophets, which was done by them, if they happened to have had names given them by their parents from some of the names of the idols, in which case you would hear them calling themselves Elias, and Jeremiah, and Isaiah, Samuel and Daniel; thus exhibiting the true and genuine Israel of God, as belonging to those who are the real Jews* (spoken of by the apostle), not only in their works, but also in their proper names.

---

* The author refers here to that passage of the apostle, Rom. ii. 28, where he draws the distinction between the mere nominal and the real Jew.

When Firmilianus had heard some name like this of the martyr, and yet did not understand the force or import of the name,
he next asked him what was his country? He gave an answer
allied to the former, saying that Jerusalem was his country, referring to that city of which Paul speaks, " but the Jerusalem
above is free, which is the mother of us all ;" also again : " And
ye have come to mount Sion, and to the city of the living God,
the heavenly Jerusalem," and it was this that the martyr meant
to signify. But the judge, fixed in thought and cast down in his
mind, anxiously inquired what country, and in what part of the
world it was? Then he also applied tortures to make him confess the truth. But he, with his hands twisted behind his back,
and his feet thrust into certain new machines, persevered in asserting that he had said the truth. Then, again, being frequently
asked what and where that city was that he had mentioned, he
said that it was the city of the pious only, for none but these
were admitted to it ; but that it lay to the very east, and the very
rising sun. And here again, the martyr in this way philosophized
according to his own sense, paying no regard to the tortures
with which he was surrounded ; but as if he were without flesh
and blood, he did not even appear to be sensible of his pains. But
the judge at a loss, was greatly perplexed in mind, thinking that
the Christians were collectively about establishing a city somewhere in opposition and hostile to the Romans, and frequently inquired where this city was, and examined where the country lay
towards the east. But after he had sufficiently tortured the young
man with scourging, and lacerated him with many and various tortures, perceiving his mind unchangeably fixed in his former purpose and declarations, he passed the sentence of death against
him. Such then, was the scene exhibited in the martyrdom of
this one. The rest he exercised with trials of a similar kind, and
finally destroyed in a similar manner. Wearied at last, and
perceiving that it was all in vain to punish the men, and having
fully satiated his curiosity, he proceeded against Pamphilus
and his associates But as he had learned that they had already displayed an unchangeable alacrity in the confession of
religion under torture, and also asked them whether they were

yet disposed to obey, and yet received only the same answer, the last confession of every one in martyrdom, he inflicted upon them the same punishment with the former. These things done, a young man, who had belonged to the family of Pamphilus, as one who had dwelt with and enjoyed the excellent education and instruction of such a man, as soon as he learned the sentence passed upon his master, cried out from the midst of the people, requesting that the body at least should be interred. But the judge, more brute than man, and if any thing worse than brute, making no allowance for the young man's age, only inquired this one thing, and heard him confess himself a Christian. On this, as if he were wounded by a dart, swelling with rage, he orders the tormentors to exercise all their force against him. When he saw him refusing to sacrifice according to his orders, he commanded that they should scrape and mutilate him, not as the flesh of a human being, but as stones and wood, or any other lifeless object, to the very bones, and the inmost parts and recesses of the bowels. This being continued for a long time, he at length perceived that he was labouring in vain, as he continued without uttering a sound or evincing any feeling, and almost totally lifeless, although his body was so dreadfully mangled with tortures. But as the judge was of an inflexible cruelty and inhumanity, he condemned him in this condition to be committed to a slow fire; and thus this youth, although he had entered upon the combat last, yet he received his dismission from this life before the decease of his master in the flesh, and whilst those that rivalled the first were yet lingering on the way. One could then see Porphyry, for this was his name, with the courage of one who had already triumphed in every species of combat, his body covered with dust, but yet his countenance bright and cheerful, and after this, with a courageous and exulting mind advancing on his way to death. Truly filled with the divine Spirit, and covered only with his philosophical garb thrown around him like a cloak, and with a calm and composed mind giving exhortations and beckoning to his acquaintance and friends, he preserved a cheerful countenance at the very stake. When the fire was kindled which was at some distance around him, he attracted and inhaled the flame in his mouth, and then most nobly perse-vering in silence, until his last breath, he uttered not another word after that which he uttered as soon as the flame reached him, calling upon Christ the Son of God, his helper. Such a wrestler then was Porphyry. But Seleucus, one of the confessors of the army, brought the intelligence of his martyrdom to Pam-philus ; and he, as the bearer of such intelligence, was imme-diately honoured with the same lot. For as soon as he had an-nounced the end of Porphyry, and had saluted one of the mar-tyrs with a kiss, some of the soldiers seized him and led him to the governor, who, as if to urge him to attach himself to the former, as his companion on the way to heaven, commands him imme-diately to be put to death. He was from Cappadocia, but among the chosen band of Roman soldiers, and one who had obtained no small share of honours.

In the vigour of age, strength, size, and firmness of body, he was greatly superior to his fellow-soldiers, so that he was noted among all for his very appearance, and admired for the grandeur and the comeliness of his whole form. At the very beginning of the persecution, indeed, he was prominent in the trials of the confessors, by his patient endurance of the scourge, and after his renunciation of military life, he exhibited himself a zealous fol-lower of those who led a life devoted to the exercises of piety, in which, like a provident father, he proved himself a kind of overseer ($\varepsilon\pi\iota\sigma\kappa\sigma\pi\sigma\varsigma$,) and protector of destitute orphans and helpless widows, and of all those that were prostrated in poverty and sickness. Hence, also, he was honoured by that God who is better pleased with such charities than the fume and blood of sacrifices, to receive an extraordinary call to martyrdom. He was the tenth after those wrestlers mentioned that were perfect-ed in one and the same day, on which, as is probable, the mighty portals of eternal life were opened to Pamphilus, in a manner worthy of the man, and presented to him and to others a ready entrance into the kingdom of heaven. Immediately after Seleu cus, came the aged Theodulus, a grave and pious man, who was of the governor's family, and who on account of his age had been treated with more regard by Firmilianus than any of his domestics, as also, because he was now a father of the third generation, and had always evinced great fidelity and attachment to himself and family. He, however, pursuing the same course as Seleucus, when arraigned before his master, incensed him yet more than the former, and was condemned to endure the same martyrdom as our Saviour on the cross. One now remaining of those who constituted the number twelve, already mentioned; after all the rest came Julianus, to complete it. He had just come from abroad, and not yet even entered the city, when learning the death of the martyrs on the road, just as he was, he immediately hastened to the sight. There, when he saw the earthly tabernacles of the holy men lying on the ground, filled with joy, he embraced every one, and kissed them all. Upon this he was immediately seized by the ministers of death, and conducted to Firmilianus, who consistently with his character, also consigned him to a slow and lingering fire. Then Julianus, also, leaping and exulting with joy, gave thanks to God with a loud voice, who had honoured him with a martyrdom such as these endured, and was crowned with the martyr's death. He also was a native of Cappadocia, but in his manner he was most religious, and eminent for the sincerity and soundness of his faith. He was also a devoted man in other respects, and animated by the Holy Spirit himself. Such was the band and the company that met with Pamphilus, and were honoured to encounter martyrdom with him. The sacred and holy bodies of these men, by the order of the cruel and impious governor, were kept and guarded for four days and nights to feed the wild beasts. But, as contrary to expectation, nothing would approach them, neither beast nor bird of prey, nor dog, by a divine providence they were again taken up uninjured, and obtaining a decent burial, were interred according to the accustomed mode. But when the cruelty exercised against these was noised abroad among all, Adrianus, and Eubulus, from the region called Manganæa, came to the other confessors as far as Cesarea, and were also asked the cause of their coming at the gate of the city. They confessed the truth, and were brought before Firmilianus. He, as usual, without delay, after many tortures which he inflicted, by scourging and lacerating their sides, then condemned them to be devoured by the beasts. After the lapse of two days, on the fifth of the month Dystrus, the third of the nones of March, the day that was considered the birthday of the tutelary divinity of Cesarea,* he was cast before a lion, and afterwards slain with the sword. As to Eubulus, after another day and a half, on the very nones of March, which would be the seventh of Dystrus, when the judge had urged him much to enjoy that which was considered liberty among them, by offering the sacrifice, he preferred a glorious death in the cause of religion, and after being cast to the beasts like the former, was the last to close the list of the martyrs that wrestled for the faith at Cesarea. It is also worth while here to state, how at length the providence of God overtook the wicked governors themselves, together with the tyrants. For the same Firmilianus that raged with such violence against the martyrs of Christ, after receiving with the others the most signal punishment inflicted on him, at length ended his life by the sword. And such, then, were the martyrdoms endured at Cesarea, during the whole period of the persecution.

CHAPTER XII.

The prelates of the church.

But the events that occurred in the intermediate time, besides those already related, I have thought proper to pass by; I mean particularly the circumstances of the different heads of the churches, who from being shepherds of the reasonable flocks of Christ that did not govern in a lawful and becoming manner, were condemned, by divine justice, as unworthy of such a charge, to be the keepers of the unreasonable camel, an animal deformed in the very structure of its body, and condemned further to be

---

* Every city was supposed by the heathen to have its tutelary divinity, who presided over its destinies, and hence called τυχη, *fortune*, by our author. The temples dedicated to these were hence called Tychea.

the keepers of the imperial horses; also, the number and severity of the burdens and oppressions they bore for the sake of the
sacred vessels and property of the churches, from the imperial
rulers and governors at the time in the midst of insult, injury, and
torment; moreover, the ambitious aspirings of many to office,
and the injudicious and unlawful ordinations, that took place, the
divisions among the confessors themselves, the great schisms and
difficulties industriously fomented by the factious among the new
members, against the relics of the church, devising one innovation after another, and unmercifully thrusting them into the
midst of all these calamities, heaping up affliction upon affliction:
all this, I say, I have resolved to pass by, judging it foreign to my
purpose, wishing, as I said in the beginning, to shun and avoid
giving an account of them. But whatsoever things are serious
and commendable according to the Scriptures—" if there be
any virtue, if there be any praise," deeming it most proper to tell
and to describe these, and present them to the attention of the
faithful, in a history of the admirable martyrs, as also, most consistent with that peace which has recently shone upon us from
heaven, I shall consider myself as most likely to decorate the
close of my work, if I present to the attention of the faithful an
account of these.

CHAPTER XIII.

Silvanus and John, and thirty more other martyrs.

THE seventh year of the conflict against us was verging to its
close, and the measures against us had gently and imperceptibly received a less afflictive aspect, and had now continued until
the eighth year, when there was no small number of confessors
collected in the copper mines of Palestine, and these were enjoying considerable freedom, so far as even to build houses for assembling together, then the governor of the province, a savage
and wicked man, such indeed, as his acts against the martyrs
proved him to be, came thither, and ascertaining the state of

things, and the manner of those that lived there, communicated the whole to the emperor, and wrote against them whatever slanders he thought proper. After this, being appointed as superintendent of the mines, he divided, as if by imperial orders, the multitude of confessors into different bodies, and sent some to inhabit Cyprus, some to Libanus. Others he scattered into several parts of Palestine, and commanded them all to labour in different works. Then selecting those that appeared to be pre-eminent among them, he sent them away to the commander of the forces there. Of these, two were Egyptians, bishops Peleus and Nilus, another was a presbyter, and a fourth added to these named Patermuthius, well known to all for his great benevolence toward all. These the commander, after demanding a renunciation of their religion, and not succeeding, committed to be consumed by the flames. Others again, had their lot cast there, in a separate place by themselves, as many of the confessors, as whether from age, or blindness, or other infirmities of body, were exempt from performing labour. Of these, the chief was Silvanus, a bishop from Gaza, who presented a venerable example of genuine Christianity. This man, one might say, was eminent for his confessions from the very first day of the persecution, through the whole time, in a variety of conflicts, and was reserved until that time, that this might be as the last seal of the whole conflict in Palestine. With him were associated many from Egypt, among whom also was John, who in the excellence of his memory surpassed all of our time. He, indeed, had already before been deprived of his eyes, and had his foot destroyed with burning irons, like the others, on account of his confessions, yet although his sight was already destroyed, he had the red hot iron nevertheless applied to him; the butchers aiming at every display of cruelty, and inhumanity, and whatever was savage and brutal. And as this man was such, one has no cause to wonder at his philosophical life and habits, as he appeared not so wonderful on this account, as from the excellence of his memory. He had whole books of the sacred Scriptures written, as the apostle says, not on tables of stone, neither on skins of animals, nor papers destroyed by moths and time, but on the tables of flesh, in the heart, in an

enlightened soul, and the pure eye of the mind. So that whenever he wished to produce any passage, whether from the law,
or the prophets, or the apostles, the historical parts or the gospels,
he could repeat and produce it as from a treasury of learning,
whenever he pleased. I confess that I myself was astonished
when I first saw the man standing in the midst of a large multitude,
and repeating certain parts of the holy Scriptures. For as far
as I had opportunity only to hear his voice, I thought that he was
reading as is usual in the congregations, but when I came near
and saw the fact, all the others standing around, with their sound
eyes, and him alone raising his mind and pronouncing without
any artificial means, as a kind of prophet, and far surpassing
those who were robust in body, I could not but glorify and praise
God. And indeed, I seemed to behold an evident and solid proof
in facts, that not he who appears in the external form is the real
man, but in truth that which is in the soul and mind. For he,
though mutilated in body, exhibited the greater excellence of
power and virtue. But as to those already mentioned, who
were living in a separate place, and were engaged in performing
their accustomed duties, in prayer and fasting, and other exercises, God himself condescended to grant them a salutary issue,
by extending his right arm to help them.

The enemy, no longer able to bear them, armed with constant
prayer to God, prepared to destroy and remove them from the
earth, as troublesome to him. God granted him, also, power to
do this, that at the same time he might not be restrained in his
determined wickedness, and they might now receive the prizes
of their varied conflicts. Thus, then, the thirty-nine, at the command of the most execrable Maximinus, were beheaded in one
day. And these were the martyrdoms exhibited in Palestine
in the space of eight years, and such was the persecution in our
day. It began, indeed, with the demolition of the churches, and
grew to a great height during the insurrections from time to
time under the rulers. In these, many and various were the
contests of the noble wrestlers in the cause of piety, who presented an innumerable multitude of martyrs through the whole
province, among those from Libya, and through all Egypt, Syria,

and those of the east, round as far as those of the region of Illy-ricum. For the countries beyond these, all Italy and Sicily, Gaul, and whatever parts extend toward the west, Spain, Mau-ritania, and Africa, as they did not experience the hostility of the persecution quite two years, very soon were blessed with the interposition and peace of God, as if his providence spared the simplicity and faith of these men. For that, indeed, which was never before recorded in the annals of the Romans, this first ob-tained in our day contrary to all expectation. The empire was divided into two parts during this persecution. Those in the one part enjoyed peace, whilst those brethren that inhabited the other, endured innumerable trials one after another. But as soon as the divine favour prepared to display to us his kind and gracious care, then at length, also, our rulers themselves, through whom these wars were formerly waged against us, changing their mind in a most extraordinary manner, sounded a retreat, and extin-guished the flame of persecution by kind ordinances and milder edicts. But we must not omit the recantation.*

---

* Eusebius here intimates that he appended the imperial revocation to this book, and prepares us for it in these closing words. But as it does not appear in this place, the book, of course, does not end here. The defect is easily supplied from the last chapter of the eighth book.

BOOK IX.

CHAPTER I.

The pretended relaxation.

THE revocation of the imperial edict that had been issued, was published every where, and in all places throughout Asia and its provinces. This being done, accordingly, in this way, Maximinus, the tyrant of the east, the most impious of men, and most hostile to the religion which acknowledges only the supreme God, by no means satisfied with these mandates, instead of issuing an edict, gives verbal commands to the rulers under him, to relax the war against us. For as he had no power to oppose or to pursue a different course, and place himself in opposition to the judgment of his superiors, he suppressed the edict; and designing that it should not be made public in the parts under him, he gives orders, without writing to his governors, to relax the persecution against us. These communicate the mandate to one another by letters. Sabinus, who held the highest rank and power among the provincial rulers, communicated the imperial will to the respective governors of the provinces, in a Latin letter, the translation of which is as follows:

" With a most persevering and devoted earnestness, their majesties, our sovereigns and most august emperors, had formerly directed the minds of all men to live and conduct themselves according to the true and holy way, that even those who appeared to pursue practices foreign to the Roman, should exhibit the proper worship to the immortal gods. But the obstinacy and most unconquerable determination of some, rose to such a pitch, that they could neither be induced to recede from their own purpose by a due regard to the imperial command, nor be deterred by the impending punishment inflicted. Since, then, it has happened that many incurred danger from a practice like this, their majesties our sovereigns, the most powerful emperors, in their peculiar and exalted piety, deeming it foreign to the purpose of their majesties, that men should be thrust into so great danger for such a cause, have commanded (me in) my devotedness* to address (you in) your wisdom, that if any of the Christians be found to observe the worship of their people, that you should abstain from molesting or endangering them, nor determine that any one should be punished on such a pretext; as it has been made to appear by the lapse of so long a time, that it has been impossible to induce them in any manner to abandon their obstinate course. It is incumbent, therefore, on your attentive care, to write to the governors and magistrates, and to the præfects of the districts of every city, that they may know that it is not necessary for them to pay any further regard to this edict (or business.)"

After this, the rulers of the provinces thinking that the resolution contained in these writings, was truly set forth to them, communicate by letter the imperial will to the controllers, magistrates, and præfects of the different districts. Nor did they urge these things only by writing, but much more by their

---

* The more literal translation of this passage may give the reader some idea of the kind of phraseology employed here. It would run thus—" have given orders through my devotedness to write to your discretion :" αγχινοια signifies acuteness of discrimination. As Eusebius gives us here a Greek translation from the Latin, it would not be surprising to find Latinisms transferred here as well as in the edict before translated by him. We have suspected the original of καθοσιοτης here, to have been in the Latin *sanctitas*, a very comprehensive word, expressing integrity, inviolable fidelity, attachment. But the classical use of καθοσιοτης, would rather be *sanctificatio*, very different, therefore, from *sanctitas*.

We have in this mode of address, also, a specimen of that kind of style in which the great were addressed by others, and by one another. Some traces of it still exist in Europe, as in *your Lordship, your Grace, your Excellency*, &c.; but it has prevailed no where to a greater extent than among the dignitaries of the German empire. Formerly almost every book that had a dedicatory epistle, abounded in this artificial mode of address; so that unless one were apprized of the fact, it would be difficult to tell who it was that was addressed. This usage among the Germans is no doubt to be traced back to a more intimate connexion with the Roman empire.

acts, to execute the imperial mandate; conducting those fortl who had been imprisoned by them on account of tl.eir faitl· they set them at liberty, and dismissing those who had been consigned as a punishment to the mines. For this in mistake they supposed to be the true intention of the emperor. When these things had thus been executed, all on a sudden, like a flash of light blazing from dense darkness, in every city, one could see congregations collected, assemblies thronged, and the accustomed meeting held in the same places. Every one of the heathen was not a little astonished at these appearances, both amazed at the singular change of affairs, and exclaiming that the God of the Christians was the only great and true God. Those of our brethren who had faithfully and manfully passed through the conflict of persecution, also again obtained great privileges with all. But those who had deserted their faith, and had been shaken in their souls by the tempest, eagerly hastened to their remedy, supplicating and entreating the strong to give them the right hand of safety, and imploring God to be merciful unto them. Then, also, these noble wrestlers of religion, liberated from the hardships of labouring in the mines, were dismissed every one to his own country. Joyous and cheerful they proceeded through every city, filled with an inexpressible pleasure and a confidence which language is inadequate to explain. Numerous bodies thus pursued their journey through the public highways and markets, celebrating the praises of God in songs and psalms. And they who a little before had been driven in bonds under a most merciless punishment, from their respective countries, you could now see regaining their homes and firehearths, with bright and exhilarated countenances; so that even they who before had exclaimed against us, seeing the wonder, beyond all expectation congratulated us on these events.

CHAPTER II.

The subsequent reverse.

But the tyrant, unable to bear this state of things, an enemy of goodness, and as far as possible of good men, who we have already said was the sovereign of the parts in the east, did not suffer this course to hold out quite six months. And thus, whilst he was devising schemes in every possible way to destroy the peace, he first attempted to restrain us by a kind of pretext from assembling in the cemeteries.* Then he sent delegates to himself† against us, through the agency of some abandoned characters, stimulating the inhabitants of Antioch to request of him, as a very great favour, by no means to permit any of the Christians to dwell at Antioch, and suborned others to do the same thing. Of all which things, Theotecnus was the cause and prime mover at Antioch, a man of a violent, artful, and wicked character, altogether the reverse of the name he bore. But he appears to have been the controller of that city.

CHAPTER III.

The new statue erected at Antioch.

After he had thus waged war against us by every means, and had caused our brethren with all diligence and care to be hunted up in their retreats, as thieves and malefactors, and had plotted against us by slander and accusation, and been the cause of death to vast numbers, he finally erected a certain statue of Jupiter Philius, with a variety of mummery and magic rites. And after reciting forms of initiation, and pronouncing dire in-

* See note, Book VII. ch. ii.

† Our author here represents Maximinus in the odd predicament of sending an embassy to himself, by suborning his agents to have this done. The original is pronounced by Valesius, *elegans locutio*, to which we may add *sale plena*.

auspicious mysteries before it, and inventing execrable modes of expiation, he even went so far as to exhibit his impostures to the emperor, by the oracles which he pretended to utter. Thus, by a flattery grateful to the emperor, he roused the dæmon against the Christians,·and said that God had commanded to expel the Christians as his enemies, beyond the limits of the city and the adjacent territory.

CHAPTER IV.

The decrees against us.

As this man who took the lead in this matter, had thus succeeded, all the rest in office that inhabited cities under the same government (of Maximinus,) proceeded to issue a similar decree. And the governors of provinces perceiving that it would be acceptable to the emperor also, suggested to their subjects to ao the same thing. To these decrees the emperor himself most readily assenting, the persecution that raged at first was again kindled against us. Hence, in every city priests were appointed for the images, and highpriests over these, by Maximinus himself; these were from among those who had been most distinguished for their public life, and had gained celebrity in the different stations they had filled. Who were also fired with great zeal for those objects that they worshipped. In short, the absurd superstition of the emperor led on the rulers under him, as well as his subjects, to do all things against us in order to gratify him; supposing this was the greatest proof of gratitude they could give for the kindnesses they had received from him, if they only exhibited slaughter, and constantly devised new plots and modes of mischief against us.

CHAPTER V.

The false acts.

HAVING forged, therefore, certain acts of Pilate, respecting our
Saviour, full of every kind of blasphemy against Christ, these, with
the consent of the emperor, they sent through the whole of the empire subject to him, commanding at the same time by ordinances
in every place and city, and the adjacent districts, to publish
these to all persons, and to give them to the schoolmasters to
hand to their pupils to study and commit to memory, as exercises
for declamation. Whilst these things were doing, another commander, whom the Romans call Dux, in Damascus, a city of
Phœnicia, caused certain infamous females to be seized from the
forum, and threatening to inflict torture upon them, he forced
them to make a formal declaration, taken down on record, that
they had once been Christians, and that they were privy to the
criminal acts among them ; that in their very churches, they
committed licentious deeds, and innumerable other slanders,
which he wished them to utter against our religion. Which declarations he inserted in the acts, and communicated to the emperor, who immediately commanded that these documents should
be published in every city and place.

CHAPTER VI.

Those who suffered martyrdom at this time.

THIS commander, however, ere long, laid violent hands upon
himself,* and thus suffered punishment for his wickedness. But
exiles and severe persecutions in the mean time were again renewed against us, and the rulers of the provinces were every
where again stirred up against us, insomuch that some who were

---

* Our author's Greek here is both elegant and nervous. *He became his own executioner ;* αυτοχειρ ιαυτου γιγονως.

more distinguished for their skill in the divine word, when taken, received the sentence of death without mercy. Three of these in the city of Emesa in Phœnicia, professing themselves Christians were thrown to be devoured by the wild beasts. Among these was Silvanus, a very venerable and superannuated bishop, who had been engaged in the ministry forty years. At the same time also, Peter, who presided over the churches of Alexandria with great reputation, an admirable instance of a bishop, both for the excellence of his life and his study of the sacred Scriptures. He was seized for no reason whatever, and beheaded, beyond all expectation so suddenly, and without any cause assigned, as if by the orders of Maximinus. With him also many other bishops of Egypt suffered the same punishment. Lucianus, a man in all respects most excellent, temperate in his life, and conspicuous for his proficiency in sacred literature. He was presbyter of the church at Antioch, and when brought to Nicomedia, where the emperor happened to be staying, he delivered a defence of his doctrine before the governor, when he was committed to prison and slain. Such were the preparations made against us in so short a time, by the malicious Maximinus, so that it would appear this persecution now raising against us, was more severe than the former.

CHAPTER VII.

The measures decreed against us, and engraved on pillars.

The measures and the decrees of the cities against us, and copies of the imperial edicts appended to these, were engraved and erected on brazen tablets, a course never before adopted against us any where. The boys also in the schools had the names of Jesus and Pilate, and the acts forged in derision, in their mouths the whole day. And here appears to me the proper place to insert the epistle of Maximinus, engraven on brass, that at the same time the boasting and haughty arrogance of the man's hatred of God, and also God's just and ever vigilant hatred of iniquity against the wicked may appear, which soon overtook him, and by which he was urged onwards; so that he did not long devise hostilities, and form decrees against us. The decree was as follows:

Copy of the translated epistle of Maximinus, in answer to the ordinances (of the cities) against us, taken from the brazen tablet at Tyre.

" Now at length the feeble powers* of the human mind have prevailed so far as to shake off and to scatter the mists of every error, and dissipate the clouds of delusion, which before this had beset the senses of those who were more miserable than profane, and enveloped them in a destructive darkness and ignorance ; thus leading us to acknowledge that it is regulated and strengthened by the good providence of the immortal gods : which things it is incredible to say how grateful, how delightful and pleasing it is to us, how powerful an evidence it has furnished of your pious resolutions, since before this it could be unknown to none, how much regard and reverence you cherished towards the immortal gods, to whom faith is exhibited not by mere empty words, but by a constant and eminent† display of illustrious deeds.   Wherefore, deservedly, may your city be called the seat and habitation of the immortal gods, for by many evidences it does appear most clearly that it flourishes by the presence and residence of the celestial gods.   So then, your city, regardless of all local interest and advantage, and omitting the petitions formerly presented to us, for its own political affairs, when it perceived the votaries of an execrable vanity again insinuating themselves, and as a funeral pile long disregarded and smothered, again rising in mighty flames and rekindling the extinguished brands, immediately without delay it took refuge to our piety, as

---

* We have rendered the word ϑρασυτης here, not according to the Greek, but what we conjecture was the original Latin. Audacity, the meaning of the Greek, seems entirely at variance with the whole drift of the sentence, even if it should be understood in the milder sense of confidence. If our author had before him the word *vis animi*, it is possible that he might have understood it in a lax sense, and rendered accordingly.

† Probably the Latin here, was *singularis*, and our author rendered παραδοξα.

to the metropolis of all religion, entreating some remedy and relief. Which salutary mind it is evident the immortal gods have imparted to you on account of your faith and piety. Wherefore, that supreme and mighty Jove, he who presides over your most illustrious city, who has rescued your country's gods, and wives, and children, and houses, and homes, from every destructive pest, has infused into you the happy counsel, showing and proving to you how excellent, and noble, and profitable it is to observe the worship and the sacred rites of the immortal gods with the becoming reverence. For who can be so bereft of understanding, and all sense, as not to perceive, that it has happened by the gracious benevolence of the gods, that neither the earth has refused the seed committed to it, and disappointed the hope of the husbandmen, with vain expectation; nor the presence of impious war has been inevitably fixed on earth, and under a corrupt atmosphere wasting bodies have been dragged and weighed down to death; nor indeed, the ocean swelling and rising on high, with the raging blasts of intemperate storms, nor unexpected tempests have burst and spread destruction around. Moreover, that neither the parent and nurturing earth has risen in dreadful tremblings, from its lowest depths, nor the superincumbent hills and mountains have sunk into its opening jaws. All which calamities, and worse than these, have, as we all know, frequently occurred. And all this in consequence of the destructive error of this hollow delusion of those lawless men, when it began to take root in their minds, and we may say has covered nearly all the world with infamy." A little after, he superadds the following:

"Let them look at the flourishing crops in the wide extended fields waving with the loaded ears, and the meadows glittering with plants and flowers, from the seasonable showers, and the temperature of the air restored to a mild and placid state. Then let all rejoice, that by your piety, and sacrifices, and veneration of the gods, the divinity of omnipotent and mighty Mars has been propitiated, and hence let them enjoy tranquillity and solid peace, be filled with pleasure and joy; and as many as have abandoned that blind delusion and perplexing error, whoever they may be, and have returned to the right and sound mind, let these rejoice still more, as those who have been rescued from an unexpected storm or severe disease, and let them enjoy the delightful fruits the rest of their life.   But should they still adhere to their execrable folly, let them be driven out and separated far from your city and territory, as you have desired.   That thus agreeably to your zeal, so praiseworthy in this respect, your city, separated from all pollution and impiety, may attend to the sacred rites of the immortal gods, according to its natural disposition, with due veneration.   That ye may also know how acceptable this request of yours respecting this matter has been, and how very prompt our mind is to confer benefits of our own voluntary kindness, without decrees and without petitions, we grant to your devotedness to desire any privilege you please for this your pious purpose of mind, and now present your petitions to have this done and to receive it.   For you shall obtain without delay.   Which, indeed, when granted to your city, will be an evidence for ever of your devoted piety to the immortal gods, as also of the fact that you obtained by our kindness, merited prizes for this your purpose of life; an evidence which will be exhibited to your children and posterity."

Such, then, were the letters that were sent abroad against us in all the provinces, cutting us off from every hope of good, at least from men.   So that, according to the holy Scriptures themselves, if it were possible " the very elect would take offence." And now, indeed, when the hope of most of us was almost extinct, all on a sudden, almost whilst the agents of this decree against us were in some places yet on the way to carry it into effect, that God, who is the defender of his church, all but stopping the pomp and boasting of the tyrant's mouth, exhibited his heavenly interposition in our behalf.

CHAPTER VIII.

The events that occurred after these ; famine, pestilence, and war.

Rains and showers which usually fell in the winter season, now withheld their accustomed contribution upon the earth. An unexpected famine came on, and pestilence after this. Another kind of sickness also followed, which was a species of ulcer called by an epithet the carbuncle, on account of its inflammatory appearance. This spreading over the whole body, greatly endangered the lives of those afflicted with it. But as it prevailed mostly about the eyes, it deprived great numbers of men, women, and children of their sight. In addition to these calamities, the war with the Armenians threatented the tyrant. These men had been the friends and allies of the Romans from ancient times, and as they were Christians, and greatly valued piety toward the Deity, and as the profane and impious tyrant had attempted to force them to sacrifice to idols and dæmons, he made them enemies instead of friends, and belligerent foes instead of allies. And all these troubles suddenly concurring at one and the same time, refuted the tyrant's boasting and blustering audacity against God. When, indeed, in his great zeal for idols, and his hostility to us, he boasted that neither famine nor pestilence nor war had happened in his times. All these then coming upon him at once, presented also the preludes to his own death.

He, therefore, together with his army, was defeated in the war with the Armenians. But the rest of the inhabitants of cities under him were dreadfully afflicted both by famine and pestilence, so that a single measure of wheat was sold for two thousand five hundred Attic drachms.* Immense numbers were dying in the cities, still more in the country and villages, so that now the vast population in the interior was almost entirely swept away, nearly all being suddenly destroyed by want of food and pestilential disease. Many, therefore, were anxious to sell their

* About 175 dollars.

most valuable effects to those better supplied, for the smallest quantity of food. Others gradually spending all their possessions were reduced to the last extreme of want. And now some even chewing remnants of hay, and others eating without distinction certain noxious herbs, miserably destroyed the constitution of the body. Also, some of the more honourable females throughout the cities, constrained by want to throw aside all shame, went into the public markets to beg, indicating the evidences of their former liberal education, by the modesty of their countenances and the decency of their apparel. Some, indeed, wasted away to mere skeletons, stumbled hither and thither like dead shadows, trembling and tottering, from excessive weakness and inability to stand ; they fell down in the midst of the streets, where they lay stretched out, and only earnestly begged some one to hand them a little morsel of bread, then drawing in their breath, with the last gasp they cried out hunger ! having only strength sufficient for this most painful cry. Some, however, of those that appeared better supplied, astonished at the great multitude of those begging, after giving vast quantities away, afterwards yielded to a harsh and inflexible disposition, expecting that they would soon suffer the same things with those begging of them. So that now in the midst of the streets and lanes, the dead and naked bodies, cast out and lying for many days, presented a most painful spectacle to the beholders. Some, indeed, were already the food of dogs, on which account, especially, the survivors began to slay the dogs, lest growing mad they should devour men. The pestilence, however, in the mean time, did not the less prey upon every house and family, particularly those however, whom the famine from their abundance of food could not destroy; the wealthy, the rulers, generals, and vast numbers in office, who, as if they had been designedly left by the famine to the pestilence, were overtaken by a sudden, violent, and rapid death. All places, therefore, were filled with lamentation, in all streets, lanes, market places, and highways. Nothing was to be seen but tears, with the accustomed flutes, and funeral dirge. In this manner death waged a desolating war with these two weapons, famine and pestilence, destroying whole families in a short time, so that one now could see two or three dead bodies carried out at once. Such were the rewards of the pompous boasting of Maximinus, and of his edicts throughout the cities against us. Then, also, the evidences of the zeal and piety of the Christians became manifest and obvious to all, for they were the only ones in the midst of such distressing circumstances, that exhibited sympathy and humanity in their conduct. They continued the whole day, some in the care and burial of the dead, for numberless were they for whom there was none to care; others collecting the multitude of those wasting by the famine throughout the city, distributed bread among all. So that the fact was cried abroad, and men glorified the God of the Christians, constrained as they were, by the facts, to acknowledge that these were the only really pious and the only real worshippers of God. Whilst these things were thus doing, God, the great and celestial defender of the Christians, who exhibited his indignation and anger against men by these calamities, on account of the excesses committed against us, restored the benign and smiling brightness of his providence toward us, so that by a most wonderful concurrence of events, the light of his peace again began to shine upon us as from the midst of the densest darkness. Showing plainly to all, that God himself has been the ruler of our affairs at all times; who sometimes, indeed, chastens and visits his people by various trials, from time to time, but after he has sufficiently chastened, again exhibits his mercy and kindness to those that trust in him.

CHAPTER IX.

The death of the tyrants, and their expressions before their end.

CONSTANTINE, whom we have already mentioned as an emperor born of an emperor, the pious son of a most pious and virtuous father, and Licinius next to him, were both in great esteem for their moderation and piety. These two pious rulers had been excited by God, the universal sovereign, against the two most profane tyrants, and engaging in battle, in an extraordinary manner, Maxentius fell under Constantine. But the other, (Maximinus) did not long survive him, being himself put to a most ignominious death, by Licinius, who had not yet at that time evinced his insanity. But Constantine, who was first both in dignity and imperial rank, first took compassion upon those who were oppressed at Rome, invoking the God of heaven, and his Son and word our Lord Jesus Christ, the Saviour of all, as his aid advanced with his whole army, purporting to restore the Romans to that liberty which they had derived from their ancestors. Maxentius, however, relying more upon the arts of juggling than the affection of his subjects, did not venture to advance beyond the gates of the city, but fortified every place and region and city, with vast numbers of soldiers and innumerable bands and garrisons in all places of Rome and Italy that were enslaved by him. But the emperor (Constantine) stimulated by the divine assistance, proceeded against the tyrant, and defeating him without difficulty in the first, second, and third engagements, he advanced through the greatest part of Italy, and came almost to the very gates of Rome. Then, however, that he might not be forced to wage war with the Romans for the sake of the tyrant, God himself drew the tyrant, as if bound in fetters, to a considerable distance from the gates; and here he confirmed those miraculous events performed of old against the wicked, and which have been discredited by so many, as if belonging to fiction and fable, but which have been established in the sacred volume, as credible to the believer. He confirmed them, I say, as true, by an immediate interposition of his power, addressed alike I may say to the eyes of believers and unbelievers. As, therefore, anciently in the days of Moses, and the religious people of the Hebrews, the chariots of Pharaoh, and his forces were cast into the Red Sea, and his chosen triple* combatants were overwhelmed in it; thus, also, Maxentius, and his com-

---

* This passage is found Exod. xv. 4. The Hebrew is שלשׁי מברחר, is rendered in our version, *his chosen captains.* It probably refers to three combatants on one chariot. On the import of the word in the Hebrew, and the Alexandrian version, see Biel. Drusius, Bochart, Gesenius.

batants and guards about him, sunk into the depths like a stone, when he fled before the power of God that was with Constantine, and passed through the river in his way, over which he had formed a bridge by joining boats, and thus prepared the means of his own destruction. Here one might say, " he digged a pit and opened it, and he fell into the ditch that he made, his mischief shall fall upon his own head, and his iniquity descend upon his own pate." Thus, then, the bridge of boats over the river being broken, the crossing began to cease, and immediately the vessels with the men sunk, and were destroyed, and the most impious tyrant himself first of all, then the guards that he had around him, just as the divine oracles declare, sunk like lead in the swelling floods. So that justly might those who obtained the victory from God, if not in word, at least in deeds, similar to those whom that great servant of God. oses led on, sing and say the same that they sang against that impious tyrant of old. " Let us sing unto the Lord, for he hath triumphed gloriously. The horse and his rider he hath cast into the sea: the Lord is my helper and defender, and he is become my salvation. Who is like unto thee, O Lord, among the gods ; who is like unto thee, glorious in holiness, fearful in praises, doing wonders."

Such, and the like expressions, did Constantine sing to God, the universal sovereign and author of the victory by his deeds, as he entered Rome in triumph. All the senate and others of illustrious rank, together with their wives and infant children, with the whole Roman people, received him as their deliverer, their saviour and benefactor, with cheerful countenances and hearts, with blessings and unbounded joy. But he, according to the piety deeply implanted in him, neither exulting in the shouts that were raised, nor elated by the plaudits bestowed upon him, well perceiving the assistance which he had received from God, immediately commanded a trophy of the Saviour's passion to be placed in the hand of his own statue. And when they had erected his statue, thus holding the salutary sign of the cross in his right hand, in the most public place at Rome, he commanded the following inscription to be written, in the Roman tongue, as follows:

" *By this salutary sign, the true ornament of bravery, I have save l your city, liberated from the yoke of the tyrant. Moreover, l have restored both the Senate and the Roman people to their ancient dignity and splendour."** After this, Constantine himself, and his imperial colleague Licinius, who had not then yet been perverted into that madness which he afterwards evinced, both celebrating and praising God, as the author of all their successes, with one consent and resolve drew up a full and most comprehensive decree respecting the Christians; and sent an account of the wonderful things done for them by God, the victory they had obtained over the tyrant, and the law itself to Maximinus, who was yet sovereign of the east, and pretended friendship toward them. But he, tyrant as he was, was greatly troubled at what he learned. Then, in order not to seem disposed to yield to others, nor to suppress what was commanded, for fear of those who had commanded, as if he acted on his own authority, he of necessity addressed the following decree, first to the governors under him, respecting the Christians, falsely and fictitiously alleging against himself what had never been done by him.†

Copy of the translated epistle of the tyrant Maximinus.

" JOVIUS MAXIMINUS AUGUSTUS, to Sabinus: I trust that it is obvious to your gravity and to all men, that our sovereigns and parents, Diocletian and Maximinus, when they saw almost all men abandoning the worship of the gods, and attaching themselves to the people of the Christians, rightly ordained that all men that swerved from the worship of the same immortal gods should be reclaimed, by the infliction of punishment and pain, to the worship of the gods. At the time, however, when I first came to the east, under favourable auspices, and ascertained that great numbers of men, capable of rendering service to the republic, were banished by the judges for said reason, I issued or-

---

* In the Greek style of this inscription, we may see some traces of the Latin original.

† Our author here represents Maximinus guilty of the double inconsistency of attempting to give a fair colouring to his proceedings against the Christians, although his conduct and procedure had wanted even the shadow of appearance, and in his very defence, saying what was in fact a reproach to himself.

ders to each of the judges, that in future none of these should behave with severity to the provincials, but rather reclaim them to the worship of the gods, by exhortation and flattery. Then therefore, whilst, agreeably to my orders, the injunctions were observed by the judges, it happened that no one of the countries in the east was either banished or insulted, but rather that they were reclaimed to the worship of the gods, from the fact that nothing severe was done against them. After this, however, when a year had passed away, I arrived under fortunate circumstances at Nicomedia, and made my stay there, and citizens of that place came to me with the statues of the gods, greatly intreating me, that by all means this people should not be suffered to dwell in their country.* But when I ascertained that many men of the same religion dwelt in these parts, I gave them this answer: That indeed, I cheerfully thanked them for this petition, but perceived this was not alike requested by all. If, however, there were some that persevered in this superstition, that each one had the option to live as he pleased; even if they wished to adopt the worship of the gods. Nevertheless I deemed it necessary to give a friendly answer both to the inhabitants of Nicomedia and the other cities, which had so earnestly and zealously presented the same petition, viz., that not one of the Christians should be permitted to dwell in their cities, because this same course was observed by all the ancient emperors, and was acceptable to the immortal gods, by whom all men and the whole administration of the republic subsists, and also, that I would confirm this same petition which they had presented for the worship of the immortal gods. Wherefore, although there have been before this, letters sent to your devotedness, and it has in like manner been ordered that the rulers should attempt nothing harsh against those provincials that are desirous of observing this course, but that they should deal mildly and moderately with them, nevertheless that they may suffer neither blows nor injuries from the beneficiaries† or the other common sol

---

* This is his account of what Eusebius had wittily called " sending an embassy to himself."

† The beneficiarii were soldiers, who were promoted by the tribunes, and had

diers, I deemed it consistent to remind your gravity by these
letters, that you should cause our provincials to cultivate their
regard for the gods, rather by exhortations and mild measures.
Whence if any one should determine to adopt the worship of the
gods, of his own accord, it is proper that these should be readily
received. But if any wish to follow their own worship, you may
leave these to have their liberty. Wherefore, it is incumbent on
your devoted zeal to observe what is committed to you, and that
liberty be granted to no one, to oppress our provincial subjects
with violence and insult; whereas, as I wrote before, it is more
becoming to reclaim our provincials, by encouraging and inviting
measures, to the worship of the gods. But that this our will may
come to the knowledge of all our subjects, it is incumbent on
you to communicate the mandate by a proclamation issued by
you." When he had thus commanded these matters, he was
neither sincere nor credited by any, but was evidently forced
by necessity, and did not act according to his real sentiments, as
was obvious from his duplicity, and perfidy, after the former
similar grant. No one therefore, of our brethren, ventured to
hold meetings, nor even to appear in public, because neither was
this the import of the writing, only enjoining to beware of ha-
rassing us; but not commanding that we might hold meetings,
or build houses of worship, or perform any of those things customary with us. And with all this, those advocates of peace and
piety, Constantine and Licinius, had written to him to permit
this, and had granted it to all those under them in their edicts
and ordinances. But this most impious ruler did not choose yielding to this course; until, driven by the justice of God, he was at
last compelled, though unwillingly, to adopt it.

certain privileges. The word, as it here occurs, forms a curious illustration of the
manner in which Greek words were formed from the Latin, βινιφιχαλιοι. The li-
quids *l* and *r* were frequently interchanged.

CHAPTER X.

The victory of the pious emperors.

Such a cause and circumstances, indeed, beset him on all sides. Unable as he was to sustain the magnitude of the government so undeservedly conferred upon him, in consequence of his own incapacity and deficiency in the qualities of a prudent and imperial mind, he administered his affairs in a foolish and disreputable manner, and yet foolishly elated in all, with a fulsome arrogance and haughtiness, even toward those who participated in the government with him, and who were his superiors both in birth and education, dignity and intelligence, and in that wisdom and that true piety which is the crown of all, he yet dared to boast and proclaim himself the first of all in dignity and honours. Proceeding at length to that degree of madness in his vanity and haughtiness, he broke the league that he had made with Licinius, and undertook an execrable war. After this he soon threw all into confusion; alarming every city, and collecting innumerable armies, he went forth to give him battle, elated with his trust in dæmons, whom he supposed to be gods, and the vast multitudes of his soldiers. Thus engaging in battle, he was deprived of the interposition and aid of God; the victory being decreed in favour of the emperor Licinius, by the one only and supreme God. And first, he lost the soldiery upon whom he relied so much, and as the guards about him all abandoned and left him destitute, and deserted to the emperor Licinius, he secretly stripped himself as quickly as possible of the imperial robes, which, indeed, he had never deserved, in a cowardly, abject, and effeminate manner, and mingled with the crowd. Then he made his escape, lying concealed in the fields and villages, and with all this caution and vigilance for safety, scarcely escaped the hands of the enemy. Thus showing in facts the reality and truth of the divine oracles, in which it is said: "A king is not saved by the multitude of an host, nor shall a giant in the greatness of his strength; a horse is a vain thing for safety, and in the greatness of his strength he

shall not be saved.   Behold, the eyes of the Lord are upon those
that fear him, those that trust in his mercy, to rescue their soul
from death."

Thus the tyrant, loaded with disgrace, returned to his own
parts, and first in the rage of his mind, he slew many priests
and prophets of those gods whom he admired, and by whose
oracles he had been induced to undertake the war; these I say
he slew, as jugglers and impostors, and above all as the betrayers
of his own safety.   Then, at length giving glory to the God of
the Christians, he immediately enacted a full and final decree for
their liberty.   However, being seized with a violent disease, he
died very soon after it was issued.   The law enacted was as
follows.

*Copy of the tyrant's ordinance, in regard to the Christians, trans-
lated from the Latin into the Greek.*

" The Emperor Cæsar, Caius, Valerius, Maximinus, Germanicus, Sarmaticus, Pius, Felix, Invictus, Augustus,—That it be-
hoves us by all means, and with constant endeavours to promote
the good of our provincial subjects, and to wish to bestow upon
them such things as are best calculated to establish the advantage of all, and whatever may contribute to their common benefit
and utility ; also, whatever is adapted to the public advantage,
and is agreeable to the views and wishes of all ; of this no one
can be ignorant ; and, moreover, we believe every one can refer
to past events, and know and convince himself of it.   When,
therefore, before this it was obvious to our mind, that by reason
of the law which was enacted under our most sacred parents
Diocletian and Maximian, that the assemblies of the Christians
should be abolished, many oppressions and spoilations were made
by those in office, and that this evil advanced daily to a great
height, to the injury of those of our provincials, for whom we
are particularly anxious to make the necessary provision ; as
their property and possessions were thus destroyed on this pretext, letters were given to the respective rulers of the provinces
the past year, in which it was enacted, that if any one wshed

to follow this practice, or this observance of the same religion, that he was at liberty to pursue this his purpose without hindrance, and without obstruction or molestation from any one; and also, that they had full liberty to do that without fear or suspicion, what each one preferred. But even now we could not but perceive that some of our judges have mistaken our injunctions, and caused our subjects to be in doubt as to our ordinances, and have caused them to proceed with too great reluctance to the performance of those religious observances which they prefer. Now, therefore, that all suspicion of duplicity and fear may be removed, we have decreed that this ordinance should be published, that all may clearly understand, whosoever wish to adopt this sect and worship are at liberty to do so, by this privilege granted by us, so that as each one wishes, or as may be agreeable to him, thus he may observe that religion to which he has been accustomed. And, moreover, liberty is granted to build their churches. But that this indulgence of ours may be the greater, we have also thought proper to make further provision by law, that if any houses and lands happened to be justly the property of Christians before this, and by order of our parents, have been transferred to the treasury, or have been confiscated by any city, or at least have been seized and sold or bestowed as present to any one, all these possessions we have ordered to be returned again to the former possession and control of the Christians, that all persons may also, in this respect, have knowledge of our piety and foresight."

These are the declarations of the tyrant, that were issued not quite a year after the ordinances against the Christians had been published by him on brazen tablets, and by the same man, to whom but a little before, we appeared impious and abandoned wretches, destructive of all society, so that we were not allowed to dwell, indeed, in a city, or even the country and the desert; by this same one, ordinances and laws were enacted in favour of the Christians. And they who a little before were destroyed by the tyrants with fire and sword, the food of wild beasts and birds of prey in the very eyes of the tyrant, and sustained every kind of punishment and torture, and the most miserable death as in

fidels and profane persons, these very same are now acknowledged by him as worshippers having religion, and are allowed
to rebuild their churches; moreover, the tyrant himself confesses
and testifies that certain rights belong to them. Having, therefore, made these confessions, as if he had actually obtained some
positive benefit, on this very account, he suffered less than was
properly his due, and being smitten with a sudden visitation of God,
he died in the second campaign of the war. But his end was not
like that of generals and military commanders, who bravely and
heroically expose their lives, and encounter a glorious death for
glory and their friends; but as one hostile to God and religion,
whilst his army was drawn up for battle in the field, he himself
remained at home, concealing himself, and received the punishment that he deserved, being smitten with a sudden judgment of
God over his whole body; so that he was harassed by dreadful
pains and torments, and prostrated on the ground, was wasted
away by hunger, whilst his whole flesh dissolved by an invisible
fire and burning, sent from God. So that this being wasted
away, the whole aspect of his former shape was destroyed, and
there was only left of him a kind of image, reduced by length of
time to a skeleton of dry bones. Indeed, all present could regard
his body as nothing but the tomb of his soul, buried in one that
was already dead, and completely dissolved. And as the heart
began to burn still more violently in the very recesses of his
marrow, his eyes burst forth, and falling from their sockets they
left him blind. After this he still continued to breathe, acknowledging many things to the Lord, and invoking death. At
length, however, after confessing that he justly suffered these
judgments for his wanton excesses against the Christians, he
breathed his last.

CHAPTER XI.

The total destruction of the enemies of religion.

THUS, then, Maximinus being removed out of the way, who nad proved the worst of all the surviving enemies of religion, by the goodness of God, the omnipotent ruler, the renovation of the churches was begun from the very foundations. But the doc· trine of Christ shining forth to the glory of the supreme God, enjoyed greater privileges than before, whilst the impious and profane were covered with shame and irrecoverable disgrace. First of all, Maximinus himself, being publicly announced by the emperors as the public enemy, was confirmed to be the most impious and detestable, as well as the most hostile to the Deity, by his public edicts. And, whatsoever paintings and representations had been placed in honour of him or his children, in every city, some were forced down from their elevation, and torn to pieces or broken, others were destroyed by having the face daubed with black paint. Whatsoever statues, also, had been erected to his honour, were likewise cast down and broken, lying exposed to the laughter and jests of those that were disposed to insult and wantonly abuse them. Then, also; all the honours of the other enemies of religion were removed. All that favoured the party of Maximinus were slain, especially those that had been distinguished by him with eminent offices, as rulers, for their flattery to him, in their insolent excesses against our faith. Of this number was Peucetius, the most honoured, and revered, and dearest of all his favourites, who had been consul twice and thrice, and had been appointed by him prime minister. Culcianus, also, who had been promoted through every grade of office, and who was also prominent for his many slaughters of Christians in Egypt. There were also not a few others, by whose agency especially, the tyranny of Maximinus had been augmented and confirmed; justice, also, summoned Theotecnus, by no means overlooking the evils he had done against the Christians. And whilst he now expected to enjoy himself, after he had erected the statue at Antioch, and

was now promoted to the government of a province, Licinius
came to the city of Antioch, and making a search for all the impostors, he put the prophets and priests of the newly wrought
statue to the torture, asking at the same time, how they came to
concoct such a delusion. And when unable by reason of the
tortures to conceal it any longer, they disclosed that the whole
secret was a device of Theotecnus. After punishing all according
to their deserts, he first condemned Theotecnus, and after him all
the partners of his impostures, to death, with the greatest possible
torments. To all these were superadded the children of Maximinus, whom he had already made sharers in the imperial dignity with his titles and statues. Also, the relatives of the tyrants
who before this were elated and boasting, and exercising their
power over all men, had the same punishments, together with
the utter disgrace of the others, inflicted upon them. As they
would neither receive instruction nor understand the exhortation
given in the Holy Scriptures: " Trust not in princes, in the children of men, in whom there is no safety. For his breath goeth
from him, and he will return to his earth again. In that day all
their thoughts shall perish." Thus, then, the impious being
cleared away, the government was deservedly reserved secure,
and without a rival, for the only two, Constantine and Licinius.
These, after first removing the hostility to God out of the way,
and sensible of the great benefits conferred on them by his goodness, exhibited ł oth their love of virtue and God, as well as their
piety and grau.tude to Him, by the laws they enacted in favou
of Christians.

BOOK X.

CHAPTER I.

The peace which was granted us by divine interposition.

But thanks be to God, the omnipotent and universal sovereign, thanks also to the Saviour and Redeemer of our souls, Jesus Christ, through whom we pray that peace will be preserved to us at all times, firm and unshaken by any temporal molestation from without, and troubles from the mind within. Attended with your prayers, O most holy Paulinus,* whilst we superadd this tenth book to the preceding ones of our ecclesiastical history, we shall dedicate this to you, announcing you as the seal of the whole work. Justly, indeed, shall we here subjoin in a perfect number,† a complete discourse and panegyric on the renovation of the churches yielding to the spirit of God, inviting us in the following manner: "Sing to the Lord a new song, because he hath done wonderful works. His right hand hath saved him, and his holy right arm. The Lord hath made known his salvation, his righteousness hath he openly showed in the sight of the heathen." Thus, then, as the Scriptures enjoin upon us to sing a new song, we shall accordingly show that after those dreadful and gloomy spectacles and events, we have been privileged to

---

* Paulinus was bishop of Tyre, and Eusebius here dedicates the work to him, as the one who suggested and urged him to undertake it.

† The number ten is called perfect, because it is the limit and close of our system of numeration; all the numbers beyond ten being only combinations of this and the included digits. Shorting has overlooked the stress which our author intended to lay on the expression. He has considered it as a mere qualification of panegyric. It may be observed, this book contains the celebrated panegyric delivered by Eusebius at the renovation of the cathedral of Tyre. But the author seems to intend the whole book as a eulogy upon the happy reverse of affairs, and therefore, a happy close of the whole work. He now seems to lay aside the historian, and to swell into the amplifications of the orator.

see such things, and to celebrate such things as many of the really pious and martyrs of God, before us ardently craved to see, and did not see them, and to hear, and did not hear them. But they, indeed, hastening on their course, obtained " what was far better;" being transferred to the heavens themselves, and to the paradise of celestial pleasures. But we freely acknowledging this state of things in our day as better than what we could expect, have been beyond measure astonished at the magnitude of the grace manifested by the author of our mercies, and justly do we admire and adore him with all the powers of our mind, and bear witness to the truth of those declarations recorded, where it is said, " come hither and behold the works of God, the wonders that he hath done upon the earth; he removeth wars until the ends of the earth, he breaketh the bow and snappeth the spear asunder, and burneth the shields in fire." Rejoicing in these things fulfilled in our day, we shall pursue the tenor of our history. All the race of the enemies of God were destroyed in the manner we have stated, and were thus suddenly swept away from the sight of men, as the divine Word again declares: " I saw the wicked lifted up and exalted like the cedars of Lebanon, and I passed by, and lo, he was not; and I sought, and his place was not found." And now a bright and splendid day, with no overshadowing cloud, irradiated the churches in the whole world with its celestial light; neither was there any indisposition even on the part of those who were strangers to our faith, to enjoy with us the same blessings, or of sharing at least in the overflowings of these as they were provided from God.

CHAPTER II.

The restoration of the churches.

ALL men, then, were liberated from the oppression of the tyrant, and those who had been delivered from the miseries previously existing, acknowledged, one in one way, and another in another, that the only true God was the protector of the pious. To us especially, all whose hopes are suspended on the Christ of God, there was an incessant joy, and there sprung up for all a certain celestial gladness, seeing every place, which but a short time before had been desolated by the impieties of the tyrants, reviving again, and recovering as from a long and deadly distemper, temples again rising from the soil to a lofty height, and receiving a splendour far exceeding those that had been formerly destroyed. Moreover, those who held the supreme power, confirmed the privileges granted us by the divine beneficence to a still wider and greater extent by their constant decrees in favour of the Christians, and epistles of the emperor were issued, addressed to the bishops, with honours and superadded donations of monies. Of which it may not be singular to insert extracts in the proper place in this book, as in a certain sacred tablet, as we have translated them from the Latin into the Greek language that they may remain recorded for those that come after us.

CHAPTER III.

The dedications of the churches in all places.

AFTER this the sight was afforded us so eagerly desired and prayed for by all, the festivals of dedications and consecrations of the newly erected houses of prayer throughout the cities. After this the convention of bishops, the concourse of foreigners from abroad, the benevolence of people to people, the unity of the members of Christ concurring in one harmonious body. Then was it according to the prophetic declaration, mystically indicating what would take place, " bone was brought to bone, and joint to joint," and whatsoever other matters the divine Word faithfully intimated before. There was, also, one energy of the divine spirit, pervading all the members, and one soul among all, one and the same ardour of faith, and one song of praise to the Deity Yea, now indeed, complete and perfect solemnities of the prelates and heads of the church, sacred performances of sacred rites, and solemn rituals of the church. Here you might hear the singing of psalms and the other voices given us from God, there divine and sacred mysteries performed. The mystic symbols of our Saviour's passion were celebrated, and at the same time every sex of every age, male and female, with the whole power of the mind, and with a mind and heart rejoicing in prayer and thanksgiving, gave glory to God the author of all good. Every one of the prelates present, also, delivered panegyric discourses, desirous of adding lustre to the assembly according to the ability of each.

CHAPTER IV.

Panegyric on the splendour of our affairs.

AND a certain one* of those of moderate capacity, who had composed a discourse, advanced in the midst of the assembly where many pastors were present, as in the congregations of churches, and whilst all attended in decency and silence, he addressed himself as follows, to one who was the best and most pious of bishops, and by whose zeal principally the temple in Tyre, by far the most noble in Phœnicia, was built.

Panegyric on the building of the churches, addressed to Paulinus bishop of Tyre.

"FRIENDS, and priest of God, and ye who are clad in the sacred gown,† adorned with the celestial crown of glory, the inspired

---

* Eusebius here means himself, and addresses the bishop of the church of Tyre. We cannot conceive how translators could make our author here speak of his merits, as Valesius and Shorting; he modestly states merely his moderate qualifications, εκ των επιεικων.

† The gown here mentioned, derived its name from its extending down to the feet: ποδηρη

unction and the sacerdotal garment of the Holy Spirit. And
thou, O excellent ornament of this new and holy temple of God
endowed by him with the wisdom of age, and yet who hast exhibited the precious works and deeds of youthful and vigorous
virtue, to whom God himself, who comprehends the universe, has
granted the distinguished privilege of rebuilding and renewing it
to Christ, his first begotten and only begotten Word, and to his
holy and divine spouse; whether one might call thee a new Beseleel,* the architect of a divine tabernacle, or a Solomon, the
king of a new and better Jerusalem, or a new Zerubbabel, superadding a glory to the temple of God, much greater than the
former. You, also, O nurslings of the flock of Christ, the habitation of excellent discourses, school of modesty, and the devout
and religious auditory of piety. Long since, indeed, we were
allowed the privilege of raising hymns and songs of praise to
God, when we learned from hearing the sacred Scriptures read,
the wonderful deeds of God, and the benefits of the Lord conferred upon men, and whom we were taught to repeat, 'O God,
we have heard with our ears, our fathers have told us, the work
that thou didst in those days, in the days of old.' But now as we
perceive the lofty arm and the celestial hand of our all-gracious
and omnipotent God and king, not only by the hearing and the
report of words, but by deeds ; and, as we may say, with our
own eyes, as we contemplate those faithful and true declarations
recorded in times of old, we may raise another song of triumph,
and exclaim, and appropriately say, ' as we have heard, so have
we seen, in the city of the Lord of hosts, in the city of our God.'
And in what city but in this newly built and framed by God ?
' which is the church of the living God, the pillar and foundation
of the truth.' Concerning which another passage of the holy
Scriptures thus, declares: 'Glorious things are spoken of thee,
thou city of God;' into which the all-gracious God having collected us by the grace of his only begotten, let each one here assembled only sing, cry aloud, and say: 'I was glad when they
said unto me, we will go into the house of the Lord;' and again,

---

* The name is written in our version, Bezaleel. Exod. xxxv. 31.

'Lord I have loved the beauty of thine house, and the place where thine honour dwelleth.' And not only individually, but all together with one breath and one soul, let us with veneration exclaim, 'Great is the Lord, and highly to be praised in the city of our God, even upon his holy hill.' For he, indeed, is truly great, and great is his habitation, sublime, and spacious, and comely in beauty beyond the sons of men. 'Great is the Lord who only doeth wonderful things, and things past finding out, glorious and stupendous things which cannot be numbered. Great is he who changeth the seasons and times, who setteth up and debaseth kings, who raiseth the poor from the ground, and exalteth the beggar from the dunghill. He hath thrust down the mighty from their seats, and hath exalted the humble from the earth. He hath filled the hungry with good things, and hath broken in pieces the arms of the proud.' He has confirmed the record of ancient events, not only to the faithful, but to the unbelievers. 'He that worketh miracles, he that doeth mighty deeds; He, that Lord of the universe, the Creator of the whole world, the omnipotent one and only God. In obedience to him we 'sing a new song, who alone doeth wonderful things, because his mercy endureth for ever; that smiteth mighty kings and slayeth strong kings, because his mercy endureth for ever'; for the Lord hath remembered us in our humiliation, and hath delivered us from our enemies.' And may we never cease to celebrate the Father of all with these praises. Him also, we would extol, and bear his name constantly upon our lips, the second cause of our mercies, the instructor in divine knowledge, teacher of true religion, destroyer of the impious, slayer of tyrants the reformer of the world, and the Saviour of us when our condition was desperate, our Lord Jesus. For he alone as the only all-gracious Son of the all-gracious Father, according to the purpose of his Father's benevolence, readily and freely assuming the nature of us who lay prostrate in the depths of destruction, like an excellent physician, who, 'for the sake of saving those who are labouring under disease, examines their sufferings, han dles their foul ulcers, and from others miseries produces grief and pains to himself,'* has saved us, not only struggling with dreadful ulcers, and wounds already putrid, but even lying among the dead, and rescued us to himself from the very jaws of death. For none of those in heaven had such power at command, as to promote the salvation of so many without detriment. But he alone, after having reached the deplorable corruption of our race, he alone taking upon him our labours, and bearing the punish ment of our iniquities, recovering us, not merely half dead, but altogether fœtid and offensive, in tombs and sepulchres, both of old and new, by his gracious love saves us still beyond the hope and expectation of others, and even of ourselves, and liberally imparts to us the abundance of his Father's blessings. He, the giver of life and of light, our great Physician, King and Lord, the Christ of God. And then, indeed, when the whole human race, once lay buried in gloomy night and the depths of dark- ness, by the delusions of execrable dæmons, and the machina- tions and influences of malignant spirits, as soon as he appeared, as the wax melts under the rays of the sun, he dissolved the knotty and entangled bonds of our iniquities, by the rays of his light. But when malignant envy and the mischievous spirit of iniquity, almost bursting asunder at such a display of grace and benevo- lence, was now arraying all his deadly forces against us, and like a dog in a fit of madness, first gnashing his teeth at the stones cast at him, and pouring his rage kindled by his assailants, against inanimate weapons, he levelled his savage ferocity at the stones of the oratories and lifeless materials to produce, as he supposed, the desolation of the churches. Afterwards, however, he issued dreadful hissings and serpentine voices, sometimes by the threats of impious tyrants, sometimes by the blasphemous ordinances of profane governors; and moreover, he himself, pouring forth death, and infecting the souls captured by him with his pestilen- tial and destructive poison, almost destroyed them with the deadly sacrifices to dead idols, and caused every sort of beast in the shape of man, and every savage, to assault us. Then the Angel of the

* This is a quotation from some poet, and seems to belong to Sophocles or Æschylus. The verses in the original are iambics; but the poem from which they are taken is lost.

mighty council, the great Captain and Leader of the armies of God, after a sufficient exercise which the greatest of the soldiers of his kingdom had exhibited in their patience and perseverance, again suddenly appeared, and destroying what was hostile, and annihilating his foes, so that they scarcely appeared to have had a name. But those that were his friends and of his household, he advanced not only to glory with all men, but now also, with celestial powers, the sun, the moon, and the stars, the whole heavens and the world.* So that now what never happened before, the supreme sovereigns, sensible of the honour conferred upon them by him, now spit upon the faces of idols, trample upon the unhallowed rites of dæmons, ridicule the ancient delusion of their ancestors, and acknowledge only the one and true God, the common benefactor of all and of themselves. They also confess Christ the Son of God, as the universal king of all, and proclaim him the Saviour in their edicts, inscribing his righteous deeds and his victories over the impious with royal characters, on indelible records, and in the midst of that city which holds the sway over the earth. So that our Saviour Jesus Christ, is the only one ever acknowledged, by the supreme rulers of the earth, not as a common king among men, but worshipped as the true Son of God, and God himself.† And all this justly too. For who of kings at any time has ever advanced to such a height of excellence, as to fill the ears and the tongues of all men with his own name? What king ever ordained laws so pious and wise, and extended them so as to be read by all men from the ends of the earth to its remotest borders? Who has ever abrogated the fierce and barbarous customs of fierce and barbarous nations, by his mild and most beneficent laws? Who is there, when assailed by all for whole ages, that has ever exhibited a virtue far surpassing man, so as to rise and flourish again from day to day, throughout the whole world? Who is there that has ever established a nation never

---

* These expressions, "celestial powers, sun, moon, and stars," may be regarded as oriental hyperbole, for the "powers that be." What immediately follows, shows that Eusebius means the reigning emperors.

† The original here is χυριος, *God himself*, or *very God*.

heard of before, not concealed in a corner of the earth, but spread over every part of it under the sun? Who has so fortified his soldiers with the arms of piety, that their souls more firm than adamant, shine resplendent in the contest against their antagonists? What king ever prevailed to such an extent, as to lead on his armies after death, rear trophies against his enemies, and fill every place and city and region, whether Grecian or barbarian, with his royal palaces and the consecrations of his sacred temples? Witness the splendid ornaments and donations of this very temple, which themselves are noble and truly grand, worthy of admiration and astonishment, and expressive symbols of our Saviour's kingdom. Truly ' he hath spoken, and they were made; he hath commanded, and they were created.' For what was there to resist the beck of the universal King. the universal Prince, and God, the Word himself.* It would require a peculiar leisure to survey and explain each particular minutely; and not only this, but to explain how great and powerful the alacrity of those who have laboured in the work, has been judged by him whom we celebrate, who looks into the temple within our souls, and surveys the building of living and moving stones, happily and securely built upon the foundation of the apostles and prophets, Jesus Christ himself being the chief corner stone. Whom, indeed, not only those of that ancient building no longer existing, have rejected; but also, those of the building now existing, that vast multitude of men, wretched architects of the wicked as they are.† But the Father having proved him now as well as then, has established him as the head of the corner of this our common church. This, therefore, the living temple of the living God, formed of yourselves, I say, is the greatest and the truly divine sanctuary, whose inmost shrines, though invisible to the multitude, are really holy, a holy of holies. Who, when he has viewed it within, would venture to declare it? But who could ever penetrate its sacred enclosures, save only the great

* The expression here, is αυτου Θεου λογου.

† Eusebius here alludes to the two dispensations, Jewish and Christian. The former building had passed away; the latter now existing, was still rejected by the multitude of the heathen world.

High Priest of all, who alone has the right and *power* to search out the mysteries of every human and rational soul? Next to him, however, the second place* immediately devolves on one alone of his equals, the presiding prelate and leader of this host, who has been honoured by the first and great High Priest himself with the second rank in this sanctuary, and has been appointed by him as his courtier and interpreter, and the shepherd of your spiritual (divine) flock, obtaining this people of yours as his portion by the judgment and allotment of the Father; a new Aaron or another Melchisedech assimilated to the Son of God, continuing and always preserved by him in accordance with the common wishes and prayers of you all. To him, therefore, alone, let it be granted, if not in the first place, at least in the second, after the first and supreme High Priest, to inspect and superintend the observation and state of your inmost souls. As he by experience and length of time has diligently examined each one, and by his zeal and care has disposed all of you to cultivate the order and doctrine of piety; capable, also, as he is above all, to give reasons adequate to the works which he himself with the divine assistance has framed. Our first and great High Priest, saith the Scripture, 'whatsoever He seeth the Father doing, these things also doeth the Son;' and whatsoever he† seeth Him doing, using these things as archetypes and examples, their images and resemblances, he has as far as possible expressed, after the most perfect likeness in his own works. In no respect inferior to that Beseleel, whom the Spirit of God himself filled with wisdom, and understanding, and whatever other knowledge and skill might be

---

* A scholiast on this expression, makes the remark και ταυτο ασιβις. Valesius videtur existimavisse scholiastem hic Eusebium quasi de Christo loquentem intellexisse. Sed vir doctus hoc errare videtur. Scholiastes Eusebium hic impietatis arguit quod, episcopo secundum gradum dignitatis a Christo attribuere ausus est, et Valesius ipse dicit in loc.; "fatendum est Eusebium nimis hic tribuisse Paulino, dum ei τα ισα διυτερικα, tanquam æquali et collegæ Christi adscribit; dum Melchisedecum vocat." Attamen si hæc excusanda sint, eo nomine fortassis excusari possint, quod Eusebius noster hic oratorem, (prope dixissem poetam) magis quam theologum egisse, videtur. Quis nescit orientalium ingenii ardorem qui sæpe extra omnes rerum fines excurrit!

† *He*, refers to Paulinus, looking as it were to Christ.

necessary, for the building of that temple* appointed and selected as the builder of that edifice of a temple of celestial types, a temple given in symbols and figures. Thus, also. he has framed and fashioned the whole Christ complete, the word, the wisdom, the light, and bearing in his own soul the image of the same it is impossible to tell with what joy and gladness, with what an abundant and liberal mind, and with what emulation among all of you, and what magnanimity among the contributors, ambitiously striving that none should be behind him in executing the same purpose, he has framed and finished this magnificent and noble temple of God, so similar in its character to the copy of that better temple, the visible of the invisible. And what also deserves first of all to be mentioned, he did not overlook this place, which had been covered with filth and rubbish, by the artifices of our enemies; but could not think of giving way to the wickedness of those who were the authors of it, though he was at liberty to go to another place, there being innumerable others in the city; and thus to find a diminution of his labour, and to be relieved from trouble. First, he prepared himself for the work. Then, also, after strengthening and animating the people, and forming all into one great body, he performed this, the first of his labours.† Thinking that the church which had been most assailed by the enemy, she that had first laboured in trials, and that had sustained the same persecutions with us and before us— this church, like a mother bereft of her children, should also enjoy with us the mercies and privileges of the all-gracious Giver. For when the great Shepherd had driven away the wild beasts, the wolves, and every fierce and savage race, and, in the language of Scripture, had broken the jaws of the lions, he again condescended to collect her children, and in the most righteous manner he raised the fold of her flock, "to shame the enemy and the avenger:" and to present a refutation against the impious audacity of those that were fighting against God. And now

---

* Our author calls the tabernacle here, by a metonymy, the *temple*.

† The original is ξύλον ηγωνιζετο, a gladiatorial phrase applied to combatants and wrestlers, and referring to the labours of Hercules, particularly that of cleansing the Augean stable.

these enemies of God are no more, because they never were. For a short time, indeed, they created alarm, whilst themselves were troubled; then suffering the severe punishment which they owed to divine justice, they overturned themselves, and friends, and habitations to the dust. So that it is confessed those declarations inscribed of old on the sacred tablets, are proved as true by facts, in which the divine Word, among others, also asserts the following concerning them: ' The ungodly have drawn out the sword, they have bent the bow to cast down the poor and needy, and to slay such as are of an upright walk. Their sword shall pierce through their own heart, and their bows shall be broken.' And, again, ' Their memory is perished with a sound, and their name hast thou blotted out for ever and ever. Because when they were in miseries they cried, and there was none to save, even to the Lord, and he heard them not. They were bound† and fell, but we are raised and stand upright.'

" That, too, which was declared before, in the following words, ' O Lord, thou shalt annihilate their image in thy city,' is truly manifested to the eyes of all. But after waging a war against God, like the giants, they terminated their lives in this manner; whilst she " which was desolate, and rejected of men," has received that consummation that we have seen, for her patient endurance in God, so that the prophecy of Isaiah seemed to utter these things; ' Rejoice, thirsty desert, let the desert exult and blossom as the lily, and the desert places shall flourish and be

---

* This expression seems to have been misapprehended by Valesius and Shorting. It simply expresses the utter nothingness of the enemies of God. No expression could represent human weakness in a stronger light when arrayed against Omnipotence. It is scarcely hyperbolical to say such *power never was*. The compound word θεομισεις, may mean either *hated of God*, or *God haters*, according as the accent is on the ultimate or penultimate. Valesius reads with the accent on the last syllable, which would justify his rendering *invisi Deo*. Besides, our author is fond of antithesis, particularly if aided by alliteration. He had called them θεομαχοι, now θεομισεις. We have given the most comprehensive sense; as men, in the order of Providence, are always *God haters* before they can be pronounced *God hated*.

† It will be recollected, we translate these passages from our author, who quotes the Septuagint. The Greek here means *their feet were bound together*.

glad. Be strengthened, ye languid hands, and ye relaxed knees. Be consoled, ye weak hearted in your minds, be strong and fear not. Behold our God has repaid judgment, and he will repay. He will come and save us. For he says, water has burst forth in the desert, and a pool in a thirsty land. And the dry land shall become a pool, and a well of water shall be in the thirsty land.' These things, uttered in ancient oracles, have been recorded in the sacred books. But, now, these things, themselves, are no longer addressed to us in mere reports, but in facts.

" This desert, this dry and thirsty land;" this widow and deserted one, whose gates they cut down with axes, as wood in the forest, breaking them down with the ax and the hatchet, whose books they destroyed, and whose divine sanctuary they burned with fire, whilst they profaned the habitation of his name unto the ground, and all that passed by plucked off her grapes, breaking down her hedges; she, whom the wild boar of the forest has rooted up, and the savage wild beast has devoured, now, by the marvellous power of Christ, as he himself would have it, has blossomed as the lily. But, even then, she was chastened at his nod, as by a provident father: ' For whom the Lord loveth he chasteneth, and scourgeth every son whom he receiveth.' Then, after being chastened in measure, as far as was necessary, she was commanded to rejoice of anew ; and she now blossoms as the lily, and exhales her divine odour among all men. For it is said, ' Water gushed forth in the desert the fountain of divine regeneration of the salutary laver. And now she, which a little before was desolate, is changed into pools, and a well of living water has gushed out upon a thirsty land.' The arms formerly languid have become truly strong, and these works are the great and expressive displays of invigorated hands. Those knees, also, that were formerly debilitated and relaxed, now recovering their former firmness, are walking in a straight course on their way, and hastening on to their proper fold of the al -gracious pastor. And are there, also, some that were alarmed and overawed by the threats of the tyrants, not even these have been overlooked as incurable by the Saviour's word, but he, thoroughly healing likewise them, raises them to receive conso

lation, as he says, ' Be ye comforted, ye dejected in mind, be
strong, fear not.'

"This our new and excellent Zerubbabel, then perceiving by
the acute hearing of his mind, the sacred oracles declaring that
she who had been desolate for the sake of her God, should now
enjoy such things as these, after her severe captivity, and the
abomination of desolation, did not neglect this dead carcase.
First of all with prayers and supplications, he propitiated the
Father with the common consent and concurrence of you all, and
calling upon the only one who can raise from the dead, as his
aid and ally, he raised her, who had fallen, after he had cleansed
and healed her from her ills. He cast around her, not the garment of old, but such as he had again learned from the sacred
oracles, clearly declaring : ' And the glory of this latter house
shall far exceed the former.' Thus, then, embracing a much
wider space, he strengthened the outer enclosure with a wall to
compass the edifice, that it might be a most secure bulwark to
the whole work. Then raising a large and lofty vestibule, he
extended it towards the rays of the rising sun ; presenting even
to those standing without the sanctuary, a full view of those
within, all but turning the eyes of those who are strangers to
the faith, to contemplate its entrance ; so that no one can pass
by, without being struck in his mind at the recollection of the
former desolation, and the present wonderful transformation. By
this, indeed, he also hoped that the individual thus smitten would
be attracted by the very sight, and induced to enter. And on
entering within the gates, he has not permitted you to enter immediately, with impure and unwashed feet, within the sanctuary,
but leaving an extensive space between the temple, (the nave)
and the vestibule, he has decorated and enclosed it with four inclined porticoes around, presenting a quadrangular space, with
pillars rising on every side. Between these he carried round the
frame latticed railing, rising to a proportioned and suitable height,
leaving, however, the middle space open, so that the heavens can
be seen, and present the splendid sky irradiated by the beams
of the sun. Here too, he has placed the symbols of the sacred
purification, by providing fountains built opposite the temple,

(nave) which, by the abundant effusion of its waters, affords the means of cleansing, to those that proceed to the inner parts of the sanctuary. And this is the first place that receives those that enter, and which at the same time presents to those that need the first introduction, both a splendid and a convenient station. After passing also this sight, he has made open entrances to the temple, with many other inner vestibules, by placing again three gates on one side towards the rising sun. Of these he constructed the midde one, far exceeding those on each side in height and breadth, embellishing it at the same time with exceedingly splendid brazen plates bound with iron, and decorated with various sculpture, superadding them as guards and attendants to a queen. In the same way, after disposing the number of the vestibules, also with the porticoes on each side of the whole temple, he constructed above these, different openings to the building for the purpose of admitting more light, and these lights or windows he also decorated with various kinds of ornamental sculpture. But the royal temple itself, he has furnished with more splendid and rich materials, applying a generous liberality in his expenses. And here, it appears to me to be superfluous, to describe the dimensions, the length and the breadth of the edifice, the splendid elegance, the grandeur that surpasses description, and the dazzling aspect of works, glittering in the face of the speaker, the heights rising to the heavens, and the costly cedars of Lebanon resting on these, which have not been overlooked by the divine oracles themselves, when they say: ' The forests of the Lord shall rejoice, and the cedars of Lebanon which he planted.' Why should I now detail minutely the skilful architectural arrangement, and the exceeding beauty of each of the parts, when the testimony of the eye precludes the instruction through the ear.

" For when he had thus completed the temple, he also adorned it with lofty thrones, in honour of those who preside, and also with seats decently arranged in order throughout the whole, and at last placed the holy altar in the middle. And that this again might be inaccessible to the multitude, he enclosed it with frame lattice work, accurately wrought with ingenious sculpture, pre-

senting an admirable sight to the beholders. And not even the
pavement was neglected by him, for this, too, he splendidly
adorned with marble, and then proceeded to the rest, and to the
parts out of the temple. He provided spacious exhedræ and
oeci * on each side, united and attached to the cathedral (palace),
and communicating with the entrances to the middle of the temple. Which buildings were erected by this our most peaceful
Solomon,† the founder of the temple, for those who require yet
the purification and the sprinklings of water and the holy Spirit.
So that the prophecy repeated above, seems to consist no longer
in words, but in facts and deeds: ' For the glory of this latter
house is truly far beyond the former.'

" For it was just and consistent, that as her (the church) pastor and Lord had once submitted to death on her account, and
after his suffering had changed that vile body, which he assumed
for her sake, into a splendid and glorious body, and had conducted the flesh that had been dissolved from corruption into incor-
ruption, that she should likewise enjoy these dispensations‡ of our
Saviour; because, having received a promise of far better things
from him, the far greater glory of a regeneration, in the resurrection of an incorruptible body, with the choir of the angels of light,
in the very celestial palace of God; above all these, she desires
also to obtain them with Christ Jesus himself, her all-gracious
benefactor and Saviour hereafter for ever. In the mean time,

---

* The exhedræ and oeci were vestry-rooms on each side of the cathedral, and
connected with it. On each side of the edifice there was a long passage to the
body or nave of the building, and these exhedræ and *oeci* were in the same right
line, and communicated with them by doors. They were also baptisteries, consis-
tories, and, in general, places intended for the various subordinate purposes of the
church. See Valesius's note on Bock III. De Vit. Const. ch. l.   Also, Bingham's
Orig.

† Eusebius takes occasion to compliment the bishop on his resemblance to the
royal founder of the Jewish temple, in the similar capacity which he had here sustained. In this resemblance, he also alludes to the signification of Solomon's name,
peaceful.

‡ The word οικονομια, here occurring, is used by our author in the comprehensive
sense, for whatever our Saviour did for our salvation. Here it is evidently applied
not only to the death but the resurrection of our Lord.

however, in the present world, she that was formerly a widow and desolate, and now decorated with the flowers of divine grace, has truly become as the lily, as the prophecy declares, and receiving the bridal garment, and covered with the crown of glory, as she is taught to exult and dance by the prophet Isaiah, proclaims her gratitude in joyous language to God her king. Let us hear her own words : ' I will greatly rejoice in the Lord, my soul shall be joyful in my God, for he hath clothed me with the garment of salvation, he hath covered me with the robe of righteousness, as a bridegroom decketh himself with ornaments, and as a bride adorneth herself with jewels. For as the earth bringeth forth her bud, and as the garden causeth the things sown in it to spring forth, so the Lord God will cause righteousness and praise to spring forth before all the nations.' Thus, singing, she exults and dances.

"In the same words, also, that celestial spouse and word, Jesus Christ, himself answers her ; Hear the Lord, saying, ' Fear not because thou wast abased, neither be thou confounded, that thou was put to shame. For thou shalt forget thy past shame of old, and shalt not remember the shame of thy widowhood any more. The Lord hath not called thee as a woman deserted and dejected, neither as a woman hated from her youth, saith thy God. For a small moment have I forsaken thee, but with great mercy will I gather thee. In a little wrath I hid my face from thee for a moment, but with everlasting kindness will I have mercy on thee, saith the Lord thy Redeemer.' ' Awake, awake, thou that hast drunk at the hand of the Lord the cup of his fury, thou hast drunk the dregs and exhausted them. There was none to console thee of all the sons thou didst bring forth, neither was there any to take thee by the hand. Behold, I have taken out of thine hand the cup of stumbling, the cup of my fury, and thou shalt no more drink it again. But I will put it into the hand of them that afflict thee, and that have humbled thee.' ' Awake, awake, put on thy strength, put on thy glory, shake off the dust, and arise and sit down, loose thyself from the bands of thy neck. Lift up thine eyes round about thee, and behold thy children are gathered together. Behold they are gathered and come to thee.

As I live, saith the Lord, thou shalt clothe thyself with them all as with an ornament, and thou shalt bind them on thee as orna ments on a bride. For thy waste and desolate places, and the land of thy destruction, shall now be too narrow by reason of the inhabitants, and they that would swallow thee up shall be far away. The children which thou hast lost shall say in thine ears ' The place is narrow for me, give place to me that I may dwell.' Then shalt thou say in thine heart, Who hath begotten me these? seeing I have lost my children and am a widow? and who hath brought up these. Behold, I was left alone. But these, where had they been?'

"Such were the oracles uttered before by Isaiah. These were the declarations respecting us anciently, recorded in the holy Scriptures. It was just, therefore, that we should at some time receive their truth in the facts themselves. Since then the spouse and word addressed such language as this to the holy church before; justly, therefore, has this our bride-man (bride-dresser,*) raised her lying desolate, and as a dead carcase, hope-less in the sight of men, and with the common prayers of you all, stretched out his hands, raised her up, and at the command of God, the sovereign king, and in the manifestation of the powers of Christ Jesus, caused her to stand upright. And when thus raised, he so ordered and established her, as he had learned from the description given by the sacred oracles. Won-derful and mighty, therefore, and beyond all admiration is this work, especially to those who attend only to the external appear-ance. But more wonderful than wonders are those archetypes, the mental prototypes and divine exemplars, the renewals of the divine and spiritual buildings in our souls, which he, the Son of God himself, framed and fashioned according to his own image, and to which every where and in all respects he imparted the likeness of God. An incorruptible nature, incorporeal, reason-able, separate from all earthly mixture and matter, an intelli-gent existence. And having once created her† and brought her

* νυμφοϛτολος here, applied to Paulinus.

† Our author means the spiritual church of which he had just spoken, using a per sonification in the pronoun *her*, as common with the Christian fathers as it is with u

into being from that which was not, he also wrought her into a holy spouse, a completely sacred and holy temple, for himself and the Father. Which, indeed, himself plainly declares and professes in the following words: ' I will dwell in them and walk in them, and will be their God and they shall be my people.' And such, indeed, is the perfect and purified mind, having been made such from the beginning, as to bear the image of the celestial Word. By the envy and jealousy of the malignant dæmon, however, she began to be fond of pleasures and fond of evil, by her own voluntary choice, and then the Divinity retiring from her, as one destitute of her protector, she became an easy captive, and easily exposed to the insidious plots of those who had long envied her felicity. And thus assailed by the batteries and machines of her invisible and spiritual enemies, she fell a hideous carcase. So that there was not one stone of her virtue remained standing, and she lay completely and entirely dead upon the earth, totally stripped and destitute of her usual and natural ideas of God. But as she thus lay fallen and prostrate, she that had been made after the image of God, it was not that wild boar of the forest that we see, but some destructive dæmon and spiritual wild beasts that laid her waste. These, inflaming her with passions, as with the burning darts of their own iniquity, set fire to the really divine sanctuary of God, and profaned the tabernacle of his name to the ground. Then burying the unhappy one with heaps of earth, they totally destroyed every hope of her deliverance. But the divine and saving Word, who careth for her, after she had endured the deserved punishment of her sins, again recovered and restored her to the full confidence of the all-gracious mercy of the Father. First, then, she gained the favour of the supreme imperial rulers themselves, and with the whole world, was delivered from the impious tyrants, those destructive and tremendous enemies of all, by the intervention of those most excellent and divinely favoured princes. Then also, the men who were his (Christ's) familiar friends, those formerly consecrated to him for life, and who, concealed as in a storm of afflictions, had nevertheless been secretly protected by their God; these were led forth by him to the light and honoured, deservedly by the munificence of his spirit. Again, then, by means of these he cleansed and removed the filth of the souls who a little before had been polluted, and with the spades and mattocks, the reproving doctrines of the divine word, he removed all the accumulated matter of impious commands.* And thus when he had made the ground of your mind clear and bright, then he committed it for the future to this † most wise and divinely favoured guide. He, as in other respects, endowed with singular judgment and prudence, well capable of discriminating and discerning the minds of those committed to his charge, from the first day that he began to build, as I may say, has not ceased to the present. In one place he applied the splendid gold, in another, the refined and pure silver, and the valuable and precious stones‡ among all, so that a sacred and mystic prophecy is again fulfilled by facts displayed in you, when it is said, ' Behold, I will lay thy stones with fair carbuncles, and lay thy foundations with sapphires, and thy bulwarks of jasper stone, and thy gates with crystal, and thy walls with chosen stones, and all thy children shall be taught of the Lord, and great shall be the peace of thy children, and thou shalt be built in righteousness.'

"Building therefore, in righteousness, he divided the strength and means of the whole people, according to a due estimate. With some § indeed, he surrounded only the exterior inclosure, walling it up with an unwavering faith. For such is the great multitude and mass of the people, that they are incapable of bearing any superior structure. But allowing others‖ the entrance into the edifice, he directs them to stand at the doors, and to conduct those that are entering, who not improperly are compared to

---

* Alluding to the measures pursued by Maximinus and his governors.

† Paulinus, the bishop.

‡ An allusion to 1 Cor. iii. 12., in which our author plainly understands by the gold, silver, precious stones, &c., the different members, as the materials that constituted the moral and spiritual structure.

§ Eusebius now gives an allegorical description of the spiritual temple at Tyre, in which he also gives the different grades of religious attainment.

‖ By these are meant the sub-deacons, whose office was to conduct all that entered to their proper places, the catechumens, penitents, into the narthex or hall, the faithful, &c. into the nave.

the vestibules of the temple. Others, however, he has supported by the first pillars which are placed without, around the quadrangular hall, by initiating them in the first elements of the literal sense of the four gospels. Then he also stations around, on both sides the royal temple, those who are yet catechumens,* and that are yet making progress, and improvement, though not very far separated from the inmost view of divine things, enjoyed by the faithful. Receiving from among these, the souls that are cleansed like gold, by the divine washing, he likewise supports and strengthens these, with columns far better than those external ones, viz., by the inner mysteries and hidden doctrines of the Scriptures. He also illuminates them by the openings, to admit the light, adorning the whole temple with one grand vestibule of adoration to the one only God, the universal Sovereign. Exhibiting, however, as the second splendour, the light of Christ, and the Holy Spirit on each side of the Father's authority,† and displaying in the rest, throughout the whole of the building, the abundance and the exceeding great excellence of the clearness and the brilliancy of truth in every part. Having also selected every where, and from every quarter, the living and moving, and well prepared stones of the mind, he has built a grand and truly royal edifice of all, splendid and filled with light within and with-

---

* Eusebius here gives the different classes, into which the people were divided previous to a full admission. The first, the indiscriminate multitude, compared to the outer wall; the second, the *catechumens*, or those who by a course of instruction were preparing; and finally, those that were called the *competentes*, or the candidates for baptism.

† That the learned reader may have a comment on these words, we here transcribe the words of a scholiast, found in the Mazarine manuscript, used by Valesius, and appended to the passage : ἀνθρωπε, τι σοι των μακρων τουτων και πανηγυρικων λογων οφελος ; η τι κερδος σοι του παντος τουδι φιλοπονηματος και συνταγματος, ουχ ομοτιμον ως ορω τον υιον τω πατρι, ουτε μην το πνευμα το αγιον συνεισαγοντι. Those that wish to read the passage will find it quoted at length by Valesius, in loc. This, however, is not the only passage where the scholiasts have given utterance to what they no doubt conceived to be a just indignation. Sic non veriti sunt Eusebium nostrum, *impium, blasphemum, atheum,* scholiis suis nominare omniaque epitheta, quæ ipse in tyrannos conjicere solebat, scholiastæ iterum in ipsum quasi hostem religiones conjecerunt. Sed pace illorum qui aliter sentiunt, hæ locutiones Eusebianæ proculdubio, *secundum quid* vel κατα τι, ut dicitur inscholis, intelligendæ sunt. Quis nescit

out.   For it is resplendent not only in soul and mind, but the body also is brilliant with the blooming ornaments of chastity and modesty.   But in this temple there are also thrones, many seats also, and benches, in all the souls in which the gifts of the Holy Spirit reside, such as anciently were seen in the holy apostles and their followers, to whom cloven tongues, as of fire, appeared, and sat upon each one of them.   But in the chief of all, Christ himself perhaps resides in his fulness.   In those that rank next to him, each one shares proportionately in the distribution of the power of Christ, and the Holy Spirit.   There may also be seats for angels in the souls of some who are committed to the instruction and care of each.   Noble and grand also, and unique is the altar, such as should be at least, that sincerity and Holy of Holies, of the mind and spirit of the priest of the whole congregation.   That great High Priest of the universe, Jesus, the only begotten Son of God, himself standing at his right, receives the sweet incense from all, and the bloodless and immaterial sacrifices of prayer, with a bright and benign eye ; and with extended hands, bears them to the Father of heaven and God over all.   He himself, first adoring him, and the only one that gives to the Father the worship that is his due, and then interceding with Him for us, that he may always continue propitious and favourable to us all

"Such is the character of this great temple, which the great creative Word hath established, throughout the whole world, constituting this again a kind of intellectual image on earth of those things beyond the vault of heaven.   So that in all his creation, and through all his intelligent creatures on earth, the Father should be honoured and adored.*   But those regions† beyond the

Dominum et Servatorem nostrum κατα τι seipsum, *Patre minorem,* et κατα , iterum *seipsum* et *Patrem unum* dicit.   Et si locutiones hujuscemodi, blasphemiam vel heterodoxiam sapiunt, quis sapit recte ?

* The Greek reads thus: ο Πατηρ αυτω (λογω) τιμωτο τε και σεδοιτο.   Valesius vertit "Pater ipsius" quasi αυτω pro αυτου sed potius videtur indicare agentem.   Versione nostra hic non redditur quia lector communis titubet nec versione Valesii assentire possumus.   Qui nexum sententiarum penitus inspexerit facile videbit Eusebium, hic filium Dei quasi curatorem adorationis Patris innuere.

† Our orator, now drawing to a close, winds up his survey of the temple on earth, by an apostrophe to the transcendant glory of the church triumphant.

heavens, are also displays of what are here, and that Jerusalem above, and that heavenly Sion, and that city of the living God beyond our earth, in which are the innumerable choirs of angels and the assembly of the first born written in heaven, extol their Maker and the universal Sovereign of all, with praises and hymns inexpressible. These surpass our comprehension, neither would any mortal tongue be adequate to declare that glory. 'For eye hath not seen, and ear hath not heard, neither hath it entered into the heart of man to conceive those things which God hath prepared for those that love him.' Of which things as we are already made partakers in part, let us never cease, men, women and children, small and great, all collectively at once, and with one breath, and one mind, to proclaim and to celebrate the author of such great mercies to us. 'Who forgiveth all our sins, and healeth all our infirmities, who redeemeth our life from destruc tion, and crowneth us with lovingkindness, who filleth our soul with good things. For he hath not dealt with us according to our sins nor rewarded us according to our iniquities. For as far as the east is from the west, so far hath he removed our iniquities from us. As a father pitieth his children, so the Lord pitieth them that fear him.' Rekindling such views now, and for all future times, in our minds, and beside the present festivity, and this illustrious and most glorious day, contemplating God as its author, and the universal author of all festivity, night and day, in every hour and with every breath that we draw, let us love and adore Him with all the powers of the soul. And now rising, with the most earnest expression of our love and devotion, let us beseech Him, that he would continue to shelter and save us as those of his flock until the end, and grant us his peace for ever, inviolate and immoveable, in Jesus Christ our Saviour, through whom the glory be to Him through all ages. Amen."

CHAPTER V.

Copies of the imperial decrees.

Now let us also, subjoin translations from the Latin, of the imperial ordinances of Constantine and Licinius.

Copy of the imperial ordinances, translated from the Latin language.

" As we long since perceived that religious liberty should not be denied, but that it should be granted to the opinion and wishes of each one to perform divine duties according to his own determination, we had given orders, that each one, and the Christians among the rest, have the liberty to observe the religion of his choice, and his peculiar mode of worship. But as there plainly appeared to be many and different sects added in that edict,* in which this privilege was granted them, some of them perhaps, after a little while, on this account shrunk from this kind of attention and observance. Wherefore, as I, Constantine Augustus, and I, Licinius Augustus, came under favourable auspices to Milan, and took under consideration all affairs that pertained to the public benefit and welfare, these things among the rest appeared to us to be most advantageous and profitable to all. We have resolved among the first things to ordain, those matters by which reverence and worship to the Deity might be exhibited. That is how we may grant likewise to the Christians, and to all, the free choice to follow that mode of worship which they may wish. That whatsoever divinity and celestial power may exist, may be propitious to us and to all that live under our government.

---

* The edict here mentioned is lost, and the reference is, therefore, subject to some obscurity. The Latin original, however, of this one is preserved by Lanctantius, in his book " De Mortibus Persecutorum," beginning at the words, " Wherefore, as I, Constantine." Valesius here, as well as in the other edicts, has no reference to Lanctantius. The Greek translation is in the main so faithful as to transfer the Latinity ; the text, however, still preserved in Lanctantius, differs in some places from that which Eusebius appears to have had.

Therefore, we have decreed the following ordinance, as our will, with a salutary and most correct intention, that no freedom at all shall be refused to Christians, to follow or to keep their observances or worship. But that to each one power be granted to devote his mind to that worship which he may think adapted to himself. That the Deity may in all things exhibit to us his accustomed favour and kindness. It was just and consistent that we should write that this was our pleasure. That all exceptions respecting the Christians being completely removed, which were contained in the former epistle, that we sent to your fidelity, and whatever measures were wholly sinister and foreign to our mildness, that these should be altogether annulled; and now that each one of the Christians may freely and without molestation, pursue and follow that course and worship which he has proposed to himself: which, indeed, we have resolved to communicate most fully to your care and diligence, that you may know we have granted liberty and full freedom to the Christians, to observe their own mode of worship; which as your fidelity understands absolutely granted to them by us, the privilege is also granted to others to pursue that worship and religion they wish. Which it is obvious is consistent with the peace and tranquillity of our times; that each may have the privilege to select and to worship whatsoever divinity he pleases. But this has been done by us, that we might not appear in any manner to detract any thing from any manner of religion, or any mode of worship. And this, we further decree, with respect to the Christians, that the places in which they were formerly accustomed to assemble, concerning which also we formerly wrote to your fidelity, in a different form, that if any persons have purchased these, either from our treasury, or from any other one, these shall restore them to the Christians, without money and without demanding any price, without any superadded value, or augmentation, without delay, or hesitancy. And if any have happened to receive these places as presents, that they shall restore them as soon as possible to the Christians, so that if either those that purchased or those that received them as presents, have any thing to request of our munificence, they may go to the provincial governor as the judge; that provision may also be made for them by our clemency. All which, it will be necessary to be delivered up to the body of Christians, by your care, without any delay. And since the Christians themselves are known to have had not only those places where they were accustomed to meet, but other places also, belonging not to individuals among them, but to the right of the whole body of Christians, you will also command all these, by virtue of the law before mentioned, without any hesitancy, to be restored to these same Christians, that is to their body, and to each conventicle respectively. The aforesaid consideration, to wit, being observed; namely, that they who as we have said restore them without valuation and price, may expect their indemnity from our munificence and liberality. In all which it will be incumbent on you, to exhibit your exertions as much as possible, to the aforesaid body of Christians, that our orders may be most speedily accomplished, that likewise in this, provision may be made by our clemency, for the preservation of the common and public tranquillity. For by these means, as before said, the divine favour with regard to us, which we have already experienced in many affairs, will continue firm and permanent at all times. But that the purpose of this our ordinance and liberality may be extended to the knowledge of all, it is expected that these things written by us, should be proposed and published to the knowledge of all. That this act of our liberality and kindness may remain unknown to none."

Copy of another Ordinance which was issued by the Emperors, indicating that the benefit was conferred solely on the catholic (universal) church.

" Hail, our most esteemed Anulinus. This is the course of our benevolence; that we wish those things that belong justly to others, should not only remain unmolested, but should also when necessary be restored, most esteemed Anulinus. Whence it is our will, that when thou shalt receive this epistle, if any of those things belonging to the catholic church of the Christians in the several cities or other places, are now possessed either by the decurions, or any others, these thou shalt cause immediately to be restored to their churches. Since we have previously determined, that whatsoever these same churches before possessed, shall be restored to their right. When, therefore, your fidelity has understood this decree of our orders to be most evident and plain, make all haste to restore, as soon as possible, all that belongs to the churches, whether gardens or houses, or any thing else, that we may learn thou hast attended to, and most carefully observed this our decree. Farewell, most esteemed and beloved Anulinus."

Copy of the Emperor's Epistle, in which he ordains a council of bishops to be held at Rome, for the unity and peace of the church.

" CONSTANTINE AUGUSTUS, to Miltiades bishop of Rome, and to Marcus. As many communications of this kind have been sent to me from Anulinus, the most illustrious proconsul of Africa, in which it is contained that Cæcilianus, the bishop of Carthage, was accused, in many respects, by his colleagues in Africa ; and as this appears to be grievous, that in those provinces which divine Providence has freely entrusted to my fidelity, and in which there is a vast population, the multitude are found inclining to deteriorate, and in a manner divided into two parties, and among others, that the bishops were at variance ; I have resolved that the same Cæcilianus, together with ten bishops, who appear to accuse him, and ten others, whom he himself may consider necessary for his cause, shall sail to Rome. That you, being present there, as also Reticius, Maternus, and Marinus, your colleagues, whom I have commanded to hasten to Rome for this purpose, may be heard, as you may understand most consistent with the most sacred law. And, indeed, that you may have the most perfect knowledge of these matters, I have subjoined to my own epistle copies of the writings sent to me by Anulinus, and sent them to your aforesaid colleagues. In which your gravity will read and consider in what way the aforesaid cause may be most accurately investigated and justly decided

Since it neither escapes your diligence, that I show such regard for the holy catholic church, that I wish you, upon the whole, to leave no room for schism or division. May the power of the great God preserve you many years, most esteemed."

Copy of the Epistle in which the Emperor commanded another council to be held, for the purpose of removing all the dissension of the bishops.

" CONSTANTINE AUGUSTUS to Chrestus bishop of Syracuse. As there were some already before who perversely and wickedly began to waver in the holy religion and celestial virtue, and to abandon the doctrine of the catholic (universal) church, desirous, therefore, of preventing such disputes among them, I had thus written, that this subject, which appeared to be agitated among them, might be rectified, by delegating certain bishops from Gaul, and summoning others of the opposite parties from Africa, who are pertinaciously and incessantly contending with one another, that by a careful examination of the matter in their presence, it might thus be decided. But since, as it happens, some, forgetful of their own salvation, and the reverence due to our most holy religion, even now do not cease to protract their own enmity, being unwilling to conform to the decision already promulgated, and asserting that they were very few that advanced their sentiments and opinions, or else that all points which ought to have been first fully discussed not being first examined, they proceeded with too much haste and precipitancy to give publicity to the decision. Hence it has happened, that those very persons who ought to exhibit a brotherly and peaceful unanimity, rather disgracefully and detestably are at variance with one another, and thus give this occasion of derision to those that are without, and whose minds are averse to our most holy religion. Hence it has appeared necessary to me to provide that this matter, which ought to have ceased after the decision was issued by their own voluntary agreement, now, at length, should be fully terminated by the intervention of many.

" Since, therefore, we have commanded many bishops to meet

together from different and remote places, in the city of Arles, towards the calends of August, I have also thought proper to write to thee, that taking a public vehicle from the most illustrious Latronianus, corrector of Sicily, and taking with thee two others of the second rank, which thou mayest select, also three servants to afford you services on the way; I would have you meet them within the same day at the aforesaid place. That by the weight of your authority, and the prudence and unanimity of the rest that assemble, this dispute, which has disgracefully continued until the present time, in consequence of certain disgraceful contentions, may be discussed, by hearing all that shal' be alleged by those who are now at variance, whom we have also commanded to be present, and thus the controversy be reduced, though slowly, to that faith, and observance of religion, and fraternal concord, which ought to prevail. May Almighty God preserve thee in safety many years."

CHAPTER VI.

Of the property belonging to the Christians.

Copy of an Epistle in which the Emperor grants money to the churches.

" CONSTANTINE AUGUSTUS to Cæcilianus bishop of Carthage. As we have determined, that in all the provinces of Africa, Numidia, and Mauritania, something should be granted to certain ministers of the legitimate and most holy catholic (universal) religion, to defray their expenses, I have given letters to Ursus, the most illustrious lieutenant-governor of Africa, and have communicated to him, that he shall provide, to pay to your authority, three thousand folles.*

---

* If the follis be estimated at 208 denarii, according to the usual computation, this sum would amount to about 10,000 dollars.

" After you shall have obtained this sum, you are to order
these monies to be distributed among the aforesaid ministers, according to the abstract addressed to thee from Hosius.   But if
thou shalt learn, perhaps, that any thing shall be wanting to complete this my purpose with regard to all, thou art authorized,
without delay, to make demands for whatever thou mayest ascertain to be necessary, from Heraclides, the procurator of our
possessions.   And I have also commanded him when present,
that if thy authority should demand any monies of him, he should
see that it should be paid without delay.   And as I ascertained
that some men, who are of no settled mind, wish to divert the
people from the most holy catholic (universal) church, by a certain pernicious adulteration, I wish thee to understand that I have
given, both to the proconsul Anulinus and to Patricius, vicar-
general of the præfects, when present, the following injunctions ;
that, among all the rest, they should particularly pay the necessary attention to this, nor should by any means tolerate that this
should be overlooked.   Wherefore, if thou seest any of these
men persevering in this madness, thou shalt, without any hesitancy, proceed to the aforesaid judges, and report it to them, that
they may animadvert upon them, as I commanded them, when
present.   May the power of the great God preserve thee many
years."

CHAPTER VII.

The privileges and immunities of the clergy.

*Copy of an Epistle in which the Emperor commands that the pre-
lates of the churches should be exempt from performing service
in political matters.*

" HEALTH to thee, most esteemed Anulinus.   As it appears
from many circumstances, that when the religion was despised,
in which the highest reverence of the heavenly majesty is ob-

served, that our public affairs were beset with great dangers, and that this religion, when legally adopted and observed, afforded tne greatest prosperity to the Roman name, and distinguished felicity to all men, as it has been granted by the divine benefi-cence, we have resolved that those men who gave their services with becoming sanctity, and the observance of this law, to the performance of divine worship, should receive the recompence for their labours, oh most esteemed Anulinus ; wherefore it is my will that these men, within the province, entrusted to thee in the Catholic church, over which Cæcilianus presides, who give their services to this holy religion, and whom they commonly call clergy, shall be held totally free, and exempt from all public offices, to the end that they may not by any error or sacrilegious deviation, be drawn away from the service due to the Divinity, but rather may devote themselves to their proper law, without any molestation.   So, that, whilst they exhibit the greatest pos-sible reverence to the Deity, it appears the greatest good will be conferred on the state.   Farewell, most esteemed and beloved Anulinus."

CHAPTER VIII.

The wickedness which Licinius afterwards exhibited, and his death.

Such then, was the divine and celestial grace, exhibited by the interposition of our Saviour. And such too the abundant bless-ings imparted to us by the peace, and in this manner our affairs were finally crowned with gladness and festivity.   But malig-nant envy, and the dæmon of iniquity was not able to endure the exhibition of this spectacle.

When therefore, the events that befel the aforesaid tyrants were not sufficient to bring Licinius to sound reason, who as long as his government was prosperous, being honoured with the second rank after the emperor, Constantine the great, and also by inter-marriage and affinity of the highest order, he nevertheless abandoned imitating a good example, and on the contrary rivalled the wickedness of the impious tyrants. And thus, although he had seen their end with his own eyes, he was resolved to follow their counsels rather than remain faithful to a better disposition and friendship. Stimulated, therefore, by envy, he waged a most oppressive and nefarious war against the common benefactor of all, not regarding the laws of nature, nor leagues, nor consanguinity, nor paying any regard to covenants. For Constantine, as a most gracious emperor, exhibiting the evidences of a true benevolence, had not refused affinity with him, and had not denied him the illustrious marriage with his sister, and had honoured him as a sharer in that eminent nobility of the imperial family, which he derived from his fathers, and had shared with him the government of the whole empire, as his kinsman and partner, granting him the power to rule and govern no less a part of the empire than himself. But he, on the contrary, pursued a course directly opposite to this, by plotting every kind of mischief against his superior, and inventing all manner of artifices, as if to return the kindness of his benefactor with evils. And first, he indeed attempted to conceal his preparations, and pretended to be his friend, and having frequently waylaid him with treachery and deceit, hoped that he would very easily gain his object. But God was the friend and the vigilant protector and guardian of the emperor (Constantine) who bringing these plots formed in darkness and secrecy to light, foiled them. So much excellence has that powerful armour of piety, to repel our enemies, and for the preservation of our own safety. But our most divinely favoured emperor fortified by this, escaped the multifarious and complicated plots of the iniquitous man. But the other, when he saw that his secret preparations by no means succeeded according to his wish, as God detected every artifice and villany to his favoured prince, no longer able to conceal himself, he commenced an open war. And in thus determining war against Constantine, he now also proceeded to array himself against that supreme God, whom he knew him to worship. Afterwards he began gradually and imperceptibly to assail those pious subjects under him, who had never at any time troubled his government.

This too, he did, violently urged on by the innate propensity of his malice, that overclouded and darkened his understanding. He did not, therefore, bear in mind those that had persecuted the Christians before him, nor those whose destroyer and punisher he himself had been appointed, for their wickedness. But departing from sound reason, and as one might say, seized with insanity, he had determined to wage war against God himself, the protector and aid of Constantine, in place of the one whom he assisted. And first, indeed, he drove away all the Christians from his house, the wretch thus divesting himself of those prayers to God for his safety, which they are taught to offer up for all men. After this he ordered the soldiers in the cities to be cashiered and to be stripped of military honours, unless they chose to sacrifice to dæmons.

But these were small matters compared with the subsequent greater ones that were superadded. Why should we here relate particularly and minutely the deeds perpetrated by this enemy of God?* how, as a violator of all law, he also devised illegal laws.† For he enacted that no one should exercise humanity towards the unhappy individuals in prison, by imparting food, and no one compassionate those perishing with hunger, in bonds, so that there should be no good man tolerated, or any good thing done, and that too, even when nature herself powerfully attracts our sympathy towards our fellow-men. Indeed, this was a most shameless and inhuman law, calculated to expel every sense of humanity implanted by nature. Beside this, the punishment was attached to those who exercised commiseration, that they should be made to suffer the same things with those they commiserated; and that those who had performed the offices of humanity should be thrust into prisons and bonds, to sustain the same punishment with the worst malefactors. Such were the ordinances of Lici· nius. Why should we, moreover, recount his innovations in mar·

---

* This is the proper meaning of θεομισει here. Valesius invariably translates *invisus Deo*. This cannot be supported. See note in the Panegyric, on this word.

† This translation may give some idea of the play upon the word νομος, in the original. Our author is fond of the figure *paronomasia*, as we have seen in more than one instance.

riage, or his novelties in regard to the dying? By means of which he dared to restrict the ancient and wisely established institutions of the Romans, and to introduce as a substitute certain barbarous, savage, unlawful, and truly lawless laws.* He also invented innumerable pretexts of exaction against the people subject to him, and every variety of method to extort silver and gold, new measurements of lands,† and means of gain by way of penalty,‡ from those in the country, who were no longer living, but had long since died. Who can tell the expatriations that this enemy of mankind devised besides these, the banishment of nobles and illustrious men, those too, whom he separated from their youthful wives, consigning the latter to be shamefully abused by certain miscreants of his own; with how many females, married and unmarried, he, though in the last stages of advanced age, gratified his unbridled passions. Why, I say, should I delay in reciting those things, when the excessive wickedness of his last deeds make the first to appear as trifles, and a mere nothing? He at last proceeded to such an extent of madness, as to attack the bishops; now indeed, regarding them as the servants of the Supreme God, hostile to his measures; but yet not openly for fear of his superior (Constantine.) But commencing his operations in a clandestine and crafty manner, by means of his governors and magistrates, he insidiously destroyed the most distinguished and approved of these. And the manner of the murder itself, perpetrated upon them, was strange, and such as had never before been heard of. But the excesses perpetrated at Amana, and other cities of Pontus, surpassed all others in savage cruelty. There some of the churches of God were razed to the ground, some were closed, so that no one accustomed to frequent them could get into them, nor render God the worship that we owe

---

* The *paronomasia* we have here attempted to transfer.

† These new surveys of land afforded new pretexts for embezzlement, &c., they were always attended by a new assessment.

‡ επιζημιον κερδος, we have rendered thus. Valesius says, *exitiale lucrum*, which is too general to reach the sense. The expression seems to refer to the unlawful levies and impositions upon estates whose proprietors were long dead; length of time, probably affording the better pretext to involve and encumber them.

For he did not suppose that prayers were offered up for him reasoning thus in his bad conscience, but persuaded himself that we did all and propitiated the Deity only for the divinely favoured emperor. Hence also he directed the violence of his fury against us, and at the same time when his parasitical governors per-ceived that they were doing what was gratifying to the execrable tyrant, they subjected some of the bishops to the same punishments as the worst criminal. Those, therefore, who had done no evil, were led away to punishment without any pretext, just like murderers and assassins. Some also endured a novel kind of death, having their bodies cut into many small pieces, and after this savage and horrible spectacle, were thrown as food to the fishes into the depths of the sea. Again then, the worshippers of God began to flee; again the open fields, the deserts, forests, and mountains, received the servants of Christ. When these things had succeeded with the impious tyrant, after this manner, he finally contemplated to renew the persecution against all. And no doubt he would have prevailed in his determination, and there was nothing to hinder him to proceed in his work, had not God, the defender of his own servants, anticipated him, and led forth Constantine, his servant, with a mighty arm amid these events, and suddenly, as in the dense and impenetrable darkness of a gloomy night, caused a light and a deliverer to arise to all.

CHAPTER IX.

*The victory of Constantine, and the blessings which under him
accrued to the whole Roman world.*

To him, therefore, the supreme God, granted from heaven above, the fruits of his piety, the trophies of victory over the wick-ed, and that nefarious tyrant with all his counsellors and ad-herents, he cast prostrate at the feet of Constantine.* For when

* Constantine obtained this signal victory over Licinius, A. D. 324, the limits of our author's history. The first war that broke out between the two emperors, was occasioned by the protection which Licinius had extended to Sinicius, who

he proceeded to the extremes of madness, in his movements, the divinely favoured emperor ragarded him as no more to be tolerated, but taking his prudent measures and mingling the firm principles of justice with his humanity, he determines to come to the protection of those who were so miserably oppressed by the tyrant ; and in this, by banishing smaller pests, he thus advanced to save vast multitudes of the human race.   For as he had exercised only his humanity, in commiserating him the time before this, a man who was by no means deserving of compassion, it proved of no avail to him, who would not renounce his iniquity, but rather increased his madness against the people his subjects.   But to the oppressed there was no hope of salvation left, in the cruelties they endured from the savage beast.   Wherefore, also, Constantine the protector of the good, combining his hatred of wickedness with the love of goodness, went forth with his son Crispus, the most benevolent Cesar, to extend a saving arm to all those that were perishing.   Both, therefore, the father and son, having as it were God the universal King, and his Son our Saviour, as their leader and aid, drawing up the army on all sides against the enemies of God, bore away an easy victory; all things being prospered to them by God in the conflict according to their wishes.   Suddenly then, and sooner than said, those that but yesterday breathed threats and destruction, were no more, not even leaving the memory of their name.   Their paintings, (their effigies) their honours received the deserved contempt and disgrace, and those very scenes which Licinius had seen occurring to the iniquitous tyrants, these same he experiened himself.   As he would neither receive instruction, nor grow wise by the chastisements of his neighbours, he proceeded in the same course of impiety, and was justly hurled down the same precipice with them.   He, therefore, lay prostrated in this way.   But the mighty and victorious Constantine, adorned with every virtue of religion, with his most pious son, Crispus Cesar, resembling in all things his father, recovered the east as his own, and thus re-

had plotted against the life of Constantine, A. D. 314, and ten years afterwards he was overthrown, and deprived of the imperial dignity, having his life spared, only for a short time at the entreaties of his wife, Constantine's sister.

store·' the Roman empire to its ancient state of one united body ; extending their peaceful sway around the world, from the rising sun, to the opposite regions, to the north and the south, even to the last oorders of the declining day. All fear, therefore, of those who had previously afflicted them, was now wholly removed. They celebrated splendid and festive days with joy and hilarity. All things were filled with light, and all who before were sunk in sorrow, beheld each other with smiling and cheerful faces. With choirs and hymns, in the cities and villages, at the same time they celebrated and extolled first of all God the universal King, because they thus were taught, then they also celebrated the praises of the pious emperor, and with him all his divinely favoured children. There was a perfect oblivion of past evils, and past wickedness was buried in forgetfulness. There was nothing but enjoyment of the present blessings, and expectation of those yet to come. Edicts were published and issued by the victorious emperor, full of clemency, and laws were enacted indicative of munificence and genuine religion.

Thus, then, after all the tyranny had been purged away, the empire was justly reserved firm and without a rival, to Constantine and his sons. Who first sweeping away that enmity to God, exhibited by the former rulers, sensible of the mercies conferred upon them by God, exhibited also their own love of religion and God, with their piety and gratitude to Him, by those works and operations which they presented to the view of all the world.

With the divine blessing, the end of the Tenth Book of the Ecclesiastical History of Eusebius Pamphilus.

INDEX

SUBJECTS AND AUTHORS, ETC., OCCURRING IN THE ECCLESIASTICAL
HISTORY OF EUSEBIUS.

The number refers to the page.

CHRONOLOGICAL TABLE,

SHOWING

ᴛHE STATE OR PERIOD OF THE MOST PROMINENT PERSONS AND **EVENTS**
OCCURRING IN THE ECCLESIASTICAL HISTORY OF EUSEBIUS.

ɪɴ this Table, which is designed chiefly to present a synopsis of the principal contemporary events and persons, it will be observed that the dates are given according to the vulgar era, or four years later than the true time. The number on the left of the column shows the year, on the right is given the page of the work

A. D.

1. Oct. Cæs. Augustus being emperor of Rome, Christ was born 28
14. Tiberius succeeds him.
33. Christ crucified   -   -   39
    Tiberius dies in the twenty-third year of his reign, and is succeeded by Caius Cæs. Caligula   53
7. James, surnamed the Just, bishop of Jerusalem, the first bishop of the first Christian church   49
    The mission of Thaddeus to Edessa   -   -   -   -   49
    The name Christian grows into use at Antioch.
41 Caligula dies, and is succeeded by Claudius.
    The famine mentioned in the book of Acts -   -   -   -   58
43. Herod Agrippa afflicts the church, and puts James the great, brother of John, to death   58
    Herod dies   -   -   -   60
    Theudas, the impostor   - 61
    Helen, queen of the Osrhoenians 61
    Simon Magus   -   -   62
    Peter at Rome   -   -   63
    Philo's communication with Peter   -   -   -   -   66
    Sedition of the Jews at Jerusalem, and consequent destruction.
    Agrippa, Herod's son, appointed king of the Jews   -   -   72
54. Claudius dies, and is succeeded by Tiberias Claudius Nero - 72
1. Annianus, bishop of Alexandria, and successor of St. Mark   79
    The first general persecution of the Christian church   -   -   79
    Peter and Paul suffer martyrdom, and Linus is the first bishop of Rome   -   -   -   82
68. Nero dies, and is succeeded by Galba and Otho, whose successive

A. D.

    reigns did not embrace more than eighteen months -   -   85
69. Vitellius acknowledged emperor, but is soon after killed, and Vespasian declared emperor   85
    The Jews oppressed by grievous famine   -   -   -   87
70. Capture and destruction of Jerusalem by Titus, the son of Vespasian   -   -   69—87
    Gnostics, Dositheus, Simon Magus, Ebion, Cerinthus.
    Simeon, son of Cleopas, the second bishop of Jerusalem. It is worthy of note that the two first bishops of this church were relatives of our Lord   -   -   99
    The family of David investigated by Vespasian.
79. Vespasian dies, and is succeeded by his son Titus.
    Anencletus, bishop of Rome.
81. Titus dies, and is succeeded by Domitian, a second Nero   100, 101
    Second general persecution   101
    Clement, bishop of Rome.
    Avilius, bishop of Alexandria   100
    John the apostle, exiled to Patmos   -   -   -   101
94. Fl. Clement and Domitilla, martyrs.
    The grandchildren of Judas, relatives of our Lord, yet living 102
96. Death of Domitian, who is succeeded by Nerva. Nerva is succeeded by Trajan.
98. Cerdon, bishop of Alexandria   104
    Clement of Rome ; Ignatus of Antioch, successor of Evodius, the first bishop   -   -   104
    Simeon of Jerusalem suffers martyrdom, and is succeeded by Justus in the episcopate   - 120

A. D.

About this time the dates of the succession in the church of Jerusalem became uncertain. The first fifteen bishops were all Hebrews. Of these, however, we know but little more than the names of the succession preserved by Eusebius - - 131
After these followed the Gentile succession, when the dates became more certain. See the tabular view of the bishops appended to this table.

99. The apostle John dies at Ephesus.

Euarestus, bishop of Rome 128
Primus, bishop of Alexandria.
Alexander succeeds Euarestus in the see of Rome - - 128

107. Ignatius suffers martyrdom.

117. Trajan dies, and is succeeded by Adrian - - - 129
Quadratus and Aristides write a defence of Christianity addressed to Adrian - - - 129
Xystus, or Sixtus, bishop of Rome.
Justus of Alexandria ; Telesphorus succeeds Xystus at Rome, and Eumenes succeeds Justus at Alexandria - - - 131
Barchochebas the impostor 131
The last siege of the Jews, when the name of Jerusalem was changed and called Ælia, in honour of the emperor, Ælius Adrian - - - 132
About this time appeared the heresies of Menander, Saturninus, and Basilides, the offspring of the heresy of Simon Magus 133
Adrian forbids the Christians to be punished without trial 136
Hegesippus and Justin contemporary writers - - 135

138. Adrian dies, and is succeeded by Antoninus Pius - - 137
Hyginus, successor of Telesphorus at Rome - - - 137
Valentine and Cerdon, Gnostics, notorious at Rome - 137
Justin addresses his apology to Antonine, by which the emperor is induced to send his edict to the cities of Asia - 139, 140
Pius, bishop of Rome, is succeeded by Anicetus - - 141

161. Marcus Aurelius Antoninus suc-

A. D.

ceeds Antoninus Pius, and is associated with Lucius Antoninus Verus, his brother - 142

163. Justin addresses a second apology to the emperors ; about the same time also Athenagoras and Tatian wrote their apologies.

166. Martyrdom of Justin and Polycarp - - - 149, 150
Fourth persecution ; Anicetus succeeded by Soter in the see of Rome, and Celadion succeeded by Agrippinus in the see of Alexandria - - - 156
Heron, Eros, Theophilus, bishops of Antioch - - 156
Dionysius of Corinth, Pinytus of Crete, Philip Apollinaris, and Melito, Musanus Modestus, and Irenæus, contemporary writers 156

169. L. Verus dies.
The Christian legion pray for rain, and victory over the Marcomanni, whence the legion is called fulminea - - - 184
Eleutherus of Rome - 168
Bardesanes of Syria - 167

177. Martyrs of Lyons and Vienna in Gaul - - - 169
Syriac and Italian translations of the New Testament are made about these times, as also those of Aquila, Symmachus, and Theodotion.

180. Antonine dies, and is succeeded by Commodus - - 190
Agrippinus is succeeded by Julian in the see of Alexandria 190
Pantænus, the philosopher, at the head of the Alexandrian school 190
Clement of Alexandria, the pupil of Pantænus - - 191
Narcissus, bishop of Jerusalem, being the fifteenth of the Gentile succession, which commenced after the invasion of Judea under Adrian - - - 192
Rhodo opposes the errors of Marcion - - - 192
Phrygian errors, Montanus, Priscilla Maximilla - 191—194
Blastus, schismatic, at Rome 194
Miltiades and Apollonius, ecclesiastical writers ; the latter dies a martyr - - - 205

A. D.

Eleutherus is succeeded by Victor in the see of Rome ; and Julian of Alexandria by Demetrius 206
Serapion, bishop of Antioch 206
Nacissus of Jerusalem, Bachyllus of Corinth, and Polycrates at Ephesus.
The question respecting the passover is now agitated - 207
Artemon's errors revived by Paul of Samosata - - 213
Natalius, Asclepiodotus - 214

192. Pertinax.

193. Didius Julius.

194. Septimius Severus, emperor.
Tertullian writes his apology 216
Fifth persecution - - 217
Martyrdom of Philip, governor in Egypt, Leonidas, and others

205. Irenæus and the martyrs at Lyons.
Origen - - - - 218
Clement succeeds Pantænus in the Alexandrian school -
About the same time flourished Judas the historian, Alexander of Jerusalem, Demetrius of Alexandria, and Porphyry, the opponent of Christianity - 238, 239

211. A. Caracalla and Geta, emperors.

217. Macrinus with his son.
Zephyrinus of Rome, successor of Victor, is succeeded by Calisthus, who again left the church to Urbanus - - - 242

218. Heliogabalus (alias Antoninus) succeeds Macrinus - 242

222. Alexander Severus, emperor 242
Philetas succeeds Asclepiades in the see of Antioch - - 242
Mamæa, Alexander's mother, favourable to Christianity 242
Hippolytus, an ecclesiastical writer - - - - 242
Heraclas succeeds Demetrius in the see of Alexandria - 247
Firmilianus bishop of Cesarea in Cappadocia - - - 247
Theoctistus bishop of Cesarea in Palestine.

235. Alexander assassinated by Maximinus Thrax, who is proclaimed emperor, and commences the sixth persecution - - 248

238. Maximinus Thrax is succeeded by Gordian.
Pontianus is succeeded by Anteros in the see of Rome, who was succeeded by Fabianus 248

A. D.

Heraclas bishop of Alexandria **249**
Zebinus of Antioch is succeeded by Babylas - - - 249
Africanus, author of the work called Cesti - - - - 251
Beryllus of Arabia - - 251

244. Gordian is succeeded by Philip the Arabian.
Origen's works on the Scriptures - - - - 250
Heraclas is succeeded by Dionysius in the see of Alexandria 252
Dissensions of the Arabians 253
Heresy of the Helcesaites.

250. Decius succeeds Philip.
Seventh persecution - 254
Alexander, bishop of Jerusalem, dies a martyr, and is succeeded by Mazabanes.
Babylas of Antioch also died in prison, and was succeeded by Fabius - - - 255
Origen's great sufferings and tortures - - - - 255
The sufferings of Dionysius 256
The martyrs at Alexandria 257
Novatus creates a schism at Rome - - - - 263
Fabianus suffers martyrdom, and Cornelius bishop of Rome 263
Cyprian of Carthage, and Fabinus of Antioch - - - 267
Dionysius writes to Novatus 268
The dispute between Cyprian of Carthage and Stephen of Rome 272

253. Gallus emperor.
Lucius bishop of Rome - 271

254. Valerianus emperor.
Stephen bishop of Rome - 273
The following bishops at this time were contemporary : Demetrianus of Antioch, Theoctistus of Cesarea, Mazabanes of Ælia, Marinus of Tyre, Heliodorus of Laodicea, Helenus of Tarsus.
Stephen was succeeded by Xystus or Sixtus II. - - 273
The Sabellian heresy - 274
Valerian stimulated by Macrianus to persecute - - 278
Dionysius bishop of Rome 302
The sufferings of Dionysius of Alexandria - - - 280
The schism of Nepos - 295

259. Gallienus sole emperor on the capture of his father Valerian **285**

Tabular View of the Order of the Episcopal Succession in the prominent Dioceses mentioned by Eusebius.

Bishops of Jerusalem.

1. James the brother of our Lord.
2. Symeon, son of Cleopas.
3. Justus.
4. Zaccheus.
5. Tobias.
6. Benjamin
7. John.
8. Matthias.
9. Philip.
10. Seneca.
11. Justus.
12. Levi.
13. Ephres.
14. Joseph.
15. Judas, last of the Hebrew succession.
16. Marcus.
17. Cassianus.
18. Publius.
19. Maximus.
20. Julian.
21. Caius.
22. Symmachus.
23. Caius II.
24. Julian II.
25. Capito.
26. Maximus II.
27. Antoninus.
28. Valens.
29. Dolichianus.
30. Narcissus.
31. Dius.
32. Germanio.
33. Gordius.
34. Narcissus II.
35. Alexander.
36. Mazabanes.
37. Hymenæus.
38. Zabdas.
39. Hermon.

Bishops of Antioch.

1. Evodius.
2. Ignatius.
3. Heron.
4. Cornelius.
5. Eros.
6. Theophilus.
7. Maximinus.
8. Serapion.
9. Asclepiades.
10. Philetus.
11. Zebinas.
12. Babylas.
13. Fabius.
14. Demetrianus.
15. Paul of Samosata.
16. Domnus.
17. Timæus.
18. Cyrillus.
19. Tyrannus.

Bishops of Rome.

Peter and Paul, according to Eusebius died as martyrs at Rome; after these followed

1. Linus.
2. Anencletus.
3. Clement.
4. Euarestus.
5. Alexander.
6. Xystus or Sixtus.
7. Telesphorus.
8. Hyginus.
9. Pius.
10. Anicetus.
11. Soter.
12. Eleutherus.
13. Victor.
14. Zephyrinus.
15. Callisthus.
16. Urbanus.
17. Pontianus.
18. Anteros.
19. Fabianus.
20. Cornelius.
21. Lucius.
22. Stephanus.
23. Xystus or Sixtus II.
24. Dionysius.
25. Felix.
26. Eutychianus.
27. Caius.
28. Marcellinus.
29. Miltiades.

Bishops of Alexandria.

The evangelist Mark established the church there, and after him came

1. Annianus.
2. Avilius.
3. Cerdo.
4. Primus.
5. Justus.
6. Eumenes
7. Marcus.
8. Celadion.
9. Agrippinus.
10. Julianus.
11. Demetrius.
12. Heraclas.
13. Dionysius
14. Maximus.
15. Theonas.
16. Peter.
17. Achillas.
18. Alexander.

Bishops of Laodicea mentioned by Eusebius.

Thelymedres.
Heliodorus.
Socrates.
Eusebius of Alexandria.
Anatolius.
Stephen.
Theodotus.

Bishops of Cesarea mentioned by our author

Theophilus.
Theoctistus.
Domnus.
Theotecnus.
Agapius.
Eusebius.

A

HISTORICAL VIEW

OF

THE COUNCIL OF NICE

WITH A

Translation of Documents.

BY

REV. ISAAC BOYLE, D. D.

———•———

PHILADELPHIA:

J. B. LIPPINCOTT & CO.

1879.

PREFACE.

THE ecclesiastical history of Eusebius extends only to A. D. 324. The Council of Nice was convened the following year. The publisher of Eusebius being about to furnish another edition of the work, and thinking that a translation of certain documents relating to that celebrated convention, throwing light on its transactions, would be interesting to the readers of Eusebius, and add some value to the new edition, the writer of the following pages was induced, at his request, to undertake the performance of such a version. But in the prosecution of his task, he perceived that the documents would be better understood, and, consequently, be more acceptable to the reader, if preceded by a short and connected view of the origin of the Arian controversy, and of the proceedings of the synod, derived from such original and authentic sources of information as were within his power. He has therefore introduced the documents by such a summary of events. In preparing it, it is very possible he may have inadvertently fallen into some mistakes, but not, he trusts, into any error of importance. He is conscious, at least, of no wilful misrepresentation of facts, nor of any intentional departure from the truth of history.

In some instances, the writer has given the descriptions of the authors, from whom he has derived his materials, with more minuteness of detail than may seem consistent with the narrow limits to which he has ɔeen restricted. But he thought that these particulars might be useful as presenting a picture of the manners and character of the times to which they relate. He has also given at length some narratives which have no immediate reference to his main design, because he considered them as interesting or instructive.

In the translations annexed, he has sought to give a faithful version of the originals, without, however, obscuring the meaning by aiming at too great a degree of mere verbal exactness. In other words, he has endeavored not to sacrifice the sense and spirit of his authors by too strict an adherence to the letter. How far he has succeeded in this attempt is respectfully submitted to the decision of those who are best qualified to judge.

A HISTORICAL VIEW

OF

THE COUNCIL OF NICE.

CONTENTS.

It was the charge of our Saviour to his apostles, after his resurrection, to "go and teach all nations." This command was,
in a great measure, accomplished by them, and those who succeeded them in the ministry, within three centuries of the time
when the gospel was first preached in Judea by its divine Author.
In the prosecution of their glorious enterprise, a great proportion
of the then known world, by the blessing of God on their indefatigable labors, submitted to the religion of Jesus. They visited
the burning climes of Africa, and the various regions of Asia, to
proclaim the glad tidings of salvation ; and a great part of Europe,
from the countries bordering on the Mediterranean to the distant
shores of Britain, received the light of Christian truth. But,
although their efforts were crowned with so considerable a share
of success, they encountered in their progress almost continual
opposition, and endured nearly every variety of hardship and persecution. Some of them were assailed by the bigotry and malice
of the Jews, and others became victims to the rage and cruelty of
their gentile oppressors. They were exposed to the lawless vio-

lence of the multitude, and suffered from the sanguinary decrees
of rulers and princes. If, under the milder sway of a few of the
Roman emperors, they enjoyed an interval of comparative repose,
it was only to be followed by a renewal of their calamities. At
length, however, a brighter prospect was opened to the Christian
world. In consequence of the victory of Constantine over the
tyrant Licinius, in the year of our Lord 323, external tranquillity
was fully secured to the Church ; and in order to confirm it, several beneficial laws were enacted by the emperor. He recalled
those who had been banished for the profession of the faith ; and
the property of such as had been despoiled of their goods was restored. He gave directions for enlarging the ancient churches,
and building new and more splendid ones. He commanded that
the clergy should be held in honor ; and shielded their persons
from indignity and outrage. The people were exhorted to relinquish idolatry, and embrace the true religion ; and many other
salutary measures were adopted, to extend the influence, and promote the welfare of Christianity.

But while Constantine was zealously employed in this lauda-
ble design, and the Church was protected from foreign enemies, a
dissension had arisen in its own bosom, which occasioned much
animosity, and long continued to disturb its domestic peace. It
happened that Alexander, bishop of Alexandria, in Egypt, disputing one day, in the presence of his presbyters and other clergy,
on the subject of the three divine persons, and being desirous of
making a display of his knowledge, remarked, that in the Trinity
there was a unity.* Arius, one of his presbyters, who was well
versed in the art of reasoning and in metaphysical distinctions,
thinking that the bishop was desirous of introducing the opinion
of Sabellius † of Lybia, inclined to an error directly opposed to it,
and replied, with great asperity, that if the Father begat the Son,
the latter must have had a beginning ; from which, he continued,
it clearly followed that there was a time when he was not, and

* Socrates, L. I. c. 5.

† It will be recollected that Sabellius, who lived about the middle of the third
century, believed in a *modal* Trinity, considering the Son and Holy Spirit as
different manifestations only of the Godhead, and not as separate persons.

that his substance was made from nothing.* These novel and hitherto unheard of opinions excited many persons to enter into the controversy. By a little spark a great fire was thus kindled. The evil which originated in the church of Alexandria, pervaded he whole of Egypt, Lybia, and the upper Thebais, and reached at length to many other cities and provinces. Numbers favored the sentiments of Arius; but no one defended them with more warmth and earnestness than Eusebius, formerly bishop of Berytus, but who had now surreptitiously obtained possession of the bishopric of Nicomedia, in Bithynia. Alexander, being greatly incensed at these proceedings, assembled a numerous council, in which Arius and his followers were deposed; and afterward wrote to the other bishops informing them of the fact.† His letters, copies of which were sent to all the cities under his spiritual jurisdiction, served only to increase the mischief, by kindling the flames of discord among those who received them. Some signified their approbation of the letter, while others expressed their dissent. Eusebius, of Nicomedia, opposed it more strenuously than others, as it made unfavorable mention of himself. The credit of Eusebius, at that period, was great, because the emperor then made Nicomedia his residence, having built a palace in that city a short time before the reign of Diocletian. Many of the bishops, therefore, were subservient to the wishes of Eusebius. He was continually writing, sometimes to Alexander, to induce him to abandon the dispute with Arius, and receive him into commu-

---

* Sozomen gives the following account of this dispute:—" Arius having declared his opinions in public, some of those who heard of them, blamed Alexander for having suffered him to advance such novel doctrines; but this prelate thought proper to leave the two parties at liberty to dispute upon an obscure subject, lest if he should prohibit the controversy, he might seem to terminate it by force, rather than by persuasion. Sitting, therefore, in the midst of his clergy, he permitted every one to say what he thought proper. Alexander inclined sometimes to one side, and sometimes to the other, but declared at last for those who maintained that the Son of God is consubstantial and coeternal with the Father, and required Arius to hold the same opinion; and because he refused to do it, drove him from the Church, together with the priests and deacons who supported him." Hist. Eccles. L. I. c. 15.

† Documents, A.

nion, and sometimes to the bishops of the different cities, in order to persuade them not to join that prelate. The churches were thus filled with tumult and disorder. Nor was the war of words confined to the pastors of the church, but the people also were divided, inclining to one or the other of the two parties. The matter proceeded, at length, to such a shameful extremity, that the Christian religion was publicly ridiculed, and afforded a subject of profane merriment to the pagans, even in their theatrical exhibitions. The people of Alexandria contended with childish petulance respecting the most sublime mysteries of our faith. Each party sent messengers to the bishops of every province, and succeeded in gaining individuals to their respective opinions. But the Meletians, who had recently been separated from the Church, espoused the cause of the Arians. They were so denominated from Meletius, one of the bishops of Egypt, who had been deposed by Peter of Alexandria, for several reasons, but especially for having offered sacrifice, in time of persecution, to the heathen divinities. His partizans were numerous; and, although he had no sufficient cause for deserting the church, he complained that he had been treated with injustice by Peter, whom he attacked with reproaches and calumny. After the death of that prelate, who suffered martyrdom under Diocletian, he transferred his abuse to Achillas, who was next to Peter in the episcopate, and then to Alexander, his successor. In this state of things, the controversy respecting our Lord's divinity taking place, Meletius, with his followers, favored the party of Arius, and supported him against the bishop. They who thought that the notions of Arius were absurd, approved of the sentence against him; and considered those who agreed with him in opinion as justly condemned. Eusebius of Nicomedia, however, and such as had embraced the views of Arius, wrote to Alexander, praying that the excommunication might be removed, on the ground that his opinions were orthodox.

On receiving intelligence of these transactions, the emperor was greatly afflicted; and, regarding the affair as his own private calamity, spared no pains to suppress the growing evil. Accordingly he sent a letter * to Alexander and Arius, exhorting them

* Documents, B.

to be reconciled, by Hosius, bishop of Corduba, a city of Spain, who was a man of approved fidelity, and greatly beloved by the emperor. He had reached the age of seventy, had been a bishop thirty years, was a confessor in the persecution of Maximian, and celebrated throughout the Church. This letter, however well intended, produced but little effect. The disorder indeed, had acquired such a degree of virulence, that neither the endeavors of the emperor, nor the influence and authority of his messenger, were of any avail. Both Alexander and Arius remained inflexible, the people disputed with still greater acrimony, and tumults became more frequent.

But there was another subject which occasioned considerable uneasiness in the Church, viz. the difference which arose among the orientals with respect to the proper day of keeping Easter, some celebrating that festival in the manner of the Jews, and others following the custom of Christians throughout the rest of the world. This diversity of practice, however, with regard to the day of observing that important solemnity, did not hinder religious fellowship, although it might cast a shade of gloom over the joyful anniversary of our Saviour's resurrection. The emperor, therefore, finding that the quiet of the Church was not a little disturbed by these two evils, assembled (by the advice of some of the prelates, according to Rufinus,) a general council, inviting, by letter, all the bishops to meet at Nice, in Bithynia, and furnishing them with the means of conveyance. In consequence, a great number of them, not less than three hundred and eighteen,* arrived from various cities and territories, attended by a vast con-

---

* The early historians of the church differ considerably as to the number of bishops assembled on this occasion. Athanasius mentions about three hundred; and in one passage of his work expressly says that there were three hundred and eighteen. Eusebius speaks of more than two hundred and fifty. Eustathius, of Antioch, who was present, as well as the two already named, and was an active member of the synod, declares that there were about two hundred and seventy, but that he cannot give the exact number, on account of the great multitude who attended ; nor indeed does he profess to have been very solicitous to ascertain it. Sozomen reckons about three hundred and twenty. The number mentioned in the text was at length generally admitted as the correct one. See Cave, Hist. Eccles. Lit. p. 223.

course of the inferior clergy. Daily and ample provision was made by Constantine for the support and accommodation of this numerous body. It is mentioned by Sozomen, that several persons were also present, well instructed in the dialectic art, for the purpose of assisting the bishops.

So great a synod was without previous example; for the Church was not at liberty to convoke such numerous assemblies under the pagan emperors. The pastors of three churches founded by the apostles, were present, Macarius, bishop of Jerusalem, Eustathius, of Antioch, and Alexander, of Alexandria. Of this memorable council, Eusebius Pamphilus speaks in the following terms.* "The most distinguished ministers of God met together from every part of Europe, Asia, and Africa. The sacred edifice, as if enlarged by the pleasure of God, inclosed at the same time within its walls, both Syrians and Cilicians, Phenicians, Arabians, and inhabitants of Palestine; Egyptians, Thebeans, and Lybians, with others arriving from Mesopotamia. A bishop from Persia was also present. Nor was the Scythian absent from this assembly. Pontus, also, and Galatia, Pamphylia and Cappadocia, Asia and Phrygia furnished representatives from their most able divines. Thracians too, Macedonians, Achaians and Epirotes, and those who resided at a vast distance beyond them, were convened. That illustrious Spaniard, who is so highly spoken of, took his seat with the others. The prelate of the imperial city, indeed, was absent on account of his advanced years, but his place was supplied by presbyters. Constantine, alone, of all the princes who ever lived, wove so brilliant a crown as this, joined together by the bond of peace, as a suitable acknowledgment of gratitude to Heaven for the victories vouchsafed him over his enemies, and dedicated it to God his Saviour, in bringing together so great a convention; an image, as it were, of the apostolic assembly. For it is related that in the times of the apostles, religious men were gathered together from every nation under heaven. Among them were Parthians, Medes, Elamites, and inhabitants of Mesopotamia, Judea and Cappadocia, Pontus, Asia

---

* Vit. Const. L. III. c. 7.

and Pamphylia, Egypt, and the parts of Lybia, which is near Cyrene; strangers also of Rome, Jews and proselytes, Cretes and Arabians. In that congregation, however, there was 'his circumstance of inferiority, that all who were collected together were not ministers of God, while the present assembly included more than two hundred and fifty bishops; but such a multitude of presbyters, deacons and acolothists accompanied them, that it was difficult to determine their number. Among these holy ministers, some excelled by the wisdom and eloquence of their discourse, others by the gravity of their deportment and patience of labor; and others, again, by their humility, and the gentleness of their manners. Some of them were honored on account of their grey hairs, while others were recommended by their youthful vigor and activity, both of body and mind. Several of them had but recently begun to exercise the functions of their ministry."

This account of Eusebius may sufficiently refute the disparaging language of Sabinus,* bishop of Heraclea in Thrace, who derides the fathers of Nice as ordinary and ignorant men. It is very probable that in so large an assembly, collected from various quarters, such a character might be applicable to some individuals; but there is no reason to doubt that there was a fair proportion of men of talents, learning and piety, in this convocation. Some were confessedly eminent for knowledge and abilities; and several of them, according to Theodoret, had exercised miraculous powers, which, though less common, it is likely, in the third and fourth centuries, than in the preceding ages of the Church, were yet to be found, in the opinion of some respectable writers, within its communion. Others were esteemed on account of their past sufferings in the cause of our holy religion, still bearing in their bodies, like the great apostle of the Gentiles, "the marks of the Lord Jesus."

Before the opening of the council, some who were experienced in the practice of disputation, began to agitate questions of theology. A layman of good sense, who had the courage to confess

* He was of the sect of Macedonius, who considered the Holy Ghost as a divine energy, and not a distinct person.

the name of Christ, in a time of persecution, perceiving that many were attracted by the force and elegance of their discourses, undertook to rebuke them by remarking, that neither our Lord nor his apostles had taught us the rules of logic, or idle subtleties, but the truth, which is preserved by faith and good works. All who were present listened. to him with admiration, and approved of what he had said. The speakers themselves became more moderate in consequence; and the noise and clamor excited by their animated declamation were no longer heard.

It is also related * that certain heathen philosophers were anxious to take a part in the dispute, some of them wishing to be made acquainted with the doctrines of the gospel, and others, to whom the Christians were obnoxious, on account of the decaying credit of their own religion, desiring to create a misunderstanding, and to foment divisions among them. One of these "seekers after wisdom," in the vain confidence of his imagined eloquence, assuming an insolent manner, endeavored to turn the priests into ridicule. But a plain and illiterate old man, one of those who had been distinguished as confessors, was unable to bear his arrogance; and, although unversed in the rules of logic and the art of disputation, ventured to accost him. This excited the laughter of some inconsiderate persons, to whom he was known, but alarmed the more reflecting, who apprehended that he might expose himself in so unequal a contest. Their respect for his character, however, prevented any attempt to hinder him from speaking. "Listen," he said, "philosopher, in the name of Jesus. There is one God, the Creator of heaven and earth, and of all things visible and invisible, who has performed all this by the power of his Word, and established it by the holiness of his Spirit. The Word, which we call the Son of God, pitying the errors of men and their brutish way of life, condescended to be born of a woman, to sojourn among them, and to die for their salvation. He will come again, to judge the actions of every one in this life. We believe, in the simplicity of our hearts, that this is the truth. Do not then fruitlessly trouble yourself, in seeking arguments

* Sozomen. I. 8.

against these things, or in attempting to discover the mode in which they may be, or not.   But if you believe, only tell me so." The philosopher, not a little astonished at this unexpected address, answered, I believe; and, thanking the old man for having vanquished him, recommended it to those with whom he had formerly agreed in sentiment, to follow his example, solemnly declaring, that the change which he had experienced was the effect of divine power, and that he felt himself inexplicably impelled to embrace the faith of Christ.

The bishops had several conferences among themselves previously to the day when they were to proceed to the formal decision of affairs, and on which, Constantine desired to be present.   Arius having been sent for on these occasions, declared his opinions as they are given in his letters;*—that God has not always been a Father, and that there was a time when the Son was not; that the Son is a creature like the others; that he is mutable by his nature; that by his free will he chose to remain virtuous, but that he might change like others.   He said that Jesus Christ was not true God, but divine by participation, like all others to whom the name of God is attributed.   He added, that he was not the substantial Word of the Father, and his proper wisdom, by which he had made all things, but that he was himself made by the eternal wisdom; that he is foreign in every thing from the substance of the Father; that we were not made for him, but he for us, when it was the pleasure of God, who was before alone, to create us: that he was made by the will of God, as others are, having no previous existence at all, since he is not a proper and natural production of the Father, but an effect of his grace.   The father, he continued, is invisible to the Son, and the Son cannot know him perfectly; nor, indeed, can he know his own substance.   Some expressions of Arius are deemed too irreverent to be repeated, but the curious reader may find them in the works of Athanasius.† The bishops, assembled as they were from so many different and widely separated countries, stopped their ears on hearing such lan-

* One of them may be found among the Documents annexed, C.

† Orat. I. contra Arianos, p. 294 and 295.

guage, and rejected this doctrine as remote and alien from that of the Church. After a protracted discussion, some were of opinion that nothing new should be introduced, and that they should hold to the faith which was received from the beginning by tradition. This was particularly the case with those whose simplicity of cha racter led them to receive religious truths without a minute ex amination. Others contended that it was not expedient to follow the opinions of the ancients without inquiry. Many of the bishops, and of the ecclesiastics, who attended them, acquired great reputation at these preliminary meetings, by exhibiting their strength in the art of logic, and their practised skill in disputes of this nature, and thus made themselves known, not only to the emperor, but also to his courtiers; and from that time Athanasius, a deacon of the church of Alexandria, who accompanied his bishop, took the principal part in this important discussion.

Constantine being desirous of meeting so great a number of prelates as were assembled at Nice, as well as of promoting peace and unanimity, repaired to that city, after he was informed of their arrival. But as it too frequently happens, many of that sacred order, as if they had met together on their private concerns, and supposing that they had found a favorable opportunity of having their grievances redressed, presented to the emperor writ-ten complaints against their brethren. As he was almost contin-ually importuned with memorials of this kind, he deferred the consideration of them all to a certain day. At the appointed time, he addressed the prelates to the following effect. "All these accusations, my friends, must be finally determined at the great day of account, by the common Judge of all men. But it does not belong to a man like myself to take cognizance of these mu-tual charges, as they are brought by bishops, who ought so to de-mean themselves as not to be judged by others. Imitate, then, the divine clemency in forgiving one another; and relinquishing your reciprocal imputations, agree to be at peace: And let us give our attention to those articles of faith, for the consideration of which, we have convened in this place." He assured them, according to Theodoret,* although this seems to have been said

* Hist. Eccles. I. 11.

at another time, that he had never read their libels. He declared that the delinquencies of the prelates ought not to be published, lest they should prove an occasion of offence to the people; and even added, that if he should surprise a bishop in adultery, he would cover him with his imperial mantle, for fear that the example of the crime should be prejudicial to those who might witness it. He then commanded them to desist from their unseemly recriminations, and ordered their memorials to be thrown into the fire.

The day appointed by the emperor for the public session of the council was under the consulate of Paulinus and Julian, the thirteenth of the calends of July, answering to the nineteenth of June,* A. D. 325. On the arrival of that day, says Eusebius,† all those who were to be present at the council, assembled in an apartment in the centre of the palace, which was larger than any of the others. Many benches were disposed on each side, and every one took his proper place. When all were seated with suitable decorum, they awaited the coming of the emperor. First one, then another, and then a third, of his attendants entered the hall. Others also preceded, not armed men, nor any of his usual guard, but only his particular friends. At the signal which announced the entrance of the emperor, all arose, and he appeared in the midst of them, his purple robe, resplendent with gold and precious stones, dazzling the eyes of the beholders. That his mind was impressed with religious awe was evident in his downcast eyes, his blushing countenance, and his modest step and movement. He was taller than any of those, by whom he was surrounded. Nor was he in stature only, but also in elegance of form, and robustness of frame, superior to the others. These external advantages were heightened by courteousness of behavior,

---

* Socrates says, that it was on the 20th of May, but Valesius thinks he was mistaken. Atticus, bishop of Constantinople, mentions the 14th of June, but the date assumed by the writer is supported by the council of Calcedon and the Alexandrian Chronicle. The reader who may wish to see a full examination of this difficulty. is referred to Tillemont, mémoires pour servir à l'histoire ecclésiastique, Tom. VI. Note I, sur le Concile de Nicée.

† Vit. Cons. III. 7.

and a princely condescension, indicative, says his biographer, of the noble qualities of his mind. When he had reached the upper end of the hall, he remained standing in the middle, between the highest places, before a small chair, burnished with gold, which was prepared for his accommodation, until he was requested to be seated by the bishops, who then resumed their places.

The prelate * who occupied the seat on the right side of the emperor then addressed him in a short speech, giving thanks and praise to Almighty God for the benefits conferred on the Church through his instrumentality. When he was seated, the spectators all continued in silence, fixing their eyes upon the emperor, who, surveying them with a cheerful and serene expression of countenance, and employing a few moments to collect his thoughts, spake to the following purport, in a pleasant and subdued tone of voice. " It was, my dear friends, my most cherished wish, that I might one day enjoy the sight of this convention. Having been indulged in this desire, I return thanks to God, the ruler of all, who, in addition to innumerable other favors, has granted me this greatest of all blessings, to see you assembled together, and united in your minds. May no malignant foe disturb in future our public happiness. After the complete subversion, by the help of God our preserver, of the tyranny of those, who warred against the Most High, let no malevolent demon again expose the divine law. in any other manner, to slander and detraction. An internal sedition in the Church is, in my apprehension, more dangerous and formidable than any war, in which I can be engaged ; nor do foreign concerns, however unfortunate, affect my mind with so sensible a grief as this unhappy affair. After I had become victorious, by divine assistance, over all my enemies, I thought that it only remained for me to render thanks to God, and to participate in the universal joy with those, whose liberation he has accomplished through my agency and efforts. But when the unwelcome news of your dissensions was brought to my ears, I conceived that the report should by no means be neglected ; and hoping that by my interference, a remedy might be applied to the evil, I sent for you all, without delay. Great indeed is my satis-

* Eustathius, according to Theodoret. I. 7,

faction to see you assembled together. But I shall consider the object of my prayers and labors as fully obtained, when I shall behold you united in the purpose of promoting harmony and concord; which, as persons consecrated to God, it is your duty to preach, and to inculcate on others. Endeavor then, my friends. ministers of God, and faithful servants of a common master and Saviour, that, the causes of your disagreement being removed, all the asperities of controversy may be smoothed by the dictates of peace. By pursuing this course, you will not only do that, which is pleasing to God, who is exalted above all, but will confer an important benefit on myself, your fellow servant." The emperor also remarked,* that the power of the enemy being destroyed, and no one remaining to make any resistance, it would be deplorable indeed, if they should now molest one another, and give occasion to those, who regarded them with no friendly aspect, to turn their quarrels into ridicule. Their business, he said, was with matters of theology, the decision of which depended on the instructions which the Holy Spirit had left them. The gospel, the letters of the apostles, and the works of the ancient prophets, teach us, with sufficient clearness, what we are obliged to believe concerning the divine nature. Let us then renounce all angry contentions, and seek in the books which the Holy Ghost has dictated, the solution of our doubts.

The oration of Constantine was pronounced in Latin, which was his vernacular tongue. Another person translated it into Greek, which was better understood by most of the fathers, as it was generally diffused in all parts of the East. The emperor then gave those who presided in the council an opportunity of speaking, and permitted the members to examine matters of doctrine and religious differences.

The opinions of Arius were first examined in the presence of the emperor. He repeated what he had said on former occasions. The Eusebians, anxious to defend him, entered into the dispute. The other bishops, who were beyond comparison the greater number, mildly required them to give an account of their doc-

* Theodoret, I. 7.

trine, and to support it by suitable proofs. But no sooner had
they begun to speak, than they seemed to be at variance with
themselves; they remained confounded, and seeing the absurdity
of their heresy, confessed their shame by their silence.* The
bishops having refuted their allegations, explained the holy doctrine of the Church. The emperor patiently listened to these disputes, which were agitated at first with considerable warmth.
He gave great attention, says Eusebius, to what was advanced
on either side; and sometimes reproving, sometimes encouraging
the speakers, he moderated by degrees the violence of the contending parties. He spake kindly to every one in the Greek language, with which he was not unacquainted, gaining over some
of them to his opinion by the strength of his arguments, and
softening others by his entreaties. He commended those who
spake judiciously, persuaded them all to concord, and reduced
them at last to an agreement on the contested points.†

A letter of Eusebius of Nicomedia was read in the council,
which evidently contained the heretical opinion, and discovered
the management of the party. It excited so much indignation
that it was rent in pieces, and Eusebius was overwhelmed with
confusion.‡ He says, among other things, that if the Son of God
was acknowledged to be uncreated, it would be necessary to admit, that he was consubstantial with the Father.§ It has been
thought that this was the letter to Paulinus of Tyre, in which the
same idea is expressed in other words.‖ The Arians also presented to the council a confession of faith, which was torn on
being read, and pronounced to be spurious and false. A great
outcry was raised against them, and they were generally accused

* Athan. de decretis, p. 251.

† Eus. III. 13.

‡ Eustath. as quoted by Theodoret. I. 8.

§ According to Ambrose, occasion was taken from this expression of Eusebius, which discovered so great a dread of the word consubstantial, to adopt that
formidable term against the Arians. "Hoc verbum posuerunt patres, quòd vide-
runt adversariis esse formidini; ut tanquam evaginato ab ipsis gladio, ipsum
nefandæ caput hereseos amputarent." de fide L. III. c. 7.

‖ Documents, D.

of having betrayed the truth.* The council wishing to set aside the terms employed by the Arians, and to use words authorized by scripture, said that our Lord was by nature the only Son of God, the alone Word, power and wisdom of the Father, true God, according to St. John; the splendor of the glory, and the image of the substance of the Father, as St. Paul writes. The partisans of Eusebius said among themselves,† let us consent to this. for we also are of God, since it is written, "there is one God, from whom all things proceed." And in another place, "old things have passed away, and all things are new, but all things are of God." The bishops, however, who comprehended their design, explained more clearly the words "of God," by saying that the Son was of the substance of God. It is true, they remarked, that creatures are said to be from God, because they exist not of themselves, nor without a cause; but the Son alone is properly of the substance of the Father. For this is peculiar to the only begotten and true Word of the Father, and therefore the expression "of the substance of the Father" has been employed.

The prelates having again asked the Arians, who seemed to be few in number, if they allowed that the Son was not a creature. but the alone power, wisdom and image of the Father, and in no respect whatever different from him, and that he is true God, it was observed, that Eusebius and his adherents made signs to one another that all these particulars might agree to men, for we too. said they, are called the image and glory of God. There are many powers, for it is written, "all the powers of God went out of Egypt." The caterpillars and locusts too are called the great power. "The God of powers is with us, the God of Jacob, our protector." We are not merely the children of God, since the Son of God himself calls us his brethren. And as to their denominating the Son true God, that occasions us, they said, no embarrassment, for he is so truly, because he has been made so. But the bishops perceiving their sophistry and dissimulation, produced a collection of passages from the sacred writings, where the

* Theodoret, I. 7.

† Athan. de decret. p. 367, et epist. ad Africanos, as reported by Theodoret. I. 8.

Son is called splendor, fountain, river, and figure of the substance; and quoted the words " in thy light shall we see light," and " I and my Father are one." Finally, they explained themselves with more clearness and brevity, in declaring that the Son is consubstantial with the Father, making use of the Greek word ομοουσιος, which this dispute has since rendered so celebrated, as expressive of the meaning of the terms and passages which have been cited. It was understood to signify that the Son is not only like the Father, but so similar that he may be called with propriety the same; and implies that the resemblance and immutability of the Son is different from that which is affirmed of us, and which we acquire by the practice of virtue, and the observation of the divine commands. Besides, bodies which have a resemblance only, may be separate and distant; as a father and a son, however great may be the likeness between them. But the Son of God was considered not only similar to the substance of the Father, but inseparable from it,—the Word being always in the Father, and the Father in the Word.

The Arians rejected with murmurings and contempt the term consubstantial, complaining that it was not to be found in the Scriptures, and might be taken in a very exceptionable sense. For, they remarked, that which is of the same substance with another is derived from it in one of these three modes; by production, as a plant from its root; by fluxion, as children from their fathers; or by division, as in abstracting three or four pieces from a mass, for instance, of gold.* The Catholics explained so happily the term consubstantial, that the emperor himself, little as we may suppose him to have been familiar, from his education and military habits of life, with theological inquiries, perceived that it did not include any corporeal idea, no division being signified of the substance of the Father, which is altogether immaterial and divine, and must therefore be understood only in a divine and ineffable manner. They demonstrated the injustice of their opponents, in objecting to this word, on the pretence that it is not to be found in Scripture, when they themselves scrupled not to

* Basil, Epist. 300.

employ expressions, which are not in the sacred writings, such as, that the Son of God was made from nothing, and had not always existed. They added, that the term consubstantial was not a new one, and that it had been used by illustrious bishops of Rome and Alexandria in opposing those who represented that the Son was a work, or creation. Eusebius of Cesaria himself acknowledges this.* It was insisted by some, that the word consubstantial had been objected to, as improper, in the council of Antioch, which was held against Paul of Samosata. But this, it was asserted, was because it had been taken in a gross manner, as implying division, as when it is said that several pieces of money are of the same metal. But the only question in reference to Paul, was to show that the Son was before all things, and that, being the Word, he was made flesh ; whereas the Arians admit that he was before all time, maintaining, however, that he was made, and that he was one of the creatures. They declared that his resemblance to, and union with, the Father, was not with regard to his substance or nature, but in a conformity of will and counsel.†

After the word consubstantial, and others the best adapted to express the catholic faith, were agreed on, Hosius, according to Athanasius, drew up the form, as recorded in the letter of Eusebius. All the bishops approved of this symbol and subscribed it, with the exception of a small number of Arians.‡ At first, there were seventeen who refused to subscribe, but the number was afterwards reduced to five, viz. Eusebius of Nicomedia, Theognis of Nice, Maris of Calcedon, Theonas and Secundus of Lybia. Eusebius of Cesarea agreed to the word consubstantial, after having opposed it the preceding day. Three of the five who have been named conceded the point at last, from the fear of deposition. Theonas and Secundus only, continued obstinately

* Documents, E.

† By comparing the above sketch of the debate on this subject, derived from Athanasius and others, with the account of it given in the letter of Eusebius of Cesarea, (Doc. E.) which is somewhat different, if not in certain particulars contradictory, the intelligent reader may be the better enabled to elicit the truth.

‡ Socrates, I. 8.

attached to Arius, and the Synod anathematized them with him.* The writings of Arius were condemned at the same time with himself, and particularly his Thalia.†

The question relating to the observance of Easter, which was agitated in the time of Anicetus and Polycarp, and afterwards in that of Victor, was still undecided. It was one of the principal reasons for convoking the council of Nice, being the most important subject to be considered after the Arian controversy. It appears that the churches of Syria and Mesopotamia continued to follow the custom of the Jews, and celebrated Easter on the fourteenth day of the moon, whether falling on Sunday or not. All the other churches observed that solemnity on Sunday only, viz. those of Rome, Italy, Africa, Lybia, Egypt, Spain, Gaul and Britain; and all Greece, Asia, and Pontus. It was considered indecorous, and as affording occasion of scandal to unbelievers, that while some were engaged in fasting and penitence, others should be indulging in festivity and relaxation.

This subject having been discussed, it was decreed to celebrate Easter on the same day, and the oriental prelates promised to conform to the practice of Rome, of Egypt, and of all the West. St. Athanasius remarks a difference of language, in pronouncing on this subject, from that which was used in reference to the faith. With respect to the latter it is said, "this is the catholic

* Philostorgius, an Arian historian, of whose work an epitome is extant by Photius, acknowledges that all the bishops agreed to the Nicene Creed, with the exception of Secundus and Theonas. But the Arian prelates who embraced the decision of the council, artfully concealed under the word ομοουσιον the term ομοιουσιον, the former signifying *of the same substance*, and differing in orthography only by a letter from the latter, which means *like*, or *similar*. The course they adopted (in assenting to the decrees of the council,) was by the suggestion of Constantia, sister of the emperor. Phil. L. I. 8.

† It was a chant set to the same measure and music as the infamous songs formerly composed for convivial occasions by Sotades, a Greek poet, proverbial for his flagrant immoralities. This was sufficient to render it odious, to say nothing of the erroneous opinions which it contained, for Arius had incorporated into it the substance of his doctrines. He composed several other airs, to insinuate his opinions more agreeably into vulgar and uncultivated minds Some of them were intended for travellers, sailors, and millers. See Phil L. II. 2.

faith, we believe," &c., in order to show that it was no new de
termination, but an apostolic tradition. Accordingly, no date is
given to this decision, neither the day nor the year being mentioned. But with regard to Easter, it is said, " we have resolved
as follows," in order to show that all were expected to obey.*
Easter day was fixed on the Sunday immediately following the
new moon which was nearest after the vernal equinox, because it
is certain that our Saviour rose from the dead on the Sunday
which next succeeded the passover of the Jews. In order to find
more readily the first day of the moon, and consequently the fourteenth, the council ordained that the cycle of nineteen years
should be made use of, because at the end of this period, the new
moons return very nearly to the same days of the solar year.
This cycle, which is denominated, in Greek, Εννεακαιδεκαετηρις,
had been discovered about seven hundred and fifty years before,
by Meto, a mathematician of Athens, and it has since been termed the golden number, because it was customary to mark in the
calendar with letters of gold, the days of the new moon. It has
been thought that the synod assigned the task of this calculation
to Eusebius of Cesarea. It is certain, however, that he had composed a paschal canon of nineteen years, and that he had explained the nature and origin of this question in a treatise dedicated to
the emperor Constantine, who gave him thanks for it in a letter.
But notwithstanding the decision of the council there were some
quartodecimans, as they were termed, who remained pertinaciously attached to the celebration of Easter on the fourteenth of
the moon, and among others the Audeans, schismatics of Mesopotamia. They found fault with the council, reproachfully remarking, that this was the first time that the ancient tradition,
through complaisance for Constantine, had been departed from.
    The Synod was also desirous of applying a remedy to the
schism of the Meletians, who had occasioned a division in Egypt
for twenty-four years, and who encouraged the Arians by their
union with the party. Meletius was treated with considerable
lenity—more, it was thought, than he deserved. He was per-

* Synod. Arim. et Seleuc. Epist. p. 873.

mitted to continue in Lycopolis, the city of his residence, but was deprived of his ecclesiastical powers and authority, being merely permitted to retain the title of bishop. But the reader is referred to the synodical epistle * for the particulars in relation to Meletius, and those who had received ordination at his hands.

Another part of the business of the council was the framing of several canons, or general laws of discipline, not, it is understood, to establish a new code of regulations, but chiefly to preserve the ancient rules of conduct imposed on the clergy, which had been too much relaxed or neglected. These canons † are twenty in number,‡ and have been acknowledged as genuine by all antiquity. The bishops were inclined to pass an ecclesiastical law in addition to the others, requiring, according to Socrates, that those who had been admitted to holy orders, the bishops, priests and deacons, and, according to Sozomen, the subdeacons also, should abstain from cohabitation with the wives whom they had married while they were laymen. When this topic was proposed for debate, and the opinions of the synod were called for, Paphnutius, rising from his seat in the midst of the bishops, and raising his voice, protested against the imposition of so heavy a yoke on the clergy, remarking, in the words of St. Paul, that marriage was honorable and the nuptial bed undefiled, and that such an excess of rigor might rather be injurious than beneficial to the Church; that every one was not capable of so entire a continence, and that the repudiated wives might forfeit, perhaps, their conjugal virtue. He added, that he considered the marriage union, sanctioned by the laws, as pure and chaste; that it was sufficient, according to ancient usage, that he, who had once been admitted to the clerical order, should no longer be permitted to marry; but that it was unnecessary to separate him from the wife whom he had espoused when in the condition of a layman. It was thus that the venerable confessor supported his sentiments, although he had not only never been married himself, but had always re-

---

* F.   † Documents, I.

‡ Some of the Eastern Christians mention a much greater number. See J. S. Asseman, Bibloth. Orient. Clement. Vatic. tom. I. p. 22, 195. and Cave, Hist. Lit. p. 224.

frained from illicit intercourse with the other sex, having been educated from childhood in a monastery, in which he was distinguished for his singular purity of life. The council acceded unanimously to the views of Paphnutius, and, without further deliberation, left those who were already married to continue in the state of wedlock or not, at their own discretion.

It will be perceived that the eighth canon of the synod relates to the sect of Novatians, who were called *Cathari*, that is, the pure. The last words of this canon are remarkable, and contain an important rule, that there should never be two bishops in the same city. The emperor, moved by his zeal for peace and union in the Church, had invited to the council a Novatian bishop by the name of Acesius. A conversation of some interest between Constantine and this prelate is recorded both by Socrates and Sozomen, which may be as well related, perhaps, in this place as in any other. When the form of faith was written, and the synod had subscribed it, the emperor asked Acesius, if he also agreed to that confession of faith, and approved of the resolution concerning Easter. "My prince," he replied, "I know of nothing new determined by the council. I have always understood, that from the beginning, from the very days of the apostles, the same definition of the faith, and the same time of celebrating the festival of Easter, has been handed down to us by tradition." "Why then," rejoined the emperor, "do you separate yourself from our communion?" Acesius explained to him what had happened under the persecution of Decius, when many fell from the profession of the faith; and spake of the rigor of the canon, which forbade receiving those, to the participation of the sacred mysteries, who, after baptism, had committed any such sin as is pronounced in scripture to be a sin unto death. "They ought, indeed," he said, "to be urged to repentance, but not encouraged to hope for pardon through the ministration of the priests. For this they should look directly to God, who alone has the power and prerogative of remitting sins." The bishop having thus spoken, the emperor replied, "Take a ladder, Acesius, and ascend alone to heaven."

Before separating, the council prepared a synodical epistle * chiefly intended for the church of Alexandria, as being most in-terested in all the acts of the Synod. It is also addressed to all the faithful of Egypt, Pentapolis, Lybia, and all other churches whatever. The emperor Constantine wrote at the same time two letters, in order to promulgate the ordinances of the council, and to make them known to those, who were not present at the con-vention. The first* is particularly addressed to the church of Alexandria, and informs them that the faith has been examined, and placed in so clear a light that no difficulty remains. Copies of this letter were dispatched to all the provinces. The second† is directed to the churches in general. He published also another letter, or more properly an edict, directed to the bishops and people, condemning Arius and his writings. He says that Porphyry, having composed impious books against Christianity, rendered himself infamous in the eyes of posterity, and that his writings were destroyed. It has in like manner, he continues, been de-creed, that Arius and his followers be called Porphyrians, so that they may bear the name of him whom they have imitated ; and that if any book written by Arius shall be found, it shall be com-mitted to the flames, that no monument of his corrupt doctrine may descend to future ages. He declares that whoever shall be convicted of having concealed any book composed by Arius, in-stead of burning it, shall suffer death immediately after his appre-hension. With whatever degree of aversion we may contemplate the doctrines of Arius, it is painful to witness so melancholy a for-getfulness in the first Christian emperor, of the benignant temper of Him, who rebuked the unhallowed zeal of the disciples, as not knowing what spirit they were of, when they would have called down fire from heaven to consume the inhospitable Samaritans. At the same time, Arius and the two prelates who adhered the most obstinately to his party, Secundus and Theonas, were ban-ished by the emperor.

The council concluded its session on the twenty-fifth day of August, A. D. 325, a month after the commencement of the twentieth year of the reign of Constantine, who ascended the throne on the twenty-fifth of July, A. D. 306 ; but it is thought

* Documents, G.   † Documents, H.

that the festival on that occasion, which was celebrated in every part of the empire with great solemnity, was deferred in compliment to the termination of the synod. During the public rejoicings, Eusebius of Cesarea, in the presence of Constantine, and surrounded by the bishops, pronounced a panegyric on the emperor. A magnificent entertainment was provided by that prince, "for the ministers of God," to borrow the graphic language of Eusebius, "now reconciled with one another, as an acceptable sacrifice offered to the Divine Being, through them. No one of the bishops was absent from the imperial banquet, which was more admirably conducted than can possibly be described. The guards and soldiers, disposed in a circle, were stationed at the entrance of the palace with drawn swords. The men of God passed through the midst of them without fear, and went into the most private apartments of the royal edifice. Some of them were then admitted to the table of the emperor, and others took the places assigned them on either side. It was a lively image of the kingdom of Christ, and appeared more like a dream than a reality." At the conclusion of this splendid festival, the emperor courteously saluted every individual of the company, and presented his guests with rich and valuable gifts, according to their respective rank and merits. When they were about to separate, he took a friendly leave of them, exhorting them to union, harmony and mutual condescension; and concluded by recommending himself to their prayers. Thus ended the great council of Nice, which, it is said, is still celebrated by the Greeks and Orientals among the festivals of the saints.

Nothing, in the preceding narrative, appears to give any countenance to that supremacy of the bishop of Rome, which was claimed and conceded in later ages. He was merely represented in his absence by two presbyters. He seems to have possessed no pre-eminence, nor any exclusive privileges. Bossuet indeed asserts, on the authority of Gelasius Cyzicenus, a writer in the latter part of the fifth century, that Hosius was one of the legates of the Roman prelate, and presided in the council; but it is generally admitted that the testimony of Gelasius is of little value when unsupported by other writers; and no earlier historian makes any mention of a fact, which, if true, would scarcely have been left unrecorded.

The remarkable unanimity of the synod on the subject of our
Saviour's true and proper divinity, the only one examined by that
convention, which excites much interest at the present day, may
be considered, under the peculiar circumstances of the case, as
affording a powerful confirmation of the truth of this important
doctrine.   Every part of the Christian world was virtually represented by men, who, from their commanding station and favorable opportunities, must be supposed to have been well acquainted
with what was understood to have been the doctrine of the apostles, on this important article of our faith.   Most of them, probably,
lived within two centuries of the death of St. John.   Could the
original doctrine have been lost in a period so comparatively
short?   Could it have been corrupted?   Could it have been
generally corrupted throughout the Church ?   If not, the fathers
of Nice must have held, in this respect, the faith delivered by the
first preachers of Christianity, and consequently the true one.
They could not have been ignorant of what was, and had been,
believed, in their respective countries.   The agreement, therefore,
on this point, of so many different nations, as expressed by their
representatives, nations of such various characters, pursuits, manners, customs and prejudices, can be satisfactorily accounted for
only on the supposition, that they had received their belief from a
common source, and preserved it pure by tradition, during the
few generations which had elapsed from the time when they first
received the gospel from the apostles themselves, or from those
who lived not long after the apostolic age.   It may be said, that
many of the members of the council might have been deterred
from expressing their real belief, as some few of them undoubtedly
were, from the fear of exile or deposition.   But they appear to
have been almost unanimous on this subject before any threats
of that kind were held out, and therefore such an apprehension
could have operated on a very small number only ; and if even a
mere majority had been Arians, the danger would obviously have
been on the other side.   St. Chrysostom remarks, that it would
be absurd to charge the council, composed as it was, in a great
measure, of saints and confessors, either with ignorance or fear.
Nor does this reflection seem to be unfounded.   For, how can it
be reasonably supposed, that in the situation in which they were

placed, and which has already been adverted to, they could be in any doubt whether our Lord was divine in the strict sense of the term, or a creature only, however exalted in rank and dignity; or that such men would have disguised their genuine persuasion, from the fear of losing their sacerdotal honors, or of missing those temporal advantages and emoluments, which they might naturally have expected to enjoy under the dominion of a Christian prince? Was it for them, men of unblemished integrity and virtue, basely to violate their consciences for "a piece of bread?" or descend, for the sake of office, from their elevated position, as "good soldiers of Jesus Christ," to the meanness of subterfuge and dissimulation? Was it for men who were born and grew up amidst scenes of pagan insult, cruelty and oppression, and many of whom, for their courageous defence of the truth, had been deprived of their substance, or loaded with chains, or confined in a dungeon, or maimed and disfigured in their persons; and who would doubtless have accompanied their heroic brethren in the faith, "counting not their lives dear unto them," to the scaffold or the stake; or would have expired in torments on the rack, or been nailed to a cross, or become food for lions, rather than "blaspheme that worthy name whereby they were called;"—was it for *them* to stoop to such moral degradation? men, too, some of whom had been distinguished by the episcopal mitre at a period when it was so far from advancing their worldly interest, that it only exposed them more surely to the "loss of all things," added to their toils, their trials and their sufferings, and served but to render them a more conspicuous mark for heathen persecution?

It may be thought that the language and actions of the prelates were sometimes harsh and overbearing, and little adapted to encourage freedom of debate. It must be confessed, that, measured by the standard of modern usage in deliberative bodies, their deportment was occasionally vehement and impassioned. But, is no allowance to be made for ancient manners, and for the fervid and exaggerated style, both of speaking and acting, when under the influence of strong emotion, so prevalent in the eastern and southern regions, of which so considerable a proportion of the members of the synod were natives? It might be asked, however, from what cause so general an ebullition of indignant feeling proceeded. Was it not that their ears were wounded by language which they considered as blasphemous, and that sentiments were avowed which they regarded as alien from the belief of every part of the globe enlightened by the gospel, and contrary to the uniform and uninterrupted tradition every where received from the times of the apostles; a tradition to which, as well as to the scriptures, they solemnly appealed; while, on the other hand, although the Arians alleged passages from the sacred writings in support of their opinion, they did not even pretend that it was sanctioned by the ancient and universal faith of the Christian Church?

It will only be added, that the greater part of the protestant community believe that the doctrine of our Saviour's divinity is satisfactorily proved by the Scriptures alone, independently of any foreign aid, on a fair application to the sacred text of the legitimate rules of interpretation. But if, on a view of what has been advanced from the words of scripture for and against that doctrine, any doubt on the subject should remain, would not the historical evidence afforded by the result of the synod of Nice, (evidence which, in secular concerns, would be esteemed of great importance in determining a question of fact,) go far to remove it, without assuming, with the Church of Rome, the infallible authority of that venerable convocation, or believing, with Constantine, that its decision was guided by divine inspiration?

The opinions of the "disputatious presbyter" of Alexandria, whose followers were soon divided into several sects, long continued to be the occasion of angry contentions and mutual persecutions, by no means becoming such as "profess and call themselves Christians." The Arians flourished, at one period, in the sunshine of imperial favor, and were involved, at another, in disgrace and calamity. But their internal dissensions hastened their decline. The faith established at Nice prevailed at length, and "the consubstantiality of the Father and the Son," says a modern historian,[*] "has been unanimously received as a fundamental article of the Christian faith, by the consent of the Greek, the Latin, the Oriental, and the Protestant Churches."

* Gibbon, Decline and Fall of the Roman Empire, Vol. III p. 334.

DOCUMENTS

RELATING TO THE PRECEDING NARRATIVE.

In the translation of the Letters, which are found in Socrates, with the exception of those of Arius and Eusebius of Nicomedia, which are recorded by
Theodoret, the edition of Valesius, by Reading, Cambridge, 1720, has been used

A.

Letter of Alexander, Bishop of Alexandria.

To our beloved, and most honored colleagues, in all places, in
the ministry of the Catholic Church, Alexander, greeting in the
Lord.

As the body of the Catholic Church is one, and as it is commanded in the divine scriptures that we should preserve the bond
of peace and concord, it is proper that we should write and signify
to one another, what happens to any of us; so that if one member suffer or rejoice, the others may sympathize or rejoice with
him. In our jurisdiction, then, there have lately appeared iniquitous men, and enemies of Christ, teaching an apostacy which
might be justly thought and called a forerunner of Antichrist. I
had intended to bury this matter in silence, that the evil, being
confined to the apostates themselves, might haply die away; and
that it might not, by passing into other places, pollute the ears of
some of the more simple. But since Eusebius, who is now of
Nicomedia. imagining that the affairs of the Church depend upon
his direction, (because, leaving the Church of Berytus, he coveted

and obtained, with impunity, that of Nicomedia,) has undertaken
to protect these apostates, and to write letters in their favor to
every quarter, that he may draw ignorant men into this worst of
heresies, and most inimical to Christ; I thought it was necessary,
knowing what is written in the law, that I should no longer forbear, but inform you all, that you may know who these apostates
are, and the unfortunate language in which their error is expressed; and that in case Eusebius should have written to you, you
may pay no regard to him. Willing now to renew through them
his ancient malignity, which time seemed to have obliterated, he
pretends that he writes letters for their sake. He shows, however,
by his conduct, that he does this for the furtherance of his own
interests. The names, then, of those who have become apostates
are these: Arius, Achillas, Carpones, Aithales, another Arius,
Sarmates, Euzoius, Lucius, Julianus, Menas, Helladius and
Gaius; and with these, Secundus and Theonas, who were formerly denominated bishops. What they advance in opposition
to scripture is this,—God was not always a Father, but there was
a time when he was not a Father. The Word of God was not
always, but originated from nothing; for God, who exists, created
him, who was not, from that which did not exist. Therefore
there was a time when he was not. For the Son is a creature,
and was made. Nor is he like the Father with respect to his
essence. Neither is he by nature the true Word of God, nor his
true wisdom, but he is one of his works and creatures, and is improperly termed the word and wisdom, since he himself existed
by the proper Word of God, and by the wisdom which is in God;
by which, as he created all things, he made the Son. Therefore, by his nature, he is exposed to change and alteration, in like
manner as other rational beings. The Word is foreign and separate from the substance of God, and the Father cannot be declared by the Son, and is invisible to him. Neither does the Son
know the Father perfectly and accurately, neither can he see
him perfectly. Nor does the Son know what the nature of his
own substance is. He was made on our account, that God
might create us through him, as his instrument; nor would he
ever have existed, unless God had determined to create us. And

when they were asked whether the Word of God could be changed, as the devil is changed, they were not afraid to reply, Yes, he can, since he is mutable by his nature, being begotten and created. Such declarations having been made by Arius with unblushing effrontery, we, with the bishops in Egypt and Lybia, having met together, in number nearly a hundred, have excommunicated him and his followers. But Eusebius has received them, endeavoring to mix falsehood with truth, and ungodliness with piety. He will not, however, prevail. The truth is victorious. Light has no fellowship with darkness, nor has Christ any agreement with Belial. For, who ever heard such things? or who, now hearing them, is not struck with amazement, and does not stop his ears, that the pollution of such expressions may not penetrate into them? Who, when he hears John saying "in the beginning was the Word," will not condemn those who assert that there was a time when he was not? Or who, hearing in the gospel the words "only begotten Son," and "by him all things were made," will not abhor those, who affirm that he is one of the creatures? How indeed can he be one* of those who were made by him? or how can he be the only begotten, who, according to their opinion, is to be included in the number of creatures? How can he be made from nothing, when the Father says, "My heart hath sent forth a good Word," and in another place, "I have begotten thee from the womb, before the morning," or how is he unlike the substance of the Father, who is the perfect image and splendor of the Father, and who says,— "He that hath seen me, hath seen the Father." But if the Son be the reason and wisdom of the Father, how could there have been a time when he was not? For it is the same as if they should say, that God was once without his Word and wisdom. How can he be subject to change and variation, when he says, of himself, "I am in the Father, and the Father in me," and "I and my Father are one?" He declared also by the prophet,

* The expression in Socrates, is ισος ειναι των δι αυτου γενομενων, the equal of those things which were made by him. But the reading of the manuscript of Leo Allatius, εις ειναι των δι αυτου γενομενων, preferred by Valesius, is followed by the translator.

"Behold I am, and change not." And although it might be said that this declaration refers to the Father himself, it may in this instance be more properly understood of the Son, because when he became man he was not changed; but, as the Apostle says, "yesterday, and to-day, is the same, and forever." And what could have persuaded them to say that he was made on our account, when Paul says, " for whom, and by whom, are all things?" But as for their blasphemy, that the Father is not perfectly known by the Son, it is not to be wondered at. For when once they had resolved to proclaim war against Christ, they despise even the words of our Lord himself, who says, "As the Father knoweth me, even so know I the Father." If, therefore, the Father knows the Son in part only, it is evident that the Son also knows in part the Father. But if it be nefarious to say this, and if the Father perfectly knows the Son, it is clear, that in like manner as the Father knows his Word, the Son knows his Father, whose Word he is. By these remarks, and by explaining the sacred scriptures, we often gained the advantage over them. But, chameleon-like, they again changed their ground, taking pains to bring upon themselves the application of what is written,—" When the ungodly man cometh into the depths of wickedness, he despiseth." Many heresies, indeed, have existed before their time, which have proceeded with licentious daring to great extravagance. But they, having endeavored in all their discourses to subvert the divinity of the Word, have justified, in a manner, these heresies, so far as it was in their power, by their own nearer approach to Antichrist. For this reason they have been publicly expelled from the Church, and condemned by an anathema. We are grieved, indeed, at the ruin of these men; the more so, that having once been instructed in the doctrine of the Church, they have now departed from it. We are not, however, greatly surprised. The same thing happened to Hymenæus and Philetus, and before them to Judas, who, having been a follower of the Saviour, afterwards betrayed and deserted him. And even with respect to these persons themselves, we were not without warning, for our Lord himself had said, "Beware lest any one deceive you; for many will come in my name, saying,

I am, and the time is at hand; and shall lead many into error.
Go not after them." And St. Paul, who had learnt these things
from our Saviour, writes, that "in the last days, some shall depart from sound doctrine, giving heed to spirits of error, and to
doctrines of demons, turning from the truth." Since, therefore,
our Lord and Saviour Jesus Christ hath himself declared, and
hath signified by the apostle, concerning such persons, we having
heard their impiety with our own ears, have justly anathematized such men, as we have already said, and declared them to
be aliens from the Catholic Church and faith. We have made
this known to your piety, beloved and most respected fellow-
laborers, that you may neither receive any of them, should they
have the presumption to visit you, nor give any credit to what
Eusebius or any other person may write respecting them. For
we, who claim to be Christians, should turn away from all those
who speak and think against Christ, as enemies of God, and cor-
rupters of souls; and not even salute such men, lest by any
means we should become partakers of their sins, as is commanded by the blessed John. Salute the brethren who are with
you. Those who are with us salute you

B.

Extract of a letter from Constantine to Alexander and Arius.

The whole of this letter is given in Eusebius's life of Constantine, but that
portion of it only which is found in Socrates is inserted here, the preceding part
being considered less important in relation to the subject in debate.

The Conqueror Constantine, the greatest, august, to Alexander
and Arius.
* * * I understand this to have been the origin of the present
controversy, that you, Alexander, required of your presbyters
what they respectively thought of a certain passage of the law, or

rather questioned them in regard to a point of useless debate; and that you, Arius, advanced that which should either not have entered into your mind at first, or after having gained admission, should have been locked up in silence; and that dissensions arising among you in consequence, communion has been refused, and the most holy people, rent into two factions, have departed from the harmonious union of the common body. Therefore, let each of you, mutually pardoning the other, embrace what your fellow-servant most reasonably advises. But what is this? It was improper at first that questions should be asked on subjects of this kind, and then for the person interrogated to reply. Questions of this nature, which no law compels us to discuss, but which are suggested by a fondness for disputation in an hour of unprofitable leisure, may indeed be permitted as an exercise of the intellectual faculties. We ought however, to confine them within our own bosoms, not readily bringing them forward at public meetings, nor rashly confiding them to the ears of every one. For how eminently gifted must be the man, who can accurately understand the true nature of such great and difficult matters, or explain them in a manner worthy of their importance? But if any one should be supposed capable of performing this with ease, what portion of the common people would he be likely to convince? or who, in the subtle management of such questions, could avoid the danger of falling into serious mistakes? In matters of this description, therefore, one should restrain a talkative disposition, lest, either through the weakness of his understanding, he should fail to explain what is proposed; or his hearers, being unable, from slowness of perception, to comprehend what is said, should necessarily fall into blasphemy or schism. Let, therefore, an unguarded question and an inconsiderate reply be set against each other, and mutually overlooked. This contention has not arisen respecting any important command of the law, nor has any new opinion been introduced with regard to the worship of God; but you both entertain the same sentiments, so that you may join in one communion. It is thought to be not only indecorous, but altogether unlawful, that so numerous a people of God should be governed and directed at your pleasure, while you are thus emulously contending with each other, and quarrelling about small and very trifling matters.* You know, if I may admonish your prudence by a little example, that even the philosophers themselves, although associated in one sect or profession, were frequently at variance on particular points. But although they differ, in consequence even of the excellence of their knowledge,† they again unite, on account of their fellowship, in the same general purpose. How much more reasonable is it, then, that you, who are ministers of the Most High God, should be likewise unanimous in the profession of the same religion. But let us examine with more accuracy and attention what has been said; let us ask, whether it be just and reasonable, on account of petty and idle disputes among you about words, that brother should be arrayed against brother, and that the venerable assembly, through your quarrels respecting things of so little importance, and by no means necessary, should be mutually estranged by an unholy contention. Such contentions are low and vulgar, and better suited to the ignorance of children, than becoming the gravity and wisdom of priests and discerning men. Let us voluntarily depart from the temptations of Satan. Our great God, the Saviour of all, has vouchsafed to every one a common light. Permit me, his servant, I beseech you, to terminate this affair, by the aid of his providence, that you, his people, may be recalled to unity in your public assemblies by my exhortations, my labors, and the urgency of my admonitions. For, as I have already re-

---

* This passage is thus written in the manuscript of Leo Allatius. τοσουτον του θεου λαον 'ον υπο ταις υμετεραις ευχαις και φρεσιν.ευθυνεισθαι προσηκει, διχονοειν ουτε πρεπον, &c. Epiphanius Scolasticus, it appears, followed the same reading, as he thus translates the words. " Tantum Dei populum, quem vestris orationibus et prudentiâ convenit gubernari, discordare nec decet, nec omnino fas esse, credibile est." It is believed to be unbecoming and utterly unlawful, that so numerous a people of God, who ought to be governed by your prayers and prudence, should be at variance. See Valesius, annotationes in Socratem.

† The original expression in this passage, ει δε τη της επιστημης αρετη, is rather obscure. The translation of Valesius, " in ipsâ scientiæ perfectione," is followed by Shorting, who renders it, " in the very perfection of knowledge." Musculus, in his version, gives " in virtute scientiæ," and Grinæus, " disciplinæ causâ."

marked, you have one and the same faith, and one opinion concerning our religion ; and as the requisition of the law, in its various parts, urges all to an agreement of sentiment, the topic which has excited animosity and division among you, since it belongs not to the essence and life of religion in general, should by no means produce discord and sedition among you. And I say not these things by any means to oblige you to be of the same opinion, with regard to this very foolish controversy, or by whatever other term it may be denominated. For the honor and character of the assembly of Christians may be preserved entire, and the same communion retained among you all, notwithstanding you may greatly differ among yourselves in matters of very little importance, since all men have not the same understanding of every thing, the same turn of mind, or mode of thinking. Let there be, therefore, among you but one faith and mind concerning the providence of God, and one worship and service of the Deity. But your subtle disputes and inquiries respecting these most trifling matters, if you cannot agree in sentiment, should remain in your own thoughts, and be laid up in the secret depths of the mind. Let your mutual friendship remain unshaken : and be firm in your belief of the truth, and your obedience to God and his law. Return to mutual love and charity. Restore to the whole people their accustomed harmony. Purify your own hearts, and renew your former acquaintance and familiarity. It often happens that friendship is more pleasant when enmity is followed by reconciliation. Enable me again to enjoy quiet days, and nights undisturbed by solicitude, that in future the pleasure of the pure light, and the happiness of a tranquil life may be reserved for me. Otherwise, I cannot but sigh and lament, and be dissolved in tears; nor can I pass without great disquietude the remainder of my days. For how can I look for repose, while the people of God who serve the same Master as myself, are torn asunder by an iniquitous and fatal contention? That you may comprehend the excess of my grief on account of this affair, I ask your attention to what I am going to say. Arriving lately at Nicomedia, I had determined to proceed immediately to the East. When I was hastening towards you, and had already performed the greater part of my journey, the news of your differences changed my resolution, lest I should be compelled to behold that with my eyes, of which I thought I could hardly bear the recital. Open therefore to me, by your agreement, a way into the East, which has been closed against me by your contentions. Permit me, as speedily as possible, to behold you and all others of the people happy and rejoicing, and to render, with you, due thanks to God for the common agreement and liberty of all.

C.

Letter of Arius to Eusebius, Bishop of Nicomedia.

To the most esteemed Lord, a faithful man of God, the ortho-dox Eusebius, Arius, unjustly persecuted by Pope* Alexander for the sake of truth, which overcomes all things, and which you also defend, greeting in the Lord.

My father Ammonius being about to visit Nicomedia, I thought it my duty to salute you by him; and at the same time to make known to you, as being naturally charitable and affectionate in your disposition towards the brethren, for the love of God and of his Christ, that we are vehemently opposed and persecuted, and every engine is set in motion against us by the bishop; so that he has even expelled us from the city as atheists, because we do not assent to such declarations as follow, publicly uttered by him. God is always, the Son is always. The Father and the Son are co-existent. The Son, unbegotten, co-exists with God, and is always begotten: without being begotten, he is begotten :† nor

---

* In the earlier ages of the Church, the title of Pope, or father, was the com-mon appellation of the bishops. But when the bishop of Rome afterwards usurp-ed a spiritual supremacy over his brethren, this title, and some others, once bestowed indiscriminately on prelates, as such, being exclusively appropriated to him, acquired, of course, an additional emphasis.

† There appears to have been some confusion of ideas in the mind of the

does God precede the Son in thought, nor by a single moment. Always God, always the Son. From God himself the Son exists. Because Eusebius, your brother, bishop of Cesarea, and Theodotus and Paulinus, Athanasius, Gregorius and Aetius, and all the bishops of the East, affirm, that God, who is without a beginning, existed before the Son, they have been condemned, with the exception only of Philogonius, Hellanicus and Macarius, heretical men, and uninstructed in the faith; who say, one, that the Son is an effusion; another, that he is a projection; and another, that, like the Father, he is unbegotten. We could not listen, indeed, to such impieties, although the heretics should threaten us with a thousand deaths. But what we ourselves say and think, we have already declared, and now declare, that the Son is not unbegotten, nor in any manner a part of the unbegotten, or of any matter subject to him; but in will and design he existed before all times and ages, perfect God, the only begotten, unchangeable; and that he existed not, before he was begotten, or created, or determined, or established, for he was not unbegotten. We are persecuted, because we have said that the Son has a beginning. But God is without a beginning. On this account we are persecuted, and because we said that he is of things not existing. Thus we have said, because he is not a part of God, nor of any subjected matter. On this account we are persecuted. You know the rest. I hope that you are in health in the Lord, and that you remember our troubles, thou true disciple of Lucian, and truly pious man, as your name imports.

bishop, if his words are correctly reported by Arius. It is probable that this passage is intended to express what is called the "eternal generation" of the Son, a phrase, however, which, itself, may not be considered as remarkably perspicuous. Possibly the original may, to some readers, be more clear than the translation. It is therefore added. συνυπαρχει αγεννητως ʽο υιος τῳ θεω, αειγενvης εστιν, αγεννητογενης εςτιν.

D.

Letter of Eusebius, Bishop of N.comedia, to Paulinus, Bishop of Tyre.

To my Lord Paulinus, Eusebius greeting in the Lord.

The zeal of my Lord Eusebius for the truth has not been concealed, but has reached even to us, nor has your silence, my Lord, on the same subject, been unnoticed. We naturally rejoiced on account of my Lord Eusebius, but were grieved much by your reserve, considering the silence of so eminent a man as our own defeat. Wherefore, I exhort you, knowing as you do, how unbecoming it is in a wise man to think differently from others, and yet to suppress the truth, to exert your mental faculties, and commence writing on this subject, which would be useful both to yourself and your hearers, especially if you follow in the footsteps of scripture, and endeavor to write according to its words and meaning. We have never heard, my Lord, of two beings unbegotten, nor of one divided into two; nor have we learnt or believed that he could suffer any thing corporeal, but that there is one unbegotten, and another truly from him, and not made of his substance, by no means partaking of his nature, nor being of his substance, but altogether differing in nature and in power, yet made in the perfect likeness of the nature and power of his Creator. We believe not only that his origin cannot be explained in words, but that it cannot be comprehended, we will not say by the understanding of man only, but by that of any beings superior to man. And we say this, not from our own reasonings, but instructed by the scriptures. That he is created and established, and begotten in the substance, (γεννητον τη ουσια,) in an immutable and inexplicable nature, and in the resemblance which he bears to his Maker, we learn from the very words of the Lord, who says—' God created me in the beginning of his ways, and formed me before the world, and begat me before all the hills." If then he was from him, that is, of him, as it were a part of him, or an emanation of the substance, he could not then be said to have been created or established. Nor can you indeed, my Lord, be ignorant of this. For that which is from an unbegotten being cannot be created nor founded by another or by the same, being from the beginning unbegotten. But if, because he is said to be begotten, it seems to be intimated, that he is derived from the substance of the Father, and has therefore a sameness of nature, we know that the scripture does not say that he alone was begotten, but also other things which differ altogether from him in their nature. For it also says concerning men, " I have begotten sons and exalted them ; but they have despised me," and, " thou hast forsaken God who begat thee." And of other creatures it says, "who is he that hath begotten the drops of dew ?" This is not saying, that the nature of the dew is divine, but that all things which are made, proceed from the will of God. For nothing exists of his substance ; but all things being made according to his pleasure, every thing exists in the manner in which it was made. For he is God, but those things which resemble him, are made so by the Word, according to his will, since all things are of God. And all things which are by him, are made by the Deity, for all things are of God. When you shall have read this letter, and have polished it according to the grace which you have received of God, write as soon as possible to my Lord Alexander If you will take this trouble, I doubt not you will persuade him. Salute all the brethren in the Lord. May the divine favor preserve your health, and enable you to pray for us.

E.

Letter of Eusebius Pamphilus to the Church of Cesarea.

It is probable, beloved, that you have already learnt from another source, what has been done respecting the ecclesiastical faith in the great Council convened at Nice, as common fame usually outruns an accurate report of facts. But as a rumor of this kind may h've represented things differently from what they actually were, we have thought it necessary to send you, first, the form of faith proposed by us, and afterwards that which was set forth by the bishops, who made some additions to ours. Our own form, then, which was read in the presence of the emperor, and appeared to be right and proper, is expressed in these terms. As we have received from the bishops who preceded us,—as we have been taught in the rudimental instructions of our childhood, and when we were subjects of the baptismal rite, and as we have learnt from the divine scriptures; as we have believed and taught, both in the order of presbyter, and the episcopal dignity itself, and as we now believe, we present to you our profession of faith. And it is this. We believe in one God, the Father Almighty, Maker of all things, visible and invisible; and in one Lord Jesus Christ, the Word of God, God of God, light of light, life of life, the only begotten Son, the first born of every creature, begotten of the Father before all ages, by whom all things were made; who for our salvation was made flesh and conversed among men; who suffered, and rose again the third day, and ascended to the Father, and will come again with glory to judge the living and the dead We also believe in one Holy Spirit; believing every one of these to be and subsist, the Father truly the Father, the Son truly the Son, and the Holy Spirit truly the Holy Spirit; as our Lord, when he sent his disciples to preach, said, " Go, and teach all nations, baptizing them in the name of the Father, and of the Son, and of the Holy Ghost." We solemnly affirm that we thus hold and thus think, and have so held formerly, and will hold even unto death, and will always continue in this faith, anathematizing every impious heresy. We testify before Almighty God and our Lord Jesus Christ, that we have believed this sincerely, and from the heart, from the time that we were capable of knowing ourselves, and now also truly think and speak, being prepared to show by sufficient proofs, and to convince your minds, that we have so believed in times past, and have preached accordingly.

Having made this representation of our faith, there was no pretence for contradiction. But our pious emperor himself was the first to declare, that it was extremely well conceived, and that it expressed his own sentiments, exhorting all to assent to, and sign it, that they might unite in its doctrines, with the addition only of the single word consubstantial; which he himself explained by asserting that he did not use the term with reference to corporeal affections, and that the Son did not subsist from the Father, either by division or abscission, since it was impossible that an immaterial, intellectual and incorporeal nature could admit of any bodily affection; but that it must be understood in a divine and mysterious manner. It was thus that our most wise and religious emperor argued on this subject. But the bishops, taking occasion from the word consubstantial, committed to writing the following form :—

THE CREED.[*]

We believe in one God, the Father Almighty, Maker of all things, visible and invisible ; and in one Lord Jesus Christ, the Son of God, the only begotten of the Father, that is, of the substance of the Father ; God of God, light of light, true God of true God ; begotten, not made, consubstantial with the Father, by whom all things were made, both in heaven and in earth ; who for us men, and for our salvation, descended, was incarnate, and was made man, and suffered, and rose again the third day : he ascended into heaven, and shall come to judge the living and the dead : And in the Holy Spirit. But the holy catholic and apostolic Church of God anathematizes those who affirm that there was a time when the Son was not, or that he was not before he was begotten, or that he was made of things not existing : or who say, that the Son of God was of any other substance or essence, or created, or liable to change or conversion.

When this form was dictated by the prelates, their expressions

---

[*] The Greeks termed the symbol of faith μαθημα, because the catechumens learnt it by heart. Leontius Bisantius, in his work concerning sects, calls the Symbol or Creed of Nice, το μαθημα των εν Νικαια.

" of the substance of the Father," and " consubstantial with the Father," were not suffered to pass without examination. Hence, therefore, several questions arose, and answers were made, and the sense of these terms was carefully considered. They admitted that the words " of the substance" signified that the Son was of the Father, but not as a part of the Father. We thought it well to assent to this explanation, as conveying the pious doctrine, that the Son was of the Father ; but not, however, a part of the Father. We therefore agreed to this opinion ; nor did we reject the word consubstantial, having in view the promotion of peace, and being anxious to avoid a departure from the right belief. For the same reason, we approved also of the words " begotten, not made," since the word made, they said, was common to the other creatures which were made by the Son, and to which he has nothing similar ; and that therefore he is not made like those who were created by himself, but is of a more excellent substance than any created being. The divine oracles inform us, that he was of the Father, by a mode of generation, which can neither be conceived nor expressed by any created intelligence.

The question whether the Son is consubstantial with the Father being thus examined, it was agreed that this was not to be understood according to the manner of material things, nor that of mortal beings, since it could be neither by division, nor abscission, nor by a change of the paternal essence and power, since the unbegotten nature of the Father is foreign from all these things. But by the expression " consubstantial with the Father" nothing else is intended, than that the Son of God has no similitude with created beings, but resembles in all things the Father only, by whom he was begotten, and that he is of no other substance or essence than that of the Father. The proposition being thus explained, we thought that we might justly accede to it ; since we knew that some of the most learned and distinguished of the ancient bishops and writers had made use of the term consubstantial, in treating of the divinity of the Father and the Son.*

---

* This assertion of Eusebius, who must have had access to many ancient writings, which are now lost, sufficiently shows, that the word ομοουσιος was

This is what I intended to say concerning the faith which was declared, and to which we all gave our consent; not, however, without inquiry and examination, but according to the senses adduced, which were discussed before our most religious emperor, and for the reasons already mentioned, unanimously approved. We also agreed without difficulty to the anathema put forth by the prelates, and subjoined to the form of faith, because it prohibits the use of unscriptural expressions, from which nearly all the confusion and disturbances of the Church have arisen. Since, therefore, no divinely inspired writing has made use of the phrases, "of things not existing," and "there was a time when he was not," and others which are added to them, it did not seem proper that they should be spoken or taught. We therefore consented also to this salutary decree, not having been accustomed, in times past, to the use of such terms.

We have sent you this information, beloved, that we may clearly show you, with what care and deliberation we conducted our inquiries and examination, and gave our assent, and with how much reason we resisted at first, and continued our opposition to the last hour; so long, indeed, as any thing being written otherwise than correctly, afforded occasion of offence. We finally embraced, without further contention, those expressions which were found to be unexceptionable, when, on a candid examination of the sense of the words, it appeared that they entirely agreed with those admitted by ourselves, in the exposition of faith which we at first proposed.

not first invented by the Nicene Fathers, nor originally used by them, as many suppose, in discussing the subject of the divinity of the Son. Tertullian, in the beginning of his book against Praxeas, expressly says, that the Father, the Son, and the Holy Spirit are of one substance, and affirms that this doctrine is contained in the rule of faith preserved by the Catholics. But wherein does the Latin phraseology, *unius substantiæ*, differ from the Greek expression, ομοουσιου?

F.

The Synodical Epistle.

The bishops assembled at Nice, constituting the great and holy Synod, to the church of Alexandria, by the grace of God holy and great, and to the beloved brethren in Egypt, Lybia, and Pentapolis, greeting in the Lord.

Seeing that, by the grace of God, and the favor of Constantine, a prince greatly beloved by him, we have met together from various cities and provinces, and have holden a great and sacred Council at Nice, we considered it highly necessary that a letter should be sent to you from the holy Synod, that you might understand what things were proposed and examined, and what was decided and established. In the first place, then, the impiety and iniquity of Arius and his associates was inquired into, in the presence of our most religious prince, Constantine. It seemed good to all, that his ungodly opinion should be anathematized, and the blasphemous words and expressions which he made use of, saying, that the Son of God was from nothing; that there was a time when he was not; and that by his freedom of will he was capable of virtue and vice. He also called him a being created and made. All this was condemned by the holy Synod, who could not patiently listen to a doctrine so impious or absurd, and to language so blasphemous. You have already been made acquainted with the result of the proceedings against him, or will shortly be informed; and we would not seem to insult a man who has received the just reward of his own error. But so great was the influence of his impiety, that it involved Theonas, of Marmarica, and Secundus, of Ptolemais, in the same ruin with himself, for they shared the same condemnation.

But after the grace of God had delivered us from that pernicious opinion, from impiety and blasphemy, and from those men who had the presumption to excite discord and divisions among a people heretofore at peace, the rashness and petulance of Meletius, and of those who had been ordained by him, still remained to be considered. And what was determined by the Synod with respect to these persons, we proceed, beloved, to make known to you. It seemed advisable to the council, who were moved by feelings of humanity towards Meletius, although in strict justice he merited no indulgence, that he should remain in his own city, but have no power either of ordination, or of designating candidates for orders, and should not appear in the country, or in any other city, under that pretence; but should retain the name only of his office.* Those, however, who were admitted by him to any clerical function, after being confirmed by a more sacred ordination,† were to be received into communion on this condition, that although they should retain their honors and ministry, they should always be ranked after those, who, being stationed in any parish or church, had been previously ordained by our most respected colleague, Alexander. They are not allowed to propose for ordination such as they may think suitable persons, or to suggest their names; or, indeed, to do any thing without the consent of some bishop of the Catholic Church under the jurisdiction of Alexander. Such, however, as, by the grace of God, and the aid of your prayers, have never been found in any schism, but have remained in the Catholic Church without spot, have the privilege of voting, and of proposing the names of such as may be worthy of admission into the clerical order; and, in short, of performing whatever may be agreeable to ecclesiastical law and sanction.

* It seems that Meletius had undertaken to confer orders in cases which did not belong to him; and had, moreover, infringed the ancient and universally received usage in regard to the ordination of bishops. For it was the custom, when any episcopal seat became vacant, for the bishops of the province, in the presence of the people, to elect and ordain a successor. But Meletius, wherever he happened to travel, made no scruple of instituting bishops, priests and deacons on his own authority. See Epiphanius, de hæres. 68.

† By a more sacred ordination, the synod intended, that the bishops and other clergy, who had been ordained by Meletius, should receive imposition of hands from Alexander. As they had been ordained without his consent, it was especially requisite that they should be consecrated by the bishop of Alexandria, according to ancient custom, which exacted obedience from all the bishops of the Egyptian diocese to Alexander, as their spiritual head.

But if any of those who are in the Church should be removed by death, the office of the deceased is to be conferred on such as have recently been admitted to orders; provided, however, that they appear to be worthy of the promotion, and be elected by the people; whose choice, nevertheless, must be approved and confirmed by the bishop of Alexandria.* And this privilege was conceded to all the others. But with respect to Meletius, on account of his former irregular conduct, and the rashness and precipitancy of his temper, it was otherwise decreed; that no power or authority should be given to a man, who might be able to renew the same troubles, which had existed before.

These are the transactions relating more particularly to Egypt and the most holy church of the Alexandrians. And if any thing further was resolved or determined, in the presence of our Lord, and most honored associate and brother, Alexander, he will him self the more accurately relate it to you, from having been a prominent actor and sharer in what was performed.

We moreover inform you of our unanimous agreement with regard to the most holy season of Easter, which was happily effected by the assistance of your prayers; so that all our brethren in the East, who formerly celebrated the passover simultaneously with the Jews, will in future keep that festival in accordance with the Romans, with ourselves, and with all those, who from the earliest times have observed that solemnity with us. Rejoicing, therefore, on account of these happy regulations, and the peace and harmony which prevail, and also that every heresy is cut off, receive with the greater honor and warmer affection, our colleague, and your bishop, Alexander; who by his presence has

---

* This passage, says Valesius, evidently refers to the bishops who were ordained by Meletius, as well as to the presbyters and deacons. For if it only contemplates the promotion of one presbyter to the vacant place of another, why did the Nicene Fathers use so much caution? Why did they make so many and such important preliminary requisitions? Why so much solicitude in regard to the advancement of a presbyter merely? Unquestionably, the words of the council have a more immediate view to bishops; in the election of whom, the suffrages of the people were necessary, and also a confirmation of their choice by the bishop of Alexandria, as the metropolitan of all Egypt.

afforded us great satisfaction, and at so advanced an age has supported such arduous labors to restore peace among you. Pray also for us all, that what has been rightly established, may firmly continue, through Almighty God, and our Lord Jesus Christ, with the Holy Spirit, to whom be glory forever, amen.

G.

Letter of the Emperor.

Constantine, august, to the Catholic Church of Alexandria.

All hail, beloved brethren! We have received a signal benefit from the divine providence, in that, being freed from all error, we acknowledge one and the same faith. Henceforth it will not be in the power of the devil to do any thing against us; for all his insidious machinations are utterly removed. The splendor of truth, at the command of God, has vanquished those dissensions, schisms, and tumults, which invaded our repose, and, if I may so speak, the deadly poisons of discord. We all, therefore, believe that there is one God, and worship in his name.

That this happy state of things might be brought about, I called together in the city of Nice as many of the bishops as possible, with whom, as one of your number, and rejoicing exceedingly to be your fellow-servant, I undertook myself to examine into the truth. Whatever, therefore, might give occasion for controversy and dissension was accurately considered and discussed. May the Divine Majesty pardon the many and grievous expressions concerning our blessed Saviour, and our hope and life, which were indecorously and blasphemously uttered by some. who declared opinions contrary to the divine scriptures, and our holy faith, and professed to believe them. When, therefore, more than three hundred bishops, not less to be admired for their modesty than for their talents and intelligence, confirmed one and the same faith, which is derived from the truths of the divine law accurately investigated, Arius alone, who first sowed this evil among you, and afterwards among others also, with impious design, was found to be overcome by diabolical art and influence. Let us receive, therefore, that doctrine which was delivered by the Almighty. Let us return to our beloved brethren, from whom this shameless minister of satan has separated us. Let us return to the common body and to our own members, with all diligence, since it is due to your prudence and understanding, to your faith and holiness, that, the error of this man, who is evidently an enemy of the truth, being demonstrated, you return to divine grace. For what was approved by three hundred bishops can only be considered as the pleasure of God, especially as the Holy Spirit, dwelling in the minds of so many and such worthy men, has clearly shown the divine will. Wherefore, let no one hesitate, let no one delay; but let all return with alacrity to the path of truth, that when, with all convenient speed, I shall visit you, I may offer, with you, due thanks to the Searcher of all hearts, that having made known to you the unadulterated faith, he has restored to you that mutual charity, which was so much to be desired.

May the Divine Being watch over you, my beloved brethren.

H.

Another Letter of Constantine.

Constantine, august, to the Churches.

Having experienced, in the flourishing state of public affairs, the greatness of the divine goodness, I thought it especially incumbent on me to endeavor that the happy multitudes of the Catholic Church should preserve one faith, be united in unfeigned love, and harmoniously join in their devotions to Almighty God. But this could not otherwise be effected in a firm and solid manner, than by an examination, for this purpose, of whatever pertains to our most holy religion, by all the bishops, or the greater part of them at least, assembled together. Having therefore convened as many as possible, I myself being present, and, as it were, one of you, (nor do I deny that I exceedingly rejoice in being your fellow-servant,) every thing was examined, until a unanimous sentiment, pleasing to God, who sees all things, was brought to light; so that no pretence was left for dissension or controversy respecting the faith.

When the question arose concerning the most holy day of Easter, it was decreed by common consent to be expedient, that this festival should be celebrated on the same day by all, in every place. For what can be more beautiful, what more venerable and becoming, than that this festival, from which we receive the hope of immortality, should be suitably observed by all in one and the same order, and by a certain rule. And truly, in the first place, it seemed to every one a most unworthy thing that we should follow the custom of the Jews in the celebration of this most holy solemnity, who, polluted wretches! having stained their hands with a nefarious crime, are justly blinded in their minds. It is fit, therefore, that, rejecting the practice of this people, we should perpetuate to all future ages the celebration of this rite, in a more legitimate order, which we have kept from the first day of our Lord's passion even to the present times. Let us then have nothing in common with the most hostile rabble of the Jews. We have received another method from the Saviour. A more lawful and proper course is open to our most holy religion. In pursuing this course with a unanimous consent, let us withdraw ourselves, my much honored brethren, from that most odious fellowship. It is indeed in the highest degree preposterous, that they should superciliously vaunt themselves, that truly without their instruction, we cannot properly observe this rite. For what can they rightly understand, who, after the tragical death of our Lord, being deluded and darkened in their minds, are carried away by an unrestrained impulse wherever their inborn madness may impel them. Hence therefore it is, that, even in this particular, they do not perceive the truth, so that continually wandering in the grossest error, instead of duly reforming their calculation, they commemorate the passover twice in the same year. Why then should we follow those who are acknowledged to labor under a grievous error? for we will never tolerate the keeping of a double passover in one year. But if what I have said should not be thought sufficient, it belongs to your ready discernment, both by diligence and prayer, to use every means, that the purity of your minds may not be affected by a conformity in any thing with the customs of the vilest of mankind. Besides, it should be considered that any dissension in a business of such importance, and in a religious institution of so great solemnity, would be highly criminal. For the Saviour has bequeathed us one festal day of our liberation, that is, the day of his most holy passion; and it was his pleasure that his Church should be one; the members of which, although dispersed in many and various places, are yet nourished by the same spirit, that is, by the will of God. Let the sagacity of your holiness only consider, how painful and indecorous it must be, for some to be experiencing the rigors of abstinence, and others to be unbending their minds in convivial enjoyment on the same day; and after Easter, for some to be indulging in feasting and relaxation, while others are occupied in the observance of the prescribed fasts. Wherefore, that a suitable reformation should take place in this respect, and that one rule should be followed, is the will of divine providence, as all, I think, must perceive. As it is necessary that this fault should be so amended that we may have nothing in common with the usage of these parricides and murderers of our Lord; and as that order is most convenient which is observed by all the churches of the West, as well as those of the southern and northern parts of the world, and also by some in the East, it was judged therefore to be most equitable and proper, and I pledged myself that this arrangement should meet your approbation, viz. that the custom which prevails with one consent in the city of Rome, and throughout all Italy, Africa and Egypt, in Spain, Gaul, Britain, Lybia, the whole of Greece, the diocese of Asia, Pontus and Cilicia, would be gladly embraced by your prudence, considering that not only the greatest number of churches exist in the places which have been already mentioned, but also that it is most religious and equitable that all should wish what the strictest reason seems to require, and to have no fellowship with the perjury of the Jews. And, to sum up the whole in a few words, it was agreeable to the common judgment of all, that the most holy feast of Easter should be celebrated on one and the same day. Nor is it becoming, that in so sacred an observance there should be any diversity ; and it is better to follow that decision, in which all participation in the sin and error of others is avoided. This being the case, receive with cheerfulness the heavenly and truly divine command. For whatever is transacted in the holy councils of the bishops, is to be referred to the divine will. Wherefore, having announced to our beloved brethren what has been already written, it is your duty to receive and establish the arguments already stated, and the observance of the most holy day ; that when I shall come into your beloved presence, so long desired by me, I may be able to celebrate, with you, on one and the same day, the holy festival, and that in all things I may rejoice with you ; seeing that the cruelty of the devil is taken away by divine power. through my instrumentality, and that your faith, your peace and concord is every where flourishing.

May God preserve you, my beloved brethren.

I.

CANONS.

The whole number of canons, universally admitted to be genuine, which were framed by the Council of Nice, is twenty. All of these were translated, with a view to insertion among the documents. But as the work has been extended considerably beyond the original design, as the canons relate altogether to matters of discipline, and most of them would probably be of little general interest at the present time, it was determined, on consultation, to publish a few of them only, which are more particularly connected with the historical view, or which may otherwise seem to claim a preference. The reader who may wish to examine those which are omitted, is referred to the Concilia Generalia et Provincialia, Coloniæ Agrippinæ, 1618, page 275, from which the following are translated.

Canon IV.—*Of the Ordination of Bishops.*

It is highly proper that a bishop should be constituted such by all the bishops in the province; or, if this should be difficult, either through any urgent necessity, or from the length of the journey, three, at least, meeting together, shall ordain the candidate, provided those who are absent shall also consent, and signify their approval by letter. The transactions, however, which may take place in every province must be confirmed by the metropolitan bishop.

Canon VI.—*Of the distinguished honors which were decreed to the chief Bishops in Ecclesiastical Government.*

Let the ancient usage prevail of Egypt, Lybia and Pentapolis, that the bishop of Alexandria have jurisdiction over all these provinces, since this is the custom with regard to the bishop in Rome.* In like manner, at Antioch, and in the other provinces, let the churches preserve their privileges. It is very clear, that if any one be made a bishop without the consent of the metropolitan, the great council has decreed that he ought not to be a bishop. But if through their own obstinacy two or three individuals oppose the election of a candidate, it being just and con-

* Here, again, it appears, that the bishop of Rome had no pre-eminence at the period of the Nicene council, being placed on the same footing only as the other metropolitan prelates.

formable to the ecclesiastical canon, the vote of the majority shall prevail.

Canon VII.—*Of the Bishop of Ælia.* (*Jerusalem.*)*

Since custom and ancient tradition require that the bishop of Ælia be held in veneration, let him have the next degree of honor to the metropolitan, without prejudice to the appropriate authority of the latter.

Canon VIII.—*Of those who are called Cathari, that is, the Pure.*

Respecting those, formerly calling themselves Cathari, who have acceded to the holy Catholic and apostolic Church, it seemed good to the great and holy council, that receiving the imposition of hands, they may thus continue in the clerical order. But above all things, it is proper that they should promise in writing to approve and follow the regulations of the holy apostolic Church, that is, that they will communicate with those who may have contracted a second marriage, and with those who, in a period of persecution, have fallen from the truth, but to whom a time is fixed and a season appointed for repentance; that they may observe in all things the decrees of the Catholic Church.

---

* Jerusalem having been destroyed by Titus, a colony was afterwards established on its ruins by Adrian, and the place was then called Ælia. As a new city, it was of no great importance, and was under the jurisdiction of Cæsarea, the metropolis of Palestine. The Christian world, however, was not unmindful of its antiquity, and of the interesting events of which it was the scene. Especially was it remembered as the sacred spot, where that divine religion, which was one day to be extended throughout the world, was first proclaimed by our Lord and his apostles. For these reasons the bishop of Jerusalem was thus distinguished, and Eusebius has preserved the succession of prelates in that city, as well as those in the other apostolic sees.

Wherever therefore, they alone may be found ordained, whether in villages or cities, they shall remain in the same order, to which they had been admitted. But if any of them come to a place where there is a bishop or a presbyter of the Catholic Church, it is evident that the bishop of the Catholic Church, shall have the episcopal dignity. But he who is called a bishop by the Cathari, shall have the rank of a presbyter, unless it shall seem fit to the bishop to share with him the honor of the title ; but if otherwise, he shall provide for him the place of a country bishop, ($\chi\omega\rho\epsilon\pi\iota\sigma\kappa o\pi o\nu,$) or of a presbyter, that he may by all means appear to be in the number of the clergy, and that there may not be two bishops in one city.

Canon XIII.—*Of those who solicit Communion at the point of death.*

Concerning those who depart this life, the ancient and ecclesiastical law shall now also be observed, that if any one is about to expire, he may not be deprived of the viaticum of the Lord. But if, in despair of life, having received the communion, and partaken of the offering, he be again numbered with the living, let him be placed with those who participate in prayer only. By all means, however, let the bishop impart the offering to every one, on examination, who desires, at the point of death, to partake of the eucharist.

Canon XV.—*Of the inexpediency of removing from one city to another.*

On account of the frequent tumults and seditions which arise, t is decreed, that the custom which exists in some parts, contrary to the canon, be entirely taken away ; so that no b'shop, priest or deacon, be permitted to migrate from one city to another. If any one after this determination of the holy synod, shall attempt any such thing, or shall engage in a business of this nature, such a proceeding shall be rendered altogether void, and he shall be restored to the church of which he has been ordained bishop, priest, or deacon.

Canon XVI.—*Of those who do not remain in the churches to which they have been appointed.*

Whoever, not having the fear of God before their eyes, and disregarding the ecclesiastical canon, shall rashly withdraw from the church, whether they be priests or deacons, or in any other ecclesiastical order, such persons ought by no means to be received by any other church, but should be compelled to return to their own parishes; and those who are obstinate, should be deprived of the communion. If any clergyman should presume to invade what belongs to another, and be ordained in his church, without the consent of the bishop from whom he had withdrawn, such ordination shall be null and void.

Canon XVIII.—*Of presbyters receiving the eucharist from deacons.*

It having come to the knowledge of the great and holy council, that in certain places and cities, the eucharist is administered by deacons to presbyters, and neither law nor custom permitting that those who have no authority to offer the body of Christ should deliver it to those who have; and it being also understood, that some deacons receive the eucharist before even the bishops, let therefore all these irregularities be removed, and let the deacons remain within their own limits, knowing that they are ministers of the bishops, and inferior to the presbyters.　Let them receive the eucharist in their proper place, after the presbyters, whether it be administered by a bishop or presbyter.　Nor is it permitted to deacons to sit among the presbyters, as that is against rule and order.　If any one will not obey, even after these regulations, let him desist from his ministry.*

* The order of deacons was instituted to serve tables, and chiefly the table of the Lord.　It is mentioned by Justin Martyr, towards the close of his second apology for the Christians, that they were employed to carry the bread and wine to such communicants as were absent.　They had the administration of the offerings, and of all the temporal concerns of the churches.　The poor received from their hands the alms of the faithful, and the clergy, their stipends and remuneration.　All this was adapted to increase their consequence, and gave them, says Fleury, a kind of authority over the priests.　The council of Arles had already begun to check the aspiring views of the deacons, by prohibiting that order, in their eighteenth canon, " ut diaconus nihil sine presbytero suo agat," from taking upon themselves any functions belonging to the priests

Twin Brooks Series

Barclay, William
Educational Ideals in the Ancient
World

Bass, Clarence B.
Backgrounds to Dispensationalism

Battenhouse, Roy W. (ed.)
A Companion to the Study of
St. Augustine

Bavinck, Herman
The Doctrine of God
Our Reasonable Faith
The Philosophy of Revelation

Beardslee, John W., III (ed. & tr.)
Reformed Dogmatics

Beckwith, Isbon T.
The Apocalypse of John

Beecher, Willis Judson
The Prophets and the Promise

Berkhof, Hendrikus
Christ the Meaning of History

Berkhof, Louis
The History of Christian Doctrines
Introduction to Systematic Theology

Bright, John
The Authority of the Old Testament

Bushnell, Horace
Christian Nurture

Carnell, Edward John
A Philosophy of the Christian
Religion

Clark, Gordon H.
A Christian View of Men and Things
Thales to Dewey

Dargan, Edwin C.
A History of Preaching

Davies, J. G.
The Early Christian Church

Davis, John D.
Genesis and Semitic Tradition

Deissmann, Adolf
Light from the Ancient East

De Ridder, Richard R.
Discipling the Nations

Dodd, C. H.
The Apostolic Preaching and Its
Developments

Eck, John
Enchiridion of Commonplaces

Edersheim, Alfred
The History of the Jewish Nation
Prophecy and History

Ellis, E. Earle
Paul's Use of the Old Testament

Eusebius
The Proof of the Gospel

Farrar, Frederic W.
History of Interpretation

Frend, W. H. C.
Martyrdom and Persecution in the
Early Church

Gasper, Louis
The Fundamentalist Movement

Gerstner, John H.
Reasons for Faith
The Theology of the Major Sects

Goppelt, Leonhard
Apostolic and Post-Apostolic Times

Green, William Henry
General Introduction to the Old
Testament
The Higher Criticism of the
Pentateuch
The Unity of the Book of
Genesis

Henry, Carl F. H.
Aspects of Christian Social Ethics
Christian Personal Ethics

Henry, Carl F. H. (ed.)
Basic Christian Doctrines
Fundamentals of the Faith
Revelation and the Bible

Heppe, Heinrich
Reformed Dogmatics

Hillerbrand, Hans J.
The Reformation
The World of the Reformation

Hort, Fenton John Anthony
Judaistic Christianity
Jerome
Commentary on Daniel
Kevan, Ernest F.
The Grace of Law
Klotsche, E. H.
The History of Christian Doctrine
Kuiper, R. B.
God-Centered Evangelism
Kurtz, J. H.
Sacrificial Worship of the Old
Testament
Kuyper, Abraham
Principles of Sacred Theology
Law, Robert
The Tests of Life
Lecerf, Auguste
An Introduction to Reformed
Dogmatics
Lightfoot, J. B.
The Apostolic Fathers
Longenecker, Richard N.
The Christology of Early Jewish
Christianity
Paul, Apostle of Liberty
Machen, J. Gresham
The Virgin Birth of Christ
Manson, T. W.
The Servant-Messiah
Mayor, Joseph B.
The Epistle of James
The Epistles of Jude and II Peter
McDonald, H. D.
Theories of Revelation
Meeter, H. Henry
The Basic Ideas of Calvinism
Niesel, Wilhelm
The Theology of Calvin
Orr, James
Revelation and Inspiration
Rackham, Richard Belward
The Acts of the Apostles
Ramm, Bernard
The Evangelical Heritage
Varieties of Christian Apologetics

Raven, John Howard
The History of the Religion of Israel
Sandeen, Ernest R.
The Roots of Fundamentalism
Seeberg, Reinhold
Textbook of the History of
Doctrines
Sherwin-White, A. N.
Roman Society and Roman Law in
the New Testament
Smith, David
The Days of His Flesh
Smith, James
The Voyage and Shipwreck of St.
Paul
Steinmetz, David C.
Reformers in the Wings
Stonehouse, Ned B.
Origins of the Synoptic Gospels
The Witness of the Synoptic Gospels
to Christ
Sweet, William Warren
The Story of Religion in America
Theron, Daniel J.
Evidence of Tradition
Trench, Richard Chenevix
Notes on the Miracles of Our Lord
Notes on the Parables of Our
Lord
Studies in the Gospels
Trueblood, David Elton
General Philosophy
Philosophy of Religion
Turretin, Francis
The Atonement of Christ
Van Til, Henry
The Calvinistic Concept of Culture
Vos, Geerhardus
The Pauline Eschatology
Westcott, B. F.
A General Survey of the History of
the Canon of the New Testament
Wilson, Robert Dick
Studies in the Book of Daniel
Young, Warren C.
A Christian Approach to Philosophy

BAKER BOOK HOUSE   BOX 6287   GRAND RAPIDS, MI 49506